Oh Dad!

A Search for

Robert Mitchum

Lloyd Robson is a writer and broadcaster from Cardiff. As a poet he has performed and been published in five continents. He's been described as '*A national treasure*' (Niall Griffiths, novelist) and '*Just not what people expect a poet to be*' (Peter Finch, poet). His first novel, *cardiff cut*, was proclaimed the first ever prose written in Cardiff dialect.

For further information, visit www.lloydrobson.com.

Oh Dad!

A Search for

Robert Mitchum

Lloyd Robson

PARTHIAN

Parthian
The Old Surgery
Napier Street
Cardigan
SA43 1ED

www.parthianbooks.co.uk

First published in 2008
© Lloyd Robson 2008
All Rights Reserved

ISBN 978-1-905762-13-2

Cover design by Marc Jennings
Inner images © Lloyd Robson
Inner design & typesetting by books@lloydrobson.com
Printed and bound by Dinefwr Press, Llandybïe, Wales

Published with the financial support of the Welsh
Books Council

British Library Cataloguing in Publication Data

A cataloguing record for this book is available from
the British Library

For all the young boys writing poems.

Walter Brennan: *'You ain't going out there just to save our necks.'*
Robert Mitchum: *'I'm tryna save my own, too.'*

Blood on the Moon

To anyone who wishes to take offence at any unintentional historical inaccuracies which may've wormed their way into this book: shove it up your ass. I have written this with absolutely no intention of disrespecting anyone except myself and, on occasion, Mitchum, who I think would've been happy to let it go, take a beer from me, and then, if he deemed it necessary, punch my lights out. So let's leave the arguments there.

Lloyd Robson

'They're all true – booze, brawls, broads, all true. Make up some more if you want to.'

Robert Mitchum

Prologue

I feel the frost descend my body. Not the frost of the outer world; the frozen atmospheric moisture; the hoarfrost, the glazed frost, the rime, but an inner freeze, of skin and bone. The quick shiver through the system; the reaction-baton handed from nerve ending to ending, from scalp to toe. Each signal, each spasm, each contraction of muscle, each mini-moment of cold notifying the body, the blood, the sinewy tissue, the sinuous dermis, the bumps and scars, the glands and pores, the remains of a soul, of a message which originated low; worked its way up to announce through the Tannoy: 'your bladder is full'. There is fire down below.

I rise from the floor. Stand and piss. Dance my dilemma; sway to and forth, back and fro. Cease. Unzip my denims. Continue the flow. Catch sight of someone in the mirror. He looks familiar. Piss-holes in the snow. He looks like my father; my dead and dastardly father – even now he will not leave me alone. I've been waiting all my life for solitude to clear my thoughts. Have muffled his voice with meaning-less drivel in an attempt to avoid facing existence; to avoid facing the inescapable: I *am* my father's son, whether I like it or no. Dreamt I would find where he ended and I began, so I could cut the paternal umbilical; slice the cord. And wrap it around his bastard throat.

'You may not think very highly of me right now, young man, but you're my next of kin.... With my name and everything that goes with it. And that's the way of the world.'

R M, *Home from the Hill*

I stare at the mirror; the bathroom mirror; the *barf*-room mirror – there are collagulating lumps in my bristles, on my clothes. For a second I mistakenly look in my eyes; the reflection of *my* eyes out of focus, my *father's* eyes, spot-on, explore. I break the look; snap the lock. Vomit once more. Continue to piss while my leg warms.

'You're feeling a little raw, aren't you.'

R M, *Home from the Hill*

The flood stops. I pull down my jeans (if only I could pull down my genes) and sit on the bowl. Hunt through the pocket-dust for substances necessary to roll a joint. I roll a joint. The taste of tobacco and grass is just about all that can break through the fug on my tongue – it has always

2

been so, when I'm ill; when I'm lost. But I have no grass, only cheap diesel hashish; a grubbing of mud. Oh, for a lump of Barcelona *chocolate*, Red Leb, squiggy black. I spark up. Spot a beer can on the floor. Drink from it, hope there's no roaches afloat. Inhale and choke. Cough blood and unspecified lumps. Spark movement from both ends of my living corpse. Life has caught up and now the quality of existence is enhanced more by a good bowel movement than by memories of delirium and deliciousness born from artistic endeavour; the onslaught of creative thoughts; the *involvement* I once felt, safe in the poetic fold.

I have memories of being a poet, of *fighting* to be a poet, against my father who would introduce my teenage self to fully-grown men I was trying to impress – in the hope I'd be accepted as a man in the eyes of men; in the hope they would accept me as one of their own. He would introduce me as his 'gay son', the 'poet ponce', the 'pox doctor's clerk'.

'I had something from my father that his father gave to him. I'm gonna give it to you.... What I'm saying is, you're gonna have to stand up and be counted. You're gonna be known in these parts as a man, or as a mama's boy.'

R M, *Home from the Hill*

Fighting against expectations and limitations; against my own ignorance; against conditioning and a whole swamp of suffocating control.

'We're all saved by the promises of our imagination. You're not the first whose future was foretold in childish dreams.'

R M, *Mr North*

Now, I am dead. Drunk. I have suckled at the breast of brainfuck and weirdness and found it a bitter-sweet experience which repeats on my ulcerous gut. I am Lord of Lost It upon my throne, a clown tripping over his own shoes in the circus of circumstance, a trapeze act wobbling between bedlam and madness; meddling and badness; malady and bedness... ah, bedness... bedness... I dreamed, once. But no more. You must sleep to dream, and sleep haunts me now. So I avoid. Get drunk. Avoid thought. Avoid feeling. Get stoned. Avoid getting caught by my own memories and thoughts. The beast must feast and its hunger, its thirst, is such that I... that I... must not... sleep... must... tired; tired of it all. If I lie naked and alone my brain will enforce reflection and history I cannot control.

I cannot remember how it feels to rest; to wake refreshed. I am scared of my bed. Night after night I lock myself into a cycle of waiting, for avoidance activities to coincide and collide; for end of drink and end of joint to align, to punctuate the night and prompt me to retire.

'You think I drink too much? Just enough to sleep. I cannot rest without it.'

Curt Jurgens, *The Enemy Below*

But when the glass is empty the smoke still burns strong;

when the butt is stubbed the glass still holds fluid escape and false warmth. Eventually I sleep, well past dawn and into the day-shift hours. It offers no relief, just otherness; just *more*.

'I always thought I had as much inspiration and tenderness as anyone in the business. I always though I could do better. But you don't get to do better, you get to do more.'

R M

I get woken by cramp and a bad fucking mood. Roydo San not a well boy, oh no. There's a joint still between my yellow fingers and a lighter on the floor. I pick up the lighter, dry it on my shorts and spark up. I try to stand but my leg is comatose – if only the lymbic had the luck of the limb. I drag it to the door. Inhale again. Choke. Return to the sink and cough up. My ulcer wakes up. Bastard. Everyone has a weak link in their chain, an Achilles' traitor, whether physical or mental. Given opportunity alcohol will find it, expose it, explore it, exploit it, explode it. Mine is a father reborn as ulcer in stomach; my old man incarnate; my peptic pater; a ghost who's chosen my gastric Gomorrah as abode. It's genetic – I come from a long line of ignoble drinkers and drunks who each have suffered the same complaint. I figure: if it's in my genes, I may as well drink and pickle the damn thing; bring on the decline at my own pace; enjoy listening to him scream as he drowns.

I'm fast becoming a drunk, despite my own warnings. A big-mouth. An argumentative, aggressive, heavy-drinking, drug-taking, football-supporting twat of a 'man' who's gonna try and get his hands in your mother's/daughter's/sister's/wife's panties as soon as I can convince her it's what she's wanted all along. But somewhere inside there is a lost, fatherless poet; a sensitive artist raised in a house run by women; a passionate compassionate, lost to anger and pain and fear of the road ahead, of what he might become. Of what he might already be. I have vague memories of being more.

I don't know how to be a man. A sensitive man. A man who is sensitive as well as, as well as whatever a 'man' is supposed to be. I was probably more 'man' when aged three, when existence was more fancy-free and I just *was*. I'm having problems in this western world figuring out just who I am and why I am and what the hell I'm supposed to be. I am sick of bumping into my self; sick of the distrust and self-destruct. I need to stop living a reaction; find a degree of free will; stop driving as if to die; stop shooting loose and firing wide; become more than dead flesh on a cold pan.

R M: *'You looked to me like you needed to learn a thing or two.'* George Hamilton: *'Well, you're my father. How come I wasn't taught?'*

Home from the Hill

The equation does not balance; the maths doesn't add up, so it's time to wipe the slate clean; to start again; to be reborn; to disassemble and regenerate and *be* once more. But first, I need revenge – on my old man.

'I've seen dogs wouldn't claim you for a son.'

R M, *Blood on the Moon*

Oh dad, you blackbeard, you long shadow, you would
not bend and you would not accept. You brainwashed me
into despising myself. So we became enemies. You, my
Moriarty; you, you narcissist, my nemesis. You projected
onto me your failings and inability to be man. So now I am
'man' in name alone. A fuck-up with cock and balls. Yes, I
need revenge, and a sherpa to show me how to carry my
own load. I need to find something, someone resembling
myself onto whom I can project and from whom I can
learn. I need to replace your negative influence and fear of
becoming you; to find some sense. I need to know who I
am; I need to be able to look my reflection in the eye and
not feel ashamed; know I am 'man', deserving of the name.
I need, finally, to grow up. And get along without your
ghost. So I can sleep and dream safe again.

You left me without faith, with no role model to trust.
I've tried others, in attempts to gain direction, to gain
acceptance, to gain what I don't know; to remove the
bruise of man, the gruesome maroon of paternal abuse; to
heal the harm caused by the incompatibility of our own
personal lunacies; to seal the emotional rust. But I cannot
trust, so convince myself they all want to screw me up in
their own image.

'I'm your father, I don't answer to you for anything.'

R M, *Home from the Hill*

7

I don't have heroes. Not even anti-heroes. Don't trust the fuckers. They're all self-serving bastards as far as I'm concerned. As a child I never had strong, male role models to guide me and still don't. Never have. No father to look up to and say, 'I wanna be like him'. No support network of men supporting men, in silence and drinking. I just barge my way through, knocking drinks and people over, making it up as I go along, getting the occasional fist in the mouth – sometimes deserved, sometimes not. But I'm no fighter, only a big-mouth. I've started my fair share of scraps, often with the biggest or nastiest bastard I could find, then walked away and left others to clean up.

Susan Hayward: *'The more bones you break the bigger man you think you are.'*
R M: *'That's right. Broken bones, broken bottles, broken everything.'*

The Lusty Men

I've walked away from fights, run away from fights, had to crawl away from fights. I've stayed and got a righteous good kicking. I've stayed and talked my ways into and out of beatings. I've stayed and made the aggressor afraid of what he has uncorked.

On occasion I could actually claim to have won, if win we can. But now I don't want to raise my fists, or my voice, because I don't have to and because it hurts. I can deal with the scabbed knuckles, the cuts, the bruised organs, sore bones, but each forced hit drains life from my soul and that I cannot reclaim. Although in that moment, in that

8

split second of getting a split lip, feeling the blood burst through my skin I am more alive than ever, like jumping off a cliff and knowing every second is immense and multidimensional and sensory and sensational and I *exist*, in every cell I exist, if only until he hits me again and my head hits the floor.

Lucky for me, these days I've got my camouflage painted good – few are brave or stupid enough to clamber through the minefields around me when there are far easier targets to reach.

I feel I have nothing to prove, and no one to prove it to, but my behaviour betrays something else. I am what I am, whatever it may be, but am I 'man' or just 'male'? Does it matter anymore? I seem to be less and less aware or certain of my role. The continued emancipation of women is wonderful and long overdue, but as women successfully redefine their roles, so my role is being redefined too. And, if I'm not careful, I might not have a say in what is expected of me. I am still beast – and thank fuck for that – lumbering after my mental existence; chasing my brain and imagination. But I am defined by my father's dismissal and I must free myself of this. Become... my own man, finally, before time is gone.

There was another man I hated as a kid. A man who seemed with every smug grin to be rubbing my face in it. The 'man' on whom I projected my bitterness, who stood as the personified enemy; as the example of 'real' masculinity I, in my father's eyes, would never match: Robert Mitchum. A man capable of doing his own thing without fear. A man who reeked of something I could never imagine achieving. An acceptance of self, perhaps. Or an authenticity. An authentic *what* remains open to question.

R M: *'How 'bout me? Am I a good man too?'*
Grazia Buccella: *'I don't care what you are.'*

Villa Rides!

I lie. I resented, not hated, Mitchum. And then only until my teens, when one midweek night the BBC showed *Night of the Hunter* at the end of the night's schedule. I was engrossed. Not in plot, but in watching this actor I had previously dismissed or avoided, be so hypnotising and alive. From that night I ceased to resent him – I just didn't trust him. Then one wet Saturday afternoon, with a choice between wrestling on ITV's *World of Sport* or international synchronised knitting on a non-football, non-rugby edition of BBC1's *Grandstand*, I tuned into BBC2 and caught most of *Heaven Knows, Mr Allison*. I didn't know what the film was called – which is just as well, it's a terrible title – but again I was fascinated by this rough and tumble, charismatic, sensitive character. Was this really the same guy as in *Night of the Hunter*? Was this really the guy I was supposed to turn into? Was I, too, supposed to be nice to a nun? I could do that. But my father had more in mind. His version of Mitchum, the man's man, is only implied in *Heaven Knows*. Ah well, at least somewhere in that earlier time my subconscious mind must've logged that you don't have to be just one or the other.

See, I was not brought up but beaten down. I was spiritless, broken. Just a weedy kid. Mitchum: barrel-chested and built like a brick shithouse. I could not deny he was a splendid example of a *physical* man – not just physique, but presence. Mitchum seemed alive in a way I thought I could never be: a fighter, a womaniser, a drinker; a fearless experimenter, explorer and risk-taker; man's man and lady's man – physically, mentally, emotionally; a normal working man, one of the boys; an imaginative man, a dangerous man, willing to follow his desires and dreams, to stand up for himself against impossible odds; a man without pretention who could still think further than most. He made me sick. I wanted to beat him; to break him, just as I had been.

So what bigger, badder, bolder bastard is there, on which to take out my confusion? Roll on up then, Robert fucking Mitchum. If somebody can shine a light for me, perhaps it is you and perhaps it is now. Stand still, you bastard, this is going to hurt me more than you. You better teach me something, *daddio*, or I'm gonna split in two.

Robert Mitchum: '*Why bother about me?*'
Robert Preston: '*Because I need you.*'

Blood on the Moon

Take 1

The moon slouches over the city and the air is hot. Restlessness jumps to the down jazz of heavy goods wagons travelling the tracks, their notes and tones clang and shudder the lines – not so much a serenade as a trembling jungle-drum threat, punctuated by an occasional air horn or maintenance gang working the night. The rapid thrust of the intercity express slowing its approach along the last few miles before reaching its stop and the staff in the tea room, the drunks on the platform and the junkies in rest-rooms shooting up, passing out and not waking up. Discovered cold and stiff on the morning tiles; hamstrung by an unusually pure batch, their corpses prodded by mops before the cops are called to sort things out.

My apartment stands on the site of a goods yard and overlooks, from the south side, the tracks which underline much of the dock city. And Rover Bridge, the rivets of which threaten to leave their clinch if the thump and rumble does not desist. It does not desist. Nor does it prevent the blackberries from crowding the cutting banks or the bats from blackening the navy-blue night before the 4am gulls demand it back. What the steel squeal and weighted back-beat does to nocturnal ears. Ultrasonic attack. It is the resonance of travel, of action, of distance. It demands my attention as I try to sleep; as I try to keep still, rest, lie, and hide in my pad.

I must leave. The trains have woken in me something deep. They threaten my foundations. The need to travel; the need to escape. The speed of my journey is of no importance, but I must depart with haste. Method unknown and irrelevant – train, plane, hitch.... It demands I turn to the greater world. To be part of it. Mitchum would understand this.

'Tell me what trail to follow, I'll find it.'

R M, *Second Chance*

From a young age, Robert Mitchum had a strong link with the railways – American railways built with technology developed in the Gwent valleys of Wales.

As a fourteen year old – his head full of poetry and the words and world of Irish-American author Jim Tully and Welsh author W H Davies – he fell for the adventure of the hobo trail. Fare unpaid and with the ambition to be a bum – a bum who had seen something of the world – he boarded a train in his hometown of Bridgeport,

Connecticut, and decided to head west. He travelled across the States nine times. To California, via Georgia in the south-east so he could go see the Okefenokee Swamp he had read so much about.

It was not the first time he left home. Aged four, he walked out and kept walking, only to be found at the city limits. He just 'wanted to see what was out there', he would claim. A concerned woman handed him over to the police – his first, but not last, experience of their hospitality. Aged seven, he ran away again, this time to Hartford – a full forty miles up the line. He returned home and began telling tales of his travel time. As a teenage hobo, a 'road kid', he smoked wild grass when it still grew wild and legal alongside the tracks, while riding on curiously-named 'reefer' refrigeration wagons. Woke to find a fellow hobo, feeling the cold, had set fire to the trousers Mitchum wore – so he sat shivering and half-bare in the cold night, alighted and stole clothes off a washing line; jumped off at Savannah, Georgia, in the search for food, only to be arrested as a vagrant and prosecuted for a robbery he did not commit. He proved his innocence, but was still sent down to the prison farm. He just wanted to go see the swamp, that's all.

Previously, while Mitchum was still a babe in arms, his army father was crushed between the couplings of box cars which rammed together, irrespective of his internal organs getting in the way. His father – a strong fighter and drinker of Celtic and Blackfoot descent – hung on to life as long as he could but died from his wounds, in his wife's arms, skewered on steel and dead spent.

15

Mitchum escaped from Georgia, bullets whistling past his ears as he ran from the chain-gang through Pipemaker Swamp and made his way, eventually, to California via Baltimore, Delaware, New York; at twenty years of age, he found himself conned by his family into auditioning for a role with the Long Beach Players' Guild. He had a natural presence on stage, by all accounts.

Along the way to LA, he was held captive by boot-leggers up in the Alabama hills; lived off the ransoms paid for kidnapped pets; came close to having a leg amputated; met his future wife – his only wife – stealing her from under his brother's nose and scaring off all the other boys who came sniffing about; sent a poem to his mother back home:

Trouble lies in sullen pools along the road I've taken
Sightless windows stare the empty street
No love beckons me save that which I've forsaken
The anguish of my solitude is sweet.

I wish I'd written that. The loner was not yet the macho hunk his screen image suggested, but neither was he scared of trouble and his quiet sensitivity was already alluring to girls. But with a grasp of what was needed to aid his survival, he kept from the masculine world his poetic persuasions and sensitive voice.

A far cry from Mitchum the big film star. Mitchum the man men wanted to be, and their women agreed. Mitchum the smouldering hero. Anti-hero. The real deal. The ex-con with a record for drugs and vagrancy. The barrel-chested anarchist. The self-proclaimed 'poontang hunter'. The Howard Hughes fantasy. The man always caught up in bar room brawls, 'accidentally'. The man who claimed he could tell any strain of US weed, blindfolded. The drowsy-eyed, somnambulistic actor who dismissed the film industry as peddling horse shit. The actor's actor who never won an Oscar®. The one who prepared the way for Brando and James Dean. The influence on Pacino, De Niro, Jeff Bridges. The one who stood up for the inexperienced. The star, the storyteller, the out-and-out liar. The tall tales, the bullshit. The life and soul of the party. The foul-mouthed, scatological saxophonist who loved to mix it. The boozer. The jazz hound. The cynic. The small-town ferret-faced kid who wrote poetry.

Where the hell did you go, Mitch, you son of a mother? And don't you go telling me 'six foot under', more like 'forty leagues' – I know your bad ass was scattered at sea. But you still better look over your shoulder, baby, cos I'm coming to get thee.

'You're not gonna find a thing, except yourself.'
R M, *His Kind of Woman*

17

Take 2

So let's open the file on this cat.

Robert Mitchum's reputation goes before him. Always has. Sometimes deserved, sometimes not. He had 'an easy way of looking as if he knew where the bodies were buried' and admitted when he smiled he looked 'like a fox in a hen-house'.

He's been described as: antagoniser and ignorer of authority, rebel, maverick, stray cannon, iconoclast, thrill-seeker, cynic who didn't give a damn about anything, least of all acting... 'the Hipster John Wayne', 'a wild son of a bitch', hemp-headed Hemingway-man... tough, virile, indifferent... a rugged individualist, 'a skeptical and sarcastic cat', 'a taciturn grump and profane crank', a 'study in contradiction'... bloody-minded, cantankerous, deadpan, sardonic... 'Mr Bad Taste', 'Trouble Himself',

'The Man with the Immoral Face'... a roughneck, a beef-cake, a scatological lout... uncouth and overbearing... a thief, con-man and saboteur who 'never backed off from anyone'... head-fucker, game-player, micky-taker, smart-ass... 'roverboy', a dirty dog, 'catnip for women'... the 'embodiment of film noir'... an outlaw, flawed to the core... an 'existentialist hero'... I could go on. OK, let's run with it: he was anarchist; button-pusher; cage-rattler and cruel Casanova; druggy, drunkard and devil's advocate; experimenter and escapee from authority; foul-mouthed fucker; groper; hep-talkin' hophead; inflammatory icon; jazz-hound and jerk; knob-head and knave; Lothario and libertine; muff-magnet; obscene offender-in-chief at every opportunity; pugilist; quoteable, quaffing, quarrelling Quixote; rebellious roustabout and raunchy ratbag; shit-stirrer supreme; thunderous thug and tarnished tartar; an utterly unorthodox, unadulterated adulterer; a violent vulgarian; wildcat and wrongdoer; X-rated extremist; yahoo and yardbird; a zoot-suited zoomorphic zinger... (give me more letters, I don't have to return James Ellroy's thesaurus just yet).

Tales of his antics are legion: expulsion from school; running with street gangs; shooting friends; in and out of prison, coming close to amputation; dognapping and rolling drunks for money; bar brawls, fighting off marines and heavy-weight boxers; drug busts and smuggling; loose-living; wannabee actresses 'throwing' themselves at him; bloody-minded escapades to get what he wanted; getting fired from movies; hanging a film producer from a lamp-post and chucking a press officer in the bay; convincing a 'journalist' he spent his spare time 'poontang' hunting, as if it were a wild animal... Mitch, *you* were the animal, you dirty fucker. Oh and he acted too, when he could be bothered.

Robert Mitchum – 'movie star'. Big deal. What's one less actor in the world? One less fat, over-paid, demanding drama queen? Shit, no great loss to anyone except his family.

'That great has-been.'

Susan Hayward, The Lusty Men

In an age when cinema was at the heart of entertainment and Hollywood actors were *the* great heroes, Mitchum publicly considered himself a movie star rather than an actor.

'There are actors and there are movie stars. Basically, that's it. And the assumed rewards and returns and claims of a movie star are the goal of the actors.'

R M

So which was he? Talented screen performer or celebrity hunk? Those in the business knew there was no question: Mitchum was among the very best movie actors of the twentieth century, who never failed to stand out amongst his peers and has served as a role model ever since. But the critics and public have consistently found it hard to be certain. Even today, whether or not he deserves his praise is still a moot point.

'People can't make up their minds whether I'm the greatest actor in the world or the worst. Matter of fact, neither can I. It's been said that I underplay so much I could have stayed home, but I must be good at my job or they wouldn't haul me around the world at these prices.'

R M

If by your friends shall ye be known, then by their co-stars and directors shall an actor. Mitchum worked with renowned directors Edward Dmytryk, John Farrow, Henry Hathaway, Howard Hawks, John Huston, Jim Jarmusch, Elia Kazan, David Lean, Mervyn LeRoy, Vincente Minnelli, Robert Parrish, Sydney Pollack, Otto Preminger, Nicholas Ray, Martin Scorsese, Josef von Sternberg, J Lee Thompson, Jaques Tourneur, Raoul Walsh, William A Wellman and Daryl F Zanuck. If Mitchum wasn't a great actor, then that's a hell of a lot of experienced directors making the same mistake.

'Mitchum is... of the caliber of Olivier, Burton and Brando. In other words, the very best in the field... he is capable of playing King Lear.'

John Huston

'He has the greatest natural sense of timing a line of anybody I have seen work before the cameras. He does naturally what most actors and actresses strive for years to attain without success.'

Lloyd Bacon

'I adore Robert Mitchum.'

Martin Scorsese

It's tempting to think Mitchum never really appeared in a 'great' movie. Lots of footage, not much substance. And yet he starred with some of the finest, most famous and endearing names in cinema history: Lauren Bacall, Yul Brynner, Richard Burton, James Coburn, Tony Curtis, Olivia DeHavilland, Robert De Niro, Johnny Depp, Kirk Douglas, Henry Fonda, Ava Gardner, Cary Grant, Rita Hayworth, Katherine Hepburn, Charlton Heston, Rock Hudson, John Hurt, Gene Kelly, Deborah Kerr, Burt Lancaster, Laurel and Hardy, Jack Lemmon, Dean Martin, Lee Marvin, Marilyn Monroe, Paul Newman, Jack Nicholson, Gregory Peck, Edward G Robinson, Jane Russell, Frank Sinatra, James Stewart, Elizabeth Taylor, Spencer Tracy, Peter Ustinov, John Wayne and numerous others.

For my money, Mitchum was a damn fine actor who wanted to be an artist, but the industry wouldn't let him. Yes, he could've forced his intentions but then he would've risked appearing precious or pretentious. More to the point, he would've risked the income needed to support his extended family. Any intention of producing art was beaten out of him by gorilla scripts so, realising his artistic desires would not be met within the movie industry, he quickly became cynical of the business. He sussed the lie of the land: churn 'em out kid, churn 'em out. And churn he did.

'I gave up being serious about making pictures years ago – around the time I made a film with Greer Garson and she took 125 takes to say "no".'

R M

It's hardly surprising when you consider the greater details. The film was *Desire Me*, the year 1947. It was one of three movies Mitchum was making simultaneously, for RKO and MGM. Director George Cukor was replaced by Jack Conway. Jack Conway was replaced by Mervyn LeRoy. Mervyn LeRoy was replaced by Victor Saville. Co-star Robert Montgomery left to work on another film, Mitchum took his part and Richard Hart took Mitchum's. The script went through so many rewrites that many elements of the story got lost in the fog. What a way to make a film. What a way to make a living.

'I think there were five directors on the film. That was a real mess. You wouldn't believe the dialogue in that script. George Cukor and Mervyn LeRoy are both exemplary directors in their own right. But together they don't spell mother.'

R M

So what happened to Mitchum's motivation and purpose? His artistic integrity and reward? Did he: offer himself up to a role, only to discover he wasn't that talented, or wasn't that appreciated, so stepped back; refuse to offer himself up out of fear or disinterest, satisfying himself with the pay-check and fame; offer himself up but claim he didn't so as to side-step criticism, failure and pain? All of the above; none of the above; something else?

'He may say he doesn't take acting seriously, but he was totally professional. He resented it when others weren't.'
Jacqueline DeWitt, co-star, The Gentle Approach

There's plenty of evidence as to his professionalism – however drunk he was the night before, he almost always showed up the next morning, clean-shaven and sober enough to work, having memorised not only his own lines, but everyone else's.

'Mitch could drink... could drink most of the night but it never seemed to affect him. At seven o'clock the next morning he was there, in makeup, wardrobe and on the set, on time. And he always knew his lines.'
Stanley Rubin, producer, River of No Return

Whether that sobriety lasted the day depended on the quality of the movie. On those occasions when he felt frustrated or let down by the quality of script, performance or production, he would allow his emotions to get the better of him and any pretentions to professionalism. But however righteously angry he felt, he was always willing to apologise if he realised he was wrong. Or when he sobered up.

'Mitchum took to drink. Who could blame him? Bob put much more violence into the action... the stunt men went flying... he went on a rampage.... there was nothing I could do except

stand there and watch and hope the fury would finally drain out of him. It didn't. It went on and on.... I started into my prepared speech... "You're a bully and a..." but Bob interrupted. "Look," he said, "I'm sorry about what happened. I apologize. What more can I say?".... "Bob," I said, "you're a son of a bitch." "I know."'

Richard Fleischer, uncredited director, His Kind of Woman

Wouldn't it be great to go to work and let rip like that, and still be employed the next morning?

'Wouldn't it be fun to be a real movie star and get to act like one... get shitfaced snockered? Wow! Just like Robert Mitchum. That'd be something else friends, that'd be something else.'

Peter Boyle, co-star, The Friends of Eddie Coyle

Those stories always find their way into print. What's often ignored is the evidence proving his good behaviour and total involvement in a role, if he thought it deserved the effort.

'[Mitchum] doesn't want anyone to realise it, but he cares deeply.'

Edward Dmytryk, director, Anzio, Crossfire, Till the End of Time

'Often they embarrass me by saying, "We think it's fine." If they say to me, "It stinks but let's make it," then I'm with them. I ain't here because I'm displaying any facility or versatility.'

R M

So he responded to how he was treated. If they gave him a film worthy of an actor, he put in his all. If they gave him a dud deserving of a studio mule, he kicked and chewed his way through it.

'[Mitchum] *simply walks through most of his pictures with his eyes half open because that's all that's called for.'*
John Huston

The great shame is not that he didn't put his full effort into every role, but that his disregard for certain films has been used to camouflage his great subtlety on screen.

What made Mitchum's portrayals so unappetising to many was that he brought realism to the screen before anyone wanted it. In the forties and fifties, when a cinema audience settled in with their popcorn, they wanted to see 'a performance'. And Mitchum looked like he wasn't performing. He didn't 'act' as such so, in a time of ham-dramatics and over-acting, his subtlety was often misunderstood. Besides, how can such a troublemaker, a roustabout, a drug fiend, a demon, a beast, be subtle? Once a man is tagged as a bull in a china-shop there is little he can do except try to remember to be himself – whichever version he might be that day.

Mitchum could do things on screen no one else mastered. Free of the ego-driven ambition to be the only 'star' that mattered, he made standing in the background an art-form; he made waiting for someone to answer a masterclass in acting – in not acting, or not appearing to act.

One of the great ironies is the ease with which critics

27

became lazy, in writing about how they perceived Mitchum to be lazy. They often dismissed his performances with yet another 'Mitchum sleepwalks through the picture' swipe, whether he was engaged and at his most remarkably subtle or just going through the motions, frustratedly awaiting a pay-check. Once his style was misconstrued, he was damned for ever.

So Mitchum's subtlety in a not-too-subtle age, a subtlety which contradicted his persona, was often misinterpreted as 'doing nothing'. And sometimes it was true. Mitchum would go through his scripts marking whole passages 'NAR' – 'No Acting Required'. Was this laziness? A lack of enthusiasm? Mitchum laughing all the way to the bank? He was the first to admit to all of these, just as he was always willing to put himself down, as an actor. Perhaps, just perhaps, it wasn't acting that was required, but naturalism; reality; a man, not a pretence. Marking scenes 'NAR' could mean 'no effort' or it could mean 'be normal', authentic. Acting is easy, compared with being. You watch how Mitchum does nothing on screen. He confounds movie-goers because he doesn't act like an actor; he acts like a normal guy, or as normal a guy as the role will allow.

'[Mitchum] *was born with what we call film-style acting. A really fine film actor does not give a performance, he creates a person and is that person. Mitchum was one of the very best at that. He knew people, common people – I think that's one thing that endears him to people. He gives that feeling.'*
Edward Dmytryk

These days, movie audiences expect a subtle approach from actors and overblown reactions can make us cringe. So although we can now see Mitchum's skills for what they are, we've also become blasé. But it mustn't be forgotten: this man was doing it before the contemporaries. Without Mitchum, the best movie acting wouldn't be what it is today.

Opinions of Mitchum have always been fuelled by what he said of himself. He was always willing to supply a self-deprecating remark which some critics took as confirmation of their own opinions. He didn't help his own case.

'I have two acting styles: with and without a horse.'

R M

He claimed he had only three expressions – 'looking left, looking right and looking straight ahead'; that the only difference between him and other actors was that he had 'spent more time in jail'; that he was highly sought after because he was cheap. Perhaps Mitchum was just getting the first punch in. He shared with Spencer Tracy a simple philosophy towards the craft: 'learn your lines and don't bump into the furniture'. He did the basics well, kept things simple and that simplicity gave room for texture and dynamic to emerge in his performance.

For me, it's Mitchum's absolute ability to be subtle, often in unsubtle roles, which really reveals his talent. Whereas most actors would approach a macho role by being loud and obvious, Mitchum underplayed, which gave his characters far greater authenticity and menace, if menace was required.

'I was trying to get a close-up of [Mitchum] *reacting... and nothing happened. So I cut and said, "You're supposed to react." "I did react." "Well, I didn't see it!" He said, "Well, it's the best I can do." I thought, "Jesus, he's pretty snotty." We run the dailies the next day and by God you look at the screen and he is reacting. It's on the screen and I couldn't see it.'*

Richard Fleischer, director, *His Kind of Woman* and *Bandido*

Mitchum made sense because he was believeable and because he wasn't like all the rest. Sometimes he just *was* and that was enough. Mind, you watch enough Mitchum movies and you soon get fed up with the sigh he developed and stuck to again and again.

Mitchum never claimed to have any great insight into the art or craft of acting and wasn't the kind of man to show enthusiasm for learned techniques or schools of thought. He considered actors to be 'narcissistic bastards' and was frequently frustrated with the likes of Peppard and De Niro who insisted on following 'The Method' or Actors' Studio techniques, or needed hours to get into character. Famously, when asked if he followed the Stanislavski method he replied, 'I follow the Smirnoff method'.

'Brando can spend three minutes saying hello.'

R M

'[Young actors] *only want to talk about acting method and motivation. In my day, all we talked about was screwing and overtime.'*

R M

While filming *Secret Ceremony* he was so detached from the cast's process that he skipped set and found his way to the home of Bob Parrish, his director on *Fire Down Below* and *The Wonderful Country*.

'*It was early in the morning. He asked for some tequila... and told us he had snuck out on [Joseph] Losey and Liz Taylor and Mia [Farrow]. They didn't even know he had left. He said they were arguing over their motivation for the next scene. They needed to know what was the character's grandmother's maiden name. In other words, he was decrying that kind of acting. He drank some more tequila and decided he better get going... he said, "I'll go back and hit my mark."*'

Kathie Parrish

Mitchum relied on his depth and humanity, on his understanding of people and the psychology of men. Real people who shit and fart. He was one of them. A man of his time, Mitchum wasn't alone in his opinions.

'*Method actors give you a photograph, real actors give you an oil painting.*'

Charles Laughton, actor and director

Equally considered was John Huston's reply to a USC film student who questioned whether he should follow the three-act formula for movie-making: 'I think you need to get yourself down to Mexico and fuck some whores.' Stop analysing process and get out there and live.

These were the opinions of actors and directors who

had first grabbed life by the throat and survived a range of experience before portraying it on screen.

Mitchum was *the* man of his generation. On screen and in life. Respected by his peers, loved by his audience, feared by his rivals. He was the original screen rebel. He didn't just act the part, he lived it, and then merely presented a version of himself on screen. Although, as a young man, Mitchum found in stage-acting a level of pleasure, enthusiasm and group expression he'd never before encountered, he shared with Humphrey Bogart and Spencer Tracy the belief that movie acting was an embarrassing thing for a 'real' man to do. In a 'man's' world, acting isn't a real job and isn't something a 'real man' should be caught doing. Next thing you know, he'll be joining a dance troupe and writing poems, prancing along the flouncy outer-limits of masculinity. Sensitivity equals weakness and lower status as 'man'. I'd love to claim these beliefs have vanished.

'One feels that way. Should be out building a bridge or digging a ditch or jacking up a tyre or something. Stealing a car or something. Not making faces; getting all painted up and making faces, pretending to be someone else.'

R M

'I like getting up at 5am and having my head painted for the cameras. What real man doesn't?'

R M

But it wasn't only the questions he himself cast upon his

masculinity which made Mitchum uncomfortable with his role as movie star.

'I'm ashamed of being an actor because people accord you the respect and fame and attention you don't merit.... A lady who teaches blind children wrote me, "My pupils believe that when you say something on the screen, whatever it is, it must be true. Your voice has the ring of honesty and sincerity in it." Stuff like that bothers the hell out of me. It's embarrassing because I'm only a survivor of the Stone Age of American middle-class culture. I'm no hero or paragon.'

R M

At least, as actors, Mitchum and Bogart played tough-man roles that remained in the public's consciousness, even when they were off set. God forbid the world discover Mitchum wasn't reliant upon acting for his artistic satisfaction. God forbid the world discover that for artistic satisfaction the big man, the all man, the man's man – Robert Mitchum – turned to poetry.

Whatever your opinions on Mitchum as an actor, there's no doubting he appearing in some great movies. *The Story of GI Joe* (1945), *Crossfire* (1947), *Heaven Knows, Mr Allison* (1957), *The Sundowners* (1960), *The Longest Day* (1962) and *Ryan's Daughter* (1970) all deserved their Oscar® wins and nominations. Others, like *Pursued* (1947), *Out of the Past* (1947), *The Lusty Men* (1952), *Night of the Hunter* (1955), *Cape Fear* (1962) and *The Friends of Eddie Coyle* (1973) never received the awards, rewards or credit they deserved.

Post-World War II, Mitchum was huge in both physical and celluloid frame; in both presence and star value. In a time when people were shorter and movie careers easy to come by and easy to lose. Actors of lesser stature tried to upstage him but the audience's attention remained on him.

At over six foot he was not to be messed with, and directors presumed he could take any punishment. He often had to do his own stunts – falling downstairs, wrestling giant sea turtles, steering a raft down the rapids. An aspect of the job which, over the years, would ruin his knees, his ankles, and anything else that hurt.

Mitchum wasn't only man's man, he was lady's man, also. Physically broad and strong (though not so toned as life went on), Mitchum's rugged, masculine frame sent women wild.

'Mitchum was really physically imposing and kept himself in great shape – he always worked out and was always quite gorgeous to look at.'

Polly Bergen, co-star, *Cape Fear*

But he also had something else – his drowsy eyes fronting a suggestion of subterranean brutality wrapped in an electric sexual presence. He was danger, he was risk, he was animal.

'Of all the post-war actors – Douglas, Lancaster, Widmark – only Mitchum figured out how to be a man's man and a woman's man at the same time.'

Carrie Rickey, film critic

'Mitchum... is MAN!'

Frances Nuyen, co-star
Last Time I Saw Archie, Man in the Middle

So potently did Mitchum's real-life activities substantiate his bad-boy image and reputation as a dangerous force; such was his standing as the sexually-alluring anti-hero; so clearly did he stand out; so attractive was he to the fantasies of acceptable society and a role model to the loner and outcast, that even a career-threatening court case for possession of illegal narcotics did nothing but aid his development, his fame, his importance, the respect his fans held for him. The women looked up to him as all man, as dangerous man; the men were threatened by him, saw him as one of their own, or looked up to him as the epitome of what they wanted to be.

'Bob... is amazingly tolerant of the fawning adulation of hysterical women, and is invariably picked on by men who are jealous of his success. He is very slow to move to retaliate, though....'

Deborah Kerr, co-star, *Heaven Knows, Mister Allison*, etc

He was seen as the bad boy both on- and off-screen. His fan club, the 'Bob Mitchum Droolettes', grew in number – all bobby-socks and young pussies eager for the screen giant to provide them with the 'real' man of their dreams; good girls wanting to escape their fathers into the arms of a bad boy. These were the days before Marlon Brando, before James Dean, before the modern-day two-bit pretenders

35

who are desperate for us to believe they are dangerous desperados. Before Mitchum, there was no 'great American screen anti-hero'; no rough and ready character who was just trying to survive. Mitchum invented it. He lived it. He brought to roles something genuine which has since been the goal of numerous outsiders, oddballs and loveable fuck-ups, pseudo or otherwise. They owe him their careers, their demand and their infamy. Mitchum didn't fit the niche, he created it. You go look at that niche, you go look at Brando and James Dean and all those misfits and anti-heroes and you'll see, you'll see they're just trying to fill a Mitchum-shaped crater, unsuccessfully.

'[Mitchum] *was cool before cool became common.*'
Stanley Rubin, producer, *River of no Return*

Before him there were tough guys, sure, but they were of a different mould: Bogart, Cagney, Edward G Robinson – greats all, as either heroes or villains – but audiences didn't associate with them so easily; found it harder to see themselves in the actors on screen. Mitchum was human.

'*You know what the average Robert Mitchum fan is? He's full of warts and dandruff and he's probably got a hernia, too. But he sees me up there on the screen and thinks, "If that bum can make it, I can become president." I bring a ray of hope to the great unwashed.*'
R M

Many of his B-movies were pot-boilers just making up the

production figures, or opportunities for Mitchum to rid himself of contractual obligations, but have since taken on a new value as classic examples of style or as markers of the period.

When Strangers Marry (re-released as *Betrayed*) has been dubbed 'unquestionably the finest B-film' (Don Miller, movie historian) and 'the model of a budget thriller' (Alvin H Marrill, *Robert Mitchum on the Screen*), and resulted in Mitchum being offered a contract by RKO. Several of Mitchum's RKO pictures can now be viewed as great examples of film noir.

'Mitchum was *film noir.'*

Martin Scorsese

In hindsight, noir seems the perfect vehicle for the real Mitchum, who led a raging existence of black and white yet was a great appreciator and explorer of grey areas.

Out of the Past has been heralded as the best film noir ever, whereas *Crossfire* and *The Lusty Men* are amongst the best the studio ever produced. Even *His Kind of Woman* and *Macao*, although structurally and technically rough-and-ready, remain entertaining opportunities to see Mitchum and Jane Russell bounce off each other.

Some Mitchum movies were unique, original, or the best of their genre: *The Locket* (1946) was the most flashback-obsessed movie Hollywood had ever produced; *Crossfire* (1947) was ahead of its time, in dealing with anti-Semitism in post-war America; *Pursued* was the first ever psychological western; *The Lusty Men* was the greatest-ever rodeo picture; *Thunder Road* (1958) was the forerunner, and greatest, of the moonshine-runner flicks; *The Longest Day* (1962) was the most ambitious war movie ever made and a major influence on *Saving Private Ryan*; *Night of the Hunter* (1955) and *Cape Fear* (1962) were complex and sophisticated dramas in which Mitchum gave brilliant presentations of psycho-sexual villains.

Whereas many of the pictures released under the bizarre leadership of Howard Hughes can be seen to have ruined RKO (including Mitchum's own films, according to the man himself), another Mitchum film saved 20th Century-Fox from disappearing up its own box office. Having overspent massively on the production of the grandioise and extravagant Burton/Taylor flick *Cleopatra*, the studio found itself in huge trouble. There was no way the studio could afford to make another film, least of all a huge star-studded project like *The Longest Day*, but so determined was studio head Darryl F Zanuck to go ahead with the project that he funded it himself. Not only did it prove to be a great war film and an Oscar® winner, it also saved the studio.

Unfortunately not all Mitchum's movies were so monumental. He sure appeared in some real stinkers, he was the first to admit it. They may've paid the mortgage but movies like *Matilda* (1978), *Breakthrough* (1982) and *Believed Violent* (1990) should never have seen the light of day. Even *The Red Pony* (1948), for which John Steinbeck wrote the screen adaptation of his own book, was a tedious disappointment. As for *James Dean: Race with Destiny* (1997), it's best to remember Mitchum was near to death and was probably trying to make some money for his family, before passing. But even when you consider the duds, the big cheques for poor product, the shambolic vomiting of scripts dumped on studios by conniving agents; even when you consider the dross and the contract-fillers, the walk-on parts and the war-time propaganda flicks, the scales are still most firmly weighted in Mitchum's favour – none of the bad films are so bad as to detract from his finest moments; the mean is still magnificent.

'I became very conscious of waste. I mean, why? Why would they [make] *a film that had so little chance, and why would they do it so badly? I was very conscious of the waste of time. I suppose it kept people employed – that's the only possible excuse.... I always felt they could do much better and I was very disappointed. For instance, during the war you could put a sign on a marquee that said "Closed" and people would queue up for four blocks to see "Closed" and at that time they could've... made some advances but instead of that they reached down to the bottom of a drawer and they took out all the dreft that they'd been gathering for years, that agents had palmed off on them, and they made it and people were subjected to it, and I don't believe that's fair, really. Truly, I think that the people deserve something for their attention.'*

R M

Still, the general consensus seems to be: if only Mitchum appeared in more quality films, rather than often being the one glimmer of quality in a couple of reels of mediocrity, appreciation of his talents would be far greater. Well, let's break this down. Mitchum broke into Hollywood in 1943, at a time when pictures were churned out en masse, many taking only a week or two to film. It was normal for actors to work on more than one film in a day. Are they technically superior? Do they have the rapid-cut pazazz of contemporary movies? Of course not. They offer a slower, more textural pleasure. But pleasure and entertainment are still there. If you consider many of the movies Mitchum appeared in, they're either genuine markers in the development of cinema or deserve to be re-evaluated as great examples of period style. If you look at Mitchum's output, decade by decade, quality and value are consistent:

1940s – the 'Hopalong Cassidy' movies; *When Strangers Marry*; *The Story of GI Joe*; *Till the End of Time*; *Crossfire*; *Pursued*; *Out of the Past*; *The Big Steal*.

1950s – *Where Danger Lives*; *His Kind of Woman*; *The Lusty Men*; *Angel Face*; *Second Chance*; *Track of the Cat*; *Night of the Hunter*; *Man with the Gun*; *Foreign Intrigue*; *Heaven Knows, Mr Allison*; *The Enemy Below*; *Thunder Road*; *The Wonderful Country*.

1960s – *Home from the Hill*; *The Sundowners*; *Cape Fear*; *The Longest Day*; *Two for the Seesaw*; *Secret Ceremony*.

1970s – *The Friends of Eddie Coyle*; *The Yakuza*; *Farewell, My Lovely*.

1980s – *Maria's Lovers*; *Mr North*; even *Scrooged*.

1990s – the remake of *Cape Fear*; *Tombstone*; *Dead Man*.

That's one hell of a lot of damn fine cinema. Who else has starred in so many good films, over such a wide period and in so many styles? Compare this list to the output, to the average quality of product, from an actor like, say, Tom Cruise....

'Mitchum delivered a body of work that now looks timeless and enduring when compared with other American screen actors.'
David Gritten, *The Daily Telegraph*

With so much respect from his peers, he must've had a shelf full of Oscars®, right? Wrong. He never received one. He was nominated once and many in the business lobbied the Academy to award him a lifetime achievement award before he died, but neither went his way.

Mitchum was nominated for the Best Supporting Actor award in 1945, for his role in *The Story of GI Joe*. Afterwards he quipped, 'You notice the Academy hasn't messed with me since.'

'When he passed away I was a little miffed that here was a guy who should've got an Academy Award or a nomination at least for a dozen different films... when we knew that he was sick we did a little push to try and get him the Life Achievement Award. Virtually ever actor he ever worked with sent in letters to the board of directors... Martin Sheen wrote him a letter, De Niro, Eastwood, Selleck, Nicholson... my father was overlooked again. Of course he wasn't around for the next one. The next one Jack Nicholson got an Oscar® and dedicated [it] to my father. The actors knew who was a good actor.'
Chris Mitchum, son

It's commonly believed that there was really only one reason why Mitchum never received an Oscar® and that was his refusal to toe the line. He wasn't pliable, he wasn't controllable. If they put him on the stage in front of a worldwide audience, who knows what he might do or say? If you award the rebels, the individuals, what message does that send out to everyone else? If the troublemakers win awards, why should anyone else behave? Mitchum could never win; could never be seen to win. That's the nature of the game, and he knew it.

Mitchum wasn't willing to perpetuate the myth of Hollywood spendour. He may've been a movie star as a job, but he didn't subscribe to the full package – his brain, his thinking, remained that of a blue-collar man who had been forged in the fire of the real world, and wasn't willing to lose sight of that amongst the glitter and glamour.

'I don't think he really understood Hollywood and all the glamour and glitz, and I think that's why he was Hollywood's first bad boy, because he never really played that game. He would be the guy who would stand up for himself and not worry if his nose got broken. He was a guy's guy.'

Bentley Mitchum, grandson

OK, we get the message. Regardless of awards and the acknowledgement from authority, his status as an actor stands. Those in the know, knew. Mitchum was the real deal. Now I gotta go figure what this cat means to me. I gotta figure out why he wrapped up the poet in the man's man guise; why he couldn't get away with being all of himself; why he *presumed* he couldn't get away with being all of himself; why being an actor or a poet was such a threat to his perceived masculinity; and why so little has changed. Good god, I need to go find this man 'cos I need to learn from him.

'Alright, he was the best, but he's dead.'
R M, White Witch Doctor

That fact ain't gonna stop me. I despised him as a kid but now, as a boy approaching forty, I need myself a role model, a guide, a surrogate. I'm going for a beer.

Take 3

Mitchum's regular film career began as an extra in the 'Hopalong Cassidy' cowboy movies, starring William Boyd in the title role. Boyd had been sinking into the swamp of alcoholism before the Hoppy's came along and resurrected his career in the mid-1930s. Mitchum, like Boyd, was chosen because he was available, and cheap.

My father liked Hopalong Cassidy. As a child growing up in post-World War II Cardiff, he'd be there, Saturday mornings in some flea-pit cinema, whooping at the screen with the other kids. He had his photo taken wearing a Roy Rogers T-shirt. Later, as a grown man, he never shook off the disappointment he felt that it was Rogers and not Cassidy emblazoned on his chest.

For all his childish inability to shake off childhood disappointment, when it came to horse operas he had

45

good taste – there are few better ways to laze away an hour or a day than with a big spliff, a comfy settee and a good-versus-bad black and white 'Hoppy' flick. Or several. And there *were* several – thirty-five in all, of which Mitchum appeared in seven, usually playing an unshaven heavy, long-legged and slim. He described these early roles as 'very little dialogue, a lot of beard'.

As with most of Mitchum's life, the story of how he came to get his first break has variations: the official version claims he was working as an extra when agent Paul Wilkins wangled a chance for Mitchum to meet 'Hoppy' producer, Harry 'Pop' Sherman; another version claims Mitchum was involved with Sherman's daughter, Teddy, and got his introduction through her; another that he wasn't *involved* with Teddy, but that she was driving along Sunset Boulevard when she spotted Mitchum thumbing a ride. She stopped and when he found out she was on her way to the studios he asked if she could get him in. She got him in and introduced him to her father. This was May 1942 and Mitchum was working at a shoe-shop on Wilshire Boulevard. Or maybe he wasn't. One version says he had already been fired, for screaming 'Beaver!' at an annoying customer. I'm tempted not to believe this but I used to flick the V's at customers when I worked for W H Smith, so who am I to throw a dim light. Another version claims he screamed 'Beaver!' whenever a female entered the store.

Peter Falk: '*Look, a guy can sell shoes for forty years, I live more in one day. I see more and I feel more. I taste more, I think more, I'm more. Understand? I'm more. You know,*

there's more to living than just breathing. Capisce?'
R M: *'Capisce.'*

Anzio

Mitchum went to meet Sherman wearing a borrowed suit held together with sticky tape. Sherman sized him up, liked the look of him (if not his suit) and told him not to shave.

The one constant throughout many versions of this story is *why* Mitchum was needed in the first place: Charlie Murphy – a regular in the 'Hoppy' movies – had his skull crushed when he fell off a stage coach during filming. Mitchum was to take his place. When he arrived, the costumer scrapped the blood off Murphy's hat and gave it to Mitchum. Yep, he made his screen debut in a dead man's hat, and you don't get any more cowboy than that.

But cowboy he ain't; *wasn't*. He may've been a regular in the saddle, but not on the back of a horse. It wasn't until later in life that Mitchum became a horse-man, breeding them at his Maryland ranch, including a World's Champion, Don Guerro.

He had 'owned' a horse as a kid, but only because it had broken loose in search of somewhere to die. Mitchum locked it in a barn where its corpse soon stank to high heaven. But as a Hollywood cowboy he was green, so when he bluffed about his riding skills to the experienced 'Hoppy' crew they sensed he was covering his tracks and put him on a dangerous horse.

Hoss. He tried to mount but it threw him off. Sensing his new job and wage were at stake, and a potential loss of face, he punched the horse full on the nose. It didn't throw

47

him again. 'I had to stick on because Dorothy was pregnant again,' he said, 'money was scarce.'

The horse operas were good to Mitchum – as well as a decent wage they also provided all the manure he could sell. For the rest of his life he would refer to his job as 'horse-shit salesman', 'movie *actress*' or 'RKO's mule'.

'It was kinda my road-game... if I didn't have another job I could always get a job on a Hopalong Cassidy because they made them endlessly, you know. I think they made two pictures every three weeks. They'd do the interiors of one and then the exteriors of both and then the interiors of the second... it was a good healthy outdoor life for a hundred dollars a week, all the horse manure I could carry home, playing cowboys and Indians, picnicing in the grass, it was OK.'

R M

Six years later, his career on an impressive rise, Mitchum's infamous answer to the question 'What is your profession?' was *'former* actor'.

Picture this: 1 September 1948 – a warm night. LAPD narcotics officers raid 8334 Ridpath Drive on LA's hip, happening Laurel Canyon....

Loaded on Scotch and sat smoking grass are Mitchum and his buddy Robin Ford. Mitchum has been under survelliance for some time and Ford is well-known to the Narc Squad who are desperate for a big-name collar. Mitchum and Ford are visiting twenty-year-old Lana Turner lookalike Lila Leeds and twenty-five-year-old dancer Vicki

Evans. Mitchum sparks a joint and throws a pack of them on the table. He doesn't want to be there; feels antsy; thinks he sees a face at the window. The police creep around the bungalow and pretend to be Evans' dogs, scratching at the back door. Evans lets them in. The police introduce themselves in their inimitable manner. Mitchum drops his joint and puts out his wrists to receive the cuffs to which he is already accustomed. Amongst the drugs found are marijuana and amphetamine. The press have a field-day; his wife goes bananas. It looks like his days are numbered.

'I figured I'd go quietly. Not like I was a virgin – it was trip number eleven for me [for] *various infractions of statutes: walking against the lines, stepping on the grass, sassing the cops – jazz like that.'*

R M

Mitchum had already appeared in an incredible thirty-five movies in five years, including successful war pictures and noir classics *Thirty Seconds Over Tokyo*, *The Story of GI Joe*, *Undercurrent*, *Crossfire* and *Out of the Past*, but he had just become the first major Hollywood star of the talking-movie age to get arrested for narcotics.

It's important to appreciate to what extent Mitchum's star was in the ascendancy. In 1948 he was receiving more fan-mail than any other Hollywood star except Ginger Rogers – around 1,500 letter a week. In the previous few years, he had his first star billing (*Nevada*); had been nominated for an Oscar® (*The Story of GI Joe*); worked with legendary directors William A Wellman, Raoul Walsh,

Mervyn LeRoy, Jacques Tourneur, Vincente Minnelli and Edward Dmytryk; had starred in the superb *Pursued*, *Crossfire* and *Out of the Past*; had appeared with established stars such as Burgess Meredith and Katherine Hepburn; had made his network radio debut; and still had his range and creative freedom unrestricted by behavioural expectation and image. Who could tell in what roles he would best be employed. Would he be hero, villain, paternal/fraternal/ avuncular rock, fall guy, comedian, lover, rat? Much was expected of him. He had a future. There was a growing momentum to a future of fame and success.

These days, the possession of marijuana is hardly headline-grabbing news, and it shouldn't have been then – 1948 was a busy year. Mud was being slung before the House Un-American Activities Committee; the US was testing new atomic weapons in the Marshall Islands; the Supreme Court ordered the state of Oklahoma to admit a black girl to law school; Communists seized power in Czechoslovakia; North Korea formed a Soviet people's republic; over two thousand people were killed in six weeks, as Arabs and Jews fought over land known as Israel or Palestine; Britain signed an alliance with Iraq, and warned Argentina to remove their forces from the Falkland Islands; 'Mahatma' Ghandi was assassinated; 'Babe' Ruth and Kurt Schwitters died. On the day of Mitchum's arrest, China announced the creation of a North China People's Government. But Hollywood stars were news, so who cared what was happening in the world. Besides, the US Goverment and media were keen to promote the perception of weed as the insanity-inducing devil's daisy since possession was made illegal in the thirties.

Such an arrest as Mitchum's would surely signal the scuppering of even the hardiest of movie careers – no studio would want to be associated with someone so socially unappealing; so immoral and illegal; so bound for the asylum. The climate was such that even the Oscar®-winning Ingrid Bergman (who many presumed was as much a saint in real life as on screen and stage) would soon be ostracised for becoming pregnant as a result of her affair with Roberto Rossellini, while still married.

Mitchum's spell of success seemed certain to be aborted. He was thirty-one, earning $3,000 a week as a movie star and was trying to convince his wife to come back to him after she had gone back east, taking the children with her because he had 'gone Hollywood and was hanging out with undesirables'. (What did *their* wives think of them hanging out with *him*?)

Once in custody, he was asked if he had a criminal record. Yes he did. He admitted speeding, drunkeness and disorderly conduct. He also had a record for vagrancy – including a five-day spell in solitary, in Texas, which wasn't mentioned.

The next morning, Mitchum had been due to speak on the steps of City Hall as a positive role model, to celebrate 'National Youth Day'. Instead, he was in jail.

The police asked Mitchum who would bail him out. He replied, 'Who knows? I've got two bosses – David O Selznick and RKO. Have you ever listened to [them] when they're peeved? I'd just as soon stay in jail.'

Once the news broke, RKO's share price dropped and

51

the studio began worrying about what to do with the millions of dollars' worth of unreleased Mitchum pictures. Far more interested in defending his investment than defending the man, Selznick – powerful head of Vanguard and co-owner of Mitchum's contract (along with RKO loony Howard Hughes) – described the star as a 'very sick man' who would 'come out of his trouble a finer man'. Sick or not, under the pressure of losing his career, his good name and – most important to him – the respect of his wife and his mother too, Mitchum became beligerent; angry, hostile and foul-mouthed. He had arrived in California in the 1930s, on the back of a freight train with only a dollar and chapel-change and was prepared to leave the same way.

Howard Hughes decided to stick with his boy and hired lawyer-to-the-stars Jerry Giesler, who had a rep for getting Hollywood names off the hook, having successfully defended Errol Flynn against a rape charge and Charlie Chaplin against a paternity suit.

Mitchum and the others were released, awaiting trial. His wife returned to face the press with him. She was furious with the intrusion.

'Everybody ought to be able to see that Bob is a sick man, otherwise he'd never be mixed up in a situation like this.... I'm indignant, though, that not only Bob but our whole family should have to suffer because he is a motion picture star. Otherwise I don't think all this fuss would have been made just because a man may have got mixed up with bad company.'

Dorothy Mitchum

Although the Hollywood press were relatively gentle with Mitchum, the same couldn't be said of those in the Midwest who saw the scandal as a great opportunity to attack the whole film industry. As far as they were concerned, Mitchum was now showing the *real* face of the Hollywood devil. And the police were happy to stoke the fires, claiming Mitchum's arrest should 'serve as a warning' and that they had other stars under surveillance. Arresting officer Alva Barr claimed, 'We are going to clean the dope and the narcotic sellers out of Hollywood and we don't care whom we have to arrest.'

Awaiting his trial, now scheduled for September, RKO decided to go ahead and release *Rachel and the Stranger*, figuring they had nothing to lose. And they didn't. In many theatres across the States, Mitchum's appearance on screen led to cheers, applause and standing ovations. Box office takings shot up. It looked like Mitchum's career could continue although, in his own words, he would have to 'resign from the local scout troup'.

Sensing a prime opportunity, RKO rush-released *Blood on the Moon* to cash in on their boy's notoriety. In this, his first 'A' western, Mitchum plays a cattle-hand caught up between two warring groups of ranchers. He narrowly escapes getting trampled by stampeding cattle; gets offered an ultimatum by gun-toting cowboys; gets shot at by a cowgirl; delivers a message to the womenfolk only to be shot at again, for his trouble; and gets told to get out – all within the first twelve minutes.

When he reaches town, he meets up with an old friend (played by Robert Preston) who explains the situation. They join forces but, realising his friend is in the wrong,

53

Mitchum – Garry – makes a moral choice and swaps sides. The friendship ends in a bar fight.

'We tried to do something for the first time in a western: a bar-room fight that was at least realistic. We said, let's have these men go at it all the way, as hard as they can, and let's have them exhausted at the end, which they would be.... *Mitchum and Preston liked the idea very much.'*

Robert Wise, director, *Blood on the Moon*

There are similarities between the relationship of the two 'friends' and that of Mitchum's and Kirk Douglas's characters in *Out of the Past*. Once again, Mitchum is the accidental hero trying to do something vaguely resembling the right thing, the other smiles and says the right things but really wants Mitchum to do as *he* wants. Neither succeeds, entirely.

'You and me together coulda licked 'em, but you always had a conscience breathing down your neck.'

Robert Preston, *Blood on the Moon*

Blood on the Moon is moody and dramatically shot. Just as *Out of the Past* takes noir from city to small town, so *Blood on the Moon* proves the classic, urban stylistic signatures of noir work just as well out on the range. It's still 'just' a cowboy film as far as plot is concerned, but it is a beautiful and impressive interpretation of the genre.

In the real world, things still weren't tickety-boo: Mitchum would have to wait until the following year to discover his fate. Further delays to the trial were incurred when lawyer Giesler was, inconveniently (some would say conveniently), involved in a minor car accident. Mitchum would not be sentenced until the following February. With the sword of Damocles, Mitchum cleaned his nails.

On 9 February 1949, Robert Mitchum was sentenced to a year in the county jail (suspended) and two years on probation – the first sixty days to be spent in the bucket with time off for good behaviour. Leeds and Ford received the same sentence, but Evans – who arranged the shindig and opened the door to the fuzz – was never convicted.

Mitchum was taken down and became prisoner No. 912345. He hadn't even brought a toothbrush.

He didn't complain about his time inside; didn't play the big star and got on OK with the other inmates. 'Oh, we just talk about our lives of crime,' he joked with the press, 'mostly the other fellows don't bother me too much... they have their own troubles.'

Mitchum was transferred to the Wayside Honor Farm where he served the rest of his fifty days (ten days off – he *did* behave). He worked hard making cement blocks, asked no favours, lost weight, slept well for the first time in years, but had to watch out for those who wanted to gain favour with the authorities by setting him up, sneaking joints and contraband under his pillow in the hope of a search. Mitchum played it safe and kept straight; flushed the grass down the pan or gave it over to the guards.

Howard Hughes would be a regular, if secretive, visitor, bringing vitamin pills and candy bars. His loyalty towards

Mitchum had a profound effect on the star. Hughes could've dumped him there and then under the morality clause in the actor's contract, but decided to keep hold of his troublesome asset. Although Mitchum moaned about his boss on a regular basis, they got on well, Mitchum referring to the secretive and elusive multi-millionaire as 'The Thin Man' or 'The Phantom'.

'[Hughes] *summoned me once to his hotel in Vegas. I walked into his room and he said, "Wait a minute, Bob, I have to make a phone call first." He walked into the next room, and that's the last I ever saw of him. Strange fellow.'*

R M

In 1951 Hughes – then the richest man in America – bought Selznick's share of Mitchum's contract and the actor became RKO's mule.

'They had drawers and vaults filled with unsung or time-wasting scripts... so they... put them on some mule like me. Every studio had its own donkey and I was RKO's.'

R M

'I went to the studio... and they said, "Bob, look. Every time we make a deal with someone it comes with another script we've got to buy for fifty grand, so we have a whole drawer full of horseshit. Every studio has a horseshit salesman. Paramount has Alan Ladd; Warners has Bogart. You want more money, you let us know. But you're our horseshit salesman."'

R M

Hughes hired a private detective to tail Mitchum, get him out of any trouble which may occur, and to report back. He also went out of his way to make things as easy as possible for his star, lending him money to cover his legal expenses and to buy a new house.

Although Mitchum resented being spied on and resented having to appear in any crap film RKO threw at him, he chose to repay Hughes' loyalty and stuck with him even though RKO was not the studio best suited to his development as an actor or his career. But Mitchum didn't really care about career, preferring to stick with the guy who stuck with him when the chips were down. For many critics, this is the decision which had the greatest effect on Mitchum's film output; the decision which kept Mitchum in second-rate movies for far too long and which, possibly, broke his optimism and ambitions as an actor.

Mitchum was no fan of the movies, of Hollywood, or of his own output. He tried to get out of appearing in several movies but contractual obligations kept him in place. He hated 'having' to do anything anyone else told him to; the obligation; the lack of escape; handing control of his own activities over to someone else. But as a family man he was aware of his responsibilites and needed the security of a long-term contract.

'I am not a person, I'm just a paragraph in a contract.'

R M

RKO continued filming *The Big Steal* while Mitchum was in jail, using his stand-in for the long shots and saving the close-ups for his release. They hoped his change in weight and newly acquired sun-tan wouldn't show up too much when they cut between takes.

In custody, Mitchum found some space to recover and regroup his energies. He had somewhere to hide, and an excuse for hiding. He couldn't be talked into anyone else's projects or plans other than the farm baseball team; couldn't be talked into giving of himself; he had no other obligations than to the prison rules, his own back and keeping his cell clean. I can see how this can provide a man with a positive opportunity to restore himself; an opportunity to take a rest from life, for a little while, before the walls start closing in.

After his release, Mitchum would comment on his stint inside: 'I've been happy in jail because I've had privacy. Nobody envied me. Nobody wanted anything.... Everyone in Hollywood is demanding – it's "gimme, gimme"... my jail term has been one of the happiest periods of my life.'

Treats for the inmates were few and far between so after his release he donated to the prison a range of vending machines. (Years later, Mitchum would arrive at a drug dealer's house and be dismayed that – against his strict instructions – there was another customer already there. The dealer had tried to get rid of him but once he heard Mitchum was due to arrive, he refused to leave. The other customer wasn't interested in meeting the 'star'; he was an ex-inmate at the farm and just wanted to thank Mitchum for the snack machines.)

What a palaver for a fist full of joints. According to the police chemist's report, it wasn't even good grass.

Following the 1951 district attorney's investigation, Mitchum was exonerated and the drugs charge expunged from his record, but nobody seemed interested anymore – the die had already been cast.

Even in 1949 the whole thing smelled of a set-up.

'The minute I walked in I went sniff-sniff, and the place was hot, man. I walked over to pick up the phone and somebody said, "Where you going?" I said, "Ah-hah, a lotta heat in this joint".... Down come the door and I went, "Uh-oh". One of the cops yelled, "Mitchum is raising his arm in a threatening manner". I said, "Hang me up, boys – I been had". Slightly yentzed. Roundly fucked.'

R M

The signals pointed to Evans being in bed with the police, who were conveniently in position and knew who they were getting. The lack of a conviction reeks of her pay-off. But then Mitchum seemed to have been more suspicious of Ford's role. Mitchum had wanted to go home that evening to read a script, but Ford insisted they call in to see Leeds and Evans.

'I'd like to know the answer to some pertinent questions. Why were the newspapers tipped off, before I even arrived at the Leeds house, that a big-name movie star was going to be picked up on a marijuana charge that night? Why did Robin Ford stop off to make so many phone calls that night? Why didn't the police raid the Leeds house earlier, since they testified they had seen Leeds smoking long before I arrived?

Why did Vicki Evans go to the kitchen door just before the police broke in, and why was she the only one of us who was never convicted? Why did half a dozen other movie stars come up to me later and thank me, saying they had been invited to a party at that house that night, but when they arrived it was already surrounded by police cars, lights flashing, so they took off.'

R M

In later years, Mitchum came to believe he had been set up as an act of revenge. In the mid-forties, Mitchum had parted company with his business manager and best friend, Paul Behrmann, because Behrmann embezzled Mitchum's savings. Behrmann claimed Mitchum must have spent it. Mitchum called this a 'monstrous falsity'.

Having been raking in the cash as a rising star, to find he was once again penniless left Mitchum feeling completely betrayed, but he refused to prosecute. His family thought he was mad and insisted he see a psychiatrist.

Perhaps his unwillingness to go to court was down to two factors: one, Behrmann had been a friend, so perhaps the actor was caught between old feelings of loyalty and new feelings of betrayal; two, he didn't want to turn to 'the man' to fight his battles. Instead, Behrmann was taken to court for ripping off another client. Mitchum and his wife were subpoenaed and testified. Behrmann was sent down.

'The guy who set me up was my ex-business manager. I wasn't even tried, you know, and in 1951 the jury apologized. But all people remember is that photo of me coming out of the

cell. What they don't know is how close I came to killing the son of a bitch....'

R M

During Behrmann's reign as Mitchum's business manager, the Mitchums received only $30 a week while Behrmann built up their (his) nest-egg to almost $100,000 – an even more significant amount in the forties. When he was eventually taken to court he threatened revenge and to 'do away with' Mitchum's wife, Dorothy. Behrmann seemed to be the answer to Mitchum's many questions about the Laurel Canyon bust.

What concerned him was how the whole episode confirmed the world's perception of him. 'After all the heat died down... it [the charge] was wiped out. Nobody cared about that, that I was innocent.'

But let's face it, *bad boy*, you weren't innocent, they just caught you illegally; you still had a lit spliff in your hand and lungs full of grass smoke – and good on you *daddio*, I'll toke to that – but don't go giving me that 'innocent' bullshit, you were as guilty as sin.

Take 4

And so the trail begins.

'I was so anxious to see the different states of America that I did not stay long in New York before I succumbed... to visit a small town in the state of Connecticut, at which place we soon arrived, with something like ten dollars between us...'
W H Davies, *The Autobiography of a Super-Tramp*

Grand Central Station, New York City. Or if you want to be accurate and pedantic: Grand Central *Terminal* – all lines end here. This is probably the world's most famous railway station, surely the station to feature most often in Amercian movies.

Grand Central is as New York as the Empire State Building, the Statue of Liberty or the yellow cab. The virgin visitor is still shocked when they first catch sight of the brass globular clock perched upon the information kiosk, and realise it is *that* clock from the movies. For years it has served as celluloid and real-life meeting place for lovers, dodgy dealers and those escaping to or from fate and the city. It is as much here as from the backseat of a JFK cab or the rails of a ship that new arrivals know they have finally reached New York.

It was from here that Mitchum hobo'd down the eastern seaboard. To here that the Mitchum clan travelled, migrating to the city like so many others out of financial necessity in the early 1930s. From here, from Grand Central's produce market, that Mitchum hitched his way out of the city in a truck heading south. To what, he wasn't sure. Unaware he was travelling from the hard worlds of his childhood – a working-class industrial town, a dust-bitten farm and the gangs of Hell's Kitchen – to Los Angeles and an adult life of fame and infamy in equal measure; a life he never asked for.

The spirit of Mitchum and all those who have felt the need to see what is 'out there' can be sensed rumbling out of the terminal, down the tracks and across the sleepers. I board the 13.07 from track sixteen – heading to New Haven, stopping at Bridgeport. It's not far; the ride should take only an hour and a half. With a quarter hour before we leave, the car is almost empty. I slide my case into the space between facing seats, settle into the polished vinyl upholstery and take out my books: copies of Jim Tully's *Beggars of Life* and W H Davies' *Autobiography of a Super-Tramp*. Both record the authors' adventures and travels as hoboes on the American railroad. Davies' was first published in 1907; Tully's in 1924. They were best-sellers in their time. Mitchum's hometown of Bridgeport and nearby New Haven appear in both books, as does the New York–New Haven–Hartford line, the remains of which I'm about to ride.

Hoboes jumped trains in Bridgeport. Tully travelled through on his way to New Haven – he had been told wealthy Yale students gave away good clothes. At New Rochelle he waited for a freight train, jumped that for a mail train bound for Boston, then returned to New Haven where he narrowly escaped a rail bull, his gun and his guard dog. His travelling companion was not so lucky and stayed ninety days longer than intended, as a guest of the state.

Tully and Davies became hoboes by choice. More accurately, they weren't so much 'hoboes' as 'road kids' – scenery bums, tourist punks along for the ride – whereas hoboes were migratory workers who would settle if they could. Neither author was looking to settle; they were looking for the world.

As well as serving his life apprenticeship as a road kid – amongst the boomers who worked for the railroads, the punk-grafters who used kids to beg, the yeggs who were criminal aristocrats of the road – Tully was also a factory worker, tramp, circus roustabout, pro fighter. As a 'library bum' he gorged eagerly on the warmth of libraries and the other worlds offered by books, educating himself between rides; he was arrested for vagrancy, and escaped; he had no qualms about exaggerating the truth for the sake of a good story. In later life, he became a well-respected –

and feared – name in Hollywood, as journalist and opinion-former.

Tully had worked for a sideshow turn called 'Amy, the Beautiful Fat Girl'. Amy, as her name suggests, was big in stature, weighing nearly five hundred pounds. Not so unusual in today's West. She was also big in alcoholic and amorous appetites. One night, when working for P T Barnum, she slapped her midget lover so hard she almost dislocated his neck. After that, she vowed to sleep with only big men.

Could this be the same midget – General Tom Thumb – who settled in Bridgeport when Barnum served as its mayor? Did he stay there, out of her grasp, tired of being slapped about by a big, drunken lass? I guess I'm grasping at straws, but Bridgeport was *the* circus town of the time.

In his early twenties, Davies left his hometown of Newport in South Wales and sailed to New York desperate to see what lay west of the Atlantic. He stayed for several years and, having fallen under a moving train, left behind a leg. He also was an avid reader, a library bum, and had a taste for the 'glove contests'.

In his day, Mitchum was also a road kid, a library bum, a factory worker and a boxer. Mitchum, who could tell a great story and tell it differently day after day. Mitchum, who would be feared by some in Hollywood, for his fist and his tongue. Mitchum who almost lost a leg escaping through the swamp and would've had it amputated if the doctors had their way.

Maybe the tales of Tully and Davies were early influences on Mitchum, inspirations; maybe they spurred on Mitchum to take a risk, leave his small world and experience the rest of it.

'There wasn't much to hang around home for. It was kind of embarrassing for me to hang around home. Moving like I did you can be just any place, rootless and, not high, but alone. Motion itself in those days was an adequate philosophy for me.... I didn't reason it out like that at the time, it just happened.'

R M

There are similarities with my own life, too. I who *had* to travel; who had to see what was 'out there'. I who hid in books, who dawdled through factory jobs and other mindless positions. I who wanted more but didn't know what.

As a teenager I hitched rides around Wales and over the border, up and down England from London to Manchester; Cornwall to Tyneside. There's a lot to be said for hitching but, after several years of travelling for the sake of it, my enthusiasm for movement and the strangers I met diminished. I got sick of chasing after cars only to have lit butts flicked in my face. I got sick of standing in the rain. Sick of being treated suspiciously. Sick of police cars pulling up. Sick of the relief of a lift quickly mutating into a different torment.

I got sick of the power brokers trying to be with 'the people'. The show-offs, the storytellers, the bigwigs and misfits. Sick of listening to the racists, the self-righteous, the zealots, the born-again Christians, the fascists masquerading as hippies and drop-outs. The bad influences. The soul sappers. The idiots. Sick of being bombarded with smarm and charm and projected goodness. Sick – ashamed as I am to admit it – sick of the drivers who needed to share their grief, their traumas, their divorces. Those I reminded of their lost sons. The desperate women. The lonely. The weeping.

I got sick of the stories. Of carrying their sadness and grief away with me for the rest of my trip, like some unshaven confessioner or exorcist.

Sick of the nutters, the criminals, the perverts. Sick of being 'invited' to get some 'rest' in a trucker's bunk – nagged to, over and over again. The insinuations of violence. Sick of sharing their cigarettes, knowing there was a 'but' at the end of it. Of defending myself against the wannabee sodomising rapists.

The suicidal drivers who needed a witness. Those who wanted to fuck with my head, for the sake of it. Sick of jumping from moving cars when my life was at risk. Of hiding behind country hedges or between parked vehicles until I was certain they'd driven on. Sick of nursing my cuts and bruises. Sick of those looking for a victim. Sick of the victims. And sick – more than anything – sick of seeing through the bullshit and learning a lesson I never wanted to learn about people.

So I decided if I had to travel – and I *had* to travel, to get away from location and attempt to get away from myself – far better to go by rail; jump station barriers and spend my journeys, ticketless, hid in a locked toilet cubicle. Sit on the seat, reading a book, a can or two of beer, blowing smoke out of the window. But I never hoboed, and never wanted to. There didn't seem much point then, on a small land mass like Britain. But Mitchum was turned on to it.

We're about to leave, the car's filling fast. Mostly guys wearing dark suits and cellphone earpieces – it's like sharing a ride with the FBI. I speak to the conductor as he strolls through the car, to ensure I'm on the right track. He confirms, but doesn't check my ticket. We discuss arrival times, he tells me it's 'all okey-dokey' and his choice of language is unexpectedly reassuring. Not that I'm worried: wherever I end up, I end up; there's always a bar, streets to walk and somewhere to crash.

The journey is quiet and smouldering. I pretend to read. We pass through Pelham. Wow, Pelham – *The Taking of Pelham 123*, I haven't thought about that film in a long time. I remember as a kid, staying up late on a Saturday night to watch it; arguing with my mam to leave it on, once they started cursing. I won, I wanted to believe, but only because my father wanted to watch it too, and his word was law; his choice ruled.

Mitchum was big on swearing and didn't care who it offended.

'Sometimes one has to choose between good taste and being a human being.'

R M, *Secret Ceremony*

When filming *Rachel and the Stranger*, Loretta Young brought a swear-box on set. A 'hell' cost 25c, a 'goddamn'

69

5Oc, etc. The money was going to a charity for unwed mothers. When Mitchum was told of the charge for each word, he demanded to know, 'How much does Miss Young charge for a fuck?' He would shove a five dollar bill in the box and just let rip. It was hardly a waste of money – he had probably known some of those mothers.

When he lived in Bridgeport, sure he was a sensitive kid but he soon grew into a foul-mouthed lad about town, swearing like a trooper from a tender age, fighting and messing and getting into situations – real childhood situations like children aren't allowed to experience anymore. He risked his life in the search for fun and adventure. These days, fewer children walk home from school, alone; fewer children fall out of trees and break their bones; fewer children eat sweets they find on the ground. Oh good, they survive – clean and careful – well done. But where does the lack of learning from experience leave them? Unadventurous? Less able to mix with their own? Less able to create their own fun and worlds of the imagination? Overly choosy? Obese and lazy? Me, I think a kid should fall out of a tree, run in front of traffic, run into roadsigns, bleed, and curse like the devil himself stubbed his toe on the steps of a cathedral. And get a clip round the ear for it. Maybe I'm just repeating what I heard myself.

New Rochelle, Larchmont, Greenwich. We travel onward, through Noroton Heights, South and East Norwalk, Westport, Southport, before slowing for Jenkins' Curve which in its day could derail a train in the bat of an eyelid, and into the Bridgeport sunshine.

The train stops next to the water and under a bridge. Sparse. Industrial. Not a great first image. No one to be seen. It's said Captain Kidd buried his treasure here, at Steeplechase Island which later became the site of a pleasure park known as the 'Million Dollar Playground'. No signs of such riches and extravagance can be seen from the steps of the train. This was the railroad on which Mitchum began his hobo'ing. From this town he ran away.

Following the death of his father in South Carolina, his mother returned the young family to her neck of the woods. This is where Mitchum spent the majority of his childhood. Here and his maternal grandparents' farm in Delaware.

I lean on the rails and look out from the land. He nearly drowned in this water, as a young boy fishing; fell off the dockside and struggled in freezing water before being rescued by a Portuguese fisherman. Iced to the core, it was only an explosion of anger which got him moving again, saving his life by getting his blood pumping.

It was here where, as a skinny kid, he suffered from the cold to such an extent as to turn blue while viewing an eclipse from Eagle Nest. He was rushed home and placed by the fire to dry off and warm. Too close to the fire. For a good few years Mitchum's ass would carry a brand, seared by the heat.

After these two events, Mitchum could never tolerate the cold again and suffered from pleurisy throughout his life.

Beneath the image of an indestructable man, Mitchum had always suffered his illnesses and head-fucks. Sure, he was a habitual moaner and 'cronic complainer' but he suffered from lifelong insomnia and claustrophobia; bouts of pellagra (black tongue fever) from malnutrition and pleurisy from the cold; gangrene as a teenager; psychosomatic blindness in his twenties; back and knee problems throughout his life; physical ailments brought on by doing his own stunts; alcoholism and associated drinking/smoking conditions, as an older man.

In the Eighties, Mitchum was paid a million to star in the sixteen-hour TV epic *The Winds of War*. At the time it was the most expensive TV production ever, so filming wasn't going to be held up by a trifling matter like Mitchum's ill health.

'I turned up on set in Los Angeles... and was diagnosed with Thai flu and a temperature of 104... then [in Zagreb] *I had picked up another virus. I told director Dan Curtis, "I'm dying." He said, "Yes, Bob, just go over there and stand in front of the camera." I developed pleurisy... I choked and sprayed blood all over the snow.... Next day, I slipped into a ditch and almost broke my shoulder. In the end, it was clear I couldn't go on.'*

R M

The doctors told him he had pneumonia. Co-star Victoria Tennant said, 'Everyone could see how sick he was but he kept working.'

Typically, Mitchum claimed, 'Slivovitz kept me alive' – a potent, Balkan, plum spirit.

In 1993, his back gave way while filming *Tombstone* with Kurt Russell and Val Kilmer. The doctor ordered him to quit. Instead of recasting, director George Cosmatos cut the role and Mitchum became the movie's narrator.

I approach a line of cabs on Water Street. The last driver in the queue spots me in his mirror and beckons me over. There's no one else in need of a ride. I put my case in the trunk and get in the cab. The other drivers watch, getting pissed at the injustice. They mouth obscenties and give us the finger. He steps on the gas.

'Where we going?'

'Holiday Inn.'

'Shit, that's just a block away.'

He doesn't want to accept such a short ride and small fare, but neither does he want to return so soon to the line of aggrieved compadres waiting for him.

The ride takes two minutes, at most. It's difficult to get much of a sense of the town. Straight-line streets, no people to be seen, everywhere closed. The cab pulls up to the hotel entrance. The driver gets out, opens the trunk, stands waiting for me to lift my own case. I tip anyway. But not much.

I'm here to search for signs of Mitchum's young life, to investigate claims he was a child prodigy in poetry, to meet my contact on a local newspaper, and to experience the town. I don't know what to expect, except that the community doesn't show a noticeable awareness of its famous son.

I had spent the morning phoning movie houses in the region to ask if they were screening any Mitchum films while I was in town. They weren't. It was a long-shot, I knew. These days, most mainstream movie houses seem to show an ever decreasing range of films and Mitchum ain't exactly retro flavour of the month. I asked if they ever screened his movies, but no one could recall.

At the local Showcase on Canfield Avenue, the young woman I spoke to didn't recognise the name.

'You never heard of Robert Mitchum?'

'No sir.'

'You know he's from Bridgeport, right?'

'No sir, I did not.'

'Are you sure you don't recognise the name but can picture his face?' That's usually the case. That and the fact only movie buffs can think of three or more films he starred in, off the top of their heads. Try it now, for yourself. Three films Mitchum starred in.

'No, sir. I'm sorry.'

What did you think of? *Cape Fear*? *Night of the Hunter*? And? And? *The Story of GI Joe*? *Out of the Past*? *The River of No Return*? *Heaven Knows, Mister Allison*? *Thunder Road*? *The Sundowners*? The appallingly drawn-out *Ryan's Daughter*? *Farewell, My Lovely*? Jim Jarmusch's *Dead Man*? Oh yeh, remember them? Remember *him* now?

The girl at the Showcase put me through to the manager. He explained they hadn't shown a Mitchum film in a *looooong* time, and the 'long' was so elongated I wanted a return on my quarter. I suggested he arrange a Mitchum film festival, here in the boy's home town. He said, 'Yeh, I'll think about that,' but this is Friday and by Monday he'll probably have forgotten.

When I phoned a movie house in Fairfield –

Bridgeport's neighbouring town – I had the pleasure of speaking to Catherine. She sounded older, husky, sexy. She couldn't remember the last time they put him on screen. I asked, 'But you do remember Robert Mitchum?'

She laughed a gritty, dirty, deep-down tone. 'Do I remember Robert Mitchum? Of course I do!' and laughed again. It sounded like I had tapped into long-forgotten fantasies. Man, I'd like to know what she was thinking. I hope some woman speaks like that of me, whether I'm dead or living. Although, preferably living, otherwise, where's the benefit?

I flicked through the phone book and called the local clairvoyants and mediums – I gotta find Mitchum one way or another – but none of them answered the phone. Perhaps they knew I was coming. Perhaps it's an omen.

I check into the hotel and take an elevator to my room. It's the only hotel in town – the Arcade long closed down. I say 'Hi' and share a smile with the maids in the hallway, open my door, dump my case on the bed, take off my jacket and shirt and roll myself a smoke. Inadvertently, I had smuggled a bag of grass into the States so it seems stupid not to smoke it all before I return. Of all places, the States. If I'd known Mary-Jane was in my case I would have dumped her at the airport. Well, smoked her anyway, before getting on the plane. If there's one country I don't want to be caught smuggling drugs into, it is the States. The United States of Paranoia. The United States of unsuccessful drugs legislature. The United States of reactionary justice (is there any other kind?). The United States where even codeine is illegal. Codeine – used in cough medicine. Sure, it's addictive, but so are caffeine and nicotine, and if you're not buzzing away on them all day then your activities are un-American. Sticks in my throat. Besides, there's plenty of domestic grass for sale so it wasn't worth the risk. But what the hey, I'm here now, so is Mary-Jane. She's in my case so I better get on hers.

Mitchum wasn't shy of shipping weed. When he arrived in Trinidad to film *Fire Down Below* with Jack Lemmon and Rita Hayworth, a journalist asked him what he was carrying in his bag. 'Two kilos of marijuana and a quart of Jewish blood... so I can stay even with those guys...' – referring to the predominantly Jewish movie producers. In just a few words he managed to shock just about everyone.

To claim Mitchum was an anti-Semite would be to completely misunderstand the man. He would frequently refer to Jews or things Jewish in his humour because he knew it never failed to get a response. When specific subjects become unmentionable, when people are afraid to use certain words just in case they are misunderstood, when fear holds us back from language, that is exactly the time when the world needs people to mention those subjects and use those words, to challenge and make people face the uncomfortable, to reclaim reference and terminology from fear.

'[David Lean would] *say "Action!" and I'd go in and do it in one take which would just, I'm sure, infuriate him. He'd be almost tearful and say, "Bob, that was spot-on! I* can't tell you how lovely, how beautiful that was – simply marvellous..." and I would say, "You don't think it was a little too Jewish?" and he'd ask, "What's he on about?" It would just drive him crazy. I kept putting him on.'

R M

'I found five young Arabs around the set one day so I told them that [Michael] Winner had demanded ten percent of our salaries to be donated to the Zionist movement. Gave them his address and told them they'd recognize the house by the effigy of Arafat hanging in the garden.'

R M

Mitchum was a coyote of Native American legend; a trickster, a buffoon, a shit-stirrer. In life, he played a necessary role. He did what amused him; what amused him more than just about anything else was winding people up, and those wheels of thought were oiled by dope.

After filming in India for *Man in the Middle*, Mitchum, director Guy Hamilton and the film crew were flying into Heathrow. Mitchum was behaving weirdly – he wasn't drinking (which was weird in itself) but he *was* off his head. Hamilton couldn't figure it, so when Mitchum returned from one of his numerous trips to the toilet he asked what was in the bag held so tightly between Mitchum's knees. Mitchum showed him. It was full of weed.

'We land and head off for Customs... I start falling behind, walking at a distance, feeling very nervous and rather sick. Bob reaches the Customs man, who recognises him, says,

"Hello Mr Mitchum, anything to declare?" Bob waves his bag and the Customs man says, "Right, carry on." Bob walked straight through... I nearly collapsed... he wasn't scared of anything.'

Guy Hamilton

I can't say I'd wanna make a habit of it, but getting grass into the States – and during all this paranoid, heightened-security bullshit designed to keep us scared – was dead easy. But I wouldn't recommend it.

I flew via Amsterdam, scheduling half a day between flights so I could take a train into the city and stroll on down to the red-light district. Get myself a smoke and do some window shopping. I mean, why travel up to that shit-house Heathrow when I could fug a few hours in the green zone of Holland?

So I get stoned outside some coffee-shop and scoot back to Schipol, thinking life is a drift. And it was, but then I was stoned and looked it. I may as well have put a neon sign on my head requesting Customs stick a German shepherd dog up my ass.

My flight gets called and I stroll over to the departure lounge, past the armed guards and sniffer dogs. One of the dogs starts walking my way. Walks beside me. Now I know this is trouble but I'm clean, right? 'Cos I made sure I smoked all I bought, so no shit on me and no shit to me. What I didn't know was there was a bag of grass at the bottom of my carry-on, left over from a recent trip to north Wales.

I look down at the dog, the dog looks up at me. I smile

innocently and say, 'Hello doggy' in one of those dumb woof-woof voices which just finds its way out of my mouth embarrassingly and unexpected. Fuck it, I doubt the dog can speak English. In my sensory periphery an armed guard is processing something. He shapes to move towards me. Me, I don't give a monkey's, 'cos I 'know' I'm not carrying. The guard's about to stop me and we both know it. I'm feeling cocky 'cos I 'know' I have nothing to fear.

Behind me there is screaming. This isn't expected. People are running. Not many, but there are rapid feet coming. There is still screaming. Young lungs. Very close. I flick a glance over my shoulder: a toddler has gained momentum on the sloped walkway and gone tumbling, landing in my wake. The sniffer dog is diverted. The speed of its initial movement is that of attack but his training kicks in within a split-second and he slows to sniff out the kid. The kid continues wailing, even more so when she gets an Alsatian's wet snout in her shell-like. Poor dab goes fall-eey-wall-eey but I carry on my merry way, whistling a happy tune, ignorantly carrying a fucking big bag of grass on my back. *Hi-ho, hi-ho, it's off to New York we go...* that'll do nicely.

When we arrived in Newark, having flown over the frozen ponds, cargo yards and oil refineries of New Jersey and through the bitter winds of our approach, Customs just waved me through. *You have a nice day, too.* Only when looking for my bank-bag of cents did I find the grass. Silly, silly me. Better skin up.

I turn on the air conditioning, run myself a bath and roll another. Pull back the mesh curtains to get a view of the town. My room looks out over Fairfield County Court with a good view of the steps. A perfect spot for an assassination. Lee Harvey Welshman, come on down. If ever the world needed to rid itself of an American president, it is now.

I soak, pull the plug, towel down and put on a change of clothes, toke one more smoke then take the elevator down to the lounge. It's pretty lively – seems there's a function going on. I walk up to the bar and wait to be served.

The barman asks, 'Open a tab?'

'Charge it to the room.'

I'll charge it all to my card; try and delay payment, although I know I'll have to meet as they come along the hidden costs of pleasure. There's always a cost. There's always a cost. I'll see if I can tap my publisher for expenses and greater financial support. I'm not holding my breath. The last time I asked he told me he'd stump up the bail bond, but only if it was absolutely necessary. When is a bail bond not absolutely necessary? He'd be just as happy to see me rot in a cell if it meant I'd meet the deadline. And besides, who says I'm gonna get in any trouble?

I take my Corona and go sit at a table I sized up as I entered. The best table in the house for my uses, within earshot of the locals yet distanced enough to offer privacy to watch and write; offering a good view of the door and the ladies in evening gowns walking past to the function room – I might even get me some eye-contact.

There's a real mix of drinkers – those still wearing their work clothes, those wearing their clean Friday-night-on-the-town wear, and those dressed formally: the ball gowns arm-in-arm with short-haired men looking uncomfortable and self-conscious in tuxedos.

Up at the bar it's like a truck-loaders' convention. As an ex-truck-loader it doesn't unnerve me but it does surprise. They're all watching the game on TV and the language is blue. It catches me off-guard, for a second. Not because they mouth curses I wouldn't use but because of the contrast their presence and language creates in the mock-elegance of the setting. The bar is smart, as is the barman. The immediate vicinity, favoured by the locals, is circled by static carousel horses. Down the steps, in the tabled area, it seems like the locals are in their wagon train, surrounded by injun' mounts, while we're sat safe as if watching on the silver screen the action unfold.

The restaurant is closed, presumably because of the function next door, so I order food from the bar menu. While I wait to eat, I scan under candlelight the Bridgeport free press and tourist brochures for mentions of Mitchum. Lots of mentions of P T Barnum but nothing of Mitchum. Perhaps this is societal retribution. A community's response to his obvious and urgent desire to escape; his desertion.

'Bridgeport is notorious as a cold-hearted town which never throws out a welcome mat or warmly receives its native sons and daughters who have made it big in television, movies or sports (Bob Crane and Bob Mitchum, to name a few).'

Harry Neigher, *Connecticut Sunday Herald*

But then Mitchum had never been from only one place, having lived and schooled in Bridgeport and Felton and Philly. When he was ready to return here – to visit 'home', temporarily – he would find economics had forced his family to move to the big city. When he joined them there, his out-of-town accent marked him as a target for the local boys but he more than held his own and although not becoming one of them he did become a leader of others; of loners and outsiders. His mother would say, 'Robert doesn't have any friends, he has disciples.'

'I don't really have any really close men friends. I'm more or less a loner anyway. I do get along well with women....'

R M

Unlike many of the young who rush from small-town surroundings ready to meet the world head-on, Mitchum bore no malice for the familiar surroundings from which he ran. He had to leave at that time in his life, he had to see what was 'out there'. As an adult, he reserved feelings of animosity not for Bridgeport but for one place in particular: Savannah, Georgia, where Mitchum claimed there was a warrant out for his re-arrest from the age of fifteen until his death, aged seventy-nine.

During his childhood and teens, Mitchum had to make himself at home as docks town boy, farm boy and city boy. I can relate to this, having been brought up in a number of environments: the relative metropolis of Wales' capital city; a rural market town which didn't know if it was Welsh or English; a sprawl of housing projects circling the concrete retail area of a 1960s 'new town' and the lonely isolation of the hills of Herefordshire, where to be Welsh was still to be distrusted. (Hereford never repealed its medieval law which claimed it fair to shoot with a bow and arrow any Welshman found within its city walls. Whether this was ever true or not, or whether it was tested or not, does not matter – the locals believed it. For generations, it has accurately reflected the psyche of an English place trying to distance itself from its Welsh heritage.)

It's easy to think of big cities as difficult places to live, if you're not from one. But cities are fine; cities are easy. It's small towns which unnerve me – full of insecurities and superstition; distrust of strangers and inbred tradition. Full of men needing to prove themselves – the new boy or occasional stranger an easy target, seen as a threat to the dominant alphas, the established hierarchies and social order. Don't dare to stand out, don't dare to be different.

I lived in this world, once. And never will again. Nearly screwed me up for good. Trying to fit in with the class system which I hadn't before encountered in city streets and housing estates. Having to hide under all that camouflage, suffocating. A rural kid moving to a city can find it a damn-sight easier than an urban kid moving further than the suburbs.

Compared to the hidden complexities of small towns and villages, city life can be simple. There, you know to be on your guard and you get surprised by the humanity and friendship you find. The smaller social environments of the rural world are expected to be friendly and simple and are happy to portray themselves as such. Only, after a short while, while trying to settle, do you realise the depth of resentment and fear held for outsiders.

People move to the city to reinvent themselves; to afford themselves a value and status *they* create, to replace the one thrust upon them. People move to the country and think their urban value translates. It doesn't. So many people like the idea of a 'simpler' life in a small rural town. They don't last two years. Rural towns exist only for locals; cities exist for the world.

Small towns can stifle creativity – it's an easy claim to make – but so can cities, unless you bring your confidence with you. A myth believed is that it's the art, expression or experiences only of the urban-informed which are worthy. What the young, rural creatives don't realise until later in life, if at all, is that most of the artists and performers in cities have moved there from somewhere else, somewhere small; from a culture the urbanites can easily dismiss, and that it is the small-town kid who often has more to say, more to express, more originality and authenticity, and more fight in them for their right to say it.

But then, it's all a matter of scale. Being used to NYC, Bridgeport appears to me as a small town, but the welcome sign outside the rail station declares it a city, and of two hundred thousand people. Whether this makes it a city or just a sprawling connurbation, I shall have to wait and see.

When Mitchum moved to the city he wasn't about to get rolled over but that didn't stop the city from trying, or Mitchum from pushing back.

I eat, read, watch, listen, drink. No need for the slices of lime in my bottles, this ain't a sipping drink.

The barman arrives at my table carrying the smallest bowl of chilli I've ever seen and the biggest basket of fries. I order another beer and, watching the smartly-dressed traffic taking a break from their function, ask what's occuring.

'You mean, next door?'

'Sure.'

'It's the annual Fireman's Ball, charity fundraiser.'

'They seem pretty sober.'

'Yeh, well they got their wives with them.'

There's a flurry of activity at the door. Cameras flash and into the bar walk Miss North-East, Miss Bridgeport and *Mrs* Puerto Rico, all three wearing sashes over their shoulders and monumentally tall tiaras on their heads. They are beautiful women, but not necessarily the shape you would expect of beauty queens.

'I believe the average woman should never wear a girdle. I believe a well-proportioned woman is an object of great beauty. I feel that the lines that nature gave us are the ones we should show.... I always have had an intense dislike for anything that detracts from the feminine qualities of a woman, and I look upon a girdle as such a device. I don't see why you should not be able to recognize a person from the back as well as the front.'

R M

There's grins and giggles from the boys at the bar. One of them asks, 'Hey Ed, how old is your daughter?'

'Too young for you,' Ed says.

The balance between humour and serious intent is

delicate but they have a good laugh and good for them.

As the night continues, the carousel horses and occasionally wild and misfitting clothes add to the vibe. It's like a carnival or pantomine but so are all Friday evenings and special nights out wherever they take place; all occasions for courting, dating, flirting, peacocking, displaying the plumage and getting it on. Pride and hope encouraging us to make fools of ourselves, to take the risk, to take a punt.

Increasingly, the men loosen their suits, their shirt tails, their ties, and watch their language in mixed company only if they remember in time. The women get given pink roses and consider the most flattering place to stick the stem.

The atmosphere flows from the function room and seems more and more like the dinner and dance functions my parents attended and pretended were civilized, when I was a child in the seventies. The photographs always showed drunken men dancing with other men's wives. Or a local disco; or an eighteenth birthday party taken over by dads. But I've yet to see a fight tonight – it's for charity, after all.

I ask the barman what's happening downtown.

'This *is* downtown,' he replies.

On first impressions, Bridgeport strikes me as a hard, run-down but friendly town. Old, blue-collar, working-class, on the bones of its ass, seen better times. You do your work and you get your cracks where you can. Then, get over your hangover and get back to work. Feed the kids, obey the wife. Or pretend to. Smoke a little herb, drink and drive. Make sure you're not caught, whatever you do. Try and forget the world turns. I respect this view. Don't wanna live it, but respect it. You gotta get by however you can.

I order a pair of drinks to take up to my room, just in case I don't retire alone. Sing as I wait the Jane Russell song from *Macao*: 'One for my ba-bee and one more for the road....'

Take 5

Ug. It is bright. I open my eyes. Sun-rays blast through the mesh curtains without dispersing – the drapes only for show. I wake in a huge bed. Stretch my limbs but still do not reach the limits of the mattress. It's easily big enough for three car-and-fast-food-addicted Americans, but still I haven't slept well.

Much like super-tramp W H Davies when he returned to a soft bed at his mother's house in Newport, I find the king-size opulence of my hotel bed unconducive to sleep. Despite myself. Or to spite myself. I've slept like a baby in bars, until kicked out; at über-volume rock concerts; on the back of a flat-bed truck; on factory shelves; in a busy Sydney convenience store; during screaming arguments; in a roadside salt bin; at funerals and weddings; even while a woman was trying to tell me for the first time that she loved me, but put me in a good bed at a reasonable hour and I can't sleep a wink.

I spent most of the night lying awake, shuffling numerous pillows in search of a position for rest; turning myself this way and that, in search of a hidey-hole from nightmares and in search of an absent woman.

Above the hum from the air conditioning there is a timbre from the street below, of pedestrian and motorised traffic. I crawl from my pit, eager to see just how busy it is but hindered by my cumulative hangover – the iron hat sits tighter, morning by morning.

It is far from hectic, but there's a sense of life to the place which was missing when I first arrived. I gather last night's clothes from the furniture and floor, hang them, wash and get dressed. Make a cup of foul tea and a half-decent joint. I tidy up to make it easy for the maid and leave a couple of bucks by the bedside. Pack my bag and prepare for my mission. Stub out and pocket the roach.

So, Mitchum, you obscene and obstreperous cur, what traces of you will I find today? Of your childhood innocence, your mischievousness, your hard-won reputation, your poetry, your history, your youth. I told you, *dad*, you won't shake me off your tail – I'm coming to get you.

'Leaning, leaning, safe and secure from all alarms
Leaning, leaning, leaning on the everlasting arms....'
R M, *Night of the Hunter*

I buy myself a copy of the *Connecticut Post* from the hotel lobby, order a coffee because there's no point dreaming of a decent cup of tea, and settle down to read.

When Mitchum lived here the *Connecticut Post* was the *Bridgeport Post* but, in the 1990s, long after Mitchum had left, and faced with a dwindling readership in an industrial town in an advanced state of decline, the newspaper's owners decided to drop 'Bridgeport' from the masthead and replace it with the wider-reaching name of 'Connecticut'.

The paper which reportedly first published Mitchum's juvenile writing and which, for years, had informed the hard-nosed population of Bridgeport, changed focus and went for the suburban, RV-driving, swimming pool-owning New England core. Perhaps this is why it is the only daily newspaper I've ever read whose Saturday edition includes a pull-out 'Religion' section. As I turn to it my heart drops – in choosing to come here, what have I let myself in for? Am I a lion, proudly yet blindly walking into the Christians' den? Oh, gods help me. Better still: gods leave me alone.

A journalist with a religious agenda is a dangerous individual, especially if he or she goes hand in hand with the politician.

Even in Britain we are well aware of the rampant, rabid hypocrisy of America's religous right-wing. It was, after all, from our shores that so many religious fundamentalists left for the New World (where they could create – unchecked by an established society – their own little extremist communities based on their personal interpretations of religion and the self-righteousness which went with it).

America has long forgotten its Welsh roots; long-forgotten all those Welsh names on the Declaration of Independence; long forgotten the troops of zealots who would no longer be tolerated in Wales. So America got them. Ships full of them. Poor old America. I feel ashamed, I feel guilty. Sure there were good guys who travelled too, but we gave you our nutters and you held them up as a guiding influence on your future. We ridiculed them so they crossed the pond and helped create a continent's mutated 'moral' consciousness.

'To parties desirous of emigrating to America
The good brig Credo of Aberystwyth'

Notice advertising passage to America from Wales, 1848

Hmm. The religious, politicians, the press – who else can I kick?

Mitchum played a journalist in several movies – *Anzio*, *The Angry Hills*, *Matilda*, and an ex-journalist in *Crossfire*.... I worked on a newspaper, too. I had worked on a monthly magazine for a few years and decided to try my hand on a daily, as staff reporter. I lasted a marathon three weeks. I had naïve notions of becoming the scoop-meister; the hard-bitten, pencil-lickin' ace reporter bringing you the low-down on all you need to know, and more. It didn't take long to realise the term 'staff reporter' is a synonym for 'under-paid rehasher of press releases' and 'he who does as he's told'. I'm not good at doing what I'm told and had little interest in what I had to write. If I – the reporter – didn't care, then nor would the readership, I thought. But the newspaper reader is often easily placated and pleased – flash of flesh, TV guide, crossword, funnies, the news often serving as filler.

They offered me a permanent post but I was already out of there, hot-footing it down to the pub – you couldn't see my ass for dust. Then I thought I'd have another go. Try and get a job with a paper which didn't put up right-wing rosettes whenever the governmental elections came around. I attended an interview. I got the job. They liked the examples of my copy I hated the most. But on the eve of my first day the editor phoned to say the paper had folded and we were all out of work. I was made redundant before I had written a word. It was then I decided newspaper journalism was not for me. Or maybe I was not for the newspaper industry. Sure, I still had the qualifications and some experience, but if I tried a third time I might get sucked in; I might grow to like it; I might become one of them; I might forget why I wanted to write in the first place. So I signed on the dole, bought myself a big bag of grass when the Giro arrived and settled down to write poetry. I had finally become a free voice; a journalist, in register and rhyme. It was now a question of having something to say.

Mitchum was a real-life journalist for a while. Even started his own newspaper – *The Gold Streak*. He was six years old, according to reports. But any respect he had for journalism would soon end. His first coverage – in the *Bridgeport Post* – not only revealed him to be sensitive and creative, but it also revealed the financial hardship his family lived in. Mitchum found both revelations humiliating. His opinions of journalists and what they'll use for the sake of a story never improved.

In the seventies, Mitchum's daughter, Trina, claimed

his distrust of journalists was compounded by an article which appeared in *Penthouse*. The journalist had followed the actor around for months, and Mitchum and the family treated him as a friend. When it was published Mitchum felt the piece was a betrayal of trust, revealing too much of the family reality.

'The thing is, it was all so private. *It hurt Dad and made him mad, too. It did all of us. Oh, it was a fairly accurate story, sure, but I don't think it was a fair story.'*

Trina Mitchum, *Rolling Stone*

I look at my tepid mud in a mug and decide to leave. Pick up the paper, read and creased. Walk down Main towards Broad Street, take the roach-ends from my pocket and ditch them in the trash, continue to the library on the corner of State. I throw down my cigarette and go inside, ask for the archive and get directed upstairs, past the sizeable portrait of P T Barnum – Bridgeport seems particularly fond of *this* famous son. I'll have to squeeze in as much search time as I can – the library doesn't reopen until Tuesday.

I am here to search for Mitchum's poems and coverage of the 'child prodigy', to find out if this early fame was justified, to discover whether the pre-teen Mitchum really was a poetic wunderkind. There are claims he was considered 'the male Nathalia Crane' – a particularly precocious nine-year-old poetess who has since been absorbed by the sponge of history.

Mitchum's mother eventually shacked up with the journalist who put the young Mitchum into print, so I am dubious it was talent alone which led to his being heralded, but I want to believe this rock of a man, this magnificent model of machismo was, even as a child, a good poet. I want his fame and fortune and all the attention he gained as both movie star and sex symbol – in the days when neither were ten-a-penny – to be a poor second choice to his first love and ambition: poetry, and achievement (in his own eyes) as a poet.

That Mitchum was at home with words from a young age is undoubtable. He could read and write when just three years old and his family were artistic, open-minded and supportive of their children's creativity. He was a rarity: a kid brought up to be artistic and free-thinking; a kid brought up to not believe everything he was told; a kid brought up to ask, 'Why?' Lucky bugger. I didn't even learn to speak 'til I was four. Been struggling with it ever since. And the idea of anyone in my family being encouraged to be artistic – man, I can't even find the words to comment. That wasn't our world.

Mitchum's sister Annette (known as Julie) was performing from a young age and Robert followed her into dance before realising he was better at writing. He was an avid reader and enjoyed not only hobo tales and comic strips but also the works of H G Wells, Jack London, Mary Austin and William Shakespeare. His favourite was the Ukraine-born British author, Joseph Conrad.

Later in life he would enjoy reading Aldous Huxley, Eugene O'Neill, Thomas Wolfe, William Wordsworth and e e cummings; would write a play called *Fellow Traveller* which he ditched after O'Neill himself sent a list of revision notes which were longer than the play (can't handle the reality of being a writer, huh, Mitch?). There was talk of him starring in a film version of Conrad's *Outcast of the Islands* until he got himself sent to prison; director David Lean was preparing a screen adaptation of Conrad's *Nostromo* when he died in 1991 – Mitchum was expecting to star in it. Throughout his life, he would quote a favourite line from *Lord Jim*: 'Loneliness is the hard and absolute condition of existence'. That's the kind of line I'd want to forget – too painful a truth.

I ask at the desk if they have a file on Mitchum. Yes they do. Can I see it? Yes I can. The librarian goes to fetch it. I sit myself down with a tray of microfilm. Where to start hunting for tracks of this cat....

'Hey, look, wad about me? Hey, don't anyone care about me? What's my name? Where'd I come from?'

R M, *Doughboys in Ireland*

OK, time to nail the basics: Robert Charles Durman Mitchum was born 6 August 1917 in Bridgeport, Connecticut, as a result of his quiet, artistic mother moving with her parents from Norway to America and falling in love with a noisy, bar-brawling, half-Celtic/half-Blackfoot soldier who would die a gruesome death less than two years after Bob's birth.

Mitchum's birth-place is a simple enough fact which, over the years, many biographical reports have got wrong. If he read his own press, Mitchum could claim to have been born in several places, which is no surprise considering his

96

transitory childhood. If he wanted to, Mitchum could claim to have been almost an *all*-American boy having spent his childhood and youth in Connectiut, Delaware, Massachusetts, New York, Pennsylvania and South Carolina, as well as short spells in Georgia, Maryland, Nevada and Ohio, before eventually joining his sister in California. He even claimed he might have spent some of his infancy in Florida.

'Six books have been written about me but I've only ever met two of the authors. They get my name and birthplace wrong in the first paragraph. From there it's all downhill.'

R M

So was Mitchum a Yankee or a Johnny Reb? He was brought up mostly in the North but never shirked or denied his Southern and Native American heritage. I reckon he'd lay claim to whichever side would oil the wheels or satisfy his contrary nature.

The librarian returns with bad news – the Mitchum file has gone missing. 'Another gentleman wanted to see it only the other day and now we can't find it.'

Hmm. Missing or stolen? Ah, missing files, stolen files, files held to ransom – the basis of so many movie chases, *Out of the Past* here we come.

The biographies don't agree on how old Mitchum was when his poetry was first published – the range they suggest is aged six to ten. One thing they do agree on is *how* he came to be published.

Mother Mitchum was cleaning her sons' room when

she found a scrap of paper shoved into a gap in the window frame to stop it rattling. She unfolded it and – *lo and behold!* – there was a poem written on it. She collected the little scraps of paper which kept appearing and built the boy's first collection. She was working as a linotype operator on the *Bridgeport Post* so it seemed logical to have a word with whoever wrote the children's page to see if she could get them published. According to the biographies, the journalist was in print under the name 'Uncle Dudley' which today would surely be a sign of a paedophile-in-office. I mean, *Uncle Dudley* – would you trust him? Anyway, good ole' Uncle Dud turned out to be nothing of the sort. He rates the kid's work and agrees to publish it.

I pull out my first reel of microfilm – *Bridgeport Post*, Jan-Feb 1923. Mitchum would've been six. I don't like working systematically, but it seems as good a place to start as any.

It starts off pretty simple: I'm looking for the children's page with some kinda headline about a local young poet with relevant photograph, but after checking through a few months' worth of copy with no sign of a children's page and no sign of the young Mitchum, my eye gets drawn to all kinds of weirdnesses.

April 22: a feature on the forthcoming 'Jewel Week' at the Poli Palace Theater. Now, Bridgeport has always been a circus town and must have seen some weird and wacky acts in its time but, according to the copy, 'Never in Bridgeport's vaudeville history has any theatre been successful in securing such a combination of high class acts'. The week kicks off with 'Midget's Monday' when

Sternard's Midgets – 'undoubtedly the greatest collection of talent small folks ever gathered together' – will feature. 'The midgets are a source of untiring interest,' writes the reporter. Really. 'Midgets have tiny stomachs, yet they are as a rule very hearty eaters, enjoying all kinds of food...' – you mean like other humans? – 'they hugely enjoy eating at cafeterias, despite the trouble they have in carting their tray around....' I am... without words.

September 1: 'Eclipse of sun, September 10 will provide thrills for all'. Could this be the eclipse Mitchum and his family watched from Eagle Nest, when young Bob turned blue from the cold?

September 22, front page news: 'Cheerful, but enigmatic of speech, former Premier Lloyd George left Waterloo Station today bound for America amid enthusiasm never before shown to a living Britisher...' (probably because he was leaving). It continues, describing David Lloyd George as 'a little Welshman' who 'it seems will never fall into the pit of indescretions....' Maybe he was just clever enough to climb out of them. Still, at least it proves the American press knew he was not English, and therefore they recognised there was a difference between being Welsh or English. So what's happened since, to America's awareness of Wales? It struggles within the swamp of more assertive cultures.

September 30, the 'Junior Bridgeport Post' nestled at the foot of the page has a map of the British Isles. There are hand-drawn fish in the ocean, sailing ships where port cities were located and in the middle of Wales, a full-to-the-brime coal scuttle – nice to know we were renowned for something. Written are the names of 'Scotland', 'Ireland' and 'England', but no 'Wales'. Take our coal but don't give us a name-check, huh? Typical.

October 6: 'Lloyd George Quits Gotham' – the 'dapper little Welshman' heads to Canada 'amid great plaudits'. Run out by Batman, no doubt.

October 15, yet another front page: 'Miss Helen Steete, Atlanta girl, is suing Edward Young Clark, imperial giant of the Ku Klux Klan, for breach of promise. She says the giant represented himself as a single man, furnished an apartment and promised to marry her'. So no problem with him being an 'imperial giant of the Klu Klux Klan', then?

October 21, an ad quotes a customer's letter: 'I had some female troubles that just run my health down so that I lost my appetite and felt miserable all the time... a friend told me to try Lydia E Pinkham's Vegetable Compound and I gained in every way...'. Good for you, missus. Bet you were farting like a loose exhaust over a bumpy trail.

Mitchum's voice pipes into my head: 'Yeh, well I've got a pink ham that'll do Lydia some good.'

Leave it out Mitch, she's dead.

'But is she still warm?'

Mitch, you sink even lower than I do.

'And I dig up more treasure.'

November 4: 'Two little graves in Mountain Grove cemetary will be visited early this week by one of the strangest groups of pilgrims that ever wended it sway [sic] to a port burial ground.... The graves to be visited are those of General Tom Thumb and [his] little wife, the diminutive ['little', 'diminutive' – yeh, we get it] Miss Lavinia Warren.

The pilgrims will be the tiny Thespians known as Singer's Midgets, who arrived in Bridgeport to fill a week's engagement at the Palace theatre....' Jesus, they liked their 'midgets' ('persons of restricted growth'; 'pituitary dwarves') in the twenties. There's a photograph too, of the 'Vaudeville Lilliputians' on the porch of the White House. If only things were like they were then, with the small-statured as guests rather than the small-witted as tenants.

The one thing I haven't found is any sign of Mitchum. But December 30, page twenty, there's a photograph of a high school musical club. On the end of the back row is a girl in a checked skirt called Julia Magnusson. Could this be Mitchum's sister? Wasn't she called Julia, and wasn't her mother's maiden name Magnusson? She might well have chosen to revert to it, between marriages. But no, I check my facts. I'm clutching at straws again. Mitchum's sister was known as Julie – not Julia – and his mother's maiden name was Gunderson – not Magnusson. Bollocks, thought for a second I was onto something.

The reels have piled up. The librarians are going through their routine, getting ready to close. Sooner I find what I'm looking for, sooner I'm gone, but I still haven't found anything linked directly to Mitchum; still haven't reached even 1924 and the library won't reopen until Tuesday. How long is this gonna take me? How long can I stare at the screen without drinking? Better draw a line under today, return these films to the right boxes; switch back to the contemporary and get on with my weekend. What to do with myself tonight in a little city like Bridgeport? First things first, I need a beer.

I'm walking down Stratford Avenue. There's a guy walking towards me. We do that eye contact thing: are you friend; are you threat; are you looking to get something; do you just wanna walk past, avoiding that annoying face-to-face shuffle as we decide whether to claim left or right of the sidewalk? He looks like Robert De Niro in the remake of *Cape Fear*. It's a good remake, but not as good as the original. De Niro plays Mitchum's role of Max Cady and plays him as an overt psychopath, muscled and tattooed – the kind with a neon light on his head flashing 'nutter'; the kind you'd cross the street to avoid if you saw him walking towards you. Mitchum's Max Cady was more subtle; the kind of guy you might figure was one of us, if you just knew him from the bar and not knowing what lay beneath; the kind of guy who might, just might, buy you a beer if he had won on the horses; the kind of guy whose dangers attracted women, but not the kind of guy you'd ever want to introduce to your sister.

'You got a spare cigarette, man?' the De Niro lookalike asks.

Everyone in America is on the scrounge for a cigarette. You can be walking through Manhattan and some couple in suits and shiny shoes and jewelry and furs and money dripping out of every orifice will walk up to the poorest-looking guy on the street and expect an affirmative answer when they ask, 'You got a cigarette?' And they ask, boy do they ask. But I'm lucky. I smoke rollies. So I offer them a rolly but they don't know what it is. So I explain to them; take out my papers and tobacco and say, 'Sure, but it'll take me a moment to roll'. Their response is always cautious; they consider it for a moment too long, reply hesitantly and walk on by, looking to ask the next guy. Scrounging bastards – buy ya own, you can afford it. The homeless I gotta dollar for, but smoke-scoungers can go blow it out their ass.

'You got a spare cigarette, man?'

To save myself the rolly conversation I lie and say, 'No. Sorry, man.'

'That's OK,' he says, and walks alongside me.

'I'm Eddie.'

'Nice to meet you, Eddie.'

'What's your name?'

'I'm Lloyd.'

'*Looooooooooooy-dah*. Huh.'

'That's right, Eddie. *Lloyd*. I got a rolly if you want it?'

'You mean rolled up?'

'Yeh.'

'Sure, that'll do it.'

'You'll have to wait a moment, for me to roll it.'

'Sure, no problem. I ain't in no rush. Ain't got anything to do, anyway – I'm homeless.'

'Yeh. How'd you find that?'

'S'OK.'

'Well, the food's not so hot, but you can't complain about the rent.'

R M, One Minute to Zero

I hand him a rolly. He lowers his head and cups his hands as I put the lighter up to the cigarette. I flick the flint. He inhales, exhales. I relight my own. We walk; reach the cross-lights. I point my thumb over my shoulder, to the north, 'I'm heading this way, Eddie.'

'Well, I'll head that way too, I ain't got nothing to do.'

We turn towards Main Street and stroll. He's looking pretty broke, and bored. Possibly lonely. Nothing wrong with that, we all live there every so often, 'cept he don't look like they're gonna let him into any singles bars.

'Anywhere open around here? For a Saturday it seems pretty dead.'

'What you looking for?'

'Anything. Shops, restaurants, bars. Somewhere I can sit in the window and watch the world go by.'

'Over on the east side – there's plenty there.'

'How far's that?'

'All the way over the bridge.'

'Sounds like a bit of a walk.'

'Ain't too far. I'm heading that way if you wanna walk.'

'Nah, I'm feeling lazy.'

We carry on strolling. Makes me feel like when I was a kid, how you could just join up with another and walk without having to hold a conversation, without having to engage, without having to impress or be anything; we could just walk in silence – company without obligation. Just kids getting along with it.

'You from round here?'

'No.'

'So what you doing *here*, man?'

'Research. You know the actor Robert Mitchum?'

'I've heard of him, I think.'

'Well he grew up here.'

'No shit.'

'No shit. But nobody seems to know it.'

'Was he white?'

'Kinda.'

'Well maybe you should try up at New Haven. This is, uh, pretty much a town of color. Puerto Rican. If you get up to New Haven with all them college students, maybe they heard of him.'

'I'll bear it in mind.'

New Haven: Yale; Ivy League money. I don't wanna talk to those pandered-asses; get bored rigid by some media student telling me why Mitchum was great; how he personifies the whole theory of *blah blah blah* – I can spout enough of that shit myself. If I'm gonna ask anyone in New Haven why Mitchum's great, it'll be somebody's grandmother; someone who can remember the thrill of wet panties on a movie-house seat.

We stop outside the convenience store on the corner of Chapel Street. I roll two more cigarettes, hand one to him.

'Hey Lloyd, you got any change for food?'

I pull out a few singles and give them to him. Apologise for the amount.

'That's OK, man. Some woman gave me a dollar earlier – it all adds up; I can get something with that.'

He walks towards the open door. I call after him. He turns. I throw him a lighter. 'Where you headed, Eddie?'

'Oh, around. You know.'

Yeh. I know. I feel kinda envious of him. And spoiled. *I* have a choice. I have *that* choice. Well what's to say he doesn't? I refuse to make that assumption. 'Well I gotta go now man, I've got work to do. You gonna be OK?'

'Sure. Hey take care, Lloyd.'

'You too, Eddie. You too.'

I turn up Chapel to see where it takes me. There's a bar ahead. Looks like it's for locals. That'll do for me.

I enter Carmelina's. Heads turn to look at me but there's no instinctive feeling I should turn tail and leave. The bar juts into the centre of the room. I take a stool and order a Sam Adams from the beautiful server. Above me, a low ceiling; below, a black and white tiled floor. Amstel, Heineken and Sam Adams mirrors hang on the walls; pool trophies on the shelves – the tallest of them lying flat; an empty and unpowered cigarette machine in the corner – one day soon the growing restrictions on indoor smoking will see these machines appearing as kitsch items. Behind the bar: shelves of condiments, the obligatory pyramid of liquor bottles, scarfs and pennants of various Portuguese soccer teams. Men around me talk *futebul* in a mixture of languages. They seem happy. The Portuguese club Benfica recently beat the English club Liverpool – posters for the game can be seen around the bar.

Liverpool gets a mention in the 1990 movie *Believed Violent*, as the home of the Wales Shipping Group. Mitchum plays an ageing professor who's rapidly losing his grip on reality. He either plays senile extremely well or fails to hide his complete lack of interest. I go with the latter. The movie is abysmal and can be summed up by one of its own lines: 'What a tragedy'. Yeh, tragedy it was ever committed to tape. Perhaps it's best summed up by another of its lines: 'Shit! Shit! Shit!'

Mitchum eventually jumps off a balcony and I get the feeling he would've done it even if it wasn't in the script. To quote Mitchum quoting his friend, the director John Huston: 'If they want bad pictures, we can do it. But it'll cost more.'

Even though Liverpool is in England, it's often referred to as the 'unofficial capital of North Wales'. This is not only due to its geographical proximity to the Welsh border but also because of the draw it held for the North-Walian working-classes who went to the city in search of work in the port and the houses of the rich. England is well aware of Liverpool's Irish heritage but not so much of its Welsh.

The similarities between Cardiff in the south and Liverpool to the north are reflected in our accents – having similar roots intertwined of Welsh, Irish and English languages and those of the world brought in through the ports. It's a heritage both cities are rightfully proud of. My American friends claim their equivalent of the Cardiff accent can be found in Boston. I may well find out.

The server stands in front of me, pouring a beer. She asks if I like soccer.

'Sure. Have you heard of Cardiff City?'

She says, 'No. Is that in London?'

'No. Not at all; it's in Wales.'

'Whales?'

'Wales.'

'I don't know Wales.'

'You know England? You know Ireland? It's between the two.'

'Ah,' she says, '*Gales.*'

'Yes, *Gales.*'

'Little country.'

'Little country.'

'But you are English?'

'No, Welsh. You know how everyone thinks you're Spanish?'

'Yes.'

'When we're abroad, people think we're English.'

'I understand.'

I take the glass and drain my beer.

'I am Estela. Would you like another?'

'Sure. Sam.'

'Your beer is Sam?'

'Yeh, my beer is Sam, I am Lloyd.'

She pours me a Sam, tells me she's a Porto fan. And so begins a beautiful friendship.

We chat until she's called to take a bottle of wine to a table of Benfica fans. I turn to check out the news on TV. In a town called Bennett a school teacher has been suspended for showing a video of an opera performed using hand-puppets to a class of elementary pupils. The palaver seems to be over it being considered too old for the pupils, rather than any obscene or blasphemous content. Suspended, for showing kids opera? This country can really do my head in. I know from the papers that today the French Government have been trying to get the arms to China embargo dropped, but there is no sign of this on Fox News. It's obviously not as challenging as showing opera to children.

Across the bar, a Portuguese guy whips out a ceramic American eagle, declares, 'A friend gave me this – it is *very* important.'

The American guy sat next to him takes it and starts playing around as if he's going to drop it.

The first guy gets aggitated. 'Do not break, do not break!' he demands.

The American he say, 'I ain't touched your goddamn seagull!'

The Portuguese he say, '*Eagle*.'

The American he say, 'That's what I said, *seagull*.'

They continue back and forth until the whole bar is laughing. It warms me to join in. But the guy's still nervous about his eagle.

'I'm most at home with the grips. You know, the old-timers who have been working behind the scenes since Wallace Beery was a juvenile. They like me. Even in Europe, the grips pitched in to buy me this [an expensive watch] *after we finished* Foreign Intrigue. *They know I talk a stream of consciousness and sometimes I fall flat on my face.'*

R M

Mitchum preferred the company of working men rather than the self-proclaimed sophisticated. I have to agree with him, to an extent. It's more about appreciating the sophistication of thought and language present in the lives of the average blue-collar worker, rather than presuming it can only be found amongst the pompous and pretentious.

'You can discuss almost anything, even philosophy and psychology, and frequently learn a surprising lot around the [hobo] jungles and the clanking box-cars, but you've got to do it in a common tongue.'

R M

You don't need to use big words to understand or express big ideas.

Estela comes back. 'Another beer?'

'Please.'

'You speak Portugeuse?'

'No.'

'I will teach you a word every day. How long you stay?'

'I'm not sure. A few days. Depends how long the work takes.'

'What you do here?'

'Research. I'm a writer.'

'You research Bridgeport?'

'Sort of. You know the actor, Robert Mitchum?'

She doesn't recognise the name. I show her his image on my cell-phone. She asks, 'Is he black?'

'Mixed race.'

'I think I know,' she says. 'What you do tomorrow?'

'Not a lot.'

'Perhaps I show you Bridgeport?'

'Sure. What time?'

'I finish at six. Where you stay?'

'Holiday Inn.'

'I meet you there.'

I finish my beer, clear my tab and we exchange phone

numbers. A guided tour of Bridgeport from a fine-looking woman – it doesn't get any better. I have a soft-spot for the southern European. Even more so, for such a warm pair of eyes.

I deserve a good meal. I go down to the bar. It's heaving and under-staffed. The servers are running around like headless chickens, the drinkers are lined up impatiently. Looks like another function on tonight. I head out of the door, stroll around the corner to Wall Street. Enter Ralph & Rich's Italian restaurant. It's packed, too. There's a stool at the bar so I take it, unbutton the jacket I bought for my father's funeral and catch the server's eye.

She says, 'Hi, anyone with you?'

I shake my head. She hands me a wine list and menu. I spin around on my stool to check out the joint. All tables are taken and along the bar there's not a spare stool in sight. Everyone appears in good spirits – families celebrating, couples romancing, a piano which looks like it's got plans for the night. I order a bottle of white and lasagne – let's see if they can do the basics right. The guy sat next to me says, 'Hey,' so I say 'Hey' back.

My wine arrives. It's cold, wet and dry and at $27 a bottle it's cheaper than the Pinot Grigio and probably better. I sip. Yeh, it'll do fine. Better put another bottle on ice.

'So what you order?'

'What's that?'

'What you order? Food.'

'The lasagne.'

'The lasagne – that's a good choice.'

The guy sat next to me introduces himself as Bob; asks what I'm doing in town. So I tell him; I tell him I'm looking for Robert Mitchum.

'Is he still alive?'

'No, but he was brought up around here. I'm looking for signs of his life.'

'Hm. Robert Mitchum.... First time I hearda drugs, it was Mitchum.'

'What, *here*?'

'In the newspapers. He informed a lot of people about stuff they'd never tried before. I never heard of drugs until he got busted.... He was older than me, but I think he went to Central High. That's where I went to school.'

'No, I don't think he went to high school here...'

'Sure he did.' Bob's made up his mind.

My lasagne arrives. I tuck my napkin in my collar, ready to dive in. Table manners are a weird concept. According to my old man, it was OK to tuck your napkin into your collar providing you were in an Italian restaurant but anywhere else it was unacceptable. So slobbering food down my shirt anywhere other than an *Italian* restaurant is OK? Nonsense. Besides, providing I don't start a food fight who cares? Anyway, I wanna concentrate on my meal. It smells good. Looks like a rich, colourful, cheese-covered beef and tomato house-brick. I'm impressed. I'm starving. I put my bread to one side and pick up my knife, slice off a corner of lasagne and fork it into my mouth. Let it sit there, see what it does. It melts, hot but fine; it folds and disintegrates as I move it around my mouth, the cheese

112

releasing the meat, neither of which is drowned by the tomato. *Bueno*, good stuff.

Bob's telling me about Bridgeport as I eat; tells me how Bridgeport used to be an industrial hot-spot – lots of business, lots of jobs; how lots of people moved here because they were 'starving in Pennsylvania'; how all sorts moved here – Slovaks, Polish, Hungarians, but not so much the Irish, although 'those Micks get everywhere'; how the dog-track serves a nice buffet; about how it's a blue-collar town.

I finish my lasagne – it hardly touched the sides. I grab a piece of bread and wipe as much of that sauce as I can gather. Nothing's gonna escape. Bob is talking and I wanna listen. The server comes over for my plate, 'Was that good?'

'Fantastic.' I order another bottle.

'So, you married?' Bob asks.

'Nah, you?'

'Not any more. I lost my, uh, *lady* and I never made *that* mistake again.'

Better leave that topic there. 'So is this a good place to live?'

'Not any more – it's corrupt. The Mayor's in jail – *ex-*Mayor...' he corrects himself. 'I'm born and bred here. I used to love this town but now I'm ashamed of it. It's all corrupt. I'm embarrassed.'

My wine arrives and I mishear, 'Did you say you're a barrister?'

'I said I'm *embarrassed*. The guy over there in the booth, he's a lawyer. I'm a ballroom dancer.'

'Is that a euphemism?'

'A what?'

'So you're a dancer?'

'Yeh. I run dances, if I didn't I would've gone by now, down to Florida.'

'Hit the sun, huh?' His glass is empty. I offer him a glass from my bottle.

'No thank you.'

He won't take a drink from me – that's a first. It encourages me to like him even more. Then I realise he's holding a martini glass. 'Can I buy you a martini?'

'No thank you. One a night, one a night. Normally I'm only here Thursdays, but I was working today, so why the hell.... So what you think of the war, in England?'

'The Iraq war? What they think in England? Well, I'm not the right man to ask...' I wanna point out I can't comment on the opinions in England, seeing as how I live in Wales, but he interrupts.

'So you English are gonna have the same problems we have – fucking Arabs, fucking Muslims, Germany, France: fuck 'em. But that Tony Blair – he's got it right.'

I nearly choke on my wine. This here's a nice, sociable guy just being friendly and I'm being friendly back, tryna get myself a little local insight. I ain't in the mood for a heavy political discussion. When it comes to Europe, it sounds to me like he don't know any more than what American TV tells him, which from what I've seen ain't gonna be much. I feel sorry for Americans – and I don't mean to patronise here, I respect the Americans I've met very much but they ain't told shit about what's going on in

114

the world, and what they *are* told is wrong wrong wrong. *Americans, listen to me! Throw your TV sets out of the window!* Americans are treated like mushrooms and that's not freedom. Me, me: I just wanna enjoy the remains of the tastes in my mouth, get Bob off the subject and have some friendly chat. Do I have the responsibility to educate? To inform? Maybe so. But I also have the responsibility to listen and learn. This guy is representing the other side of the world and me, sat here with my bottle of wine, well I'm in school right now, learning. Besides, he's had his one martini; he's pulling on his coat.

'Well, I gotta go now. Nice to meet you. Good luck looking for Mitchum.'

'You too. Good luck with the dancing.'

Cha-cha-cha. I call the server, give her a ten and ask her to buy Bob a martini, next time. I waltz outside for a smoke.

Opposite the restaurant, outside the side-door of the Holiday Inn, people in tuxes and ball-gowns are also smoking.

I ask another diner, 'What's happening over there?'

'The Mayor's Ball.'

'I heard the Mayor is in jail.'

'No, that's the ex-Mayor. He was eating his Thanksgiving dinner when the Feds came for him – imagine that.'

'In front of his family?'

'Yeh. That's why the local police don't get along with the Feds – they don't give a shit.'

'A bent Mayor, huh. Who woulda thunk. You remember Robert Mitchum?'

'The actor? Sure.'

'Well,' I inhale from my cigarette, 'he once said, "there are three times in life when it's useless trying to hold a man to anything he says: when he's madly in love, drunk, or running for office".'

'That's some true shit. Robert Mitchum said that?'

'Yep.'

'Shit.'

'Ain' it. The wisest he ever said.'

'I recognise your accent man, where you from?'

I tell him.

'That Dublin?'

'No. Other side of the water.'

'That where the Beatles are from?'

'No, but close enough.'

'Man, the Beatles were alright shit. You say hello to them for me, alright?'

'Sure, whatever I can do.'

Back at my seat, the server asks if I want any more to drink. I may as well order another bottle, not like I got far to stumble.

'So where you from, England?' she asks.

'I'm from Wales.'

'*Wales*? You're from Wales?!'

'Yeh. Heard of it?'

'Tom Jones country?!'

I give out a Mitchum sigh, 'Yeh, that's just about it.'

Her excitement is palpable. I might get a shag out of this.

'Oh, I wish I'd known! I love Tom Jones,' she repeats,

'you should say hello next time you see him.'

'I'll be sure to do that for you.'

The pianist settles in for a set at the baby grand (I pray to god he doesn't break into a Tom Jones number). He begins wrapping scales and notes around the corners of my head. She better hurry up with that bottle – I like to drink with my music.

A guy at the end of the bar inadvertently offends the server and in doing so pisses off his wife. She chides, he defends, they descend from a loving night out into the red mist of a row barely concealed behind clenched teeth. Ah, that old favourite. How quickly pleasure turns on one poorly worded phrase. Bane of my life. You have my sympathy, mate. They pay up and leave. He won't be getting any tonight.

The place is getting more crowded by the minute. I ask the Tom Jones fan if she'll watch my stool while I go out for a smoke, I gotta roll me a joint.

I roll in the men's room, go outside to spark up. The crowd outside the door are discussing the Cayman Islands. I presume they mean holidays, not bank accounts.

A huge guy comes up to me, 'What you smoking there?'

'It's just a rolly,' I say, defensively.

He laughs his ass off. 'I never heard it called *that* before!'

I pass him the joint and he inhales. Inhales again. Inhales again. Holds it in. Passes it back. Exhales. 'Thanks,' he says. 'Here,' he takes the Mardi Gras beads from around his neck and puts them around mine. He's

117

gotta be a foot taller than me so they land like a halo falling from the sky – a halo too big for me. He hands me his business card. 'Next time you in town, you give me a call.'

'Sure.' I inhale and look at the card. He's a politician. I hand him the remains of the joint and walk inside.

The pianist is blowing a horn. What is that? Ain't no trumpet, ain't no French (I mean 'freedom') horn, certainly ain't no sax or trombone. I'm running through the list, tryna think of what it could be as I squeeze past three women stood at the bar. They're in their forties and talking loud, their buzz filling the room.

One says, 'Hey, how are you?'

'I'm good, thanks.' I reply. 'You?'

'Oh we're great. We've just been to see *Hair*.'

The server hands her a Stolli and lemonade – four shots of Stolli, a splash of lemonade.

'Jeez, is that still running?'

She starts prodding my face with her finger and says, 'There ain't nothing better than a hippy – and you're a hippy.'

I'm wearing a shirt and a suit; OK, no socks but, still, real shoes. 'Lady, I'm no hippy, I just haven't cut my hair for a while.' There's no difference as far as she's concerned. I ask if she's ever seen a hippy in a suit. 'Sure. In court.' Her friends laugh.

Their husbands join them. One sizes me up, presumably for talking to his wife, and continues his own conversation with the other men in the group.

'Let me know when you want to party. We're gonna break down someone's house next weekend.'

'Scheduled or surprise?'

'Oh surprise, obviously.'

'OK, let me know, we'll enjoy ourselves.'

Some poor bastard is gonna have a house party whether he likes it or not.

There's a woman at the end of the bar giving me the eye. Either that or she's trying to regain focus. She seems pretty drunk. Her husband is standing next to her. They are not talking. He looks at her. Follows her gaze and finds me on the end of it. Gives me the dirty look. Nothing to do with me, buddy, speak to your missus.

'I've seen the way you look at your husband, I see the way you look at me.'

R M, *The Wonderful Country*

I'm bored of that fucked-off stare I get from husbands. Oh, *dad*, what can I do? I was only admiring her necklace.

The pianist comes to the bar, orders himself a drink.

'Hey, nice playing.'

'Thanks.'

'Seems pretty lively tonight.'

'Yeh, the people are enjoying themselves. What you doing here?'

'I'm researching Robert Mitchum.'

'The actor?'

'That's the man. He was born here.'

'In Bridgeport?'

'In Bridgeport.'

'I didn't know that.'

119

'From what I've heard, no one does.'

'I knew you were up to something.'

'Is it that obvious?'

'Yeh. You're obviously not from around here.'

We introduce ourselves and talk jazz and local politics. Turns out it's not just the Mayor in the bucket, but the Governer too. I ask what brass he's blowing. He tells me it's a fugal horn. I tell him Mitchum blew a mean sax. He didn't know that – why would he? But it's true, Mitchum was given a choice: either learn an instrument or get kicked out of school. It was expected to focus him. It didn't work.

We get joined by one of the restaurant's owners. Mike the musician introduces me to either Ralph or Rich. I ask him if he remembers Robert Mitchum.

'Sure. He's from 'round here.'

'Do you remember him?'

'No. but I think he used to box at St Nick's.'

It's a possibility – I should investigate. Mike goes back to his piano, picks up a flute. Ralph, or Rich, goes back to the kitchen – he's got a lot of work to do, the place is kicking.

Everywhere I look there's wedding rings, which wouldn't be so bad if I wasn't still getting vibes from their husbands. I can't help it – drunken middle-aged women like me. It's how it's always been. I seem to amuse them; they want to mother me – *Der Mutter Komplex*.

Mike's back on the piano, breaks into a few bars of *Jesu Joy of Man's Desiring* and then slides into *Bye Bye Blackbird*. I'm beginning to slide off my stool. Drinking doesn't make me drunk, talking does. If I stay silent I can drink forever. Soon as I engage in conversation my speech disintegrates and my stammer takes over. And it ain't just my speech that stammers but my thoughts and actions, also. Think maybe I should finish this bottle and be done. I'm a resident so the hotel bar should still be open. Back to the nest I fly, whistling my mating call.

'Blackbird, ciao, ciao.'

Peter Falk, Anzio

Take 6

'Seems to me I remember something about that wine.'

R M, *Pursued*

Urrrraaaaggh. Sunday ain't gonna happen – I know it as soon as I wake. There's a banging and a muffled voice. I pull the pillow off my head, clamber out of bed, twist my trousers around the right way, straighten my glasses which are bent out of shape, again.

Yul Brynner: *'Hurry up, get your pants on.'*
R M: *'How?'*
Yul Brynner: *'First one leg then the other.'*

Villa Rides!

I open the door and try to focus. A woman is talking but I

123

don't understand. I ask her to hang on a minute, take off my glasses, wipe them on my shirt, put them back on and ask her to say it again. She is the most beautiful woman I've seen for hours – a delicate beauty not expected in a maid. She asks if I want anything. Baby, you have no idea. Perhaps she could clean my brain.

'Yeh, you know where I can find Robert Mitchum?'

'Excuse me?'

'Nothing. You got any pens?'

'Sure, how many you want?'

'As many as you can spare. And paper. You got any milk?'

'No milk.'

She hands me a grabful of hotel pens and notepads.

'Cream?'

'For your skin or for your coffee?'

'Coffee.'

'You need anything else?'

I look up from the cart, follow her slim arm, the poppers between her breasts, the shape of her neck. How I'd like to kiss her flesh, hold her head, feel her thick hair against my face as I kiss my way up to her ear. She giggles. I look at her face, her just-open mouth, her dominant nose, her deep brown eyes. I guess I'm making myself obvious again. My ulcer twists my insides, as a reminder of my flaws. 'Don't ask.'

'You sure?'

'No, far from it; just about as unsure as I can be. Come back later?'

'I won' be here later. Don't say I didn' ask.'

I watch her ass as she pushes her cart down the hallway, watch her disappear around the corner to the ice machine and elevators. God-damn, another missed opportunity – good morning ulcer, you're up early today.

There's not much I can do when my ulcer kicks in. It reacts just the same way as my old man used to. Nothing he'd enjoy more than stepping in and messing things up when I was chatting to a woman. He'd see me as a threat and try to muscle in, even when his wife was listening. It wasn't so much that he wanted the action, just didn't want me getting it.

I need fuel; need a bacon sandwich but there's no way my gut will take it. No good eating fruit – all that acid. No good drinking water – fries my ulcer like a wicked witch. No good having an early beer, no good at all. The doctor recommended cranberry juice. Screw that. Guess I better take my pills and try to get back to sleep. You gonna let me do that, ulcer? No sleep, huh. Thought as much.

I settle for a cup of tea – I brought my own bags. Sit on the bed and roll a joint, waiting for the water to boil. I inhale and choke. It confirms my existence and the limitations of my throat. I feel like a cross between Stephen Hawking and Keanu Reeves: the air of intelligence in which Keanu drifts with the vocal ability of the bloke in the chair. I say 'God-damn' to prove I can and my voice is gravel-toned – too many cigarettes, cigarillos, cigars, spliffs, bongs, bottles, buckets, hot-knives over the years; too much tooting the Virginian crop circle, too many leaves rolled on the thighs of Cuban virgins, too much Mary-Jane, *daddio*, too many *just-one-more* toots.

I pull out of my mouth a flake of tobacco, before it gets stuck in my throat. Empty my pockets. Find a scrunched-up piece of paper on which a phone number is written – hope it's not my own. Strip down and run a bath. Pull out a pile of handwritten notes and drop them on the bathroom floor. Pull the lid off the creamer and pour. From the colour I can tell the tea's gonna taste poor. You gotta have milk in tea, not this crap. I'm caught between calming the ulcer and wanting to wind up my old man. Fuck it, call room service for a couple of Coronas – I need a wet brunch.

I try to write in the bath but my glasses steam up. So I lie and soak. I'm struggling between the inertia and antsy demands of a hangover – the after-effects of different substances pulling me in directions of their own. I need this bath to soothe my bones but I need to move also, to zone-out my nerves. I try figure what to do. Bridgeport's a little city but there's got to be a masseuse. Maybe I should hit the pool.

I get out of the bath – no point drying off, I'm only gonna get wet again – pad feet to my case and delve in looking for shorts. Pull 'em out, pull 'em on. Toss a towel over my shoulder, grab the key and head off down the hall to the elevator, get out on the right floor and follow the screams to the pool.

There's a family playing silly buggers and splashing about so I veer off to the gym. All these machines look like hard work. There's a stereo in the corner – tune the radio to a local station, plonk myself down on a rowing machine and put my feet up. Take a snooze. Wake and go back to the pool. No one about. The only signs of life, the water on the tiles from bombing and dunking. Dip my toe. It's warm, it's empty, it'll do. Drop my towel and slide in. Do a few lengths, grab the lifebelt, squeeze my ass in, put my head back and float. And drift. And snooze. And bang my head on the side of the pool. Do a few more lengths underwater and refresh the brain, drown the fool, wake the parts which try to refuse. Get out and feel like living again.

'I feel clean now. My whole body's just a-quivering with cleanness.'

Shelley Winters, Night of the Hunter

Don't know the time but I know I gotta meet my contact soon. I slip out of my shorts, try and wrap the towel around my waist. Should've grabbed a bath towel instead of this little thing. Still, with the swimming pool shrivel it just about covers all it needs to. Gotta remember to take short strides. I slop my way over to the elevator and wait for the 'ding'.

It dings, I get in, careful not to catch my towel in the doors – I've seen that in too many films. In the elevator there's a middle-aged American-Asian couple. She's an elegant busty – big, deep eyes matched only by her cleavage. He's a short-ass in an expensive suit. I bet they have great fun dancing. They stare at me. I am cheerful, I am happy. I smile and wish them a good afternoon. The wife lowers her head, her husband clears his throat. He presses a button and the doors re-open. We haven't moved but they get out. The husband gives me one last look. He doesn't approve. What have I done now? Polite, happy, clean, sober, didn't say anything wrong. I catch sight in the mirror: the towel reveals more than it should. I geddit. The old 'cocko revealo'. Sorry about that. Once again, Mitchum has invaded my subconcious and is leading me astray.

Back in my room, I shower and dress. Roll a smoke and gather notes, get a call from downstairs – my contact is in the lobby.

Joe Meyers is the movie columnist on the *Connecticut Post*. We shake hands and introduce ourselves. He recommends a little Mexican place he knows. Sounds good to me, I need to eat.

I order black beans and tortilla, Corona and Corona. Joe sips from salt-edged glasses of margarita. We discuss Mitchum's films and reputation; possible contacts and whether or not they're still living; whether or not they might talk to me.

Joe knows his stuff; can pull from memory favourite Mitchum scenes and off-screen anecdotes. I get my facts wrong as usual but he's too polite to point out my errors and moves the conversation on. He's originally from Delaware so we discuss Mitchum's old haunts, Camden and Rising Sun. I join him on the margaritas.

On the drive back we discuss Bridgeport and its awareness – or lack – of its Hollywood son. I find it strange that in a community this tight, a city this small, it has so little awareness of Mitchum. More so, that it doesn't exploit the link, especially considering there are towns in the States which declare themselves home to such delights as 'the world's biggest ball of string'. Surely Mitchum's more interesting than this?

Joe drops me at the hotel and agrees to stay in touch. I doubt he believes I'll finish the book. I'm not so certain, myself.

I get back to my room and find Estela's number on the bathroom floor. Phone her. She's just finishing work. I offer to walk to Carmelina's, eager for another beer. She says she'll pick me up in twenty minutes. I go downstairs and hit the hotel bar. The barman asks, 'Two Coronas?'

I nod. He delivers.

A red RV pulls up outside the hotel. I know it's her – I can spot her grin from halfway down the street. She is intriguing and absorbing. I get in.

'*Como estas*?'

'Well. How are you?'

'OK...' She sounds tired, she's been working.

'*Esta muito bonita*, Estela.'

She looks at me, holds my eye for a moment, laughs as we pull away. '*Maluca*,' she calls me, but she knows I tell the truth.

We drive around and out of Bridgeport, to Captain's Cove. Cables rattle masts, canvas flaps and the mist comes in heavy. It is ghostly and deserted. Estela drives slowly through the boat-yard, the engine kept low. Yachts, tall out of water, tower like cursed sentinels awaiting the sound of invaders. We drive on to a little place she knows run by a Portuguesa.

We talk of our lives in Europe. She speaks of her wine-growing homeland, the food, the weather, the people. *Her* people. Her losses. I trust and feel safe in her company.

I am open and honest. She is beautiful, alluring. Younger – in her mid-twenties – but with a mature head on her shoulders.

We pull into the parking lot at Dolphin's Cove. A dog barks, the mist thickens. We climb the wooden steps and are greeted warmly by staff and drinkers. I lose her to language but this doesn't matter. Everyone is eager to listen and she enjoys the audience. It warms me to hear her fluent. Her laugh disables me – makes me strong and weak, simultaneously. I like a strong woman.

She turns every so often to make sure I'm OK but I don't feel offended, I don't feel excluded. I drink my beer. One ear on her, always.

She takes me onto the patio. We stand under the restaurant's lighthouse and she tells me about the lobster and crab they catch and serve fresh every day.

'You must come back to eat,' she instructs. Whatever you say, baby, you got me. 'But in the summer,' she adds, 'it is full of American tourists.'

I share some secrets. She says, 'If you have bad feeling about the past, your feelings for the present must be stronger. Forget the past, be strong. Be very strong.'

I wake from my best sleep in months. The bed is warm. *Bom dia*, world. I feel happy, energetic, eager to get on with the day. I want to investigate and experience something; want to continue feeling while the feelings are positive. I look out of the window. Snow has fallen.

It has the feel of a holiday. I ask at reception. It's just another Monday. The library is closed and I don't want to waste life sat at a computer. I ask the receptionist to call me a taxi.

I step outside and light a cigarette. The sun is out, the snow is melting. Main Street is lively. Mamas talk on the sidewalk, officers lean on a cruiser. Some middle-aged guy zooms into my vision, asking for spare change. I offer him a single.

'Yeh man, thank you.'

Another approaches, 'You got a dollar, man?'

My wallet's open so I'm over a barrel. I give him a single and as he takes it I spot the bling watch on his wrist – *sell the fucking gold, man!* – but what the hell, it's gonna take more than a dollar to make me lose my rag today. But it ain't the dollar that costs, it's the guy feeling he's got one over on me. Well he might feel like 'the man' for a moment, but what the hell else he got to feel good about? Pride in himself, scrounging a dollar? Me: money comes, money goes, it don't define my person.

'Robert Mitchum (who grew up in Bridgeport) made millions in films but isn't impressed with it all, believing money's only important when you don't have it. "The second million looks exactly like the first, except that the second goes to pay the bill you incurred making the first".'

Alan Neigher, *Connecticut Sunday Herald*

So take my dollar, *dad*, go win the lottery and ruin your life for good.

I'm figuring on waiting inside for my cab – the sidewalk is too expensive – but a young kid asks politely for a cigarette and his manners deserve reward.

'Sure, just give me a moment to roll it.'

He looks shifty, he looks nervous; backs away, looks over his shoulder, asks, 'What's that – pot?'

'No man, it's just a rolled cigarette, it's got a filter and everything.' I pull out a Rizla paper and begin rolling. His face drops with fear.

'I'm sorry man, I'm sorry....' He backs off, arms out front like I just pulled a gun.

'It's just a rolly, man; just a cigarette I make myself. It's legal. Here, look...' I show him the inside of my tobacco pouch but he doesn't want to see.

'No, man, no,' he is one scaredy-cat to be out on such a fine morning. He turns and walks fast down the street. I watch him. Toss my butt and light the one I rolled for him. Seems only the homeless will share my smokes. Still, saves me a fortune in cigarette generosity.

A cab pulls up. I go to sit in the front seat but a dog is already there. It barks at me. OK, dog, I'll sit in the back. I ask to be taken to Logan Street.

The driver introduces himself and his co-pilot, 'I'm Jim and this here's Coco.'

'Hey Jim, hey Coco.'

The dog barks back.

'You from 'round here?'

'Who, me or Coco?'

'Whoever can answer my questions.'

'Well, try me first and if I can't help, we'll ask Coco.'

'OK Jim, so you from 'round here?'

'Sure.'

'Know anything about Robert Mitchum?'

'Who?'

'The actor Robert Mitchum.'

'Sure, but he ain't from round here.'

'Yeh he is, he lived on Logan, that's why we're heading there.'

'I never knew that. He's the guy who did that ad with the battery on his shoulder, right?'

'I don't know about that. I know he did the beef ad – "Beef – it's what's for dinner." Remember that?'

'Heck, sure, everyone remembers that. Hey, I've seen Paul Newman around.'

'Yeh?'

'Yeh, he's from Westport. And Diana Ross lives in Greenwich.'

This is the irony of the city: Fairfield County is one of the richest suburbs in America, Bridgeport is its poor heart. The area has produced a steady supply of Hollywood names and faces – Michael Douglas and Mia Farrow grew up in Westport, and Paul Newman, Bette Davies, Arthur Kennedy and Joanne Woodward all lived there. Meanwhile, the biggest New Englander of them all, Katherine Hepburn, hailed from Hartford.

Bridgeport rose from nothing to become an industrial hub in a blink of an eye, and has been in decline ever since. Placed at the mouth of the Pequonnock River on Long Island Sound, it became a city of rail and sail, within easy reach of New York City and New Haven, with a port deep enough to allow cargo ships to take and bring goods all over the globe.

Bridgeport used to be known as the 'Ethnic City', with sixty or so different ethnic groups inhabiting, attracted by the jobs on offer. World War I saw the city experience an economic boom. It has been home to Remington Arms, General Electric, Singer Sewing Machines, Underwood Typewriters, Columbia Records, as well as tin works, boat-yards, helicopter and submarine production. And it's the birthplace of the frisbee.

We drive under the Lordship Boulevard, circumnavigate the harbor and head for the east side.

Jim brings me back to the famous: 'And one of the Globetrotters – you know the basketball team? – he was from around here, somewhere.'

We pull up outside McKinley School, on Logan. I get out and take a few shots. According to reports, Mitchum schooled here about 1923-27. These days it's a primary school with about five hundred pupils – seventy-five percent black, twenty-four percent hispanic, one percent white.

We drive down the street, slowly, so I can take note of the house numbers. The numbering is strange: 476 is what I'm interested in – a black and white wood-slat house, taller than it's broad and with a front porch which didn't exist in Mitchum's day. There's mail in the box, police and neighbourhood-watch stickers in the window and a car on the drive. No signs, no plaques; nothing to show that the Mitchums lived here.

This is where Mitchum was born – blond, hazel-eyed, into a poor but strong family. His mother moved to Bridgeport in 1910 – seven years before Mitchum's birth.

Young Bob was christened in this house by the minister

of Newfield Methodist Church, which no longer exists. Although Mitchum would experience a pillar-to-post existence as a child, it is this house that served as the nearest thing to a geographical and cultural constant in his young life. This is the house where the windows were wedged shut with Bob's poems. This where his wanderlust would first become apparent.

As a child he read voraciously of travel and adventure and heroic men. Perhaps, as a fatherless child, he grabbed whatever role models he could. Later, he would tell of how he suffered 'the psychic abrasions, broken windows and bloodied noses of boyhood'.

'I was always jealous of boys who talked about their dads taking them fishing or camping or teaching them how to play ball.'

R M

His mother would remarry, believing boys need a father. Her husband, Bill Clancy, was a journalist and secret poet but he was also a violent drunk with gangster/bootlegger connections.

'I'm coming down the steps one night and I hear these guys talking. I look around the stairway and I see "Al Capone" and another guy sitting in the living-room having a beef about "receipts". I knew enough to go back upstairs.'

R M

It was a short-lived relationship. Clancy disappeared after

trying to kill mother Mitchum – the boys arrived home to a home destroyed. She had been saved by a local butcher and his cleaver. The events would culminate in Mitchum running off to Hartford, aged seven.

Later in life, sister Julie would claim her brother often left on his travels just before Christmas or his birthday. It wasn't so much that he ran away but that he was too embarrassed to accept presents, so would leave town to avoid the situation. If it's true, then he was one self-conscious, introverted kid.

'The idea that I was hiding and running away never quite died out.'

R M, *Pursued*

I take some shots of the house and get back in the cab. When we reach the top of Logan, Coco spots a dog on the street and goes mental, climbing all over Jim as he tries to turn the corner.

'Coco, you can't play with every dog you see.' He looks at me in his mirror. 'Normally I have a system,' he says, 'if I see another dog, I give her a little treat just to keep her head down, otherwise she goes crazy.'

Talking over Coco I ask, 'Is this a good neighbour-hood?'

Jim pauses before answering. 'It *is*... if you're a man of color.' He's not comfortable with his own statement. 'It's kind of a slum area. See,' he points down a street, 'that's Stratford Avenue – a lot of shootings, drugs, drinking. At night a lot of white people go there to get their drugs and get themselves shot or robbed. The police have cleaned it up but you can never get rid of that kind of stuff. You and me, we don't wanna be out here at night, but if *he* grew up here it was probably half-way decent, then.'

Stratford Avenue. This is one *long* street, stretching all the way from downtown to here, it seems. It's where Mitchum's brother John got knocked down. Robert was supposed to be looking after him but John ran out in front of traffic. While he lay bleeding on Stratford Avenue, with broken bones and cracked skull, Robert ran home and told his ma, 'Jack's been run over by two cars! But he ain't dead yet!'

'So how about the town?'

'There's a lot of unemployment but there's also a lot of lazy people who say they can't find jobs.' Jim thinks for a moment. 'If you really want a job, you can always find something.'

He asks if I want to go anywhere else. I think about visiting the grave of Mitchum's father Jimmy but considering I ain't bothered enough to fetch my own father's ashes it seems like a dumb idea, risking too many questions of my own.

'No, just take me home.'

'My ideas about fathers came from other neighborhood kids. One old man used to whack 'em if they got in a fight, and he'd whack 'em again if they lost.'

R M

Mitchum didn't consider himself a very good father. He

described himself as 'an absentee father... [like] *my* father...'. When an interviewer asked if he believed there were rules to being a good father, he replied, 'I should think so, yes. I do subscribe to them, morally, but unfortunately I don't fulfill them.'

His children admitted he had faults – notably his absence.

'Dad's always had the reputation of being an outrageous oddball – "the last of the iron-assed loners", blah-blah-blah, but he's always been pretty straight with me... my Dad's a pretty fair man, actually. Difficult to understand, but he's a fair man... when I was growing up, he wasn't around too much, so I had a lot of freedom... there were no strict church training or any regimentation like that. The only thing Dad would get upset about was if one of us did something stupid. Then he got mad. Dad has a very low tolerance for stupidity.'

Trina Mitchum, daughter

Oldest son Jim said of him, 'Dad's not a demonstrative man. What emotion he can show, he saves for the screen. But what love he feels, he saves for us. I only hope I can be half the actor and half the man he is. Not because he's my father, but because you can ask anyone and they'll tell you the truth: Bob Mitchum is one helluva nice guy.'

Mitchum was one lucky man to have a son willing to say that, and his son is one lucky man to have a father deserving of such sentiment.

I head to Carmelina's for a beer. The football's on TV and Estela's behind the bar. She smiles at me. It feels good, like walking into sunshine. She pours me a beer and introduces me to Carmelina.

Carmelina is immaculate and proud. She takes me on a tour of the restaurant and the sports room, with its pool tables and bacchi alley. 'You play bacchi?' she asks.

'Can't say I do. Played skittles with my uncle once or twice.'

'Skittles? Candy?'

'No. It's like bacchi, in Wales.'

Carmelina goes back to the restaurant and while I wait for my food I read the *Connecticut Post*.

'What you reading?' someone asks. It is Jack, Carmelina's husband. He shows me a newspaper cutting; shows me a photo of him on a boar hunt.

'We kill many,' he says, 'much meat.' He is proud of his prowess and I can't say I blame him. I've always liked animals, never been a hunter, but part of me – the adult me – is desperate to line something up in my sights. I feel a need to hunt, to track, to target, to beat, to provide, to live my animal life. It is an instinct much-distorted as it presents itself in this modern, urban life in any way it can, and those ways appear negative: gang warfare, hooliganism, road-rage.... We can be as intelligent and refined as we like but we are still animals and *that* needs an outlet. How I'd love to be a sniper hidden under a bush. It's not bloodlust but base achievement; satisfaction for the primeval me.

Some men use women as their prey. Hunt them down and enjoy their flesh as if it were fresh kill. Me, I'd rather the animal manifested itself in the shared physicality of fucking – it's a team sport in my arena, in which we hunt not each other but ourselves, safely. Any other animal needs I have are satisfied by testing the limits of my mental health and my body's capacity for toxins. One day I'm gonna get caught by my own trap.

While filming up in Colorado Springs, Mitchum took the opportunity to entertain himself at the expense of a cub reporter who asked whether he enjoyed hunting and fishing.

'I fish for relaxation.'

'You don't hunt?'

'My brother and I spent our stripling years hunting the elusive poontang.'

'What's a poontang?'

'A furry little creature – small, if you're lucky – that hides in crevasses, rocks and rills throughout the land.'

'Did you get any?'

'Practically decimated the breed.'

'Were they good eating?'

'Mighty like a rose!'

The interview was published. Five hundred copies were printed before the presses were halted. The studio bought all available copies and destroyed them.

Mitchum starred in two great hunting movies: *Track of the Cat* (1954) and *Home from the Hill* (1960).

In *Track of the Cat*, he plays the not-so-young-blood intent on exerting his power and making his mark on the world. On the surface it's the story of a man hunting a panther but it is so much more than that. It is a tale of man versus nature; a man versus himself; a materialistic, dysfunctional family at each other's throats; the moral society versus itself.

The family unit is complex: one domineering, manipulative parent hiding under religion; the other hiding in drink; a greedy eldest brother – Curt (Mitchum) – who, at thirty-seven, is still bully, coward and parents' favourite; a middle brother, Arthur, who acts as balance between the extremities of the clan (that Curt calls him 'Art' may represent more than mere familiarity); a younger brother who, with the help of a 'good woman', proves himself stronger than them all; and a sister, who fears for them all but feels powerless.

The rare black panther Curt hunts is symbolic of his expectations and fears; his battle against nature and the assertion of his masculinity. He ends up running from himself.

While all alone in a wilderness of snowy mountains, Curt reads from Arthur's collection of John Keats poems before burning the pages to keep warm. He quotes a line before tearing out the page and throwing it on the fire, 'When I have fears that I may cease to be...' then growls as it burns, 'The only good that ever came of your moaning, boy'. Whether this is a reflection of Curt's overly masculine nature – too scared, too manly to show a need for art or an appreciation of poetry; too scared to accept his own fears of death, of failure, of fear itself – or an informed comment on the work of that particular poet, or both, is for the viewer to decide. I go with the former.

There's a dialogue between Curt and Arthur which never fails to suck me out of the film and into my own mind. It reminds me of the argument between Sir Thomas More and William Roper in Robert Bolt's *A Man for All Seasons*.

Sir Thomas More (who wrote *Utopia*) was friends with Henry VIII but even this didn't save him from execution for refusing to voice an opinion, any opinion, on Henry's divorce. No Fifth Amendment back then.

I first read the play as a thirteen-year-old and the argument has never left me, although I'm yet to make full sense of it as its meaning keeps changing as my life – and my need to make sense of it – changes. The argument is this: More argues that however necessary or just our reasoning, if we cut down our morals and everything important to us ('the thickets') in an attempt to find our prey, in our attempts to find that which haunts or threatens us, then when that prey turns on us we will have nowhere left to hide. For More, the prey was the devil and the thickets the law of his god. For me, the prey is my own personal truth; to find who I am, as a man and as a beast.

Every so often I get close to it; catch sight of its tail on the edge of a clearing, a desolate zone, a personal ground zero, and it scares the living shit out of me. It knows I am watching but bides its time, drawing me deeper into the thickets, encouraging me to raze them to the ground. Be careful what you wish for? What other option is there, than to search for myself?

'Here comes the hunter, home from the hill.'
Robert Louis Stevenson

In *Home from the Hill*, Mitchum plays the middle-aged hunter intent on making a man of his son the only way he knows how. On the night his son was born, Wade

Hunnicutt (Mitchum) promised his wife raising the boy would be down to her, as long as she stayed. But when the boy reaches seventeen, Mitchum decides to make a man of him, teaching him to hunt and passing on some of the rough and rowdy to layer on top of the sensitivity, politeness and intelligence his mother encouraged in him. His mother accepts defeat, but believes he will keep hold of one sure trait she gave him: an ability to think for himself. In truth, neither parent is right. The boy's gonna be at his best given the chance to combine their influence and the two sides to himself.

Home from the Hill is one of those great, Southern, gingham and pick-up family sagas. Dramatic, powerful, merging love and brutality. Young men trying to prove themselves amongst their elders; the elders behaving like they're still young men. Women bearing the brunt of their mistakes.

'I want my son to be a better man than I am. I don't want him to make the same mistakes I have.'

R M, *Home from the Hill*

Mitchum fits well into the role of pipe-smoking king of the hill; landowner, father, best hunter in the county of both boar and woman. He gets shot at by an aggrieved husband and shut out by his wife. His acceptance is sought by sons both recognised (George Hamilton) and bastard (George Peppard). He's a real bootlace-tie Texas dawg.

While trying to learn his own lessons, Hamilton gets tarred by his father's reputation. His son needs the truth.

143

His son loses the scales from his eyes; sees his father for what he really is.

George Hamilton: '*I don't want any part of you.*'
R M: '*Better have a good reason for talking to me like that, boy.*'
George Hamilton: '*You mean I'm not showing you enough respect? Well what makes you think you've got any coming?*'
Home from the Hill

The son sees the 'failure' of his parents' marriage and, scared of repeating their mistakes, decides to cut off a major chance of achieving his own happiness. In making his decision, he unwittingly walks away from his pregnant girl.

'*The fruit don't fall too far from the tree.*'
Denver Pyle, *Home from the Hill*

Sometimes the harder we try to be different, the more we prove we're the same. Maybe we should focus on our wants, instead of our fears. I'm trying to convince myself, here.

Having gone in a matter of weeks from an idyllic, innocent, trouble-free life of a boy, to the angry and confused harsh slap of manhood; having gone from fear and respect for his father, to hatred and disgust for something he doesn't want to be, the son's attitude is best summed up by a line of the father's; by Mitchum's first line of the film.

'Who the hell did this to me?'

R M, Home from the Hill

The son spins out and fucks up. The father knows his own faults and seeks acceptance from his son.

'I'm not a perfect man. When you're in your forties, you won't be a perfect man, either. You can't live that long without hurting some and disappointing others. I guess feet of clay are pretty much standard equipment everywhere. I've got mine just like anyone else. I'm only human. But there's one thing I reserve for myself and that's the right to make my own mistakes without being judged for them. So don't judge me. Just be a son to me and take me as I am.'

R M, Home from the Hill

I talk football with Jack. He is a Sporting Lisbon fan. I ask if he's heard of Cardiff City; if he remembers the great John Charles – the 'Gentle Giant'. He doesn't. I remind him we beat Sporting in 1964. He doesn't remember. My food arrives and Jack buys me a beer.

Estela is working late tonight so I leave her to her shift and decide to walk off my food; stroll to wherever I end up.

A homeless guy, Bob, on the corner greets me. A fat woman strolls between us, towards the convenience store. We both turn and watch her ass; get caught in its wake.

'Striking, huh?'

'So are the Teamsters, but you don't see me sticking my dick in *them*.' I give him a quarter and he lights my smoke.

'So where you staying? Not the Holiday Inn! Man, that must be killing you!'

'Yeh, it is.'

'Whadda they charge? Like a hundred-twenty a night? For what? A swimming pool? I'll tell you what to do: walk a couple of blocks, take a left at Dunkin' Donuts, go down to the station, get a cab, tell him to drive you to the Camelot in Stratford. They charge about sixty a night and they got all the porn you could want. And a payphone, too.'

Cheers, Bob. Shame I didn't meet you last week, you could've saved me a fortune. I got plenty to put on the pyre, but not money to burn.

476 Logan Street, Bridgeport

McKinley School, Bridgeport

Take 7

Tuesday. I rise early and with enthusiasm.

*'When I awake in the morning and pee and it doesn't burn,
I figure it's going to be a good day.'*

R M

Except it ain't so great. Another day of finding nothing of
Mitchum the child poet. I leave the library and wonder
what to do next. There are few remaining signs of the town's
nightlife of old; of the Commodore Grill, the High Hat bar;
Sylvester Poli's theatre empire of the Hawes, Poli's, the
Majestic and Globe, but on the corner of Congress and
Broad sits the Savoy Bar and Grill, on the site of the old
Savoy hotel and movie theatre. Maybe Mitchum watched
films here. I better pop in and have an investigative drink.

147

I sit at the bar. It's not too busy. Suits sit at tall tables and laugh with their colleagues, the barman wipes beer-taps. I catch his eye and order a beer. He pours me a Sam with a big head, but promises to top it up. Which he does. I take a gulp. He tops it back up. I like him already. He asks me where I'm from. I tell him.

He nods. 'I've been there, a couple of times.'

'Yeh, when was that?'

'After I got back from Vietnam. On my way back from Ireland.'

I try and figure the geograhical link but decide I don't have enough information. He asks if I'm working. I tell him I'm investigating Robert Mitchum.

'I met him.'

He says it all matter of fact and I nearly choke on my beer as I try not to fall off my bar stool.

'Don't tell me you went to school with him.' I mean it: don't tell me that, having found nothing all day I'm not in the mood for bullshit.

'No. In Dingle. They were filming *Ryan's Daughter*.'

This sounds more like it. I ask him his name.

'Brendan. I'm originally from Ireland. I was in uniform and there was a dance – a friend told me to go out in uniform, but I didn' wanna. But I did, for the dance. He was a big fella, Mitchum – I didn't realise.'

Ah, just how tall was Mitchum? Reports vary, from six foot to six-foot-five. *The Story of GI Joe* director William A Wellman asked Mitchum how tall he was:

R M: *'Six foot.'*

Wellman: *'Come on, every actor who comes in here is at least six-foot-three, Alan Ladd is six-foot-five.'*
R M: *'My police department measurements say six feet and they're good at that sort of thing.'*

In some ways, his height was irrelevant. It wasn't that he was the tallest, but he was certainly one of the broadest.

'He asked me where I was from. I said "Bridgeport" and of course he's from Bridgeport so he was arms around me and he bought me a shot. I don't drink shots, but if Mitchum's buying... and that Sarah Miles, she was beautiful. Is she still alive?'

'I think so.'

'But he's dead, right?'

'Right.'

'Yeh, Billet's Hotel, Dingle.... He was a big man.'

The biographies state he stayed at Hotel Milltown or the Mill House hotel, but what do I care. Perhaps the dance was at Billet's.

The movie was loosely based on Flaubert's *Madame Bovary* but set in twentieth-century Ireland, exploiting the so-called 'troubles'. Mitchum didn't want to do the film. Screenwriter Robert Bolt suggested Mitchum to director David Lean because, having seen him in a TV interview, he had been impressed with Mitchum's 'dignity and mildness as against his swaggering tough-guy image'. When Bolt phoned to try and convince Mitchum to take the role of Charles Shaughnessy, Mitchum said he wouldn't be available because he had planned to commit suicide. Bolt was taken aback but, thinking on his feet, replied, 'If you would just do this wretched little film of ours and then do yourself in, I'd be happy to stand the expenses of your burial.' Or words to that effect – each biography phrases it differently. The reply made Mitchum laugh and that was enough to get him to sign on, although the idea of working in Ireland for three months was not something he was looking forward to. It got worse: three months turned into twelve.

'After ten days on the film we were already seven days behind.'

R M

Mitchum was miscast as the impotent schoolteacher. Audiences refused to suspend disbelief to such a degree as to accept Mitchum couldn't get his old fella up and give Sarah Miles a good seeing to. *Mitchum impotent? Give us a break.* The common belief was you can claim many things of Mitchum, but not that. He was still sex on legs. But David Lean was adamant his choice was a good one.

'A quiet, smooth-sweet character actor in the part would have been totally wrong and, even worse, deadly boring. Whatever one thinks of Bob Mitchum, he has never been boring.'

David Lean

'Dunno why I'm playing an Irish schoolteacher. For a fraction of what they're paying me, they could have a real one.'

R M

150

Mitchum starred opposite Sarah Miles, who at the time was married to Bolt. She and Mitchum had great respect for each other and there were rumours of an affair. When asked if there was any truth to the gossip Mitchum replied diplomatically, 'I think you should always make out with your leading lady if you have a chance. I've discussed it several times with Dorothy – unfortunately my old lady doesn't agree.'

Miles would say, 'Robert Mitchum and I were soulmates. We were very close, but we weren't "doing it".'

Mitchum arrived in Dingle in January 1969 and stayed for eleven months – the schedule all to cock because Lean wanted to nail every shot perfectly and because the ever-changeable Irish weather made continuity so problematic. Bored out of their minds, Mitchum and his co-stars Trevor Howard and Leo McKern were often shit-faced – their drunken performances providing sly amusement when it came to viewing the daily rushes.

'In Ryan's Daughter *the director insisted I examine some footage.... The first thing that comes on the screen was Leo McKern completely gassed in a pub. Then the scene shifted to a shot of Trevor Howard staggering up the beach, absolutely stoned. And then Lean cuts to a shot of me on the beach, wiped out. All I could say was, "The camera never lies".'*

R M

Mitchum also entertained himself by hosting dinner parties, usually doing the cooking himself; establishing a marijuana factory in the hotel greenhouse (the results of which he

151

shared liberally, even with the local police); and shipping in cheap skirt.

'Mitch's girls would fly in from all over the place, real rough-looking birds. It was convenient that all the rooms had a number because it was a useful way for him to remember who was who. He'd often say to me something like, "Number eleven's hot, she flew in last night."'

Sarah Miles

Mitchum, possibly in an attempt to cover his own back, said of Miles, 'She's wild, that Sarah. Sometimes she's... wakened me at three in the morning and in those refined English accents asked, "Bob, can I procure a woman for you?" That's some girl, I'll tell you.'

When Mitchum was told they had formed a Robert Mitchum fan-club in Dingle, he suggested, 'The membership is largely unwed mothers and their brothers.'

One day, Mitchum got hold of a couple of lobsters out of season, so invited people around for dinner. Miles didn't like the idea of the crustaceans screaming to a pink death so 'liberated' them by returning them to Dingle Bay. Mitchum went mental. Can't say I blame him. Your own moral choices are your own moral choices but you can't enforce them on others without payback. Even Miles couldn't blame him, claiming, 'He just went bananas, and quite rightly so... it was a dreadful thing for me to do... he's never been the same about me, since.' To the contrary, Mitchum considered her one of his favourite co-stars and they would later appear together in *The Big Sleep*. But Mitchum threatened revenge for his lost lobsters and revenge he got, by telling reporters Miles drank her own piss. A typical Mitchum thing to say and it probably would've been brushed off as such had Miles not admitted she *did* drink her own piss. Full marks for owning up.

Ah, *The Big Sleep*. This is the Mitchum-movie critics love to hate because they consider director Michael Winner took gold – Robert Mitchum as Philip Marlowe – and turned it into shit. If so, it's a remarkable feat.

So where did Winner go wrong? Well, the movie was based on great Raymond Chandler material but was onto a hiding to nothing as it was always going to be judged against the 1946 Bogart/Bacall/Hawks film noir classic and Mitchum's earlier portrayal of Marlowe in the 1975 release *Farewell, My Lovely*. So to make it stand out Winner set his version in 1970s England. Chandler, whose stories are sunk so deeply in LA, reset in 1970s England – the alarm bells sound.

For a start, the stakes are raised because *The Big Sleep* had an all-star cast: Mitchum, Miles, John Mills (reunited after *Ryan's Daughter*), Oliver Reed, Edward Fox, Joan Collins, a whole host of well-known British actors and the great James Stewart.

It's possible to interpret certain aspects of the movie as cap-doffing to film noir, which had a habit of taking what could be seen as filmic flaws and turning them into stylistic signatures. So maybe Winner's version – which has taken so much abuse from critics – deserves a second look.

The sudden editing into and out of close-ups hints at

film noir, and works in that genre, but without the lighting and style appears here as obvious and clumsy. And, for all the big reps, most of the acting lacks subtlety – again, something which works in film noir, up to a point, but not in 1970s remakes. One big name getting away with a bad performance is understandable, but so many? Fox is miscast, Collins is abysmal, even the six-line taxi-driver overacts. Mills does well, as do a couple of the bit part players. Ollie Reed plays the club owner like an urban and urbane Lee Van Cleef and, ironically enough, Mitchum – who was perfectly happy to put in a stock-standard performance – comes out pretty well. Perhaps, just perhaps, this was down to some loyalty to Bogart, or to Raymond Chandler whom he knew in LA when they were both skint and unknown, before their careers flourished. They hung out in the same bookstores and cafés on Hollywood's Wilcox Boulevard.

'I thought he [Chandler] *affected a British accent and he was always wearing white gloves. But then I learned he'd gone to school in England and wore the gloves because of a skin disorder... he was a nice guy, but distant, suspicious of everybody.'*

R M

As well as the usual film fare of people shooting handguns with impossible accuracy and a high speed car chase taking place at what must've been pushing hard on fifteen miles per hour, the action is laughable. As for location: the mansion works, but to see Mitchum staking out a house complete with slanted stone-clad wall in a 1970s cul-de-sac more fitting to *Abigail's Party* than a Marlowe movie, shows a degree of poor judgement beyond belief.

Still, everyone's allowed to screw up now and again. And at least Candy Clark strips off. And that's how best to view it: as a disappointing cheap thrill, or as a half-decent find when you're stoned and flicking through the channels at four in the morning. As a remake of a noir classic, it's sacrilege; as a movie in its own right, it's typical 1970s British fare. It could be a lot worse. And it did manage to do something no other movie had done before: team Mitchum with Jimmy Stewart.

During filming, seventy-year-old Stewart was having problems remembering his lines. Mitchum said of his co-star, 'The picture is all about corpses but Jimmy looked deader than any of them.' He was universally criticised for the remark – not only was it distasteful, but it was said of an actor, a man, who was revered and unimpeachable. Once again, Mitchum's actions were deemed beyond the pale, but for my money he was just reworking a line from the movie: in the voice-over, Mitchum says of General Sternwood (played by Stewart), 'He was used up; he looked more like a dead man than most dead men look.' So many times, when interviewed about a particular movie, Mitchum continued to use the heart of his dialogue but then those words were reported as if entirely his own. When he was criticised for remarks he made after the filming of *This Championship Season*, he claimed the journalist knew he was responding in character (that of the old-fashioned, small-minded, bigoted school basketball coach he played in the movie). But I guess there's no story in that.

Whatever the truth of that particular situation, there are questions to be asked regarding how Mitchum's interviews should be perceived. The reader must ask who they are listening to; which voice? The person, the actor or the role? Was Mitchum using this device as camouflage, playing games with the interviewer, or was he unaware of the fuzzing between his roles on screen and in life? And if he *wasn't* aware, well then is this a doorway into some psychological profile or is it simply a result of being stoned his whole adult life? I don't know. Give me a joint and I'll think about it.

'Bob was two people... quite a rowdy fellow, but most of the time he was a very quiet person, read a great deal; read poetry, important books. He used to write poetry... he was a very intellectual person.'

Michael Winner

Brendan offers me another beer. I zoom back to Bridgeport.

'You see this bar?'

I'm leaning on it. 'Yeh.'

'This bar used to be over there,' – he points to a long-forgotten bar towards the other end of Main Street. 'This bar was christened by Jack Dempsey. Soon as the place opened – 1932 – he was the first to have a drink.'

'Then I'll drink to Jack Dempsey.'

'You do that.'

And hope there ain't a short-ass lurking, mistaking me for Kirk Douglas.

I ask Brendan about Bridgeport and its neighbours; Southport, Westport and the riches there.

'I know Paul Newman lives there,' he says, 'Robert Redford, too.' He tells me Bridgeport's beginning to crawl back to its feet. Even over the last twelve months there's more bars, more companies. The Bank of Scotland have moved in. As have the FBI.

'They usually come in for happy hour. Keep themselves to themselves, mostly.'

The FBI. Huh. I bet they take the train.

Take 8

I crawl from dreams of assassination, the FBI and Robert Mitchum. How much sleep did I have? An hour? Two? Spent most of the night trapped between the need to sleep and the inability. Hours getting roped back from the verge of nodding off.

'I loathe people who can go to sleep immediately. I sometimes regard my wife with great rancour and bitterness because, hm, how dare she? I lie there and stare... I've spent a lot of time trying to get to sleep. It opens up all sorts of avenues of interest.'

R M

Smoke a couple and get back to the library. I gotta find him soon. I don't know what day it is, but for me it's 1925.

I approach a librarian to ask for today's batch of microfilm. She's got a grin on her face. 'We found the file!' she says, 'the Mitchum file – we found it.'

Fantastic, now we're getting somewhere. She pulls it out from under the desk and hands it over. I open it there, remain standing.

Photocopies of baby Bob in a sailor suit; lanky teen Bob with his brother; and in swimming costume on a beach with his wife. Photocopies of the suited actor in court, awaiting the outcome of the drugs case; quotes about smoking dope: 'The only effect that I ever noticed from smoking marijuana was a sort of mild sedative, a release from the tension when I was overworking. It never made me boisterous or quarrelsome. If anything, it calmed me down and reduced my activity.... My attitude with respect to the future... is that I will not use marijuana at any time whatsoever.'

Except when you're stoned, huh Mitch? We both know that was a big fat lie for the sake of the court, the press and the studios. Mitchum continued smoking grass for the rest of his life. In the seventies, Sarah Miles claimed, 'As long as [Mitchum] had his dope he wouldn't need money at all.'

He continued to discuss his sentence: 'It is my feeling that a transgression of the law should be punished. It is my belief that I have already received, both before and after my conviction, far more punishment than the law itself would have envisaged for a first offense of this kind.'

May 1950: An article in the local *Herald* bitching about Mitchum's unwillingness to cooperate: 'Mitchum was unavoidably detained on the set, along with several other actors and actresses, all of them sitting around a round table playing poker.' The journalist eventually got to ask Mitchum if he ever returned to his home town. 'I was around there a couple of years ago, but I don't know a soul in Bridgeport.'

'Movie star Bob Mitchum by-passed his birthplace, Bridgeport, on the way to New Haven yesterday for the Yale Law School's Mitchum Film Festival. (Mitchum has never returned to Bridgeport for a look-see-again since he left it at age 15).'

Alan Neigher, *Connecticut Sunday Herald*

A 1965 photo of Mitchum and John Wayne on the set of *El Dorado* with their real-life mothers. Mitchum's mother looks elegant, strong and attractive at sixty-two years of age.

Articles on the Logan Street house. Built 1893. A Victorian, one-family house with full cellar, attic, back yard, front L-shaped alcove. Received basswood plaque stating 'Mitchum Estate' September 1982 from the East End Historical Society. There were plans to turn the house into a museum. It remains a private residence, with no plaque.

In 1959 the then-occupants, A J and Rosa Pettway, invited Mitchum to return. He declined but recalled, 'In my mind's eye, I can see the old street between Stratford and Connecticut avenues, the Logan grocery on the corner... just thinking about it makes me nostalgic.' Much of the building had changed but, according to Rosa, 'the bathtub [was] the same one Mitchum used.'

Doris Seibel, who lived in the house as a child, recalled, 'Every day some girls would come to the house, ring the bell and ask, "Is this Robert Mitchum's house?" We'd say yes and they'd do like they did for Frank Sinatra, and squeal.'

Ah, Sinatra. Mitchum once said the only man he would never mess with was old Frank, and with the Mafia putting the 'Sin' in Sinatra who can blame him. When a man's up against another man, big or small, the worst that'll happen if it's a good clean fight is you take your kicking and maybe next time you'll think twice and keep your mouth shut. But when you're up against a little man with a chip on his shoulder, a chip supported by powerful, vicious and vindictive associates, then, man, you've got trouble. Nothing more dangerous than a little man with a chip on his shoulder: he doesn't know when to stop or will get someone else to take and dole out the licks. Sinatra was a little man, but a friend to Mitchum.

Some claim it was the mob who decided Sinatra would appear in *From Here to Eternity* – a picture which resurrected his career and won him the 1953 Oscar® for Best Supporting Actor.

Mitchum and Sinatra worked together on the 1955 release *Not as a Stranger*, along with Broderick Crawford and Lee Marvin. The film marked Stanley Kramer's directorial debut and he described working with the three boozy stars as 'ten weeks of hell'.

Lee Marvin said of Mitchum, 'The beauty of the man. He's so still. He's moving, and yet he's not moving.'

'Lee was a tough ex-Marine, a hard-drinking bastard.'

John Mitchum

'Lee, I baby-sat for Mitchum at MGM and he'd drink until six in the morning. He'd arrive on set at seven and not miss a line. You have two beers and you don't know your ass from the Grand Canyon.'

Tyrone Cabeen to Lee Marvin

According to Mitchum, Crawford drank Sinatra's wig: 'He's got this hairpiece half-way down and he takes a glass of vodka and downs the goddamn thing. So I called Frank: "Guess what? The Crawdad just drank your wig". He said, "Good, I don't have to show up Monday".'

One morning, Sinatra's lying in the dressing room with a hangover. Mitchum mixes a cure – a glorified bloody Mary – and pours it into Sinatra. Sinatra opened his eyes and uttered a solitary word: 'Mother'.

'I see Frank Sinatra occasionally. He sort of adopted me, and every year he sends a telegram on Mother's Day.'

R M

He wasn't joking. Every year, Mitchum received from Sinatra a Mother's Day message addressed to 'Mother' or 'You mother'.

In amongst the Mitchum-as-family-man promo shots and film reviews, a photocopy of a census leaps out at me. The Fourteenth Census of the United States for the county of Fairfield, compiled on 2 January 1920. I'm excited and engaged. I expect it to act as a solid source of information. I scan down to the name 'Mitchum'. The details confuse me; do not match up to commonly believed 'facts'. Names, birthplaces and the list of family members are wrong. When it comes to Mitchum hiding the reality of his early life, it seems the authorities did their best to do it for him. The whole thing stinks of a compiler's liquid lunch.

I run the file through the photocopier and hit the Savoy. In honour of the census compiler I enjoy my own liquid lunch – I need a break from the microfilm for a few hours. I pore over photocopies, pour beer down my gullet. A piece I mistakenly presume is a reworking of yet another promo-puff turns out to be something far more interesting. It is an edited version of Mitchum's appeal for probation, which he wrote in an attempt to get out of jail early following his 1949 conviction for conspiracy to possess narcotics. It covers most of two pages, which in newspaper terms is pretty substantial. It details his life in Delaware; his arrest in Savannah; meeting his wife for the first time; moving to California; and the period he spent working for Lockheed. It is the nearest thing to Mitchum's autobiography I am likely to find.

It's been well reported that when asked if he would ever write an autobiography Mitchum replied, 'What for? Who needs it? The Los Angeles police station has it all.' Previously, there seemed no reason to believe this to be anything more than a flippant and self-deprecating remark typical of Mitchum, but now I'm wondering whether he perhaps had in mind this detailed report of his early life – he had *already* written an autobiographical account of his

164

pre-fame life and this was it. Everything that followed had been or would be sucked into the public domain because of his fame. There was nothing more he wished to add to what was already known. His poetry – if I ever find it – was to stay private. He admitted later, 'I suppose I've excused myself by coming to the conclusion, forcing the conclusion, that what I have to say or what I feel is really of very little importance to anyone else'.

My initial excitement is tempered by realisation: the document was written to portray himself as innocently as possible, so this too must be taken with a pinch of salt. Touched up or not, the report didn't help his appeal – probation was denied. But it does reveal fascinating insights into the man, if you want to believe them. This, on the effect of his new-found fame:

'The new popularity brought new faces with endless requests for assistance – requests which were always met. I suppose I honestly believed that it was helping to erase a moral debt by granting aid to others of the same social-financial back-ground... at any rate, the rumor spread that I was a "soft touch"....'

I find this easy to believe, that it came from real life. The 'moral debt' rings too much of truth.

And of achievement:

'Although progressing famously in my profession, I was constantly obsessed with the phantom of failure...'

165

He was, after all, an insightful, sensitive and withdrawn child who happened to have grown into the shape of a man. However his feelings towards acting and art may have changed later in his career, when he wrote this document his young drives of artistic ambition, excitement, enthusiasm, engagement, *involvement* and a belief that he could achieve the levels of artistic expression necessary for him to deem his life successful, through the job of movie actor, were not yet swamped by cynicism and harsh realisation. That phantom still meant something.

And this on receiving psychiatric treatment – treatment he didn't believe necessary but agreed to because his mother, sister and wife persuaded him to convince him he was losing it and in a worse mental state than he was:

'Dr Frederick Hacker adjudged me rational, but suffering a state of over-amiability in which failure to please everyone created a condition of self-reproach. He told me that I was addicted to nothing but the goodwill of people, and suggested that I risk their displeasure by learning to say "No" and following my OWN judgement.'

Yeh and I bet he followed his own judgement too far; I bet his re-evaluating of other people's acceptance led to him being aggressive and anti-social; I bet he dismissed them too much. One extreme to another.

I think I understand the man. Some might read hints of a bi-polar condition in Mitchum's behaviour – extremes of sociability and isolation; giving himself to people versus self-deprecation, but I am not in a position, or a condition, to comment on this. But look at the history books, read the biographies, the police reports – it happened. Read between the lines if you want to, reach your own conclusions. Make this 'hero', any 'hero', into any shape you need them to be.

My emotions are confused; I don't know whether to be excited or not. I don't know if I'm just projecting onto him my own shit or if I'm achieving a genuine level of understanding. I better hit Carmelina's.

I brood at the bar, unsure where to go after Bridgeport. Back to New York or onward? It makes sense to continue east, to Fall River. Fall River is Portuguese – Estela has not been here long but Carmelina has, I'll ask her if she knows how to get there. Her fingernails are painted clear except the tips, which are painted white. Women here sure do go to a lot of trouble with their nails. She recommends I go to Providence first and travel from there.

I pick up a copy of the Portuguese and Spanish *The Immigrant* newspaper and start reading. Estela leans over for the horoscopes. She asks me my star sign. I tell her, *Touro*. She translates for me. Apparently, it's a good week for '*amigos e amores*'. She is a *Leão*. She tells me it says she must 'play the game and have fun'. I'm getting to like horoscopes.

She serves some customers in Portuguese. They swear in English. I scribble some notes. She comes back, tries without success to read my handwriting, turns over my scrap paper – on the other side is a section from an earlier typed draft. She asks, 'Can I read it?' but when I reach over to take it back, to see if I want her to read it or not, she retracts her hand and keeps hold of the paper. She laughs at my empty grab. So I read with her. Or, rather, as she reads I scan fast, trying to remember what I've written. I see her name halfway down the page. I don't know if she intends to read it all and I don't know how she'll react to seeing herself mentioned. She continues to read and then, 'Oh! I see my name!' half-amused, half-curious. What I have written are pleasant things but these too could work against me. She stops, puts the paper down on the bar, gives me a gentle, fleeting slap on the cheek. It feels like a kiss. I grin and hide my face in the act of drinking.

Jack tells Estela she's needed to work late so we agree to meet tomorrow. I settle my tab and leave. Walk off my food. Stroll the snow and find myself stood outside the Savoy. Enter and drink. Stumble back to the hotel. Order my Coronas. Take them to my room. Who knows, I may even get to sleep tonight. Without a woman in my bed, a coma will do.

Take 9

'My head feels like a, a giant racer – up and around, over and down, aching, pounding...'

R M, *Where Danger Lives*

I wake early with a sore bonce. I look in the mirror – there's a bleeding cut on my forehead. That bastard Mitchum, it's gotta be. Who else is gonna attack me when I'm asleep? I dress and get down to the library. The sun is out – ah, 'hail the gladsome spring' – and considering there's still snow on the sidewalk, today is hot hot hot and I'm sweating like a mule at Customs.

I gotta get back to the library and 1925: pray I find what I'm looking for. More than ever, I'm on a mission. I want to get this nailed down and get on with things; I need to move on.

Microfiche loaded, I skim the Sunday editions of the *Bridgeport Post*. A whole year of nothing. I jump to 1927.

January 3: 'Man Found Frozen to Death... in Lesbia St' writes its own punchline.

January 17: 'Prohibition's sixth anniversary was celebrated yesterday with more or less of a splash...' ho, ho, bleedin' ho, what's so funny about a dry bar?

There's a list of the latest public library books. Number eight on the list is *Poet's Alphabet* by one W H Davies – so they were definitely stocking his titles.

Page thirteen – unlucky for some – but hold on: 'Bridgeport's Youngest Poet Publishes Small Newspaper'. Now who's this little bugger? I stop reading. I'm expecting another disappointment. I'm trying to figure it out when I spot the photograph: little boy, notepad and pencil, flat cap, big ears, droopy eyes. It's Mitchum. It's little Bobby Mitchum. Little bloody Bobby bastard Mitchum – found ya! I don't quite know what to do. I want to read it but I want to print it too, in case I suddenly lose it again. I want to read and print and run around the place and sink a beer in celebration. I found him – and it's only the third week of January, I don't have to scan through the whole year. But I'm scared to read. The copy is laid out in columns. I see nothing that looks like a poem. I print and settle down at a desk.

'Bridgeport has produced several youthful genii within the last few years who, starting from obscure beginnings are now well on the road to fame.... The latest of the budding geniuses to shine over the literary horizon of Bridgeport is Robert Mitchum, the young son of Mrs

William Clancy of 476 Logan street, a member of the composing room staff of the Post Publishing company, who is blossoming out as a youthful poet of much promise.'

'Genii' and 'geniuses' – where are you proofreader?

'Master Robert, who is a few months over 8 years of age...' so definitely not aged six then, 'has, according to his mother, developed an extraordinary taste for writing... a glance over some of the products of this youthful brain indicates that here perhaps is a young poet who is gifted with original ideas...'

'Among the sonnets... and most of his inspirations are composed and written for his mother to whom he is devotedly attached... are "Waiting for the Dawn", "In the land which water smothers", this latter desciding in vivid form the effect of a flood and the vain efforts of man to stop the ever-encroaching waters....

'In the land which water smothers' is a lovely, lapping line.

Ah-ha, something that looks like a poem, albeit only an extract:

> *'Next comes the winter*
> *With a blanket of white*
> *And children are playing*
> *From morning till night.'*

Well, it ain't gonna rock the world but for a eight-year-old kid writing way back in 1926, that's not too bad. There are adults churning out verse today who should be pleased if they achieved a flow as easy.

The copy continues: 'And yet this small child seems to prefer to sit at home and compose poetry to his mother, and with pencil poised in slender fingers dreams of big things, big futures and big successes, with a mind that is already developed far above his years'.

And then an extract from a war poem:

> *'Through mud and snow I wander,*
> *Pulling guns to save others' lives,*
> *I fight in the mountains yonder,*
> *I'm imprisoned in dusty dives.*
> *I seek adventure and find too much,*
> *Oh, if I were only rich*
> *I'd not be in this terrible "dutch"*
> *And fighting in this ditch.'*

Yu'know, that's pretty good going for a kid. It scans well; shows an understanding of alliteration, assonance and rhyme; there's action and reflection; there's mature thought – 'I seek adventure and find too much' – man, it's taken me thirty-odd years to realise that's how I've spent my life. Precocious little sod.

Other poems mentioned are 'The Lord's Work', 'The Holy Star' and 'There's No Place Like Home', which ends:

> *'And when you're out and away,*
> *No matter where you roam,*
> [You can see where it's going, can't you?]
> *No matter what time of week or day,*
> *There's no place like home.'*

It also makes reference to Mitchum's newspaper, *The Gold Streak*, the previous edition of which included news updates, poems, limericks 'indicating a strong sense of humor' and a short-story called 'Adventures of Sure-Shot Shorty'.

The copy ends with 'When he is not attending the McKinley school [he] is covering sheets of paper with childish writing, in which there lies latent the unmistake-able genius of poetic success.'

Ah, love him. Underneath all that shyness and attitude I bet he was proud as punch.

It's strange to think of Big Bad Bob as this little, poem-writing mama's boy and yet it makes sense. Once Mitchum was photographed and featured in the papers as a 'poet' I bet the local boys were looking to give him a righteous kicking; I bet he had to stand his corner or get crushed by his male peers and role models, or withdraw into himself and hide away. Men, boys, don't take kindly to that kinda talent in one of their own. They don't trust it; don't trust the strength it gives the individual; don't trust the inevitable questions of sexual orientation – sensitivity in a boy means he's queer, right?

If I had to put my money down, I'd bet the foul-mouthed little bugger stood his ground and fought his corner. I can't see this kid shrinking. I can believe he tried to keep it to himself but I can't see him bending under the force of expectation or mockery.

'I think it might've hurt him and it might've confused him, angered him. Maybe he felt misunderstood.... I think if

anyone called him a derogatory term, or a poet, he would've
smacked them in the mouth. Whether the guy was a grown
man and he was twelve, he wouldn't have been afraid... it
would've given him the hurt and anger to be able to smack
that guy in the mouth.'

Bentley Mitchum

There's a map of the world on the library wall showing where their visitors have come from. I press a red tack slap-bang in the middle of Cardiff. It seems I'm the first visitor from Wales. I give the librarian a copy of the Mitchum coverage, say my goodbyes and head downstairs. I stop to take one last look at the portrait of Barnum. Someone has scribbed in the corner, 'Anthony ♡ Juleen'. Perhaps it was Anthony. Perhaps it was Juleen. I decide to stroll until I get somewhere.

I'm feeling pretty sated – my search justified; I found what I was looking for; I've reached the truth of things: Mitchum was eight when he was first published, not six; the feature wasn't on the Children's Page – because there wasn't one; wasn't published on a Saturday; and carried no by-line, let alone any mention of 'Uncle Dudley'. Nor is there any mention of Nathalia Crane. But best of all, I found the original, first publication of Mitchum's poetry. It *did* happen – I know, because I've seen it. Proof is mine. The *Bridgeport Sunday Post*, January 17, 1926, Vol. XV, no. 3, circ. 22,000 on the previous Sunday, 'forty pages – 5 cents' – I love you. Under the surface of the silver screen's biggest, baddest, boldest, bullshitting, bar-brawling bruiser there was a poet. The epitome of a man's man...

was a poet. Sex on legs... was a poet. The shy little kid who wrote poems for his mother... was a man waiting to happen.

I don't feel superior to him, I don't want to ridicule him, I just want to absorb the facts. I'm feeling so energised, so full of myself, so righteous, I'll probably walk around the corner and straight into a kicking. Well, bring it on – nobody's putting my ass on the sidewalk, today. I've got Mitchum on my side.

Take 10

'There are no rules in my end of the business, except maybe one: never stay in one town too long.'

R M, *Man with the Gun*

I have to leave Bridgeport but I know I'll return. Check-out time is a workable and reasonable 12 noon. In the UK it's an inconsiderate 10am. Whoever decided on that should be shot at dawn. How are you supposed to make the most of your last night and be up, packed and out by ten?

I pack up my kiestera and check out. Head down to the station and out of town. Now that I'm leaving the snow has gone, but the cold cuts to the bone. I am tired – physically, mentally, emotionally. Physcially, I am suffering the combined effects of several months' drinking and a lack of sleep. Mentally, the search is draining me – what it might mean to me, what Mitchum might represent. Emotionally, more than anything else I want some beautiful, compassionate woman to take me in her arms, to her bed, to love and reassure me and to make me feel well. I want to wake with my arms around her and, preferably, without cramp, her knee in my back, her snoring in my ear or a hangover. I can but dream.

'That man right there needs direction, needs affection, needs love's resurrection
That man right there, he looks a lot like me.
Is there anyway he can start all over, somewhere?
Yeh it's gotta be, if only he can find a sweet, brave angel to care.'
R M, *Little Ole Winedrinker Me*

The 86 Richmond–Virginia to Boston–Massachusetts arrives, having travelled the bulk of the north-east corridor. I board and grab myself a seat. The last time I saw Mitchum on a train was in *Thompson's Last Run* (1986). He played an old safe-cracker, handcuffed and travelling into Texas under the watchful eye of an old adversary played by Wilford Brimley. We travel away from the coast to New Haven...

'Alas what a disastrous end was ours! When we reached the town of New Haven, we began to beg from passers-by in the open streets and in less than an hour were in jail.'
W H Davies, *The Autobiography of a Super-Tramp*

And on to New London. Mitchum's mother schooled here;

learned to speak English here. According to Mitchum, she achieved record high grades for a girl of her age. It looks a pleasant enough town – houses with their widow's walks around the roofs, so they could see when the ships were coming in. Providence is about twenty-five minutes away. It's 4.45 and the mists are coming down. A good chance of a train smash in this weather.

We'll soon be leaving the Constitution State and into Rhode Island, the Ocean State. The mists roll in fast and vision is fading. These states are smaller than I expected. The one I'm in is too big.

'Thanks be to Providence.'
>   W H Davies, *The Autobiography of a Super-Tramp*

I decide to delay Boston and alight at Providence. Ask the taxi driver to take me to a cheap hotel. He takes me to a brothel. I couldn't see any working girls but they charged for the room by the hour. My bed buckles under the weight of my bag, the springs exhausted.

'It was one of those transient motels, somewhere between a fleabag and a dive.'
>   R M, *Farewell My Lovely*

The TV shows only poor-quality porn so I hit the bricks. Spend the evening entering and leaving dodgy Irish bars, gay bars, student bars, pretentious wine bars. Try to get me a session with a psychic but she slams the door in my face. Denied the world of spirits, I rely on the physical. Soon grow bored of listless strip-joint routines. Take my chances on some shallow sleep. Wake early, check out, take a taxi. I can't see me missing much if I stayed here a year.

Providence to Fall River is only eighteen miles. From Fall River to Boston only fifty-three miles, by Bonanza bus. I board and we head back through downtown Providence, past the cemetery with its big gravestones for Griffith and Jones, through the classic American architecture and over the bridge where the Stars and Stripes flies upside down – a signal for critical times. We soon enter Massachusetts, pass signs advertising 'Gas Food Lodging' and exits to Newport and Swansea.

Newport: home to the summer domiciles of the privileged land-owners. One of *the* places to be seen, to be accepted. This was the setting for the 1988 release *Mr North*. It was a family project: John Huston was executive producer, co-writer and was due to appear in the movie alongside his daughter Angelica, Anthony Edwards and Lauren Bacall. The director was Huston's son, Danny.

Before filming began, Huston telephoned Mitchum to ask a favour. Huston knew he was dying and knew he wouldn't be able to complete filming so he asked his old drinking buddy to fill in for him *if* necessary. Mitchum was soon to receive the call: Huston had contracted pneumonia and had been rushed to hospital in Fall River; Mitchum was needed after all.

He went to visit Huston in hospital and commented on how he didn't look so ill. Huston replied, 'Best hoax I ever pulled, kid.'

The nurse complained he wasn't eating enough, which Huston contended. Mitchum suggested, if he could prove he wasn't eating enough, would Huston at least admit it? Huston agreed. Mitchum got the nurse to lift her skirt in front of the patient. Huston admitted he wasn't eating enough. A fair example of their shared humour.

'I was in Ireland once and went round to see him [Huston]. *He was wanking this monkey. I said, "What are you doing?" he said, "Well, he likes it, kid." I like Huston, great fun.'*

R M

Based on Thornton Wilder's novel *Theophilus North*, *Mr North* portrays a civilised section of society and their staff; specifically, a 'most unusual young man' and his effect on the community. It's a pleasant little tale and a harmlessly enjoyable movie – a considerable feat considering filming was overcast by Huston's worsening condition and eventual death.

The movie was filmed entirely on location in Rhode Island, at Blithewold Gardens and several mansions in the state which illustrate the wealth that gathered there.

Huston died on 28 August, 1987 – after Mitchum had finished filming.

'All I can say is, they better drive a stake through his heart.'

R M, on hearing of Huston's death

The pair had a lot in common. Huston was a trouble-maker, a trouble-shooter and a 'rare bird'; had been a boxer and

181

reporter, a down-and-out and writer. He was an artistic child and first had a short story published as a teenager, in 1928 – only a few years after the *Bridgeport Post* first published little Bob Mitchum. Huston was also a highly respected professional and individual, heavy drinker, fighter (he broke two of Errol Flynn's ribs), womaniser, man's man and creative force. He made his directorial debut in 1941 with *The Maltese Falcon* (as debuts go, it's up there with Charles Laughton's); directed and co-starred with Bogart in *The Treasure of the Sierra Madre*; won the 1948 Academy Awards for Best Director and Screenplay (*Sierra Madre*) and, in 1983, the eleventh annual American Film Institute Lifetime Achievement Award.

Mitchum spoke at the AFI's award ceremony, saying he had, 'total admiration for my friend. I tell people I was led down the garden path when I first signed on [in Hollywood]. They said, "You get to meet a lot of pretty people and you get to make a lot of money and have a lot of fun." Well, the pretty people all go home at six o'clock; "the man" comes and takes the money; but John made it fun... and, honest to god, [he is] one of the few people who sees the real basic fun in the genre of motion picture-making and communication, and I adore him for that.'

We cross the Saronnet River, close to Swansea. Travel along the Eisenhower Interstate towards Somerset. 'Cape Cod 40 miles'. As we reach the bridge entering Fall River a sign suggests, 'Lonely Confused Depressed Suicidal call Samaritans'. Not a great way to greet visitors but the sun comes out as we reach Fall River.

Mitchum came to Fall River in 1932, aged fourteen, with dreams of high seas adventures. Some stories claim he ran away, but I believe as a teenager with a sense of responsibility to help lessen the pressure on his mother and family in the dark days of the Depression, Mitchum hitched from Delaware to Massachusetts to find work. His mother even packed his case. Fall River was a busy port and industrial town and, lying about his age, he found his first job as a deckhand on a salvage vessel called *The Sagamore*. His presence onboard broke the state's child labour laws and he was soon sent on his way. Mitchum claimed when the free food ran out so did he.

I walk down the hill to the water; down Columbia Street then back up and along Main; past Santo Cristo Square, Nobregas Market, Medeiros Square, Chaves Market, Casa Luso, Mundo de Bé Bé, Caravela Family Restaurant. A Portuguese town, just like they told me in Bridgeport. Never would've guessed it. I bet the food here is splendid.

A sign reading '*Cerveijaria Melo Abreu*' gives me a great idea but another saying '*So Para Membros e Convidado*' deters me. (Beer – members and guests only.)

Ponta Delgada Boulevard, Machado Green, Division Street – come Saturday night, I bet there's some fights there. Morgan Street – even amongst the Portuguese, the Welsh find a place.

Statues of saints and soldiers. The first time in weeks I've seen dogshit on the sidewalk. Run-down but living, breathing, free of pretention. A quiet town but not bland nor dull; a worker's town, down on its luck.

Fall River was once a big textile centre – even made the

183

uniforms for the civil war. Lots of mills, lots of jobs, but now it's all gone. The only signs of this past are closed little shops stocking communion dresses.

In *Macao* – the movie which reunited the on-screen pairing of Mitchum and Jane Russell – a lot of the action takes place at the Hotel Portugeusa. *Macao* often gets a bad press. Directed by Josef von Sternberg, the production was a shambles. On completion, Mitchum complained that the edit left him 'meeting myself coming through doors'. Nick Ray was brought in to reshoot it, Mitchum was drafted in to rewrite it.

'So... I wrote the days' work and... we shot in the afternoons. Did that for almost ten days. At least they could release it. Before that it was a flat impossibility.'

R M

Von Sternberg tried to shift some of the blame onto Russell, bringing into question her acting ability.

'Joe was really something. He told me, "We both know this is a piece of shit and we're saddled with Jane Russell. You and I know she has as much talent as this cigarette case." I replied, "Mr von Sternberg, Miss Russell survives so she must have something. Lots of ladies have big tits."'

R M

If the stories about Howard Hughes' bisexuality are to be believed then Mitchum and Russell together – 'the breast and the chest' or as Louella Parson's described them, 'the hottest combination that ever hit the screen' – created his ultimate fantasy, and Mitchum did become something of a gay icon. That hunk of man just sent the boys a'shiver. That he had an incredible sexual presence is undoubtable so no wonder he excited both sexes.

In *Macao*, as with *His Kind of Woman*, the chemistry between Mitchum and Russell works well, which considering they were deep and genuine friends is hardly surprising. Mitchum nicknamed Russell 'Hard John' and they remained friends until his death. When his ashes were scattered off the coast of California, Russell was the only non-family member on board the boat.

Here in Fall River there are no clear signs of Mitchum's presence. I have yet to see a hotel so it looks like I'm moving straight on to Boston. I trudge back towards the bus depot, call into the bookstore on South Main. There's plenty of photographs of film stars on the walls – many of them autographed – but none of Mitchum. I ask the guy behind the desk if he has any books on big Bob.

'Aah, no man, and he's one of my favorites. Where are you from with that accent?'

'Wales.'

'Wales! Oh my god, we got someone from Wales in the shop? What are you doing in Fall River?'

I explain I'm looking for Mitchum.

'Mitchum? But why here?'

I give him the run down.

'Wow, Mitchum was here!'

He introduces himself to me and me to his regular customers, offers me a seat and a coffee but I've got a bus

185

to catch. We discuss film and TV. Like many Americans I've met, they have a high regard for the BBC. I guess it's all relative. They ask about Wales, show real interest, but they seem to know quite a bit already. They know about Caernarfon, Port Talbot, our actors and the jug-eared prince. I explain he's not Welsh. They take my word for it.

'Where are you going?'

'Boston.'

'Boston? Oh, you'll like Boston.'

I'm not interested in Boston, yet. Ask about Fall River: on the up or on the down?

'Nah, it's on a down. Used to be a mill town, now there's no jobs, lotta welfare. Immigrants, but no jobs. Here, let me give you something. You gota have something to read on the bus.'

He gives me a biography of James Dean which I had scanned for references to Mitchum. There weren't any, even though if it wasn't for Mitchum the likes of Dean would never have reached the screen. I decide I'll enjoy the book all the same, but not as much as I enjoy their hospitality. After the chill of Providence, the Fall River bookshop warmed me.

I board the 2.40 'Quick Fink' out of town, take photographs of the warships in the dock just because it's so easy – heightened security my ass; watch the town disintegrate as we head north on 79. Empty factories, 'For Lease' signs, smashed windows, rusted metalwork, derelict stacks. Oh, Fall River – I'd kiss you if it would quicken your pulse.

Take 11

The bus chugs along. I flick through the James Dean biography. Mitchum's very last movie was the 1997 production *James Dean: Race with Destiny*. It's no better than its title suggests.

We travel through south-east Massachusetts; past scrapyards, malls, Friendly Restaurants and Dunkin' Donuts, fleamarkets, food and lodging. The native names of Watuppa, Massasoit, Assawompset, Ponkapog still present amongst Somerset, Bridgewater, Taunton, Plymouth. Past the dog tracks, the wholesale clubs, Bob's Discount Furniture, Furnace and Quincy, the *Boston Globe* offices. Arrive South Station 3.35pm, fifty-five degrees, snowing.

Mitchum was in Boston to film the 1973 release *The Friends of Eddie Coyle*. It's another solid, desolate and lost Mitchum movie.

Mitchum plays Eddie 'Fingers' Coyle, a small-time underworld character feeling old under the pressure of an up-coming court case and the inevitable prison sentence so, in search of a solution, he gets deeper into the criminal world while trying to angle deals with the authorities. Coyle has a noir-ish resignation to fate, knowing, whatever the outcome, it won't be ideal. But unlike the noir characters Mitchum played as a younger man, there are none of the wise-cracks or witty, gritty, devil-may-care attitude of youth left in Eddie Coyle. He's seen it, done it, got nowhere and nothing except the scars, and now he's tired. He's got responsibilities to consider, and hopes to see some kind of future outside of a prison cell.

'[Eddie Coyle] *left me saddened. For the first time I saw the deep scars that had long been hidden in Bob's life, take over on the screen.*'

John Mitchum

Unlike his Hollywood peers, Mitchum wasn't shy of playing the losers, the pathetic, the washed up, knowing they were more real and more valuable than heroes. 1973-75 saw a change in how the press perceived him.

'*Now, at last, Mitchum achieves a kind of apotheosis. At fifty-six, when many of his contemporaries are hiding out behind the remnants of their youthful images, he has summoned up the skill and the courage to demonstrate a remarkable range of talents.*'

Time

On location was journalist Grover Lewis, writing a piece for *Rolling Stone*. Lewis was also a poet and his collection *I'll be there in the morning if I live* has as much of a Mitchum title as you can get. He described Mitchum as 'a massive hulk of a man, with a jowly face battered as a used VW bus'.

Lewis asked why, following the success of the Mitchum-penned movie *Thunder Road*, he didn't write more. Mitchum replied, 'How come I haven't done more of that sort of thing? How come I'm not out diggin' a ditch between takes? I choose not to work. I've got a gig goin' that's probably not the most satisfactory expression in the world – nor is anyone's – but it's the course of least resistance.... I mean, I do my good works quietly elsewhere, and I can't make a profession of it. It's denied me.'

If ever Mitchum's cynicism was in doubt, this quote should answer it. Not only does it reveal a perception of reality which shows Mitchum the man trapped by Mitchum the star and the expectations placed upon him, but also that there was part of him which was dealing with the struggle of all writers: that satisfaction with your output is temporary; that you never quite get the expression nailed good. To me that's the sign of the real McCoy – in intention if nothing else. OK, *dad*, that's my interpretation, dismiss it at will.

'You don't understand like I understand.'
                                        R M, *The Friends of Eddie Coyle*

Everyone told me I'll like Boston. Even me. It's one of those places which has always intrigued me without knowing why. I promised myself I'd visit. What else has it been home to? The strangler, the crab, the tea party, the *Cheers* bar, Ivy League Harvard, the Kennedys.

I traipse around the station looking for local gen. Spot a tourist information office, hang around, get approached by someone I immediately and instinctively don't trust. He's asking if he can help me but there's something behind his eyes. I'll flow with it for now.

'Yeh, I need somewhere to sleep, cheap.'

He gives me the spiel about how everywhere's booked up but he can do me a favour and find somewhere, like real cheap but good quality. Just get on with it buddy, I wasn't born yesterday. He offers me only one place. Makes the call. He's on first name terms with the woman who answers. I'm suspicious but too bored to bother, figure I'll check it out first. I just wanna dump my bag, take a shower and hit the town. At seventy-five stones, fish, clams, greenbacks a night it's cheap, but not that cheap. He draws me a map, sends me off to the subway.

I board the red line to Park Street, change to the green C towards Cleveland Circle, get off near Coolidge Corner. Boston's subway is the oldest in America but it feels more like a tram service compared with the NYC subway – most of its lines appear to be above ground and we duck in and out of the dark like wombles.

I stroll through the snow to a townhouse which the guy promised me is a hotel but my instinct suggests is a bed and breakfast. I hate bed and breakfast places; hate my intrusion into someone else's home, the projected pressure to join in, be sociable. Goddamit, I wanna drift in and out anonymously and drunkenly, not be part of their circle of friends from around the world. And I wanna smoke and B&Bs rarely allow it.

I walk up the steps, open the door and the owner's husband greets me.

'Here, here,' he says, directing me to a bench, some bullshit doll's house furniture. 'Take a seat.'

Take it? I'll put it on the bonfire. The upholstery is covered in plastic. Oh Jesus, this is gonna be one of those pain-in-the-ass places where the owners are so proud of their abode and gods help anyone who's human enough to rip or spill or piss themselves. I sit like a kid who's just wet the bed.

'Wad he tell you, sixty or sixty-five?'

As I recall it was seventy-five but say 'Sixty-five', figuring we're even.

His wife enters, voice first: 'Seventy-five, including tax. You must be Robson?'

'*Mister* Robson, that's right.' Man, I never refer to myself as anything other than 'Lloyd' but if you're gonna get all brief on my ass then I'm gonna get some respect for my purse.

'*Mister* Robson. That's right.'

It's *my* fucking name, missus, of course it's right.

'OK, what's your first name?'

She got one of those smiles plastered over her face which spreads from ear to ear but is as friendly as a dog's snarl or the widening jaws of a snake. Lady, if you're gonna false-smile me you should shut your eyes – the cavernous shadows are all I can see.

191

'Lloyd.'

'Lor...?'

'*Lloyd.*'

'Huh?'

I spell it for her, slowly.

'Oh, Lloyd! well Robson, what are you doing in Boston?'

I'm asking myself the same thing. Is she thick or taking the piss? She's crept into my personal space and her beady little eyes are staring up at me. I wanna say I'm a dog killer or snake charmer or laxative salesman or something to get her out of my face but I, like a dumbo who should know better, say, 'I'm a writer'. Dagnabit, that is one sure way to encourage their probing. Tell her you work for the IRS or you're a health inspector.

'A writer! Are you writing about Boston?'

'No, Fall River.'

I say it more to throw her off the trail and realise, in doing so, I am voicing preferences and a prejudice against Boston I never had previously.

'Oh, how wonderful.' Now I know she's being insincere. Although *I* had good vibes for Fall River there's no way this woman would be seen dead there. And for that Fall River should be grateful. 'So are you staying one night or two?'

'I don't know yet. I'll decide tomorrow.'

'Oh, well, that'll be $150.'

She's trying to nail me for two nights and I'm just trying to figure out how to react and whether she's rude, stupid or thinks I am. 'Oh, you know what, Robson? I've just realised I've made a terrible mistake. I thought tomorrow was Thursday. But that's OK you can stay close by, with a friend. She's *very* special. She'll like you.'

Was that an added emphasis on 'she'll'? Well, baby, feelings mutual. And 'special' could mean anything – Max Cady was 'special', Preacher Powell was 'special'; if by 'special' she means transparently insincere with an untrustworthy inability to deal with her 'guests' in a non-clawing, money-grabbing manner, then I can see why she's her friend. I wanna walk out right now but I sense a challenge, I wanna see just who can wind up the other the most. I ask if they take Visa.

'No,' the husband says forcefully, 'cash only.'

Of course they don't.

'OK, well I'm gonna pay you for one night because your boy here didn't tell me you don't take Visa. Which is a little weird for a "hotel" don't you think?'

Before she has chance to answer I pull out my wallet and wave the green in front of her face. Her attention is diverted. I walk towards the stairs and make a vague claim to pay her the rest tomorrow. I reach the first step and I'm confident I've escaped but the husband blocks my way. I'm hoping he's going to carry my case but no offer is made and I'm not holding my breath.

'I won't be here in the morning...'

I'm pleased to hear it, *dad*.

'So let me explain how to get to the other place.'

The wife is now by my side and waving a piece of paper in front of my face. 'Here,' she says, 'I've written a map.'

I try to take it from her grasp but she's not finished yet. The husband's staring at me, demanding eye contact so he can give exact directions to somewhere no more than a hundred yards away. His wife is going over her map with a pen, rewriting again and again a big 'R' and an arrow where I should turn right, adding a church and some store names. Between them I am being bombarded with directions as they repeat themselves. It's like being attacked by verbal termites, killer ants, mutant insects burrowing under my skin. Right now, Providence seems so inviting yet so far away and all I have to remind me is the hangover I woke with. I've been travelling most of the day; stomped through Providence, trailed my case up and down the slopes of Fall River, crossed Boston – I'm sweating and need to unload. Refresh. I wanna get this nerve-system overload out of my face, just give me the map you weird fuckers, and let me go to my room.

I take hold of the corner of the map and raise it slowly above the vicious midget's head so she has to let go. Say 'thank you' without feeling, broaden my shoulders, take control of the eye contact, instruct them 'I'm going to my room now' and haul my ass upstairs.

Behind me the two of them are still talking over each other, both trying to direct me to my room. Up the stairs, turn left. Yeh, I get it. Climb back in your lair. I reach my room, enter hurriedly and lock it behind me.

The furniture is the same crap as downstairs, there's even a bench covered in plastic. The bed and chairs are covered in fake leopard print. Now if *this* were a brothel I'd understand. Perhaps that's it: maybe this place hosts

194

elderly sex parties; senior generation orgies; fancy dress frolics – all Venetian long-nosed masks, walking frames and strap-on dildoes? I can't help feeling I'm being optimistic – and in this country I really should put a stop to that. But, Jesus, if the thought of the old bird wearing a strap-on is optimistic then pass me the pills, quick.

I lift the leopard print to see if there's a plastic sheet on the bed. There isn't. I must remember to piss on it before I leave. I take a seat. Gather myself and try to figure what I'm feeling. I've been in Boston less than an hour and already I've been patronised, insulted and taken for an idiot. Something tells me, me and Boston, we ain't gonna be the bosom buddies I expected.

I strip off and look for the bathroom. There's a tiny TV, more tassles than on a double-D stripper, but no door to the bathroom. I get dressed again and unlock my door. I open it a creak. My eyes rise from the lock and I find myself face to face with the husband, stood waiting outside my door. I cannot step forward without walking into him.

'Where's the bathroom?'

'Upstairs.'

His wife's voice comes up from somewheres unknown, 'Across the hall.'

Which is it, dimwits? I'm confused but not so much about where the bathroom is – I'll figure that out myself – but by why he is stood outside my door. How did he know it would be opening? Can they hear everything? Are there cameras installed? Or is he gonna stand guard the whole time? I know the vents carry sound around these American buildings so I'll have to test them out with some well-chosen splenetic invectives while I shower. Presuming there is a shower. The wife pops her head out of the room next to mine. Why is she there? Why don't they leave me alone? Haven't they ever seen a Welshman before? I pull myself up and out to let the guy know he should step aside. He doesn't so I nudge past him, ever-so-gently getting into his space so he has no choice but to get the message. I lock the door behind me and stride away, not quite sure where I'm going.

Across the hall there are two doors, one of which is open. I figure the easiest way to find the bathroom is to allow my eyes to enter through the open door without committing myself to following them. There, sat on the edge of a bed staring at me is another old woman, frail in her nightgown. Just sat there, staring, like I was a midnight burglar or an asylum porter. I smile at her but there's no change to her expresssion. Perhaps she came here much like me and has never been allowed to escape. I open the door to the other room and lock it behind me. Thank fuck it's the bathroom. I put towels over the mirrors, draw fully the shower curtain and strip.

I'm clean, I feel better. But the atmosphere soon clings again and twists my mental nipples. Of all the places I need to smoke, this is it. I'll dress, hit the street, get pissed, come back, sleep because I've given them my money and tomorrow find a real hotel where I can exist in privacy. That guy from the tourist desk better pray I don't catch up with him.

I'm looking for a bar called Dillon's – the owner reckons he knows some fine women in Brookline. I call into

196

Angus O'Leary's. As I'm in Boston I figure I should try the Tremont ale – Tremont being from the earlier French name for the city, 'Three Hills'. It's a good beer with a strong perfume in its aftertaste. I down it quick. St Patrick's Day is getting ever nearer and behind the bar there are paper shamrocks signed by drinkers, with dollar bills pinned to them. The barman pours me another and says, 'I detect a bit of an accent. You English?'

'Welsh.'

'I'm from Dublin. Been here twenty-eight years.'

'You like it then.'

'I guess I do.'

I ask about the city's nocturnal delights. Angus shares a glance with the guy sat next me to me, ponders for a moment then explains, 'Boston's not known for its nightlife, I think it's fair to say that.' This surprises me. I've always thought of Boston as a 'big' city, inasmuch as in Britain the insinuation is that every US city has more to offer than ours. But here everything closes about eleven except a smattering of bars which serve until 1-2am, if you're lucky. No later than that, 'unless you know the right place and right guy'. And I don't. The idea of an early return to the hotel depresses me.

I consult the map in search of a downtown area with a lot of bars. Angus and the guy sat next to me recommend I hit the Faneuil Hall/Government Center area, Landsdowne Street, Kenmore Square. I down my beer, give Angus a tip and hit the street.

The moon is big and low over Boston. I'm staying close to JFK's birthplace. My father gave my brother 'Kennedy' as a middle name. I share a second name with Mitchum.

I catch the subway. The driver is kicking shit out of his slot machine in an attempt to get it working, so I get on for no fare. Ah, the old luck is still there. It's nice to know I've still got something in common with Mitchum: the ability, the luck, the timing to travel for free. Even if it is only half a mile or so. I sit and consult the map. Monmouth Street – I won't be going there. I'm heading for six stops away.

I get off the train, stop a guy outside the station and ask directions. He points me towards the lights in the trees, the statue of Sam Adams, and tells me to turn left. I turn to continue my trek but he hovers around me. I guess he's looking for a dollar. He tells me how cold it is. And it is. This is not the town in which to wear a linen suit, Mitchum-style or not. Fuck Chicago, *this* is the windy city tonight. The wind off the Atlantic is freezing.

'What do you need?'

'Well, I need some food. So a couple of dollars would be good.'

I delve into my pocket, 'I can give you a dollar.'

'A dollar-fifty will take me straight to McDonald's.'

And that's a damn fine reason not to give him a dollar-fifty, but the boy needs to eat and at least sitting in McDonald's will warm him up. I give a buck-fifty and he compliments my shoes.

'They're not mine.'

'Whose are they?'

'Robert Mitchum's.'

'Robert Mitchum's? I remember him. Man, you're not big enough to wear his shoes.'

Yeh, tell me something I don't know, *daddy*.

But still the shoes take me to the 'Purple Shamrock' – these guys don't even pretend to be diverse.

For me, Boston started badly and didn't get any better. Apart from *Eddie Coyle* there's no real Mitchum trail to sniff and, as for nightlife, the place is a grave. I try and make the most of it but all I get are the brush-off, the cold shoulder, gravy stains on my suit and my beer stolen whenever I step outside for a cigarette.

I scrabble together some change and pour myself out of a taxi. Drag out the doorkey and let myself in. Step quietly up the stairs, aware the wood will probably creak. As I approach the top stair I poke my head around the bannister – the coast is clear, but by the time I reach the landing she's there, stood in front of my door. What the fuck does she want now, it's gotta be 3am. She's getting close. Hope she doesn't think I'm taking her to bed. She's very close but still far away, being short. I have to work hard to focus. 'What do you want?' I say, looking down at her.

She gives me forty words when one will do – she wants money.

'I gave you money.'

Another two hundred syllables spit from her poisonous, ulcerous slit of a mouth. Some bullshit about how I'm being so unfair to her 'special' friend.

'Listen missus, I'm drunk. I'm going to bed. We can discuss this in the morning.'

She continues to whitter away. I put a hand under each of her armpits, lift her out of my way.

'I'm not listening, woman. I'm going to bed.'

Whitter, whitter. Oh, I'm such a bad man. Yeh, yeh, whatever, you old witch.

'Do you hound all your guests like this?'

Whitter, whitter. Rude, yes I know. Dreadful. Bad Welshman, bad Welshman.

'You know what I need, baby? I need a good leaving alone, that's what I need.' I shut the door in her face. Fuck me, Christ help the boys of Boston if their girls' mothers are all like this. I hope I snore like a bear through a megaphone or scream blue-murder in my sleep.

I wake on leopard print, still fully clothed and drunk. My first memory-hunt is to specify location, the second to pin-point time. I sit up, bend my glasses back into shape. Wonder why I'm in my suit. Search my pockets for clues – half-smoked cigarettes, pens, pencils, unused condoms – that pisses me off but I'm grateful there's no used ones.

I remember I'm in Boston. I need the bathroom. Gotta wash and get out of here. Reach the door and pause – who's gonna be waiting out there? I remember the late night conversation, if you can call an old witch waiting up and nagging an innocent drunk a conversation. I take a deep breath, figure I'm leaving anyway so I've got nothing to lose. I open the door and for the first time since I arrived get two seconds peace. The door to my fellow guest's room is shut – the old girl could be hiding, dead or locked in. Sensing a swing in the power balance I stride bullishly to the bathroom and lock the door behind me. As I wash I sing loudly. Charlie Rich's 'The Most Beautiful Girl in the

World'. Continue singing as I stroll across the hall. Come and have a go then, you old harridan, bring your husband with you and your 'special' friend – I'm in the mood for a right good rumpus and it'll take more than the three of you to shut me up.

I toss my junk in my case, put on my suit jacket, figure the steak stains don't matter, go downstairs. Wait for a moment – no one jumping out at me, no one screaming from above or below, no guests looking sheepishly as if they expect to pay for my rebellion. I write in the guestbook 'what a fuckin' joke' and get out of there. Cross to the subway stop and light myself a smoke.

It's sunny this morning and the hangover won't wake until this afternoon. To quote Mitchum when he stayed in Boston, 'Hot damn, *dad*, it's great to get up durin' the day.'

The train pulls up. I open my wallet but there's nothing there. I pull a stashed twenty from the lining of my coat and ask the driver if he can change it.

'Coins only,' he says, letting me on for free. Another free ride – Mitch, this one's for you, baby.

I wasn't called to the meeting, didn't get the memo, but I've realised I've decided not to find another hotel but to get the hell out of town. Maybe it's unfair to judge a city on only one night but when the instinct says 'nah' it deserves to be listened to. Let's bugger off somewhere decent.

If I were going straight to New York I could catch the Chinatown bus for only fifteen dollars from gate twenty-five, but I want to return to Bridgeport first so I catch the

13.55 arriving at 18.45. Five hours on a bus is a pain in the ass but maybe I can sleep through the hangover.

We drive through Boston, past Fenway Park – home of the Red Sox. Pull off the Massacheusetts turnpike into Newtown.

Hopkins Hill road. Stops at Providence, Foxwoods Casino Resort – a lot of people get off and on here but none of them look happy.

I'm spread over two seats, expecting to get some sleep. A sizeable guy boards and plonks himself down right behind me. Fair enough. But within moments I can tell he's a noisy breather. Something I could never fathom: how come, whatever noise is about, you can always hear the heavy breather. The engine's chugging, people are talking, but still I can hear his breathing. He obviously has respiratory problems and I feel for him, I do, but I don't want to hear him. Once noticed it's impossible to block. I can't handle it. His every in- and exhalation permeates the pores and resonates down the hairs in my ears, bangs on that drum like that little Polish bastard in the Günter Grass novel. So now I've got nasal gargle and slurp to contend with every couple of seconds, I know it's only a matter of time before I have to change seats or cave in his skull. That's not a reaction I'm proud of but noise gets to the core of me, makes me feel like my marrow's being scraped. See, I can usually sleep through anything, but once I'm aware of those minute human noises, there ain't no shaking 'em. So I'm the guy who'll turn off your pacemaker if it disturbs my sleep. Live and let live? Of course, great idea, but you ever disturb a bear in his cave? I'd make a great dictator. I'd erect a fence around myself and would never be seen except by women. Quiet women. Women who don't breathe heavily except when aroused. Women who don't snore (are there any?).

I move to the back of the bus where there's no noisy breathers and settle in. I close my eyes and begin to drift. There's a guy going through every possible sound effect his cell-phone can make. Now this *is* his fault and he *can* change it, so maybe I can take this hangover out on him – it's beginning to hurt like a bastard.

So I do so and he is unsure how to respond. I have no qualms with people thinking I'm a miserable git as long as I get some peace and quiet. Denied his noisy toy, now my fellow passenger is just gonna have to think, quietly, while I snooze.

I wake, look out of the window. Where we at, *dad*? We pull out of The Mohegan Sun Casino. Signs warn 'Speed Checked by Aircraft', 'Speed Limit 50' – and they call this the *express*way; 'Do Not Stop – Correctional Facility', 'Hitchhiking Prohibited' – ah, the freedom of the road.

The wooden houses of Quaker Hill Village, Society Road, the woods and ponds of Connecticut; Old Saybrook, Stony Creek, Thimble Island, Pearl Harbor Memorial Bridge and into New Haven. The obliterated remains of the coliseum. Come and See 'Em at the Coliseum – wrecking balls all week.

At the station I take the opportunity to step off and smoke. Not out of need but as an excuse to stretch my legs and grab some fresh air – yeh, I'm aware of the contradiction. Unless they line the roads with dancing girls, five hours on a bus spells boredom in New England.

Boston will remain for me a shadow of a city. Still, the beer's not bad. As for Boston having an accent like Cardiff's, well there are similarities like adding an 's' to verbs, but in the words of Eddie Coyle, 'I don't knows that I like it'.

Take 12

I get off the bus and light a cigarette. I have no more business in Bridgeport but I felt a need to return. I find it hard to stay away from the place – it feels like a home to me. And I want to see Estela.

I walk down State Street. The lines on the road appear green – mine eyes are surely betraying me. The scaffolding above my head creaks and the wind tries to lift the boards. OK, Mitch, I'm coming. I'll be in the company of a beer and a beautiful woman before you know it – you can't be more eager than me.

I call into the Savoy to wait for her. Order a beer. My *bonita* is late but I don't mind waiting. I order another drink. My cell-phone vibrates. I don't need to read her message, I know she is close.

She arrives looking beautiful; even more impressive

than usual. I stand as she sits and slip without thinking into a Mitchum quote from *The Big Steal*: '*Hola, chiquita*'.

I expect her to say Jane Greer's line, 'You don't call women *chiquita* you've only just met,' but Estela hasn't seen the movie.

I call the server. Estela questions her on their wine list – no plonk for the Portuguesa. We catch up. She's all laughs and smiles. She asks me about Boston; is curious as to my rapid return. I shy away from some of the telling. We are hungry. I ask where she would like to eat. She's never been to Roberto's but warns it might be expensive. Who cares for expense when the company deserves it.

We stroll to the end of the block and enter Roberto's through two huge bronze doors. There is space aplenty in the marble hall. The setting is grandiose; elegant but strangely informal. The doors through which we stepped were deemed so distinctive they were displayed at Tiffany's in New York before being installed here.

The restaurant seems empty but there are murmurs from diners sat, unseen, on the other side of the Savings Circle – a remnant of its days as a bank.

This will be my last meal in Bridgeport. We sit, eat, drink, talk. I know I am in search of something – and not just Mitchum – but I'm just not sure what it is. These days, I cannot trust my emotions. The complexities aren't clearing and my brain doesn't help. An escape from the past, perhaps, or the hunt for a future? I feel on the edge of things, like the suicides making their final decision on Sikorsky Bridge.

Estela listens intently. Tells me I need to have a child.

'Whether with me, with someone else – it doesn't matter. But you need a child – for yourself, for your sanity. Forget the past, you are a man now, you must be strong. Forget the past and have a child, have a future, have some point.'

Estela, *bonita*. She's the nearest thing I've had to a guiding voice in a long, long time. Whether she is right or not, I do not know.

Nightmares fill my shallow sleep. Every person I have ever known, every past I've experienced, every possible future I may ever have, visit me and ensure I wake exhausted.

'I was scared the way only a kid can get. I was in a dark, cold place. I had my eyes closed to get away from some bad dream. The same dream I've been having all my life. I've never understood it... but my father wasn't there.'

R M, *Pursued*

I wash, pack, check I've left nothing behind. There's an atmosphere in the air I don't understand. Something is happening in Bridgeport today, or maybe it's in my mind.

I go down to the lobby. It is full. It is confusing. I go to the desk to sign out, pay my bill, ensure they haven't charged me for parking. Ask what the hell's going on.

'St Patrick's Day. The parade passes right outside.'

Boston comes back to me in a flash of green. Gods save me from the emerald-green army.

A woman screams after her children in a domineering American screech, 'Siobhan, Sean, Niall....'

I think I'm going to vomit. I expose myself, briefly, to

the parade, just so I can say I've done it. All bored police-men lining the route, kids in ill-fitting uniforms and grown men in tartan skirts. I make for the train back to NYC. It leaves right on time. From here, the only way is down, to the South.

Take 13

At Grand Central I avoid drowning in a sea of green and dive down to the subway, queue for a Metrocard, push against turnstile, grab the 1 and drop my shoulders in the warm squeeze of the car. I stand amongst a press of passengers trying not to lean against the sitters' knees and hang from the handrail. The woman sat below me is reading *Group Portrait with Women*.

I get off at West 103rd. Spring may have arrived but the air is as cold as a witch's tit. The wind blows blossom from trees which falls through the sidewalk grills and rains on the tracks like confetti on a metal wedding. Graffiti on a pillar reads 'Jews are the opium of NYC'. Go figure.

Between subway lines there's a build-up of batteries tossed from a million gadgets. The leaking acid confuses the twitch of the rats.

I climb the steps into light. A pile of thirteen paperbacks sit near the curb, their string undone. On top: *Group Portrait with Lady* by Heinrich Böll. There's a store advertising sports bras – 'Buy 1, get 50% free'. A homeless guy asks for a quarter but I can't respond, my brain is boggling at the thought of a woman who needs three cups to her bra. My thoughts are interrupted by the words of a couple walking past. He knocks my arm as they march along the sidewalk.

'But I just don't wanna see you anymore, Dennis.'

'But I love you baby.'

A small dog on a leash barks at me. His owner drags him away. A bus roars past. A sticker on its chrome warns, 'Do Not Fall in Love'.

'Hey, big man. A nickel, that's all I ask.'

He's talking to me.

'For calling me big man you just earned yourself a dollar.'

'Thanks man. He knows you're comin', you know.'

'Does he now. Thanks for the heads-up.'

'No problem.'

'Hey miss, a nickel, that's all I ask....'

A return to the city means revisiting old haunts. Gotta get my feet back under the table; drink where I once felt at home. Wet my whistle then make a few calls. Jingle the old girlfriends. Find out who's in town and not tied up in schedules. Re-establish a foundation from which to explore, further than before.

I head south; switch every few blocks between Broadway and Amsterdam just to reaquaint myself and decide where to stop first.

I return to the Raccoon. Only it ain't the Raccoon no more; now it's the Crossroads. Now there's a name to put a man under pressure. Apart from a new paint job and the slot machines changing position, it's just about the same as it was the last time I was here.

I try and figure just what the hell I'm doing, chasing a dead actor through the bars of New York.

An aggressive tone of voice drags my head from my beer.

'Who the hell do you think it was, George Custer?'

I scour the line-up sat at the bar. Who said that? Who the hell's taking a pop? And is it at me?

Sat at the bar there's an angry man with more than a passing resemblance to said general. He's wearing cowboy boots, Stetson, long white hair and beard. Obviously no one's mentioned the similarity in appearance today, so he's yelling the comparison into his cell-phone. OK, *dad*, you've got our attention. So you've modelled yourself on a national hero and pompous failure: well done, but you're at the Crossroads now so it's time to take that arrow and be done.

Maybe Custer was the only role model this guy could muster. Maybe the modern American male leaves him cold or flustered. Maybe he's trying to find himself, or escape himself. I shouldn't be so quick to judge. I wish he was imitating Mitchum.

One of the things I really admire about Mitchum the cowboy is that he never wore the coolest, or cleanest, hat. He began his career wearing a blood-crusted hat in the Hoppy movies and was happy to never lose touch with that. Which was in contrast to most of his peers. You watch any cowboy film – so much is implied by the quality and style of a character's hat. Mitchum didn't care. He'd appear in some shabby, unsophisticated, absurdly mis-shaped hat which was far more realistic than the stylized headgear chosen by other actors. Mitchum needing to play 'the man in the white hat'? Nah. Where's the fun in that?

In *The Wonderful Country* (1959) – for which Mitchum was executive producer as well as the star – the showgirl even has the audacity to sing 'Where did you get that hat, where did you get that hat?' It had to be an in-joke. Mitchum played the man who couldn't escape trouble however hard he tried; a man with a history – the boyhood shooting of his father's killer. His hat – a huge, floppy sombrero – made its own statement: he takes it off when speaking to women but leaves it on when speaking to authority.

Mitchum appeared in all kinds of westerns and cow-boy movies: tales of pioneering trailblazers; hero vehicles; anti-hero vehicles; revenge missions; real, roister-doistering shoot-em-ups.

In *Pursued* (1947), Jeb Rand (Mitchum) is saved from the slaughter of a family feud and brought up by his dead father's lover. It was her family – the Callums – that butchered his, so out of love for his father and guilt for what her family have done, she brings him up as her own.

Rand grows up knowing something's lurking in the shadows of his brain; feeling there's always someone or something on his tail, not realising the Callums are waiting until he grows up, before killing him too.

He fights with his foster brother; falls in love with his

foster sister; loses the toss of a coin and is drafted into the army; mounts his horse and rides off into the night, only to return home to a hero's parade with war wound, limp, Medal of Honor, nightmares and all. The fights with his foster brother continue, both punching out years of envy and resentment.

Rand feels the need to uncover his past; to dig away at lost memories and realise his truth. To know who he is, why he is, and what he has been through. His foster mother discourages him, hoping the past will never again raise its destructive head.

'I don't belong here. I don't know why. I always have the feeling something's after me. It's a bad feeling I can't explain. Lots of times I'm happy, but it's still there.'

R M, *Pursued*

Add to this a liberal dose of flashbacks and haunting, traumatic memories and you'll understand why it was dubbed the first ever psychological western (as with *Track of the Cat* it's a 'western' only in geographical, temporal and cultural setting). It is without doubt a great film; one of Mitchum's best. Once again he played a man trying to swim through the swamp in his head, while others kept trying to drown him.

As with *El Dorado* which teamed Mitchum with John Wayne to play two old stallions of the western stock, *The Good Guys and the Bad Guys* (1969, directed by Burt Kennedy) has an intentional comedy element. The cowboy movie had had its day and so the old guard who had spent

213

hours in the saddle, chasing bandits or being chased by the sheriff, were mopping up the last of the genre. They were no longer the rugged heroes and menacing villains riding the range or taking the trail through the mountains. Now they played the ageing sheriff, the tired villain, the drunk.

Mitchum would not feature in another western for over twenty-five years, eventually narrating the opening and closing scenes of *Tombstone* (1993). Then, in 1995, he appeared in Jim Jarmusch's *Dead Man*. It would be his final film of note. Mitchum's first cinema release was a western and so was his last.

I move on to the Dead Poet. Settle on a stool at the bar. I've got some guy on my shoulder looking at the cigarette I've just rolled and placed on my book on the bar.

'What you got there?'

'It's just a cigarette man, look, it's got a filter and everything.'

'No, no, the book.'

'It's about Robert Mitchum.'

'Mitchum?'

'Yeh, you know: the actor.'

Yeh I know Mitchum, man, but why read in a bar – you some kinda screen freak?'

'I'm writing about him.'

'You writing about Mitchum? Man, he was a dog.'

'You're telling me.' I rattle off a few stories about bastard Bob and it's all new to this guy's ears.

'Hell, I knew he got done for weed but I didn't know he grew his own. That's my kinda man.'

He introduces himself. Chuck, yes 'Chuck', is a dealer. But he doesn't smoke it. He tells me he runs it up from Georgia for profit.

'But they don't look like you and me, man; my drivers are clean-cut boys. They drive straight, don't drink, don't smoke, stay in the speed limit. I stay here, they bring it up to me. Man, I've got a 400% mark-up, you can't turn your back on that kind of trade.'

Dealer-speak leaves me cold. Celebrity dealers get held up as heroes, but they're just self-serving money-men not martyrs for a cause. I go outside to smoke. Chuck follows.

'I got this buddy, we call him Canadian Dry. He power-surfs across the great lakes, loads up in the States, then power-surfs it back home again. He makes even more than I do.'

Surely only in America would a dealer talk to a stranger about how much they make from drug deals. But then, maybe I appear not as a stranger. Wherever I go, people presume I smoke weed. It can be useful – people like to share their smoke. But it can also bring unwanted attention.

In the months following his drugs bust people would slip joints and bags of grass into Mitchum's palm mid-handshake; or into his pockets; into his turn-ups. Someone broke into his car and left a couple of joints in the ashtray. Was it a fan? A sympathetic smoker? Or was it another set-up? Someone waiting for Mitchum to return to his car, drive off, get pulled over, joints found in the ashtray. His denials would be useless – he already had the rep.

Years later, he hid nothing. He was well known for

smoking between stints on set and had joints sandwiched between the pages of his script. He would offer joints to interviewers and on one occasion, while speaking to a group of journalism students, he offered round a big bag of grass. Well, if you've already got the reputation....

'Hey!'

A woman is shouting but this is New York so we ignore her.

'HEY!'

On the other side of the street she is stood with her man, both wearing big, green Paddy's Day hats.

'Wass up?'

She pulls up her top and shakes her breasts at us. And magnificent breasts they are. She gets whoops and applause from up and down the street.

'Do it again! Do it again!'

She does. She's relishing the attention. Her boyfriend seems pretty pleased, too.

'Do you know her?'

'No way. Wish I did.'

She flashes a third, a fourth, a fifth time. She has brought a huge stretch of Amsterdam Avenue to a standstill. Drinks remain in hands; cigarettes burn fingers; pedestrians stand, having forgotten where they were going; trucks and cabs would collide had their drivers not screeched to a halt at the first sign of flesh.

'I bet it's crazy in the Village tonight.'

'Who wants to go to the Village, man? That's where New Jersey drinks.'

Her boyfriend nudges her into a cab and we fade back

into the bar, the air full of blue whoops of laughter. Jaigermeisters all round.

After a few shots, I slope out of the Dead Poet and find my way to Yogi's – at $3.75 for a pint of Bass it was only a matter of time.

'We're in a very exclusive rendezvous... in order to get in here you gotta push the door.'

R M, *Till the End of Time*

Yogi's is a cheap dive and rightly proud of it. It's nice to hear its jukebox is still full of country and western and see the seven-foot-tall wooden bear, the graffiti, bottle-top-covered furniture and, most of all, the stunning smile of the American-Asian barmaid.

I take a chair where I can watch both legs of the L-shape. Tap my foot along to Johnny Cash and June Carter singing 'Jackson'. Scan the room. At one table there's a happy foursome. The women spot me and swap chairs with their men, so as to have their backs to me. I don't know what I've done, wasn't even checking them out. Presumptuous and egotistical if you ask me. Potentially troublesome. Perhaps this is what they want – an opportunity to test their men. One leans over to her boyfriend. They talk tight. He gets up, walks over, stands behind me. Stares at the back of my head. I ignore him. Seen it, done it, no longer get intimidated. Keep supping my beer.

'You looking for a girl?'

I don't turn my head; don't dance to his tune.

'Hey, I'm talking to you.'

Kenny Baker: *'Who me?'*
R M: *'I don't mean your Uncle Fud.'*

Doughboys in Ireland

'You looking for a girl?'
   'Not in here.'
   'You looking for a boy?'
   'No.'
   'So what you looking for?'
   Now I look at him. 'I ain't, I only look when there's something to see.'

   He doesn't reply. I guess he has no grounds for further motion. The poker-stare has to be broken, but not by me – he's the guy with something to prove; an audience waiting for action.

'Blow, shiester.'

Robert Ryan, *The Racket*

Silently and unsure what to do next, he returns to his seat; to his group. All front, no substance. People often back off in New York – it's called survival.

   They huddle over their beers on the table. None of my business, *dad*; none of yours, either. I ain't accepting responsibility for unsettling his missus when all I've done is sit where I can watch the gorgeous server. I figure telling him I'm looking for a six-foot-something, barrel-chested, baritone-voiced man would be asking for trouble.

   They down their beers, gather their coats, head for the street. The boys barge my table, but not so much as to disturb my beer. The girls turn the other way. I guess they wanted their men to stop drinking and go home, or to spice up their evening. Me heap big excuse.

Mitchum was always getting accused of something. When you got the rep you make everyone's life easier – they don't have to question who you are any more. I guess they leave that for you to do yourself. But those who knew him were aware of his willingness to please, and how that was often exploited.

As with many well-meaning people, Mitchum got burned so turned to cynicism; turned his back on his natural reactions and did what was best for himself. And, boy, did he get burned. A perfect example occurred in 1952. Mitchum emerged from a theatre where he had been promoting *The Lusty Men*. A crowd was waiting for autographs and photographs and a word or two with the big man himself. He did what was required and was charming. Suddenly, a woman threw her baby at him; threw her own little child into the air, risking its safety and health. Mitchum reacted, caught the tot before it fell to the floor. Flash-bulbs popped. The evidence existed. The woman filed a paternity suit against him. Presumably for an easy life, Mitchum made a nominal offer but claimed that if anyone pulled the same trick twice the child would have to 'take its chances on the pavement'.

Time to change venue. I step outside and light a smoke. On the corner, a guy asks for a light.

'What you smoking there?'

'Just a roll-up.'

'You want some grass?'

'Sure, what you got?'

We slide into a doorway. He pulls out a baggy and opens it up. I fill my nostrils with a smell mighty-fine. He puts the baggy back in his pocket.

'How much?'

'Thirty.'

I weigh it up; know I've only got a twenty in my wallet.

'I'll give you twenty.'

'No man, it's a thirty-buck baggy.'

'That? Nah, that's a twenty, man, if ever I seen one.'

'It's thirty or nutin'.'

'Then it's nutin' cos I only got me a twenty.'

'You only got twenty. Huh. You got an ATM card?'

'Sure. But I still only got twenty.'

'Then let's go to the ATM.'

'No deal *daddy*, that ain't happening. That's a twenty-buck baggy. You wanna take a little out to smoke on the way home, that's fine, but I'm only gonna give you twenty.'

'You're only gonna give me twenty? I'm taking that twenty. And we walkin' to the ATM.'

The mood has changed. He ain't bartering no more, he's demanding.

'We go get some money.'

'That ain't gonna happen, brother.'

'We go get some money.'

'You ain't listening.'

'I ain't askin'. Let's go get some money.'

Just when I'm minding my own business life keeps happening to me. So let's go get you fucked, my brother.

You robbing me ain't gonna happen in this lifetime.

> *'You tryna shotgun an innocent boy.'*
>
> R M, *Home from the Hill*

'Gimme your Visa.'

Oh *dad*, this boy's getting ahead of himself.

'I said gimme yo' fuckin' Visa card.'

This kid thinks I'm some hick straight off the haystack simply 'cos I ain't from the borough; thinks he can rob me of my hard-earned and drain the overdraft too. Oh *daddy*, bad move. New Yorkers keep on making the same mistake – believing their own press. I guess I have to accept responsibility for his education and teach him a lesson. It's a risk, but what the hey.

> *'You're substituting guts for good judgement.'*
>
> R M, *The Lusty Men*

'OK, I tell you what. I'm in a foreign country, a long way from home, so there's no way I can give you my Visa card, OK? That is just not an option, so get over it. Even if you get my card, I ain't giving you my number without putting up a fight. You wanna put on a British accent and fake my signature – good luck. You wanna sell it – it'll be listed within the hour and whoever buys it will use your guts for garters.'

'My guts for *what*?'

'Forget it; listen. You gotta consider your options and weigh up what you can get against the grief of getting it. I ain't a rich man and I ain't stupid either – I don't need no trouble. You let me take another smell of that weed so I can make sure it's still the smokeable and you ain't swapped it for something nasty, maybe I can give you that twenty and dig out a ten from my pockets.'

'This deal's gonna cost you a lot mo' than thirty.'

'OK. Maybe I might have a full fifty here somewheres.'

He don't look happy but he knows he's onto something. Yeh, my line, sucker. And I'm reeling you in.

'Maybe I might find a couple of traveller's cheques in here, too. You could walk away with a hundred, hundred and fifty, without this going any further. I get the grass and keep my Visa, you get fifty for the grass and a couple of traveller's cheques for your trouble. So let's keep this civilised, yeh? We don't want no misunderstandings now; wouldn't want anyone thinking this was a robbery, right?'

'Thass right. Jus' a lil bitta business. So you got fifty, huh? And traveller's checks.'

'Twenty in my wallet, thirty in my jacket pocket, a couple of traveller's cheques folded up and stashed,' I tap my chest, 'right here. You get the lot. All it costs you is a twenty-buck baggy.'

He laughs at my insistence it's still a twenty-buck bag. He knows he could hold out for the lot but he's also realised I'm no pushover; it ain't worth the hassle. But he still thinks I'm stupid. Still laughing, he slips his hand out of his pocket and drops that baggy in my palm. Oh you poor delusional amateur. The second that baggy hits the palm of my hand I am stone gone out of town – he don't see my ass for dust. All he's left with is a Welshman's laugh bouncing off his drums. Boy, didn' your daddy tell you?

Don't fuck with a fucker. I've had years of buying Class A's from Cardiff's finest dodgy characters, it's been a while since I was a soft touch.

I sprint a few blocks, switch left. Sprint a block, switch right for two. Sprint a block, switch right again. After ten, fifteen blocks I slow into a doorway. It's amazing how fast a smoker can run, providing there's alcohol and a relevant situation to help unlock the door to those hidden stores of energy. I pull out the baggy, take a good sniff. It's grass all right. And good, too. I skin up a small one and laugh to myself. The laugh breaks into a choke. The choke breaks into a cough. The cough into a breathless, tar-exuding retch. Gob it out, son, gob it out.

I stand erect. Take a deep breath. Put the baggy back in my pocket. Light up and inhale. Somewhere south of here there's a guy stood on a street corner wondering what the hell just happened. I swear I can hear a faint, 'God damn' echoing through the night.

I stroll up Broadway enjoying the weed. This was Mitchum's territory as a kid. I know the details; I know where he lived. But I also know I ain't gonna find him tonight. In a place this full of existence, this busy with people living and moving, with so many characters and so many memories, it's hard to tell one ghost from another. I guess he's here in spirit, in the empty bottles on the subway steps; in the corner seats and bar spills; the street fights; chat-up line and cab to her place.

And just as I'm least expecting it, there he is. There he is! Mitchum! It's him. He is here. Here, on this street! Or his name, at least.

Opposite me, across the street, is a boarded-up store. The boards are pasted with posters proclaiming his name. I can't believe it. I cross and press my hands against them. Feel they are real. Smell the paste. Step back so I can read them. They speak of him; make inexplicable declarations:

'If you feel hypnotically drawn to construction sites, you're a Mitchum man.'

'If you're personally offended by bad parallel parking, you're a Mitchum man.'

'If you'd like to drive a street cleaner at least once before you die, you're a Mitchum man.'

So is this it? Are these the answers I'm looking for? Is this what it means to be a man, Mitch? Or is your name being taken in vain in order to sell a range of personal hygiene products? Whatever. Mitchum, you fine-smelling, well-parked street-cleaner, I salute you. The moment is yours. Enjoy it.

I sit on the curb and grin. Rest my forehead against the palm of my hand. The grin turns into a giggle. The giggle turns into a laugh. The laugh turns into a roar. I sit on the curb and laugh and roar at the absurdity of it all. So all these years I've been fuelled and fucked-over by my abject failure to match up to my father's image of what a man should be – Robert Charles Durman Mitchum, at his finest – when all I had to do was learn to park properly. Well, Mitch me old son, me old mucker, oppo, butty *bach*, la, my right-hand man, now I've found you on the Upper Westside of your youth, now I've found my answers on how to be a man, how to be my father's son, now I know not only what I've done wrong but also what I must do to make it right, well now I guess I better find me a beer to drink to your health and drown the old bastard from whose seed I sprung. Lead on, McDuff, it's my round.

I find myself in the Tap a Keg, drinking the dregs of the night, blowing the head off a new day. A female voice asks, 'You having a good night?'

'I'm having a fantastic night, thank you very much.'

I turn to look at her. If this was a Mitchum film some stunning broad would be stood there, a classy grin on her face, a cab waiting outside to whisk us back to her place. But this isn't a Mitchum film and I'm not Mitchum. Still, she has a nice smile and carries her two-twenty pounds well.

'You local?'

'I used to be.'

And here's the call: 'Where do you live now?'

'In Queens.'

'Girl, you're a long way from home.'

'Not as far as you are. *I* can get a cab.'

How do you know where I'm from?

'I listen in. People say things. So, man from Wales, you ever been to Queens?'

And there's the response.

'Can't say I have, but I'm always up for a new experience.'

'Always up, huh?' She smiles. 'Are you good for sharing a cab?'

'As long as you're there with me.'

We head for the door. I feel I'm robbing myself of a final beer, but at least I'll get somewhere warm and soft to sleep tonight. 'Lead on, MacDuff.'

'What did you call me?'

'It's a quote from somewhere.'

'OK, 'cos you don't know my name. You haven't asked.'

No. I haven't. I haven't asked. And still I don't ask. 'Well, you haven't asked mine.'

'I don't need to. You're the Welshman, looking for Mitchum.'

'You *have* been listening in.'

She waves down a cab. Puts her mouth close to my ear and whispers one simple line, *'Out of the Past.'*

It's gotta be code for something. I better find out.

She pulls up her legs, pushes herself forward and lies on her front. Cradles her chin and continues watching the film. I stroke the back of her calf, the back of her knee. She parts her legs a little. I clamber towards her, lie alongside her, stroke her neck, follow the line of her spine down to her ass, slide my hand between her cheeks, brush her ass-hole, slide my fingers down her lips. She's wet already. Her low hum turns into a giggle. I stroke her clitoris and she wriggles down onto my fingers. I probe and stroke. She raises her knees and pushes her ass in the air. I kneel behind her.

I pull open the drawer beside the bed. There's a

shamble of condoms of different kinds. I tear open the foil, roll down the condom and slip myself inside her. Get used to her shape. Establish a hold on her hips. Concentrate on her flesh and her movements. Begin gentle probing. She continues to watch Mitchum; pushes against me and so I push my hips forward and my cock further into her. She makes no sound. She's engrossed in the movie.

Mitchum is drinking bourbon, sat on a stool in an Acapulco bar called Pablo's.

'I knew... she wouldn't come the first night but I sat there, grinding it out.'

R M, *Out of the Past*

I stroke her cheeks, slide my finger down between them and tickle around her asshole, down to her lips for their wetness, back to her asshole, lubricate its tension with her own juices until I can slip my finger inside her. She shudders and moans, I pull it back, push it in. She welcomes it. I continue. Simultaneously slipping finger in ass and cock in pussy. Alternate for a while, timing one after another so some part of me's inside her continuously. Then back to simultaneous thrusting. Her lips tighten around my cock, her ass loosens around my finger. She joins in with the conversation on screen.

Jane Greer: *'Shall I take you somewhere else?'*
R M: *'You're gonna find it very easy to take me anywhere.'*
Jane Greer: *'Wanna try me?'*

Out of the Past

I take her prompting. Withdraw and slip my cock up her ass. She moans before continuing to quote with the movie.

Jane Greer: *'I prefer it like that.'*
R M: *'Chunk it in.'*

Out of the Past

So I keep going. I get into my stride; push harder and harder. She pushes her ass back further until a squeal jumps her forward. We re-establish a mutual, comfortable, rising tension and tempo. I concentrate on her ass and the small of her back, rubbing and stroking and grabbing and holding and working myself further inside her. Establish ideal direction and rhythm.

Mitchum and Steve Brodie are slugging it out over Jane Greer. The woman I'm in has risen up on one straight arm. Her breasts swing beneath her. Her other arm finds her own place. Her fingers flick rapidly against her clitoris, my balls bang against her hand. The strain on her straight arm is making her wobble. The movement of her other arm, increasingly faster. I've got one hand on her shoulder and the other on her hip, pulling her back and onto me. I'm on the verge of hysterical laughter brought on by the mix of near-orgasmic tension and the utter absurdity of it all. I thrust into her faster and faster, she screams out the dialogue.

A string section breaks out to punctuate the action. A shot explodes. A low rumble emerges from below me and her quivering body takes over. Her asshole almost impossibly tight around my cock, her shudders bring me off and we tense and flush and push for everything on offer until the invisible elastic snaps and we remain static and caught in orgasm. Then exhale. And cease. Steadily reverse the arch of our backs. Re-establish where our muscles should be.

Action draws to a close. Brodie lies prone, Mitchum lights a cigarette, Greer is satisfied and out of the door.

I slowly slip out my cock and she shivers as my last leaves. Her elbow snaps shut and she falls face down into the bedcovers. I fall back on the pillows.

'What was left of the day went away like a pack of cigarettes you smoked....'

R M, *Out of the Past*

Take 14

I wake to a flickering light and the sudden brass of a buzzing erection. The volume is high. I stretch out and find my glasses, raise my face from the pillow and put them on. Turn to see where the noise is coming from. It's a TV. The erection is RKO's black and white transmitter mast. The movie is *Out of the Past*. Again. I look around, listen, feel. There's no one else here. It's time to leave. I roll out of bed, drag my clothes from the floor up my legs and over my head, reach into the bedside drawer and pocket a fistful of condoms. Now to get the hell out of Queens.

I get off the 7 and climb the steps to Times Square. Stop to buy a soda from a Chinese mama who don't speak the lingo. I take a slug. It's cold. Too cold.

The air makes me choke; turns my lungs black. I feel

heady and weighed down with city grime. I've got the hot and cold sweats and the sticky sheen of sex and alcohol clogging my pores, not aided by the jumps into and out of the coldness of the street winds, the stuffy subway air and the extreme heat of buildings. Maybe I should find a bar on 56th called Pablo's, close my eyes and think of a joint in Acapulco.

In Times Square, on 'The Great White Way', a crowd has gathered on the north-west corner of West 45th. The hormonal mass consists of screaming teenage girls, as well as the occasional parent or teenage boy. They spill off the sidewalk and stop traffic. Numerous illuminous members of New York's finest insist people move along. They don't; they just shuffle position, awaiting attention from some boy-band who are currently being interviewed on the otherside of the glass. Everytime a TV camera points towards the crowd they all jump and squeal, yell and wave their arms and halo themselves in the flashing of digital cameras. Mitchum knew this world only too well – the Bob Mitchum Droolettes came out in force wherever he went. And if they weren't there, then their mothers were. Women threw themselves at him. No wonder he didn't stay faithful.

This corner is now home to MTV, serving as a Mecca to teen and pre-teen fashionables. But in 1931 it was the site of the beaux-arts style, eleven-storey Astor Hotel – which attracted few teenagers. One of them, though, was Robert Mitchum. He worked behind the lunch counter, not making much money but at least making something to help his family through the Depression. On Christmas Day, the hotel treated him to a hamburger and soda – it was his biggest meal in months.

I schlep down 42nd Street until I reach Madame Toussaud's. *Hm*, wonder if they still got Mitchum in there? Carry on past theatres and show posters block after block. *The Lion King*, *Chittychittybangbang* – all the big family pleasers. I cross the street and climb the stone stairs at the front of the New Victory Theater, away from the sidewalk and tourists. I roll myself a smoke and dodge pigeons. Each time I raise a cigarette to my mouth, I think of the woman in Queens. Her scent still lingers on my fingers. I should wash, but don't want to. Her smell makes me laugh and smile. My opinion of her is balancing out. I guess Mitchum did the hard work and I got the benefit. I should keep hold of her number; give her a jingle. Watching *Out of the Past* will never be the same again. The next woman who wants to watch it had better be prepared.

The New Victory is New York's oldest active theatre. Built in 1900 by Oscar Hammerstein, it was originally named Theatre Republic and opened with Lionel Barrymore on stage. Later shows would feature the likes of Lillian Gish (who later starred with Mitchum in *Night of the Hunter*), Tyrone Power and Mary Pickford. It became a vaudeville house in 1914 until 1932 when Billy Minsky turned it into Broadway's first strip-joint. In 1937, Mayor LaGuardia banned burlesque shows so the theatre became a movie house called the Victory, showing old movies until the 1970s when it became 42nd Street's first XXX-rated cinema. These days the New Victory houses youth theatre, possibly as an attempt to make up for its previous reputation and cleanse its soul.

Mitchum felt at home with cabaret and burlesque shows. When he moved to California his intention was to make a living from writing. Not just poetry, but plays and material for club acts. Some of his early plays were staged and his first won an award at the Pittsburgh Festival of Arts; he wrote incidental music for an oratorio organised by Orson Welles and staged at the Hollywood Bowl; he wrote many of the songs and jokes for his sister's cabaret act; and material for various comedians, transvestite performers and risqué acts performing up and down Sunset Strip.

I enter the theatre and speak to the girl in the box office.

'Hi, you know Robert Mitchum?'

'No, I don't.'

'Let me put it another way: do you *remember* the actor Robert Mitchum?'

'No. Is he famous?'

'New York has forgotten me, New York has forgotten me.'
R M, The Last Tycoon

'You *don't* remember Robert Mitchum?'

'No, sorry, I don't – I don't know any famous people.'

'This was Minsky's Burlesque, right?'

'I don't remember all the names, but this place has been many things.'

'Minsky's was a... saucy club.'

She laughs for the first time, 'Yeh, I knew that.'

'Well ask your mother about Robert Mitchum – she'll

remember him. He was a famous Hollywood actor. The story goes, he lost his virginity in this very theatre, underage and backstage with a sympathetic showgirl who was a friend of his sister.'

'Well, I don't know if I wanna ask my mother about *that*.'

I ask her what she's doing tonight. She's working.

'Do you get a break when the show's on?'

'Sure.'

I'm thinking I could follow in Mitchum's footsteps, here.

'Is there a backstage area, or a staff room you can go to?'

'There's a little place, yeh.'

'Well, I was thinking, I'd love to be able to do a little research behind the scenes...'

'Forget it honey, I know where you're going. You may have that sweet accent going on but you ain't getting behind my curtains.'

Spotted, torpedoed, sunk. *Glug, glug*.

I head west towards the Port Authority Bus Terminal, then north to 56th Street.

In 1929, the Gunderson–Tetreault–Mitchum's Delaware farm was failing so, after a brief stint in Philadelphia, the Mitchums decided to join Julie in New York where she was earning a living on stage. They moved into an apartment on West 56th – Hell's Kitchen.

The mean streets! In those days Hell's Kitchen had the rep of being the toughest NYC had to offer, where Mitchum discovered being a tough guy out in the sticks means

235

nothing on the streets of the city; where he had to take his licks and toughen up quick. And he did. He got his nose broken, again. He developed an even more aggressive and hostile nature in order to survive; caused trouble; ran with a gang when he needed to but remained, fundamentally, a loner.

It's tempting to say this is where Mitchum came of age, and in some ways he did. But, hell, he was used to having to fight for his right and defend his brother. He had stood out in Bridgeport, in Delaware, in Philadelphia, so I doubt he expected anything else of New York.

These days, Hell's Kitchen should be called Hell's Wi-Fi-Enabled Lo-Fat No-Carb Wheat-Free Smoke-Free Organic-Vegan Co-operatively-Farmed Soya-Bean Eat-All-You-Can Bar & Buffet. It is no longer the seedy muck-oven it was.

Exactly where on 56th the Mitchums lived is difficult to discover. It is a street of tall tenements, one half in shadow throughout the day. It ain't pretty, but it's safe. And it could never be mistaken for any other city.

At the junction with 10th I head north until I reach 59th. Here I find the old Haaren Cooperative High School which Mitchum attended only when he was forced to – how fitting that 'mitching' was once Welsh slang for skipping classes.

'It was a finishing school to end all... they had monitors on the door to keep you in... because you'd flee at any given opportunity. I tried to transfer up to George Washington but they wouldn't let me in because I was from Haaren. They

said, "We've heard about those cats. No way!"'

R M

Once again, Mitchum found formal education lacking so spent a lot of days educating himself in the hallowed halls of the New York Public Library and the city's many museums. Although, not always.

'We used to just take off and leave school.... I used to come back and deliver reports to my English teacher and tell her of some fancy trip to the museum or something educational... and we would be at the movies... at Loew's 72nd Street.... You know, it was sort of a haven for the jobless.'

R M

When he did attend, he engaged himself in making trouble and was soon expelled. This suited Mitchum but legally he had to go to school and, as Haaren was hardly for the elite, they took him back. Not that they wanted to. One time, his mother had to appeal to the school board. They were sceptical but she pleaded that, if they could find some way to engage him, he would behave. She suggested music. They took him back and Mitchum began learning to play the saxophone. In an incredible act of support and leadership, Mitchum's mother decided she would also learn the instrument, to keep her son on track. Both found it easy. In later years, if there was a sax in the joint Mitchum would surprise those present by picking it up and blowing out a tune. He began referring to himself as 'the poet with an ax'.

237

'They gave me a saxophone to entertain myself and it changed my whole life.'

R M

All went well until a school performance of the 'Poet and Peasant Overture', during which he tossed a firecracker into a sousaphone. There's the door, Master Mitchum, and your last day at Haaren. Instead, he went to work as a lyric arranger for a local radio station.

Named after a superintendent of schools, Haaren was built on the south-west corner of 59th and 10th in 1906, as a boys-only school. It closed in 1969 and today it's home to the John Jay College of Criminal Justice, where students go to study for the police force, the DA's Office, Corrections, pre-law school or the ball-scratching, hair-splitting jobs of the legal industry.

I open the main door. Once inside I get stopped by security. I show them an out-of-date University of Wales staff ID card and explain I'm researching the building. They let me in and direct me down the escalator to the Lloyd Sealy Library. I take my time and scout around; seach for signs of him. As with many old schools, embedded in the plaster and architectural detail is the haunted tinge of desperate interns which renovation cannot conceal. I can imagine Mitch bursting to get out of here.

I enter the library. The students may be studying to become police officers but still the walls are covered with signs warning of the theft of cell-phones and laptops. I approach the saints behind the enquiry desk – man, I love librarians. A more deserving and under-rated resource I

238

cannot imagine. I fall for all the stereotypes.

I get settled in at a workstation. The librarian explains she's not supposed to do this but gets me onto the system. I search the Law Enforcement News for John Jay, the *New York Times* historical files, the National Criminal Justice Reference Service, the National Archive of Criminal Justice Data, but Mitchum's police records are nowhere to be found, at least nowhere I am allowed to look. Access restricted and denied.

I stroll around as much of the building as I can, just to see if anyone stops me. No one does. I get bored and go outside. Take photographs of the exterior. What with the question being raised of who supplied al-Qaida with a video tape of the World Trade Center, I find myself stood on a busy sidewalk taking photos of a New York school for cops and wondering just how obvious a target I am making of myself. Best I get out of here, I suppose. Instead, I stride into the middle of road and take photos from there, making myself as obvious as possible. Apart from drivers taking the opportunity to hit their horns – as if an excuse were needed – no one pays a blind bit of notice. There may be more cops on the subway and they may have a free hand to search whomever they please, but more specific targets seem open. Perhaps those cops ride the rails just to reassure the people.

I should return to my hostel; shower and change. I stop at the Amsterdam Brewery. The server asks me what I want to drink. On the shelf is a bottle labelled La Fin du Monde – The End of the World? Are you sure that's gonna be female? There's also a bottle of Arrogant Bastard. It's difficult to decide which to go for. Mitch would've ordered two of each, stripped off and danced on the bar. Your shadow is too large, my man. Ask me later.

I take a few beers and schlep back to the hostel. Use the payphone in the lobby. Slip in a quarter and phone an ex-girlfriend in Brooklyn. I've caught her on the right day – tomorrow she leaves town on a work project. She agrees to meet me later. I take a shower and skin up.

She pulls up outside the hostel in a cranky 4x4. The last time I took a ride with her we were both on her pushbike, pedalling in a hysterical, drunken fury through five-inch snow on Bedford Avenue. Three o'clock in the morning and whooping like lunatics, wobbling and skidding, almost falling over, sticking out a foot and steadying ourselves at the last second. She liked that, she said later. Said that, even though a fall looked certain, and even though I was always drunk, I always seemed to be looking after her. We fucked well into the morning. It was a glorious time of life, straight out of the movies.

We hug and kiss and smile at each other and check out the level of eye-contact. It's good to see her again. Things didn't go so well between us but we've remained friends. She asks me where I'd like to go.

'Just drive for a while. Then find me a beer.'

'Ha! Still drinking huh?'

'When I'm not in bed.'

She laughs and accuses me of not having changed. Oh, I've changed, baby. I've changed a lot. I've lost some anger and lost some love. I've gained in cynicism and am coated in a deeper crust. And I'm looking to break out of it.

She turns to me. 'But you've lost weight – how can you do that when you drink so much?'

I can't answer. I just want her to keep her eyes on the road. Stop-lights mean nothing to her. She bombs across junctions, steams through pedestrians, swerves violently between lanes and hits her horn. She drives like a man and she's proud of it.

We head downtown, over the bridge and into Brooklyn. This is where *When Strangers Marry* premiered, at The Strand. Mitchum rightly took third billing, as befitted the role, but as Mitchum's star continued its rapid rise the movie was re-released as *Betrayed*, with Mitchum topping the bill. Made in ten days, it's a dodgy tale of robbery, murder, secrets, lies and deceit.

We park up outside a French restaurant in Fort Greene and I sneak a quick cigarette as we walk to the door. Take a table and order. I know what she'll ask for: something vegetarian and a shared bottle of pinot grigio. I order rabbit – I could do with getting greasy and sucking flesh off a bone.

She tells me about her chaotic worklife, her chaotic lovelife, her ups, her downs. I tell her about Mitchum. About my battle with conditioning and paternal expectations.

'But isn't your father dead?'

'As a doornail. But that makes it worse. You ever tried fighting a ghost?'

'But why fight at all?'

'That's the thing, sugar. I'm not fighting anymore. I'm conducting an exorcism.'

241

'Wherever the spirit takes you, huh?'

'I'll drink to that.'

We know we don't work as a couple but an attraction remains and is palpable.

'So you had sex lately?'

She laughs. Looks at me from under her deep, curly hair with those beautiful green eyes, looks away, sips her wine, looks again, laughs. That's fine, baby. Play it any way you want. This is not conflict, a hunt or a conquest; it's two old lovers fortunate enough to remember good times, who don't have to deal with each other on a regular basis. We pay the bill and slip into the night.

We pull up outside a late-night joint on Bedford Avenue. She puts on the steering lock, programmes the car alarm, locks the doors. Kneels to unlock the shutter hiding the door to her building. Rolls up the shutter, unlocks the door. The apartment's just as I remember it. Photographs and tiny artworks all over the walls; shelves full of audio tapes and records and books; tables covered in computer and camera equipment; the marble breakfast bar with the corner snapped off, separating the living and kitchen areas; the glooping refrigerator, and high above her clothes and stereo, a studio bed, its wooden steps partly covered in papers and pot plants. Searing heat throughout.

'I see your heating still only works on extremes. Mind if I take some clothes off?'

'I wondered how long it'd take you. Hang on, I'll open a window.'

I toss my coat and shoes to one side. She unlocks the window, pulls up the sash and calls me over. We poke our heads into the night air.

'Remember dancing out there?'

The last time I was here it was New Year's Eve. We celebrated by dancing on the low roof of the next building, drinking champagne under the gaze of the trains rumbling the rails on the Williamsburg Bridge.

She leans down and pulls up a bottle of champagne. 'For old times' sake.'

I uncork the bottle. She fetches two tea-cups from their hooks. I pour. We clink and toast.

'It's good to see you again.'

'You too.'

We climb out of window and sit on the roof, drink champagne and catch up. Retell old jokes and tales. Re-establish the link.

Jazz from the club below smooths the dark hues of the night. Any silence between us is comfortable. We realign our senses to each other's company. It's good to revive old feelings, for a night.

The champagne runs dry and the wind picks up. We clamber back inside. Leave the window open to stay in touch with the night. I'm ready to kiss passionately for the first time in years, get undressed and climb the wooden ladder, lie alongside her, hug and kiss and refamiliarise myself with the her skin and shape, the tender bits, the ticklish bits, the heat, the hair. But she ain't having any of it.

'It's good to see you,' she says, 'but some things are best left to history.'

She throws a me a blanket and nods towards the sofa.

'But I don't want to drive a street-cleaner.'

She shakes me awake, hands me a cup of tea. I sit up, sip. It's good, it's hot, it's normal breakfast tea. But there's something weird about it.

'What's in this?'

'Rice milk.'

Typical Williamsburg. I take my tea out onto the roof. Roll myself a joint. Wave to the train passengers heading into the city and work. They stare, but no one waves back. The tea lubricates my throat so the first smoke of the day mixed with the cold morning air doesn't burn and choke.

Her head appears at the window. 'I'm making breakfast. You want any?'

'No thanks.' The chances of a vegetarian making me a bacon sandwich are limited.

She leans out of the window, bites into an apple. 'What ya doing?'

'Smoking, watching the world go to work.'

'You got any plans for today?'

'Thought I'd give you chance to reconsider last night's rash decision.'

'Huh?'

'I thought I'd shag you senseless.'

'Ha! As pleasant as that may be, I don't think it would do either of us any favors. But if you shave and sober up you might find a wife.'

'I'm not looking for a wife.'

'You are *so* looking for a wife. It took you about a day to fall in love with me. How many times have you fallen in love this year?'

'I'm claiming the Fifth Amendment.'

'Exactly. You're not just an easy fuck, you're loose, emotionally.'

'Better than not caring about those I sleep with.'

'Is it? You suck women in with your loose emotions but then you change focus too easily and fall in love with the next one to come along, and what happens to the first one?'

'I don't mean to hurt anyone.'

'I know, but you do. Just because you care for them, doesn't mean you don't hurt them.'

'Did I hurt you?'

'Yes. But then I hurt you too, didn't I.'

She sure did.

'You should stop giving your heart so easily, and try giving it to only one woman at a time. It doesn't do them or you any good.'

'But I'm greedy. For nice things. And I try to be nice back.'

'And you are nice. Randy, drunken, rude, but nice. Why don't you try being faithful again?'

'Because one woman isn't enough. If I stick with one person I become only their version of me, but if I'm emotionally involved with more than one, I expand and grow.'

'Bullshit. You might grow but so do your regrets.'

I walk back to the window. 'Listen, if we're going to dissect my emotional and sexual behaviour, you should at least get up to speed with what it's like to sleep with me.'

'You really should settle down with one woman, don't

you think?'

'If that one woman is an all-girl finishing school in Switzerland, I agree.'

She punches me in the stomach. 'Be serious. Sober up and find yourself a gorgeous woman with the patience of a saint.'

'But they're all gorgeous, that's the problem. And as for the patience of a saint: are you a patient woman? Are any of your friends patient women? Because, in my experience, they're pretty hard to come by.'

'So are sober poets.'

'It's in the job description. The poet's heightened awareness of existence and the human condition drives said poet to shroud his senses and instincts in drink. Otherwise it hurts too much.'

She laughs. 'Always with the answers. You know you're full of shit.'

'That's the problem. I have plenty of answers but they don't fit the questions asked of me.'

'So what are you going to do?'

'Head south.'

'South?'

'Head for the swamp. Hit it face on. But first...' I put my hand on her cheek and kiss her gently on the lips. She responds, momentarily, then pulls away. It is enough. One kiss triggers the full memory of her tastes, her smells, her touch. 'For old times' sake.'

She drops me back at the hostel. She's working out of town for a few weeks so kisses me goodbye and tells me to phone her when I'm next back in the city. I watch her drive away. She waves as she careers up the avenue. It's good to have women I can trust and turn to, but her words keep coming back to me. What would I do if there was only the one? Trust her, implicitly? I'll hand the file over to my subconscious and let it do the graft – instruct it to get back to me when it's found the answer.

New Victory Theater

The old Haaren High
School building

56th and 9th

Take 15

I stroll and smoke along 42nd, east towards 5th. I need to think; I need to write. What better place to escape the city; what better place to write about Mitchum on a cold afternoon than surrounded by the glories of the New York Public Library.

It is a beautiful, classical, Beaux-Arts building. Behind it is Bryant Park, named in 1884 after the poet William Cullen Bryant. Both park and library sit on the site of the 1776 battle between Washington and the British. In the 1930s it was here that Mitchum came to escape school and embrace education.

As my bag is searched – for what the security guards will not tell me – I read the names carved in marble, of famous and wealthy benefactors who made this free library a reality: the Astors, the Carnegies, the Lenoxes, the

Rockefellers, the Whitneys. I'm given the all-clear to continue.

I absorb the surroundings of marble floors and wood panelling, of echoing air and liquid trickling from brass, lion-head water-fountains. I can see young Mitchum bending to take a drink; staring up at the statues, the paintings; entering side rooms, now locked, to examine rare books and artifacts. I can see him admiring greatness.

I stand in front of display cases containing histories of literature, printing, art, science and religion; Sigmund Freud's corrected typescripts; the handwritten notebooks which formed Jack Kerouac's *Book of Dreams*.

So much space in which to think, to feel, to imagine; so much to muse over; so much to inspire. An open doorway into dream and time-travel. No wonder those 'library bums' – Mitchum, Tully, Davies – found refuge here.

Now that my brain has been opened it is time to write. I stride past a painting by Welsh artist Augustus John and head for the reading room, my juices flowing. I take a seat, plug in my laptop, depart this world.

The library is closing. My wrist aches. My head is empty. I need a cigarette, I need a drink, I need to find a phone booth. I need to get the blood back into the cheeks of my ass.

I take a seat away from the crowd at the bar but in full view of the door. I'm early, should be on my second beer by the time she gets here. I've arranged to meet a writer with whom I've only communicated by email. I got a vibe, a personality, from her her phrasing. I've already decided I like her.

I pop outside for a cigarette. A homeless guy sat on the next-door stoop asks me for a dollar. I've got nothing smaller than a ten. I sit and roll him a cigarette. Ask him if he remembers Robert Mitchum. He doesn't. A woman walks past and stops in front of the bar. She lowers the umbrella from above her head, shakes off the excess water and retracts it back into itself. She is slender, with shoulder-length hair. Neatly dressed – simple lines showing neither ostentation nor a lack of style. She prepares herself; attempts to shake off the troubles of her day before entering a realm of pleasure. She reaches out for the door handle.

'Corby?'

She turns, looks for the source of her name. I stand up.

'Are you Corby?'

'Lloyd?'

'Yeh. Hey, have you got a dollar you can lend me?'

She's thrown by the request but says, 'I guess,' before opening her purse and rooting around for a dollar. She hands it to me. I hand it to my smoking partner. He wishes us a pleasant evening. I tell him to get out of the rain.

Inside the bar, I figure best I explain myself – after all, the first words spoken between us in person consisted of me asking for money. It wasn't a glorious introduction. We need to take a seat and begin again. I order some drinks, give the server a tip and offer control over to Corby. 'Where would you like to sit?'

She leads me to a table in the back room. I apologise again and refund her dollar before pocketing the rest of my change. Now we can meet.

She tells me she's had a busy day – just another busy day amongst a busy life, glossing over the details – and asks about me.

I tell her about Mitchum.

'Why Mitchum? Is he your dream man?'

'Excuse me?'

'You know, are you secretly gay? Are you interested because you lust after him?'

She doesn't mince her words, this one.

'Well, that's a sensible question. Many did. Obviously he was surrounded by homosexuals in Hollywood and he had a substantial gay following...'

'You're avoiding the question.'

'I'm not avoiding it, I'm just trying to find a polite answer.'

'Just give it to me straight.'

Oh, mama, I'd like to.

'I'm a rabbit fancier.'

'Excuse me?'

'A bunny fan, a cunny chaser. From Coney Beach in Wales to Coney Island New York, I chase that fluffy tail into her burrow.'

'Are you saying you like women, or animals?'

'Is there a difference?'

'Hell, yes. Women don't sink their teeth into the carrot.'

She grins and I can't help but laugh.

'Well, I'm straight. The reason I'm looking for Mitchum

is because he was seen as a "real" man, whereas when I was a kid my father considered me gay or effeminate because I was "a sensitive kid" who wrote poetry. Well, guess what: Mitchum was also a sensitive kid and also a poet, so does that mean he was gay, or that I'm a "real" man, or that it's all bullshit?'

'It means it's all bullshit. You can be both if you want.'

'I know I can. I know I am. So did Mitchum. But it doesn't make it any easier. I was not brought up to think that way; I'm still trying to learn, to remove the negative conditioning. The truth is, even in the cheesiest of Mitchum pictures, there's more wisdom than any father gave to me, and the off-screen Mitchum is providing a role model I never realised I needed. No, not a role model; a previous example of someone vaguely – and I do mean "vaguely" – like me. There's still a need to hide something of myself from the world, from men – and from some women – who can't see how or are challenged by a man being more than one thing. There's a dichotomy between conditioning, role models and societal expection, and reality or potential. Listen, I can argue the academic and intelligent toss all night long but that's not what I'm interested in. I guess... I'm trying to bring all the parts of myself together. I don't feel I have to prove anything, but something inside me still does. And I'm tired of it. I need to lay to rest some ghosts, strengthen my foundation, reach conclusions and close the file.'

'Why?'

'Excuse me?'

'Why? You think you're any different to anyone else?'

'Not at all. I'm different; I'm the same. Just like everyone else.'

'But why do you need to find an answer to this, now?'

'Because that – your question, right there – is the question I really need answering. I don't know why I have to do this now. Perhaps it's my time of life; perhaps I'm bored or tired of carrying all this nonsense; perhaps my subconscious had deemed this challenge necessary before I can achieve whatever it has planned for me. I don't know. My search is not really to discover the truth about what makes a man – I know the answer to that: I am a man through default, nothing except a transexual change in my form and self-image can alter that. I am man, full stop – period. But that's my intelligence talking, not me.'

'So what do you lack?'

'Listen, this is the first time these thoughts have come into focus so I'm gonna have to think about that. But perhaps it's stability, stoicism, reliablity. Perhaps I lack people to rely on me, to need me, to define me; people to whom I can prove what I am or could be. People who give a damn. Perhaps my life lacks structure, a family, children. Perhaps I need something, or someone, to protect. Perhaps I need to shed feelings of not being protected as a kid. Perhaps I need to bring to an end my self-led existence. Perhaps I should be a father. Perhaps I should be more of a brother or an uncle or a son. Perhaps I just need to grow up. Perhaps I need a heroic, Herculean labour against which I can prove myself – to the world, to other men, to the ghost of my father and his father and his father, to myself or to someone who matters. I don't know. Perhaps I just need to shut the fuck up and get on with it. It depends who I ask.'

'Perhaps you should buy me another drink.'

'The wisest thing I've heard all night, all this talking has made me dry. And the thinking has made me thirsty.'

I return from the bar with two drinks and a question to ask her.

'So what do *you* look for in a man?'

'Something real.'

'So you want a "real" man?'

'I don't believe in "real" men. Sure I'd like one, but I don't recall ever meeting one. I certainly haven't had a relationship with one. All the men I've been emotionally involved with have been whingers. Sure, when I first met them they seemed like "real" men. They wanted me to believe they were "real" men but once they get you they suddenly need so much – they want constant soothing and nurturing and mothering, without reciprocating in kind. They expect me to listen to them and their problems but they won't listen to me and mine. Somebody give me a "real" man for chrissake! Instead of these sissies.'

'So is that what's happened here? You've sat listening to me whinging on about my own fuck-ups, just like you have your past boyfriends?'

'No. I asked the questions, you kept answering. That's all. If you were whinging, if you were using me as audience, I would've left by now.'

'So let me ask you something. Would you like a "Mitchum man"? A protector? A rough and tough, reliable

255

god in male form? A sensitivity-coated physical presence? Someone to put his arms around you and protect you from the wolves, the stalkers, the sharks, the abusers – actual and potential – and scavenger gangs? A hero to care for and protect you?'

'I guess, but I'm not holding my breath. Especially here in America.'

'Why especially America?'

'Well, American men... you've seen what American men do in bars, right? How they speak? Can you – if you were gay – can you imagine sleeping with them? Listen, I went out with this guy for six years. One night he told me he was a man first and a person second. That, to me, is obviously not a man. He was so wrapped up in his own grunting and farting, watching football and drinking with his buddies, safely acting like every other man around him, that he forgot to grow up. He wasn't a man, he was a little boy hanging around with other little boys so that strength in numbers would save him from having to think for himself or challenge who he was.'

'So why did you stay with him so long?'

'God, if I knew the answer to that I could solve all of women's problems.' She takes a drink. 'You ever meet a "real" woman?'

I consider my answer. 'I guess. One or two. But not enough, or not for long enough for me to discover they weren't.'

'So what makes a "real" woman?'

I wish she'd get undressed so I can find out. 'Expectations being met, I guess. Honesty, maturity, compassion. A woman who knows how to love and be loved; who knows when to stand up for herself and when to allow her man to stand up for her. A woman who doesn't need to create dramatic situations just so her man has to rescue her.'

'Do women do that?'

'You better believe it – not all, but some. The worse thing: they don't even realise they're doing it.'

'What else?'

'When she realises it's time to get the next round in.'

She clocks my empty glass and laughs. 'Test one, huh?'

'It's a practical examination.'

'Then I better get to the bar. You will let me know if I've passed, won't you?'

'Get served quickly and I'll give you a gold star.'

I watch her at the bar. She's not pushy but she's no pushover either. The barman serves her, looks for the eye contact, drags it out as long as he can, follows her ass as she carries the drinks back to our table. Sexy and intelligent – a great combination.

She's a good woman. Has made an impression as dramatic and unexpected as the sparkle and glisten of the black sand in the butt-bucket outside the bar. She's got me thinking. I haven't even had to pretend to be interested.

I need a smoke. She's concerned about me standing in the rain. Christ, I'm Welsh, rain doesn't bother me. She does a quick flick through her mental files on the drinking holes of NYC and says, 'Hey, I know a cool smoking bar, it's expensive but you can smoke inside.' So we head there.

Even though smoking in bars, restaurants and clubs is illegal in the city, there is a loophole that allows bar owners to permit smoking on their premises provided they don't employ anyone else. Or that's the general gist as I understand it. Whatever the detail, it means I can sit opposite the beautiful woman who brought me here, get served a good mojito and smoke to my heart's – if not my lungs' – content. That's the thing about the American way: the state can lay down as many laws as they like but the people will always find a way to do what they want.

We stay and drink and talk far more than either of us intended. We've discussed what makes a man and what makes a woman. She's told me about growing up in the South. We've discussed travelling, self-education, sex abroad, politics and religion. She asks, 'What else can we do that's taboo?' The tension is palpable. It's not lust as such that's driving me, it's attraction to a person who fortunately exists in a beautiful body.

I walk her to the subway, kiss her on the cheek, say I'll contact her again. She says, 'Please do, I enjoyed myself.' We haven't come close to discussing any other possibility than her going home alone and me, presumably, crawling off to another bar. I want to ask if I can spend the night with her but the potential loss is already too great. As befits my modus operandi I am prepared to walk away from a woman who has captured me and in whom I am truly interested. It's not the prospect of lost sex which unnerves me, it's the sadness of lost intensity. I hover and delay. I do not want to walk away yet nor do I want to risk losing the opportunity to explore her further. If I ask her if she wants to spend the night together, will the evening appear as mere preparation for fleeting sex?

The rumble comes up from below. A train is arriving. She slides her metrocard through the reader, pushes the barrier; is caught between rushing for the train and saying goodbye. She stops, turns, doesn't catch my eye, calls, 'Come on!' and runs down the stairs.

I drag my metrocard from my pocket, slide it and push the barrier. It doesn't move, the reader bleeps. I slide it again. Again with the bleep. I wipe the card on my sleeve, curse angrily, slide it again, push the barrier. It moves. I run down the stairs. Reach the platform. She isn't there. Scan the cars. She's laughing and waving at me. I jump on the subway. Get caught between the doors. They reopen momentarily and shut on me again. They open again, I move into the car. The doors shut, the train begins moving. I am stood in front of her. She is laughing. Pats the seat next to her. I sit and she puts her arm through mine. I don't know where we're going or what will happen when we get there, I just know the night and the contact, the intensity of emotion and the adventure of discovering another person isn't over yet. And it's glorious.

We travel the C to Lafayette Avenue, Brooklyn. Get back to her shoebox apartment where she rustles up some pasta. We settle into conversation and German *weiss bier*. A mouse runs across the wooden floor – there's always a chaperone when you least need it.

'All my neighbors have cats so the mice come in here. They know it's safe. Every so often I have to clean out my

259

range. It's warm in there so they make themselves at home, then I cook something and after a day or two my kitchen smells like roast mouse flesh.'

'But this is a nice building.'

'Yeh but this is New York. Streets full of rats, apartment blocks full of mice and roaches. Doesn't matter how much you pay, you can't get away from them.'

We discuss dead fathers – both mine and hers. There's no getting away from those, either. The conversation reaching its natural end and we're left to consider what happens next. I don't want to fuck her; I want to explore her, her body, her pleasures, what she likes, what she wants, what makes her come and what makes her tick. I'm willing to wait but we're both adults – I should just ask where we stand.

'I need to sleep.'

And what does that mean? Does it mean 'let's go to bed', or does it mean she needs to sleep?

'OK, where do you want me to sleep?'

'The sofa folds out, you can sleep on that...'

'OK.' So there's my answer. Not the one I wanted, but an answer. She walks towards her bed and sits on the end of it.

'I made my pitch, the lady just didn't buy.'

R M, *The Lusty Men*

'But I'd rather you slept here with me.'

I laugh. She got me. 'With pleasure.'

'Gee, I hope so. It'll be a damn shame if it isn't.'

260

I walk over to the bed. Sit next to her, kiss her. She kisses me. We fall backward onto the sheets and forward into discovery.

I wake. It's still dark. Corby is sleeping. I listen. No unusual noises; the usual combination of traffic and sirens and the city's nocturnal activities drift in through the open window. The extremities of the building's communal heating cooled by the night breeze. Do I need a piss? No, I don't need a piss. Then why have I woken? I lie, listening to the city and her breathing, watching shadows on the ceiling, feeling the warmth of her body pressed against mine. This bed, this situation, these surroundings, already feel like a home to me. My ex's words return: it took me less than a day to fall in love with her. I've hardly spent half of that with Corby and I'm already hurting over what might or might not be come morning.

I slide out of bed, gently. Creep over to the kitchen, open the icebox, take out a beer, open it, swig. Wipe my mouth. Swig again. Shut the icebox door and creep over to the window. Roll myself a joint. Stand naked, swigging beer, blowing smoke into the night air and watching her sleep.

I put my head out of the window. Flick ash and watch it float towards the sidewalk fourteen storeys below. Let my eyes follow the lights across Brooklyn – the borough of churches, Fort Greene, Navy Yard, the Williamsburg Bridge, the East River, the Lower-East Side, Manhattan. I can see the Empire State Building. If I lean further into the night I can see the Chrysler, too. If I alter the angle of the open window I can place the reflection of the Chrysler Building over shorter buildings in Greenpoint and Queens; reconstruct the city as I please.

Corby stirs, peers at me, rolls over. I stub out my joint. Blow the last of the smoke. I'm satisfied to have found this moment.

Take 16

I get woken by a beautiful American bringing me a cup of English breakfast tea with one percent milk. I couldn't ask for more.

'Hey shitbag, I brought you a cup of tea, you being British an'all.'

'So are we at the intimate nicknames stage already?'

'What happened to your face?'

'It turned to stone at the thought of waking without you.'

'No, I'm serious. Your lip, you've been bleeding.'

I touch my lip. It's crusted with blood. I peel it off.

'Ow! Don't do that.'

'It's important to feel the pain, it tells me how badly I'm hurt.'

'So look in the mirror.'

'I'm fed up of seeing the same person.'

'Well this person's gonna start bleeding again if you keep picking it. And don't you go bleeding over my bed now.'

'Can I smoke in here.'

'I told you, you can smoke out of the window. Anyway you haven't answered my question. What happened to your lip?'

'You didn't hit me?'

'No I didn't hit you!'

'Then it must've been Mitchum.'

'Mitchum? What, Mitchum did this? He rose from the grave to hit you?'

'He has no grave, his ashes were scattered at sea.'

'Oh, so his ashes travelled the oceans of the world, climbed ashore, dried out, amalgamated, schleped over to Brooklyn and took the elevator up here just to hit you?'

'He always waits until I'm asleep. He knows I'm on his trail and he knows, whatever he throws at me, he can't shake me off in the day. So he waits until I'm asleep. Disturbs my dreams. Gives me a fat lip for having the cheek to question him.'

I crawl across the bed to the window.

'You better stop smoking that stuff or hurry up and finish the book because one or both are fucking with your mind.'

'They're fucking with my mind in a different way to how it's usually fucked.'

'And last night you seemed such a sane young man.'

'And here's the rude awakening, baby.'

264

She leans over and kisses me.

'Drink your tea.'

I watch her walk away. Watch the sway of her purple silk negligee; the delicate rise and fall of each hip partly hidden; the tone of her thighs; the tension in her calves; the angular refinement of her ankles. It's always a relief when the woman still looks fine the next morning.

I look down at the sidewalk. A trash truck is loading up, beneath me. Opposite, the names of the buildings are carved in stone above their doorways. One of them is called Roanoke.

'Hey is Roanoke in Virginia?'

'Uh-huh.'

'I have to go there.'

'Why?'

'Mitchum.'

She's getting dressed. I watch and she sees me watching; tries to deflect my attention. She points out the paintings on the walls – her paintings; hands me photographs, collages, poems. I take them but continue watching her dress.

'What so you're not interested in my art, only your own?'

'I'm interested. I'll take a look in a minute. I'm currently watching art in motion.'

She turns away from me. Decides if she's gonna have an audience, she may as well make a show of it. Bends and sticks out her ass.

I stand and walk towards her. Put my hands on her arms before she can put on her sweater. Look in her eyes, not just to look in her eyes but to see if she'll let me. She does. I kiss her. Put an arm around her. Hold her tender neck. We kiss again. She squeezes my ass then pushes me away.

'I told you, I gotta go to work.'

We head down to the subway and wait for the C to the city. People sit or stand, talk, read books, listen to their music. The posters are graffitied. One urges New Yorkers to 'Do Something Different Today', under which someone's written 'Jerk Off'. I stand behind Corby and put my arms around her shoulders, lower my face and rest it against the back of her head. She allows me to stay there. We say nothing, and plenty.

As we pull in to Broadway-Nassau, she squeezes my hand and says, 'This is me.'

We kiss and she stands up to leave.

'What you doing tonight?'

'No plans.'

'I'm working late. Meet me in Moe's at ten.'

'Sure.'

That's great – two nights in a row. It doesn't seem forced, it doesn't seem desperate. It just seems right. And now I've got all day to look forward to tonight. I call after her, 'Hey!'

She stops in the door, passengers pushing past her.

'Where's Moe's?'

'Pretend Mitchum drinks there – you'll find it.'

She allows herself to get swept along with the departing throng, leaving me with a challenge. Now I've got to find a specific bar, rather than stumble into the first one I find.

I return to the hostel for a change of clothes. Open the window, roll a joint, stare at the walls. Refill my pockets with supplies from Britain; business cards and cigarette papers. Jump the 1 and head downtown. Change to the 2 and get off at Fulton St. I head towards the river, to walk the Brooklyn Bridge. Mitchum walks it in *Two for the Seesaw*, isolating himself, killing time, saving money and taking in one of the free pleasures of the city.

Picture it: opening scene, black and white, 1962. It's early morning, Mitchum has gone walkabout; has deserted his previous life and run away to New York City in a quest to prove he can stand on his own two feet. He strolls towards Manhattan, across the Brooklyn Bridge. We see a shot of the old Fulton ferry landing, then St Mark's in the Bowery; the Metropolitan Museum, Egyptian Wing; the Financial District; the New York Public Library on 5th; Pete's Tavern on Irving Place. It is a visual list of some of the city's landmarks and historical, literary references: Fulton Landing is where the old ferry would beach – as documented in Walt Whitman's 1855 poem, *Crossing Brooklyn Ferry*; Pete's Tavern is where short-story writer O Henry used to drink and wrote *Gift of the Magi* in 1904, St Mark's in the Bowery is where Allen Ginsberg *et al* established the still-relevant Poetry Project in 1966.

I walk away from the city, towards the city of Brooklyn. Japanese tourists take photographs of each other stood between the dynamic lines of cables. I don't stop to take in the sights. I don't form opinions or think. I am too absorbed in my mood, and it is all I know.

267

I reach Brooklyn, stroll through Fulton Landing and Navy Yard. This is no longer the violent blue-collar setting described in Hubert Selby Jnr's *Last Exit to Brooklyn*. This stretch of the riverside is now an environment of reclaimed warehouses housing those who have been squeezed out of Manhattan by the rumbling, expansive demands for corporate real estate. City rents are flying high so Brooklyn is being cleared, treated, cleansed and colonised; gentrified. Meanwhile, Brooklyn moves east, resentfully. But that's New York: blink and it's different; it's a city of constant destruction and construction; a city you can live in all your life but never get to know.

The ferry landing was a pleasant neighbourhood until the Brooklyn Bridge was constructed and the area beneath it became a slum. The landing has recently been refurnished with benches and decking, public art etched with excepts from Whitman's poem. Same shit just different poem, different city.

I stop and take a seat. Roll a joint. Look out over the river towards Manhattan. There are so many places to stop and watch the world go by. Or above. The bridges flank the landing and their rumble fills the space below.

Two for the Seesaw was first produced on Broadway, but the screen version starred Mitchum and Shirley MacLaine. It is the tale of a man, Jerry Ryan, who runs to the city following separation from his wife of twelve years. She comes from a wealthy family. His job as lawyer was achieved with the string-pulling of his father-in-law. He feels... kept; unnecessary; worthless and castrated. He is not needed to provide since his financial and social status is reliant upon his wife's family. He cannot fulfil the traditional roles of man. His wife still loves him. He still loves his wife. But he must find an environment in which he can assert his masculinity. He must be man, in his own eyes. He must be needed, vital, necessary.

At a Greenwich Village house-party he meets Gittel Mosca, a New York Jewess living the bohemian life. She is a dancer, Village-hectic and poor. He is independent but needing. He telephones under the pretence of buying her refrigerator. The conversation moves on. He confuses her. She telephones back. He is incapable of expressing what he wants, what he needs; eventually admits to being lonely. They meet for dinner at the Peacock on 4th. It is his birthday. He doesn't reveal this until later, when trying to get her into bed. He plays infuriating mind-games and messes with her head. She cedes and prepares to spend the night with him. He realises and leaves. He has created in her a want and then denied her the release. He needs to feel powerful; denies his vulnerability, preferring instead to shine a light on hers. He wants it both ways: to receive help and support but without having to ask for it. He is a confused and complex man who relies on the role of possessive and patronising manipulator. He casts a long shadow as he walks down the street. He deserves a slap. And reassurance.

Mitchum was criticised for his performance. Even director Robert Wise thought he was wrong for the role, but he does bring something believable to it. As the big man squashed into a grey suit, he appears uncomfortable with himself; not quite in tune with his power. And this is exactly what the role called for – the man who feels he has been robbed of his manhood; the man who needs to find more of himself. For me, it's one of the best movies Mitchum ever made.

Initially, he had rejected the role but when he heard he would be working with MacLaine he accepted. Their understanding and chemistry can be witnessed on screen. Off-screen, their ability to play off each other entertained the crew to such an extent as to drive Wise crazy.

Mitchum was never one to stand in the way of nature so the chemistry soon developed into a full-blown affair. It lasted three years, out-growing the usual leading man–leading lady tête-à-tête and the passing sexual entertainment of a much-wanted man. The situation provided him with profound emotional rewards and challenges and was the only relationship to really threaten his dedication to Dorothy and put the skids under his marriage. They really had something going.

'He had a way of teasing me with just enough poetic artistry that I felt I'd be missing the adventure of a lifetime if I just... walked away from what I intuitively knew was a deep and stormy fragility.'

Shirley MacLaine

According to brother John the only reason Mitchum went after MacLaine in the first place, while filming *Seesaw*, was because he was scared she'd blow him off screen but, were that true, why didn't Mitchum end it as soon as shooting had finished? Besides, MacLaine was no starry-eyed film fan, she was running with the rat pack of Sinatra and Davis and Martin and had a growing fame of her own. But she also had a thing for Mitchum. He was of her father's generation and she had grown up watching and wanting him. And here he was, within reach. But MacLaine was still too wily and intelligent to get involved just because he was a film star. Mitchum showed enough of his inner self, enough of his sensitivity, to show he was whole. Perhaps it was this that attracted the real woman in her.

'I found him to be a complex mystery... shy to the point of detachment, and incapable of expressing what he personally desired.... He made me feel like it was incumbent upon me to draw out his sensitivities and prove to him that it was safe to express them.'

Shirley MacLaine, *My Lucky Stars*

So, perhaps it was a case of, 'You know and I know there's more to me, but you don't get that bit unless you work for it; unless you make it safe for me.' I can wrap my head around that. Perhaps that's the deal with any man in camouflage; any person who feels the need to hide their full self. This is where you come from, this is who you are, but *this* is where you've got to, this is your intelligence and this is your potential. That can cause a huge amount of inner conflict. This was a man who had a substantial insight into the workings of art, especially literature, music and performance. Yet he was just another booze-and-pussy hound; yet another dirty-talking numb-nut. Sophisticated and base. Textural and bland. Emotional and intelligent. Man and animal.

After three years, as the threat to his marriage grew without his reliance on wife Dorothy subsiding, the affair with MacLaine had to end. Again, according to brother John, Mitchum relied on the written word:

Dear Shirley

As I walked in the evening on the Pacific's shore, the winds brought faraway smells of places long forgotten. The roar of the surf brought back sounds of long ago, sweeping over me like a miasma. Loneliness!

I walk in loneliness, Shirley. I cannot bear to ask that you share that loneliness. I must walk to its beat alone! Please understand.

Ever, Robert

John told Shirley the letter was a standard Bob 'kiss-off'. If there's any truth to this then Robert Charles Durman Mitchum should've been ashamed of himself. I don't know what's worse, the cowardice of hiding behind a letter or the cheesiness of the writing. 'As I walked in the evening on the Pacific's shore...' – oh come on, give me a break. I can understand needing to shake yourself loose of a relationship and trying to avoid the complete grief and hassle you're gonna get for it but let's face it: what's sweeping like a miasma ain't loneliness, ode-boy, it's bullshit; long-horned, Texas-crossing, Lazy-J steer-patties piled high and shovelled into an envelope. I bet even the ink was cringing. *Woe, woe!* my ass.

I stroll past Borough Hall and up Fulton, where Whitman had his printshop and published *Leaves of Grass*. I head east, past Jay Street, across Flatbush, and towards Lafayette. On the corner there's a bar and a subway. I could jump on the ghost train and head up to Greenpoint or I could stop for a beer. All this walking has made me thirsty.

I take a stool and order a beer. The barman places it in front of me and tells me it's happy hour, so the second one's free. It would be rude of me not to accept it so I settle in.

Behind the bar there are Photoshopped images of George Bush Jnr fixed to the wall with 'Out of Iraq' stickers. One is a blow-up of a nudey-girl playing card with his face scanned over hers. It's a very confusing image – he's got a great rack.

I leave my beer where it is and go outside for a smoke. The window is covered in ads for yoga classes, reality TV show contestants and benefit concerts. The only constants throughout New York bars are the smokers by the doors, the 'Choking Victim' posters detailing the Himlich Manoeuvre and the CPU kits behind the bar.

'Hey, you new to the city?'

'No, sir.'

'You from Canada?'

'No, Wales.'

'Wales! Man, I knew you were from somewhere.'

'We're all from somewhere, whether we like it or not.'

'You a musician?'

'A writer.'

'Man, I knew you had the creative juices.'

'Do I smell of them?'

'Well, I don't know about that. I'm homeless, you know? And people keep giving me a quarter or a half-dollar...'

I give him four quarters.

'OK, a dollar, God bless you.'

'You too, man. You too.'

I'm getting mighty bored with having to put my hand in my pocket everytime someone approaches me on the street. It ain't the money, it's the regularity of it. But if I can't spare a dollar for my brother, then what kind of failure have I made of my life?

Alan Hale: '*A man's luck's bound to change sometime.... Many a man's been down to his last dollar before the change does come.*'

R M: '*I guess you just want this dollar. Well, go ahead and take it.*'

Pursued

I go back into the bar and finish my drink.

'You want another of those?'

'Sure.'

He brings me a refill.

'Hey, what's the name of this place?'

'This here's Moe's.'

Moe's, huh. Who woulda thunk. Seems Mitchum drinks here after all. Now I've found it I can relax. All I gotta do is remember my way back for tonight.

I return to Manhattan; get off the 4 at Union Square. It was here, June 1953, that over five thousand people protested as Julius and Ethel Rosenberg were fried in the chair at Sing Sing prison for allegedly passing secrets of the A-bomb to the Soviets. They never once admitted guilt; never once offered a political defence; they protested their innocence right up until they were strapped in. Sizzle sizzle. Eisenhower refused to intervene. Death in case of guilt. Praise god for justice. Their lawyer was charged with making un-American statements at their funeral. The campaign to reopen their case continues to this day.

I enter Pete's Tavern on Irving Place and hit the bar. It's crowded. The booths are full of diners and all but one barstool is taken. I grab it and order a pint of House. The lighting is low and the wood is dark. The wall of liquor is busy. Behind me, 'Pete's' is painted on the window. Above, a moulded tin ceiling. Below, a worn tile floor. The place looks larger in *Seesaw*.

According to the bar's promo puff, Pete's is the longest continuously operating bar in NYC, but who logs these things? Pete's appears early in *Seesaw* and, with Mitchum the only drinker, it's the emptiest you'll ever see it. Although the walls are now lined with photos of the famous actors and sportsmen who have drunk here, I can't find a photo of Mitchum or reference to the film. It's not surprising. Pete's has appeared in numerous movies and TV shows since, including (spit) *Seinfeld*.

So this is where short story writer O Henry hung out. Real name William Porter, O Henry was originally from North Carolina but it's as New York's answer to Charles

Dickens that he's remembered. He was yet another American writer who began by publishing his own newspaper, *The Rolling Stone* – although not the same *Rolling Stone* that would feature the face of Mitchum on its cover in 1973. As with Barnum and Mitchum, O Henry served time in jail. It was there he began writing short stories before moving to New York in 1902. He died a drunk eight years later.

It was here (actually *there*, in the booth on the other side of the doorway) that O Henry penned the story *Gift of the Magi*. There's no way he could do that now. You can't sit at a table unless you're eating and there's enough of you to warrant a booth, so I'm scribbling on a scrap of paper slapped on a soggy bar knowing any second now the fat woman in the puffa jacket (although she could be a slim woman in that jacket) is gonna strike up a conversation with me. Which may be what *she* wants, but it sure as hell ain't my desire.

'Hey, watcha writing?'

And here we go.

'I just gotta make some notes while I remember.' (So please leave me alone.)

'You know, O Henry used to write in the corner.'

'Yeh. I heard that.'

'Are you English?'

'Welsh.'

'Wow, Welsh huh.'

She doesn't know what it means.

'So how come you're in New York?'

'I'm working.'

'Oh wow, what do you do?'

'I'm a writer.' When will I learn.

'Wow! Really! What do you write?'

Not a lot unless you shut up and leave me alone.

She doesn't wait for an answer. 'I'm a writer, too.'

'Yeh.'

'Yeh. A friend of mine's a writer and she's just won a Pulitzer so I figure well if *she* can do it, sure as hell I can.'

'Great.' I never realised it was so easy.

'You know Tony's a writer too.'

'Really.'

'Hey Tony, Tony! Hey get over here. Come meet – what's your name honey?'

'Lloyd.'

'Hey come meet Lloyd, he's a writer from England.'

'Hey Tony. I'm from Wales; not England.'

Tony's too polite, confused or uninterested.

'Tony's a poet. Show him your book, Tony.'

Tony grins and holds up a copy of a book called *How to Write Poetry* or *Poetry Made Simple* or *The Bluffer's Guide to Poetry* or *Poetry for Idiots* or *Poetry for People with Fat Friends in Puffa Jackets who Completely Ignore the Reticence and Body Language of Strangers who Want You to Piss Off and Leave Them Alone.*

'So is this a regular writer's hang-out?'

'Oh sure. Well, me and Tony drink here.'

Memo to self: down your beer and go find a real tavern where the suits aren't queueing for a table and the bar isn't full of people who want to be 'writers' (as opposed to those who want to write). Bad tempered, anti-social, self-righteous, miserable bastard – me? You better believe it. There's a time to be social and a time to be left alone. And when there's a beer in one hand and a pen in the other – read the signs. I can fully understand why approaching Mitchum in a bar was taking your life in your own hands. Leave the guy alone.

After an hour of writing and drinking I become aware of a presence by my shoulder. I ignore it, figuring he's gotta work for his way in.

'Hey, watcha writing?'

And here we go again. See, this is the problem when I put away the fuck-you face and allow a pleasant or neutral vibe to escape my body: people think I'm approachable. This guy seems to be weighing me up rather than deeming me an immediate buddy. I'll give him some respect for that.

'I'm just making some notes, man.'

'Yeh? You a writer?'

'Yeh. I'm a writer.'

'Huh. I'm a writer too.'

'You don't say.'

'What you write?'

'Bit of poetry, bit of prose.'

'Huh. I wrote a book – it got published in England.'

He tells me about his book published in England. It doesn't sound too bad. He was a fireman called to the World Trade Center on 9/11. At least he had something to say for himself. On another day I would happily get drunk with him but right now my brain is demanding privacy. Some might say *he* and his comrades are today's epitome of manliness – especially the huge number of homosexual men who applied to join the FDNY after 9/11. Personally, I can't get past the belief that anyone in a uniform is hiding from something. Besides, I gotta find me some quiet so I can vomit out whatever's buzzing around my brain before I forget it or lose the end of the string. I pay the barman, make my goodbyes, stroll out into the evening. Sometimes, being a writer can be a pain in the ass.

I head back to Brooklyn; get off at Lafayette and grab a slice at Not Ray's. It's a good slice – more meat than on a butcher's block. I sidle into Moe's, still wiping the tomato from my face. The place has filled up since this afternoon. The same barman is working. He recognises me, but is no more friendly than is due.

I drink and watch the custom. There's a real mix in Moe's – of race, gender, volume, activity, group involvement, reasons for drinking and dress code. I'm early so pick up the latest issue of *The Onion*. Step outside for a smoke. Use up the last of my lighter. Cross to the store for a new one. Return inside to my beer. It's where I left it. Sit back down and realise I'm being starred at. Corby is stood in front of me.

'I've just followed you in here, don't you ever look behind you?'

'I've learned not to.'

I order her a glass of red.

'So you found it OK?'

'It's like you said, leave it to Mitchum.'

I ask her about her day. She's stressed. I expected nothing less – she's a working New York woman. And hungry. We down our drinks and I take her for *sushi* at

One Greene, where she pours out her frustrations in private. This woman has it all, except a man to listen and love her. I know I'm in danger but I can't help feeling I fit the description. We'll see where this leads me, and her.

Take 17

I lean out of the window. Amongst the traffic and sirens and the helicopter beam I can hear the strains of the Lizard's harmonica. The artist is drunk again and enjoying his existence and Moe's is calling. I put on my jacket, kiss my sleeping woman and smoke on down a block to South Portland.

As usual, the bar is full of funky drinkers, sounds, artists, writers and musicians. The Lizard is holding court at the bar, swapping between his harmonica, sketching in his pad and downing shots of whiskey. I put my hand on his shoulder. He takes my hand, shakes it and explains from the get-go that he is drunk, then moans to the barman about why the hell is he not supposed to play harmonica in a Yankee bar. I grab the next stool and order a beer.

When Moe's shuts, I join the Lizard for a stroll up

Lafayette, South Oxford, DeKalb. Outside Alibi I stop to chat to Bobby who greets me like he knows too much about me already. I palm him a dollar and enter the bar. Shake hands with Steven and Owen, the ex-pat Celtic barmen. Order me a beer. The Lizard has already lined up the Jameson's. I take the shot, order two more. The Lizard keeps leaving and returning, as does everyone else. This smoking law has turned bars into bus depots.

I am celebrating. After a few weeks of shared nights and fun, of listening and talking and caring for each other, of meeting her from work and riding the subway home, Corby tells me I may as well have my own keys. All matter of fact. And I may as well fetch my stuff from the hostel. It didn't seem dramatic and it didn't scare me off. It just made sense. And it made me feel happy. So I returned to the hostel where I hadn't spent a night, tossed my kit in the bag, paid up and left for the last time.

She cleared some table space so I could have somewhere to write. Told me what foods she can't eat, in case I felt like going to the store. I figured if I'm staying rent-free the least I could do is feed her. So I do. While she's in work, I write. And when I'm not writing, I'm unblocking her toilet and bath, fixing her shelves, replacing dead light-bulbs, rethreading their drawstrings, tidying up and cooking. I'm turning into a right little *haus frau*. It's my own choice. Having been living out of a rucksack since gods know when it's refreshing to be in a domesticated setting, and it's been good to show care through practical action as well as romantic gesture. It didn't faze Mitchum so why should it faze me? Between films Mitchum would head out on his own for days at a time, go drinking with his buddies or take his sons hunting. And when he wasn't doing that he was at home baking cakes for his wife or cooking for his family, mending the fence, decorating. He combined wild and domestic and found solace in so doing. He created a balance to his life and this is something I'm still trying to achieve. I've done the domestic and settled, I've done the drunken drift. I haven't yet learned how to do both, simultaneously. I can still slide out in the middle of the night to walk the streets or drink in Moe's and Alibi until the small hours of the morning. Neither of us is contemplating the effect this arrangement will have on us when I leave for the South, but that day is soon approaching.

'I've laid around and I've played around this old town too long and I feel like I've gotta travel on.'

R M, *Gotta Travel On*

And now it's five in the morning and Alibi is closing. Steven and Owen are wiping down surfaces and kicking out customers. And that includes me. I thank them, hit the night air and spark a smoke. The Lizard has evaporated or disappeared somewheres. I stroll down DeKalb to South Oxford. Reach Corby's building, press for the elevator, say goodnight to the Super. Stagger out on the fourteenth floor, take my new keys from my pocket and fumble with the locks. Open the door, quietly. Only I don't. I don't open it quietly because it will not open. I try swapping the keys around even though I'm certain the smaller one opens the top lock. This doesn't work either. I swap them again. Still I'm in the corridor. Swap them again. Check I'm at the right door. I am. Swap them again. I'm getting bored of this and I'm about to piss my pants. Swap them again. Swap them again. There's only one solution: I should phone and ask her to open the door.

I take out my cell-phone. Find her number in the memory and press dial. It rings. I hop from foot to foot. She answers but I cannot understand what she's saying.

'Is that you?'

'Of course it is, you just called me. Where are you? What's wrong? Are you in trouble?'

'Yeh.'

'What is it? Where are you?'

'I can't get in.'

'Can't get in where?'

'To your place.'

'Where are you?'

'In the hall.'

'My hall?'

'Yeh, I'm just the otherside of the door but the keys don't work.'

'You called me from the otherside of the door?'

'I can't get in.'

'I was asleep.'

'But I can't get in.'

'I should leave you out there.'

'You can't, I'm bursting.'

'I thought you were in trouble.'

'I am. Just open the door.'

She goes silent. I listen for the pad-pad-pad of small feet reaching the door but I can't hear it. Then the noise of bolts turning and the door opens. She doesn't look happy to see me.

'Thanks, I'm bursting.'

I rush to the bathroom. She locks the door behind me and goes back to bed. I finish and follow her. Start getting undressed.

'Sorry. Couldn't get in. Must be the keys.'

'It's not the keys. And if you think you can wake me every night because you're too drunk to open the door, you can fuck off back to the hostel.'

R M: *'Are you drunk at least?'*
Shirley MacLaine: *'Yes. I had a couple. I had this terrible thirst all nite and then, you know, I didn't stop to think. Or didn't think to stop.'*

Two for the Seesaw

I wouldn't say I'm drunk exactly, a little jovial perhaps. But I cannot deny she has a point. However much I apologise now it won't be worth a jot so I just let her rip me a new one. It seems only fair, only it's proving very difficult not to laugh as she's doing so. Even in my haze, I know to laugh outloud wouldn't be the wisest course of action. She's already furious with me but I seem quite pleased about it. There's a hint of sabotage in the air. She's still going for it and all I can do is nod in agreement and apology. I want to tell her the truth – that it really isn't my fault; that had Alibi not tossed me out I would've stayed until breakfast and she could've had a night of undisturbed sleep. But I guess she doesn't want to hear excuses. I slope off to the sofa in a state of contrition. Fuck it, deal with it in the morning. I'm celebrating here.

I get woken by cold and noise. The radio is blaring, the water is running, the window wide open. The banging of pots and pans bombards from the kitchen. Why is everything so loud? Why is everything so cold? Why am I on the sofa? I roll over and pull the cushion over my ears.

'Get up.'

I grunt.

'Come on, get up. You woke me up so now I'm waking you. And you've got some explaining to do.'

Oh fuck.

'Cup of tea.'

'Get it yourself. But first I want you to know something: you CANNOT do that again. If you think you can wake me up at five-thirty and...'

R M: *'Good mornin'.'*
Yul Brynner: *'Not good.'*
R M: *'What?'*
Yul Brynner: *'I said not good. What's the matter with you, don't you understand the language of men? Not good.'*
R M: *'Having a little trouble with the wife?'*

Villa Rides!

She's earned the right to let rip. I can't complain. Staying out 'til whatever time she said is not the issue, it's waking her up when she's got work the next day. Bad Welshman, bad Welshman. You've got some making up to do. I wait until she's run out of steam and then, quietly, raise my head.

'You're absolutely right. I know I was out of order but I didn't know what else to do. It was either wake you up or sleep in the park.'

'Next time, sleep in the park.... I was worried about you. Why would you call at that time unless you were in real trouble?'

'I'm sorry, I didn't mean to give you grief.'

'If you EVER do that again, it'll be your balls you're looking for, not Mitchum.'

Before I can stop myself, I laugh. 'Fair do's.'

She smiles, 'And don't laugh while I'm chastising you.'

'Yes, miss. Can I go now, miss?'

'Shut *up*.'

'If you come with me next time, I won't have to wake you up when I get home.'

Her look is a mix of amused, bemused and furious. She shakes her head and goes for a shower. Looks like I got away with that one. Better figure some way to make it up to her, though. So this is domesticity, huh? It's more fun than I thought.

I drag myself off the sofa and slope off to the bed. Climb in. Her side is still warm. This is nice. I ain't getting out of here until she's gone to work and I'm safe.

I wake in an uncomfortable state. The Jameson's is repeating on me. Not my drink of choice. I get up and make a cup of tea. The kitchen's a mess. I could clear this up, that'll be a brownie point or two. I open the refrigerator. We could do with some food. So I'll hit the store. Providing, bringing home the beef – isn't that what a man's supposed to do?

> *'Beef – it's what's for dinner.'*
>
> R M, TV ad

I don't know. What am I supposed to do in these situations? If I try and be nice and make up for it, I'll be acting like a creep. If I dismiss it and act as if everything's the same as normal, I'm an uncaring bastard. If I promise I'll never again sneak out when she's asleep to go drinking, I'll be lying. I guess the only option left is to talk to her. It's not that I mean to take the piss, I'm just used to living to a different timetable to most people. I could offer to meet her from work but that wouldn't be wise – the journey back on the subway would not be the place to talk so the silence would be loaded. I guess I better just clean the place up, clean myself up, hit the store. Get some good food ready for when she gets home – nothing fancy, just wholesome and healthy and hot. Just to save her from effort. Then we should talk.

I shop. I buy vegetables, beef and good bread. A bottle of red wine. I make stew. Good, healthy, reinvigorating Welsh stew. Leave it on a low flame. Open a Corona. Sit by the window, sip my beer and roll myself a joint. I figure if I stay here, when she gets back it'll be like entering her own private space again, and I'll be right at the back of it.

I hear the locks turn. She struggles with the door, eventually gets it open, closes it behind her. I guess now is not the time to point out that even for her, sober and well-practiced, the locks stick.

'Hey.'

'Hey.'

That tells me nothing.

'Smells good. What is it?'

'Welsh stew.'

'Huh. What's Welsh about it?'

'I made it.'

'Anything else?'

'It's got leeks in it.'

'Is it, like, a traditional family recipe?'

'Of course,' I lie. The only tradition in my family is the hangover. 'Listen, get comfortable. I want to talk to you.'

'Oh Lloyd, I've had a hard day and I'm hungry. Let's not make this any more difficult than it already is.'

OK, so attempt to come clean unsuccessful.

'I just wanted to apologise...'

'Good.... Look, I think I already have a good understanding of who you are and what you do. I know you like to drink and I know you like to smoke and I know you like to take drugs and I know you like to stay out late and if you haven't got all that out of your system by now then you probably never will. But that's not how I live my life. So you have to remember to consider me. As long as you do that, as long as you consider the effects your actions have on me and that I have a life too, you can do whatever you like.'

'Seems I am in the market for a whole human being, after all.'

R M, *Two for the Seesaw*

Finally, I feel humbled.

'Can I kiss you?'

'Feed me first. And if the stew's good, you can kiss me.'

The stew does the trick. We take the remains of the wine into the bathroom; share a bath. It's a good size tub, easily big enough for two. She lies with her head on my chest; tries to shape the hairs on my legs into patterns. I wash her hair, her neck, her arms, her armpits, her breasts. She leans forwards and I soap her back. She stands up so I can soap her ass, her legs, her hair. She sits back down and swills herself. Tells me to dunk my head and begins shampooing my hair.

'So what you doing tomorrow?'

'I was hoping to stay in bed with you.'

'No go, Emo. Some of us have to work.'

'I gotta work too.'

'Yeh, hard life you lead. That beer doesn't drink itself.'

Shirley MacLaine: *'So you're not working huh?'*
R M: *'I wouldn't say that. Getting unstuck from a piece of flypaper can be very hard work.'*

Two for the Seesaw

'Well, I don't have no office to go to so I have to sit in bars.'

'You could go to the library.'

290

'Yes I could, but I need to do some more research, first.'

'Is that liquid research?'

'More fluid than liquid.'

She pours water over my head without warning, and laughs, 'You're full of bullshit.'

I wipe my eyes and splutter, 'I don't pretend otherwise.'

'No. No you don't. Quite the opposite. Why do you allow people to think that's all you are?'

'We all need our camouflage, baby.'

We dry each other and fall into bed. Make love, both passionate and compassionately. Oh, my Brooklyn bombshell; my coquettish confederacy of chaotic charm; my Southern savante; my Virginian of virtuous voltage. You continue to impress me; both calm and excite me – in the right places, at the right times. I'm staying home, tonight.

I wake to find I'm hugging her. I'm loathed to move, but I know her alarm will go soon and she'll be grumpy without coffee. I slide away from her and hit the kitchen. Her alarm wakes her up. I leave her coffee by the bed. Hit the window. Roll myself a smoke.

I look down on South Oxford, the spire of Layafette Avenue Presbyterian church and the pedestrians directly below me reflected in the third storey windows of the buildings opposite. Silently, she has risen. Comes up behind me and grabs my ass, wraps her arms around me. I wrap my leg around hers, cradle her Achilles tendon between my toes and accept her affection and warmth. It's a cold, dreary day in NYC but there's a blip of a heatwave building. I turn and kiss her, she kisses back. I undo her robe and we fall easily on the bed and start the day as everyone should start every day – in affection and desire and as one. We make love and get the day's moans out of our systems so we may take reasurance and comfort and a safe haven out with us onto the streets and into the city.

Take 18

It's time to mop up the remaining Mitchum sites.

I return to Grand Central and the market. The brothers Mitchum left Delaware to come here, then left in the back of a truck and travelled all the way to Florida. Then to Birmingham, Alabama.

Well Mitch, you wouldn't recognise the market now. They jazzed it up good, *dad*. I search amongst the 'British bangers', bratwurst, knackwurst, weisswurst, Llangloffan cheese and Thuringia mett, but I find no signs of you.

I figure I should return to Pete's Tavern – it's unfair to judge a bar on just one visit. I return to Union Square and head up Irving towards Gramercy Park.

I take a stool in the middle of the bar. Two elderly women stand next to me at the bar. There's no spare seats. I offer them my stool. They decline, gratefully. They ask me where I'm from and what I'm doing here. I tell them.

'Robert Mitchum!' one proclaims.

The other adds, 'My, I haven't heard of him in years.'

Their eyes are alive and their faces glowing.

'Do you remember how huge a star he was?'

'How could I forget! There was one time I was on the bus with a school friend, and out of the window we saw Robert Mitchum just walking down the street. This was after his trouble with drugs. Well, we just had to stop the bus and get off. I forget which avenue it was, but we followed him all around town, block after block, all the way back to his hotel.'

'Did you speak to him?'

'Oh no, we didn't dare. We were just... fourteen, I guess. And he was, well, he was Robert Mitchum. We just wanted to be near him.'

I stay silent, not wishing to disturb her drift into memories long-filed.

Eventually she returns. 'Oh you must let me know when your book is published, I'd love to read about him again.'

I give her my card. 'You know he was a naughty boy, don't you – in more ways than one.'

'Oh yes, he always was. That's why we loved him.'

A server approaches to tell them there's a booth available. We wish each other well and I remain at the bar, still able to hear them talking about Mitchum.

Time to hit the bricks. I finish my beer, leave a few bucks on the bar, say goodbye to the older women. The Mitchum fan shakes my hand and reiterates her enthusiasm for my subject matter.

'I'll tell him you said "Hi" if I catch up with him.'

'I'm sorry but I think he's dead, dear.'

I cross town on the F and get off at West 4th. Walk a little way, consider the landmarks and street length, pull out the production stills. What was a parking lot in the movie is now a bank. I choose my spot carefully. In *Two for the Seesaw*, this was a Chinese restaurant called The Peacock, where Mitchum brought Shirley MacLaine on their first screen date. The restaurant's not even here, let alone Mitchum.

I head past the basketball court and into the Four-Faced Liar, settle on a stool in the corner and consider where to go next. Stare out of the window, watch the world go by. The locals on their way to or from work, the Jersey crowds hitting the city; the dollar snobs and beggars; the Africans, Asians, South Americans, North Americans, Australasians and Europeans. New York City has a habit of fooling you into believing you're taking part in something big. If nothing else, you're taking part in a cultural experiment; an exercise in tolerance and diversity. This is probably the only city in the world where you can be considered a valid part of the city yet not be a citizen of the host country; you might not be an American, but you are a New Yorker.

So where do I go next? There's always the Cowgirl on Hudson. He could be in there – it's often full of women. That means walking up Bleecker and across 7th.

R M: *'7th and Bleecker isn't a very friendly neighborhood, I better come along.'*

When Strangers Marry

You're out of date, Mitch. Anyway, where have you just come from?

R M: *'I'll leave town, captain, if that's what you want.'*

The Wonderful Country

His voice disappears as quickly as it arrived. Bizarre.

I stroll and smoke to the Cowgirl, squeeze past the smokers and hit the bar. This isn't so much a pose-y bar, as a possee bar. Posters and pictures of cowgirls, a Stetson hanging behind the bar, but no Mitchum. I go downstairs to the restroom and there, hanging over the urinal, is an ad for the Mitchum range of personal hygiene products.

> *'If you've ever urinated for 60 seconds straight you're a Mitchum man.'*

Does that include passing out and pissing your pants?

And there's Mitchum, sat at the bar. What the hell is he doing here? I pull up a stool next to him.

R M: *'How did you know I was here?'*

The Ambassador

'Your name's over the latrine.'

My ulcer's kicking in. I order a vodka and use it to

swill down a stomach pill.

R M: *'What's your problem?'*
Shirley MacLaine: *'I've got an ulcer.'*
R M: *'Isn't that supposed to be a man's disease?'*

Two for the Seesaw

'Shut up, Mitch, you got me into this.'

R M: *'I'm neither ready nor able to be responsible for anything these days.'*

Two for the Seesaw

'These days? You mean something's changed? When I want to talk about responsibility I'll let you know. Until then, all you're responsible for is my next drink.'

R M: *'Sometimes that's all it takes.'*

James Dean: Race with Destiny

'All what takes? Look, I was in a pretty good mood here. Yes, my stomach's playing up but it's nothing I can't drown. And yes I've gotta leave New York soon and I'm not sure I'm ready to go. And I just need to come to terms with all that, OK? So if you've got something positive to say, I'm all ears. If not, pipe down.'

He holds his thoughts; offers a toast.

R M: *'Your physique, wrecked though it may be.'*

Two for the Seesaw

'In your eye. You should know better than most, Mitch, sometimes a man likes to drink alone.'

R M: *'I never found out much listening to myself.'*
Out of the Past

'How can I listen to myself with you whittering in my ear?'

R M: *'Let's have a drink.'*
Georges Hubert: *'Yes that's a good idea. Let's have a drink.'*
R M: *'That's what I said.'*
Georges Hubert: *'I know, it's a good idea.'*
Foreign Intrigue

I signal to the server and ask for another. 'Better make that two – one for my friend here.'
'Oh, you with someone?'
'Private joke.'

R M: *'You alright?'*
Michael McGreevey: *'Nothing wrong with me. I'm going crazy thass all and don't try to stop me.'*
R M: *'Oh I never stop anyone from doing anything – that's just about the only principle I've got.'*
The Way West

'So you've got principles now?'

Kirk Douglas: *'What does he want?'*
R M: *'He wants justice....'*
The Way West

Oh Christ, not Kirk Douglas as well. 'Fuck off Douglas, you're not even dead.'

Kirk Douglas: *'It's hard to believe that your grief has so corrupted your guts.'*

The Way West

'It's just an ulcer, that's all. If I drink enough it'll stop its screaming.'

R M: *'Well, offhand I'd say you're a born victim. Of yourself.'*

Two for the Seesaw

'Oh, not the lecture; save me from the lecture. There's nothing worse than a dead boozer warning you of the dangers of drink.'

I down my vodka.

R M: *'These things are like water.'*
Barman: *'They creep up on you.'*
R M: *'Bring me a couple more.'*

Where Danger Lives

The server brings us a couple more.

R M: *'Shall I tell you something that no man ought to have to tell another? You're a little bastard... you could be the best, but I'm betting against it because inside the man there's a little snivelling boy, a cry-baby kid who's afraid to grow up and be a man and join the team.'*

James Dean: Race with Destiny

'Is that it? Are they the great words of wisdom I've travelled thousands of miles to hear? Christ, even my father could do better than that.'

R M: *'I can be useful to you, very useful.'*

Villa Rides!

'Great. Order more drinks and shut up.'

R M: *'You know, you're talking to an old hand at this sort of thing.'*

Home from the Hill

R M: *'I want you to tell me everything you can.'*

Crossfire

'Listen, I've been caught in this trap before. I spill the beans and then you tell me what a fuck-up I am for having beans to spill. No deal, *dad*.'

R M: *'The longer you keep putting it off, the more I want an answer.'*

Man with the Gun

'Shove it.'

R M: *'Tell me.'*
Neil Hamilton: *'You're not interested.'*

When Strangers Marry

R M: *'I'll straighten everything out. Now you have another drink.'*

Foreign Intrigue

'Thank you for your understanding.'

R M: *'You just bury those yesterdays as deeply as you can.'*
Second Chance

'And that's supposed to help? Burying things alive when they're perfectly capable of scrambling back up to the surface and biting me on the ass when I least need them?'

Curt Jurgens: *'Reason is twisted. Its purpose is dark. It's not for a simple man.'*
The Enemy Below

'That's very deep, Curt, thanks. I can see why you're a *sub*marine comander.'

R M: *'Well, it'll soon be over.'*
Man with the Gun

'You reckon? How so? How do you know? How do I bring it to a close?'

R M: *'You do whatever you have to, young man.'*
The Ambassador

'Screw this, I'm going outside for a smoke.'

301

I slap some notes on the bar.

R M: '*You all take it easy, ya hear?*'
Mitch Ryan: '*Naturally.*'

Thunder Road

R M: '*There's always* mañana.'

Second Chance

Ye gods, I wished for Mitchum but on my own terms and with answers. Instead I get an ulcer and always with the riddles. Lesson number one: be careful what you wish for. When will I ever learn? I spark a joint and walk away.

Rock Hudson: '*Now what?*'
R M: '*We wait.*'

The Ambassador

I take the subway back to Brooklyn, begin to relax again. I've got Mitchum's number. I don't blame him for trying to shake me but now is not the time to let go. I let myself into the apartment and join with my woman. This is my last night in town so we make the most of the time. Depths are reached, fears calmed, ideas planted and futures sown. A good crop is expected, so don't go digging around, Mitchum, keep your dirty nose out of my plantation. At least for now.

Take 19

Corby walks me to the subway.

'You know, they normally call this escorting me to the city limits.'

'I'm just seeing you off.'

We kiss and split. I drag my case down the steps.

'Call me when you get there.'

'Get where?'

'Wherever you're going.'

The rumble of the subway drowns our last moments. I disappear down to the platform.

I arrive at the Port Authority Bus Terminal – another central hub for the city's transport system but without the grandeur of Grand Central. I'm early. Step outside to smoke. I'm being eyeballed by someone, I can sense it.

Who's looking at me? I turn and look south. A small, slight woman, the creases on her face hiding her true self amongst the folds of age, approaches me with a steely look in her eyes. I don't recognise her but she seems to have an issue with me. I don't prepare myself because I don't know what I'm preparing for; don't broaden my shoulders or soften to her size. I can only presume she wants a dollar.

She stops and stands very close to me. I look down to her face. She looks up at mine, stares into my eyes.

'Satan.'

'Excuse me?'

She moves along with a rapidity belying her age. Turns to look at me one last time. Spits, 'You are Satan.' Disappears in the crowd.

I've been called some things in my time but never the Dark God. I turn to the woman smoking next to me. She smiles, lets out a 'Ha!' and a lungful of smoke. 'Crazy woman.'

I'm reassured. The world around me has not ground to a halt. No lynch mob is gathering, no curses uttered or crosses hurled. The only woman to notice carries on smoking, dismissing the accuser rather than questioning me. I mean, who the hell would mistake me for Satan? I'm only his offspring.

I toss my butt and go back inside. Join a queue. I need to check my baggage but the woman in front of me is arguing with the assistant.

'You can't take that on the bus.'

She replies in Spanish.

The assistant raises her case from the scales and puts

it to one side. 'It's eighty-four pound – you're only allowed fifty.'

Again, in Spanish.

'It's the rules. You'll have to take something out.'

'No rules, you motherfucker.'

Oh, so now she can speak English.

'Don't you curse me.'

'Fucking motherfucker.'

'You cursing me or MTA? As long as you ain't cursing MTA, lady.'

'Fucking fucker.'

'That's it. End of conversation. Take your case and get out of here.'

He turns his back on her. She storms off, screaming and cursing. He turns back, 'Get out of here, you mother-fucking crack whore.'

'I no crack whore, motherfucker!'

Her children are crying. She grabs her case and drags it away. Grabs her kids by their hair and pulls case and children down the concourse, swearing in English and ranting in Spanish, away from an argument she cannot win.

We pull out of the terminal at 13.45. Delaware, here we come. I'm giving you a four-hour warning.

I feel knackered. I am loaded down with the knowledge I'm walking away from unfinished business in New York and that there's a whole lot of work still to come.

The traffic concertinas at a laborious pace from block to block, restricted by heavy traffic and pedestrian speed limits. It's just as well there's lots to look at. 'Don't block the box' read the signs. Nobody takes any notice. Drivers are reluctant to move aside for fire trucks and ambulances, their sirens demanding like spoilt brats. The urban turbans sit in their cabs, ignoring the bitching of passengers. Bumper stickers proclaim 'Failure is not an option' and 'Say no to drugs'. All I know is I'm sat on the bus and driving it ain't my problem.

I try to snooze but everytime I get close to sleep my elbow slips off the window frame. So I stuff my face with Mike & Ike's to keep me awake. It doesn't work. I grab restful snatches between noises. I can't remember the last time I had a full night's sleep but at least there's been good reason to stay awake.

I think of the woman I woke with this morning. Our bodies still buzzing from the night before. The physical memory of her flesh still present in my every nerve ending. Feeling her lying in my arms, her breasts against my chest, her leg over mine, her hands touching. I'm getting hard. This could be a long journey.

Take 20

'I got off the Greyhound bus in Delaware in my thin ice cream suit and panama hat and promptly fell on my nose in four feet of snow. Dorothy picked me up and I told her the whole sad story, and she said, "Look, you don't have too much direction, you don't have too much sense. I don't think you're fit to be let loose any longer. I suggest we get married."'

Robert Mitchum on Dorothy Spence

We cross St Jones River, pull off Route Thirteen. The bus draws up at the back of a gas station. I disembark and wait for the driver to drag out my luggage. I wish he could drag out my baggage. I wish I could leave it on the bus.

Dover, Delaware. This is the closest Greyhound stop to where Mitchum first met his future wife, Dorothy Spence. Dorothy was dating Mitchum's little brother until big brother muscled in. I say 'muscled' but at the time the only Mitchum muscle developing well was his tongue; he was still a skinny kid. Although they weren't exclusive, brother John claimed his heart belonged to her. Robert had recently returned from his adventures in Savannah. He was in a bad way. His leg was cut up from the chain-gang shackles and infected from his escape through the swamp. He would hobble around on crutches for months.

Mitchum claimed he and Dorothy met on a blind date in the back of her cousin's Model A Ford.

'Returning to Delaware... it appeared our family was in most desperate circumstances.... Accordingly, I left school and went to work as a garage mechanic, determined that my younger brother's education should not be uninterrupted. That same autumn I met the girl I was later to marry, Dorothy Spence.'

R M, 1949 probation plea

I get some quarters from the food mart and wait for the payphone to free up. I walk away from the pumps and light a smoke. It's a sunny evening. The breeze relaxed. Three policemen in uniform leave the Where Pigs Fly restaurant – speciality ribs and wings – and walk towards a black UV. They eyeball me so I reciprocate. They drive past slowly, zip down a blackened window and let me know they think they've got my number.

I call a cab. It arrives immediately – a busy town, obviously. We drive a couple hundred yards along DuPont Highway to the Howard Johnson motel. The driver charges me ten bucks.

'Ain't that a little steep?'

He turns and hands me a business card, takes my money, 'Fixed fare within Dover limits'.

I rip up his card. Memo to self: avoid Dover cabs. He may be available twenty-four/seven but you only get to rip me off once.

DuPont Highway. *Hmm*. A gorgeous woman once told me Delaware ain't so much an American state as the fiefdom of the DuPont dynasty.

'While the DuPont family has a whole wing of a Washington hospital reserved for them in case any one of them gets ill, humanity is facing a world crisis.'

R M

It seems in coming from Bridgeport to Delaware, Mitchum moved from the doorstep of one major war supplier to another – Bridgeport was home to Remington, Delaware is home to DuPont. Remington made guns and ammunition, DuPont made gunpowder. DuPont became essential; diversified; became one of the largest corporations in the world. A-rootin' an' a-tootin' all round. *Yee-haw*, America had a use for them.

I wheel my case to the lobby. The woman at reception takes my passport and credit card, asks where I'm from. Look at my passport, baby.

'So what brings you to the States?'

'Research. For a book.'

'On Dover?'

'On Robert Mitchum. Remember him?'

309

'Can't say I do.'

'He was a movie star, a sex symbol. He grew up in Felton.'

'Felton, Delaware?'

'Uh-huh.'

'Oh! That's why you're here?'

'That's why I'm here.'

'Richard *who*?' She continues tapping her keyboard.

'*Robert* Mitchum.'

'Well I ain't heard of him.'

'He's dead now but he was big in the '40s, '50s, '60s, '70s, '80s. Ask your mother – she'll remember him.'

'My momma didn' grow up around here.'

'Believe me, she'll remember him.'

'OK, I will. So he still live around here?'

'No, he died in '97. He was seventy-nine years old.' I'm rattling off facts too easy.

'So how come you hooked into him?'

'There are... similarities, differences, factors to be considered.'

'So you guys grow up together?'

'Uh, no. He would be pretty old now.'

'Oh! That's right, you said.'

'Yeh, unless I'm ageing particularly well for an ninety-year-old.'

'Yeh!' She hands me my room key, passport and credit card, 'You're very good looking...'

'Thank you.'

'For a ninety-year-old.'

Thanks a bundle sister, you have a good day too. I

wheel away and take an elevator.

'I've aged considerably in the last five minutes.'
R M, Where Danger Lives

I search for the light switch in my room, turn on the TV, dump my case on the first of two double beds and hang my suit. Run a bath and roll a joint. Flick channels in search of black and white; find re-runs of *Lucy*, switch to TCM in the hope of spotting Mitch. He's keeping himself low, it seems.

There are guests at reception. I ask them if there's somewhere near I can eat. 'Sure, there's plenty of places,' one says, recommending a chicken joint about five miles away.

'Anywhere within walking distance?'

'You're walking?'

'Sure.'

They turn to each other, then back to me. They're confused. *Wal-king*. 'There's an Arby's a little way down.'

'I mean a restaurant.'

'Arby's is a restaurant.'

'Sure it is. Thanks. I'll check it out,' but Arby's ain't no restaurant, it's a fast-food joint. There's people live in this motel for weeks at a time, there gotta be somewhere decent to eat.

I stroll out to the Dover nightlife – 'Where the Fun Begins' according to the sign outside the derelict bowling alley. On one side of the motel is a nightclub (only open on weekends), a K-Mart and a Discount Cigarettes. Opposite

311

there's a gas station; a pawn shop; a huddle of old slat houses the backs of which overlook the lake; and in place of a sidewalk a line of yellow flags pegged in the grass mark out the path of a buried pipeline, leading the eye towards Payday Loans, Amco Cash Checking and Lawal Prosthetics. I guess credit here costs an arm and a leg. I turn right and follow the line of drive-in ATMs towards the Delaware Agricultural Museum and find myself a Japanese restaurant. Jesus in a gymslip – an oasis, I loves ma *sushi*. I'm in the mood for quality and I'm willing to spend some time with its pleasures.

Ichiban is almost empty. I bow to the server and say '*Sumimasen*', take a seat at the food counter; overlook the privacy of a booth for the pleasures of watching food preparation. A row of raw fish provides a perfect vista and competition for the wall-mounted TV. The staff introduce themselves but don't give their real names, only the Western alternatives. I order a cold Asahi and a flask of hot sake. Sake is my downfall. It is my bromide in the soldier's tea. I can drink it all night without it affecting my ability to chopstick or appreciate every grain of rice, but like no liquor it gets under my skin; into my system and cuts to the bone; reduces my cock to floppy flesh, a waste of cells and desire. Still, I've got a woman in New York to whom I said I'd be loyal. She told me I'm expected to behave myself. I told her it'd be difficult. I raise my cup and toast 'loyalty', the chef offers '*kampai*'. I down my sake and beer and order another of each, for the sake of fidelity. Sake is a good thing, at the right time. But I can't help feel if a man's cock is asleep then he loses some presence and

312

participation in the world.

Mitchum was a drinker and, in later years, completely impotent. I say 'later years', we're talking the last score. That's a long time to be soft. He still chased the women – saw it as a challenge. The old man trying to prove he can still pull the birds. He could, but that's as far as it went. I don't want to think of Mitchum as a shadow of himself. Younger, he had more women than he could count, more drinks than I could spill. Thank god he didn't live to take Viagra – no one else would've got a chance.

Good food. *Hmm.* Food and sex and booze. Ambitions in life? Emotional stability, acceptance of self, continual good sex for the rest of life, some health, to love and be loved, to be able to eat without rushing, to dunk my rice in the soy without dropping a grain.

With a title like *We've Never Been Licked* (UK: *Texas to Tokyo*), it's tempting to presume the Mitchum movie is a Howard Hughes innuendo flick, even more so on discovering the producer was called Walter Wanger. If only it was. Instead, it's a stomach-churning exercise in wartime propaganda vomited out by Universal Studios. It hardly ever deviates from its purpose: to big-up US forces and a Texas agricultural college which specializes in churning out cannon-fodder. If it deviates at all it's to ram home the message that the Japanese are an underhanded and untrustworthy foe. I mean, why bother to watch the movie when you could just go and enlist.

Mitchum plays Panhandle Mitchell, a hard-ass college officer. The plot revolves around a stumbling, bumbling Jimmy Stewart-type hero played by Richard Quine who,

313

having lived in Asia, is positive towards Japan and its people. The movie tries to convince us he's naïve in his opinions – he's betrayed by his Japanese friends, led into treacherous behaviour (for which, inexplicably, he's merely kicked out of college), joins the Japanese propaganda department but comes good in the end, sacrificing himself for the good ole U S of A. The message is clear: if only he hadn't trusted those damn foreigners in the first place.

In 1944 Mitchum was filming *Thirty Seconds Over Tokyo* at a Florida airbase for MGM. The plot was simple enough: a re-enactment of the World War II 'Doolittle Raid' on Japan by the American army airforce. It was Mitchum's twenty-fifth film in two years but he had played the lead in only one. He was still seen as a new boy, a potential star on the rise. The studio expected him to be as controllable as all the other wannabees in their stable. Right.

During filming Mitchum was living on base and spent his spare time drinking, pulling pranks, banging a film exec's secretary and fending off abuse from the servicemen who resented the actors and civilians in their midst. Also starring in the film was Mitchum's friend Steve Brodie. Brodie called Mitchum 'the Gentle Giant' because of his willingness and ability to walk away from the goading of gorillas – up to a point.

One evening Mitchum, Brodie and some of the crew were sitting around drinking when in comes a sergeant too drunk or too dumb to keep his mouth shut and his fists in his pockets, accusing them of bottling out of the war and general Hollywood homosexual antics. There was uproar. Mitchum exploded. He jumped on the airman, burst out of the barracks – taking the doors off their hinges – and beat him to the floor. It took three men to drag him off. A few days later the sergeant offered an apology. Mitchum refused to accept it. The sergeant explained he was acting under orders. Mitchum still refused and told the sergeant to send his commanding officer next time. Then Mitchum got Brodie blamed for banging the exec's secretary.

Mitchum *was* drafted into the army, in 1945. The studios claimed he had repeatedly tried to enlist but had been rejected for health reasons.

'Are you kidding? I still had the porch-rail under my finger-nails. I kept trying to tell them I was a fruit.'

R M

The decision to enlist was forced upon him. It was either the army or jail.

The whole situation was bizarre. Mitchum was arrested for being drunk in his own home; for being 'in an intoxicated condition on private property'. If that's a crime we're all due for a life sentence. His lawyer advised he plead guilty and take the ten dollar fine. The judge wanted to make an example of him, so instead of a fine Mitchum was given a six month sentence. In an attempt to avoid prison he claimed it would prevent him joining the army so the judge ordered Mitchum be taken to enlist, returned to custody for the weekend, then taken straight to the troop train. He may as well have been press-ganged.

As with most things in Mitchum's life, there's various versions of what happened that night. The most bizarre,

315

and least likely, comes from Mitchum's probation plea from his infamous 1948 drugs bust.

'Five days prior to my induction I was jailed. Out to obtain a prescription for a sick child, I called my wife to discuss the prescription and my sister answered the phone. She refused to allow me to talk to my wife and hung up the receiver. There followed several attempts, all of which had the same results, until finally, knowing my sister to be hostile to my wife (who was also ill and bedded), I told her that I would come to talk to Dorothy and demand an accounting before her. Pressed for complaint, my sister refused to sign, and at my own demand for justice, I was arrested, roundly beaten and booked at the Fairfax Avenue sheriff's station.'

R M

Elements of this are easily believed but as a probation plea he may as well have claimed the dog ate his homework.

Later, he admitted he was drinking on his porch when a man ran up to him and shone a torch in his face. Mitchum broke the man's nose and knocked him down the steps. The man was a police officer at the wrong address. Mitchum was furious.

'If the cops are going to come and hassle you, then I wanted them to take it all the way. I mean, what the hell? Let's go through with it, right?'

R M

As righteous as this stance may be, jumping into the police

316

car shouting, 'Let's go downtown right now, mother-fuckers!' was just asking for trouble. They beat shit out of him, breaking two of his ribs. The troop train to Fort MacArthur was waiting.

Mitchum claimed to have served as an army drill instructor and then an orthopaedic examiner. In interviews, this mutated into 'rectal examiner' – a member of the 'keister police' – assigned to examine 'the asshole of every G I in America', in search of 'piles, hemorrhoids, bananas, grapes, dope... you name it'.

In 1945, Mitchum found himself back on civvy street. After eight months of part-time soldiering/acting, the war was over and Mitchum was released due to financial hardship – his family of wife, two kids, sister, nephew, half-sister, grandmother, mother, and step-father were all reliant on his earnings. He went out celebrating his release and straight into filming *Till the End of Time*.

Mitchum, Guy Madison and Bill Williams played three marines returning home from the war. Williams has lost his legs and Mitchum has a plate in his head.

The subject matter was certainly relevant at the time: boys returning home as men, uncertain of how to live life or fit in to a peace-time society; vets presuming their disabilities destroyed any hope of a meaningful or useful existence; a domestic society unaware of a soldier's need for post-war rehabilitation. The movie also deals with prejudice. When our returning heroes are invited to join a vets' organisation it's on the understanding they're not black, not Jewish and not Catholic. Our heroes whoop ass – at a cost. Mitchum gets a bottle across the head, dislodging the plate and putting him in hospital. Will he pull through? *Gasp*.

Although a little old-fashioned, the movie still carries a valuable message: survive; keep fighting your limitations and whatever shit hits the fan.

My main course arrives. *Chirashi* – steamed rice and *sushi*; a range of complementary colours, textures, tastes. I sit upright, pause to sample the food with my eyes, pour myself a sake, toast my food silently, thank the chef, pick up my chopsticks, split and brush the splinters, hold them low and to the side. Try not to lean forward but to pick up my rice bowl and place it below my mouth. Swap between rice and fish and vegetation. One or two tastes at a time.

I finish my meal and pay. The beautiful server says, 'See you tomorrow'. I wish, baby, I wish. I wish I could get these pictures out of my head.

I hit the bricks. I am the only pedestrian. There are cars but no sidewalks. I stroll the grass and roll a smoke. Reach Mulligan's Pizza, a good old Italian name if ever there was one.

I spot goths smoking outside a back door. Spot roadies unloading gear from a truck. I sniff a venue, I sniff a club, I sniff a late bar. So there is nightlife in Dover after all.

I pay my five bucks, uncertain of what to expect. It's called Bubba's and I'm trying not to presume the worst from the name. Inside, it's crowded. Baseball caps and cell-phones, bottles held by necks and an inordinately large number of people on crutches.

'Cold Beer, Good Eats.' I sit at the bar and open a tab,

order a Bubba's Brew – you gotta try the local produce. It ain't too bad and at a dollar a draft it's a bargain, too. No purchase tax, I guess. Hell, I'm getting to like Delaware. The beer is light and the club is dark but I sense no atmosphere of threat. I relax, tune into the game on the set. Detroit are battling Miami. It's 57–58.

A flier on the bar tells me tonight is 'Local Band Night'; I'm too late in the month for 'Trailer Park Casanovas' but I may return for the 'Lima Bean Riot'.

From the sound-check taster I'd say it's a thrash night which after the serenity of the restaurant could be a shock to my system. But I've been here before; I've roadied and reported and lived to hear again.

I spot people walking past a bouncer to a back room. I'm expecting questions from the guy but he lets me stroll past and I see why: the back room ain't no sex dive, no poker hide, no hidden world; it's a brightly lit sports bar with pool tables, table hockey, arcade machines. Man what a combination: alternative music venue and all-American goody-two-shoes hangout in one. It'll do.

I sit at the back bar and order another beer. Pull out my copy of the Dover Post and check out its stories: 'Casino Expansion' – 'Growth needed to keep up with nearby states' (man, this country is hot for the slots); 'Dover police seize eight pounds of marijuana'. Same shit, different state. There's 'Jill Jackson's Hollywood' column (Mitchum had a Hollywood column – its activities often got him into print).

I turn the page. 'Harkins likely to be released from prison soon'. Yet another politician – a former Delaware

Secretary of State; a Republican sent to prison for 'abusing *his office*'.

Some guy walks up to me and asks, 'You're a writer, right?'

'Right.'

'Man, I knew it. I knew you were a writer or something.'

'Right – something.'

'You're in movies, right?'

'Not really.'

'You are, right? You're in movies – I can tell these things.'

'I'm writing about an actor, that's as close as it gets.'

'Man, I've got this great idea for a movie – you could turn it into a real hit. It's a real Delaware story, man no one's ever written about us. You see all these dumb-ass states in the movies but no one writes about Delaware and we've got things going on here the same as anywhere else, let me tell ya...'

He doesn't go into plot but he's determined to talk me into fighting his cause. I listen with interest, buy him a beer. He's barking up the wrong tree. 'Man, it sounds great but I ain't in the movies. You should write it yourself.'

'Oh man I ain't no writer, I couldn't do that.'

I try to convince him to record his ideas rather than allude to them in conversations with drunken writers in bars – there's a danger they may wake tomorrow and think the ideas were theirs. But he ain't having it. He calls over his friends, invites me to watch him try beat his own record on Hoop Fever. He holds the house record. He's proud of it.

The bank of screens behind the bar is giving me a montage of athleticism: basketball, boxing, ice hockey, ice skating, NASCAR, wrestling. No soccer. No god-damn soccer.

Mitchum was a boxer for a while. In 1936 he was fired from his friend's father's car plant in Toledo. He was seen as a bad influence and everything about Mitchum wound up the boss, even his refusal to wear socks. So, unemployed, he returned to Delaware to see Dorothy. Then he headed to California to hook up with his family. En route, he stopped off in Nevada and found himself earning a living as a fighter.

'I want folks to know I was licked. I hate fighting – it's too painful. It's not good for me. I much prefer the quiet life.'

R M

Although John was considered the family boxer, it was Robert who had to teach him the skills. When they lived in Philadelphia John got into a fight over a girl. And lost. They arranged a rematch and Robert coached his younger brother. The rematch ended in the same result. Almost. Having watched his brother take a pummelling Robert decided to even things up, knocking the victor to the ground and bouncing his head on the pavement, presumably to ensure his brother wouldn't become a permanent target. John would recall, 'It's a terrible blow to one's ego to be beaten twice. It's even worse to find that your brother can dispose of your conqueror so easily.' Depends what your brother does with that power over you; if he uses it to build you up or put you down.

'Most of the legends about Mitchum had a basis in fact, definitely.... The brawl with Primo Carnera at the Somosa Café – validated by many people I've spoken with. You have to appreciate guys back then who could live that large life and for a long time.'

Eddie Muller, President of the Film Noir Foundation

Mitchum brawling with Carnera – an Italian-born, some-time actor – doesn't sound like much, but before his career change Carnera was a professional boxer. Not just any only old boxer. At the time he was the biggest heavyweight champion in the history of the sport. In 1933, the 6' 6" champ killed an opponent with a punch.

Mitchum played a boxer in *Second Chance* (1953); a barnstorming prizefighter scared to use his right after killing a man in the ring. Out of the ring he's trademark Mitchum – square-shouldered suit and knitted tie.

Linda Darnell – another member of Howard Hughes' harem – played a moll hiding out in Mexico before having to testify against her gangster ex-lover. Jack Palance played the gangster's bodyguard who wants her for himself even though he's been sent to silence her. Mitchum sets out to seduce, unaware of the dangers she brings. Two tough guys, one broad. You can smell the trouble from here.

Filmed in Technicolor and 3-D, *Second Chance* was the last picture Mitchum made for RKO but not the last to be released. It's a pretty good, enjoyable thriller. Simple yet dynamic; high on action, low on suspense. During the film's finale, Mitchum, Darnell and Palance take a ride on the cable car 'Amor' to the Mountain of Contentment.

Disaster strikes and the cable car hangs from a snapping cable.

Mitchum and Palance have a life-or-death set-to. Mitchum socks him and Palance falls, silently, to his death. It became difficult to tell scripted hits from real ones.

'If one of the fighters varies his timing by a fraction, you can get a real wallop. This happened with Jack Palance. He miscounted during one of our fight routines and laid me flat for a full count. During other scenes, one boxer was so backward in his arithmetic I got knocked out three times.'

R M

The short-sleeve standing next to me keeps knocking me and even though it ain't my drinking arm it's still the kinda shit that gets me riled and *involved*. If he knocks me again we'll have to have words. I know I'm searching for Mitchum and I know if there was a bar brawl he would probably be near but I prefer a quieter life, if only I could keep my mouth shut. I'm aware this guy's local so I'm at a disadvantage already. I could just move my arm a few inches but, man, we're talkin' bar territory; man stuff. Other times it don't matter a jot. I turn to check out the size of him. He's got *big* fists. I guess I'll let it slide this time.

Lake Forest High, Felton

The old Felton Station

Take 21

It's vaguely pre-noon. Too late for breakfast. The sun is breaking through the window. I'm a few moons from forty and right now I feel it. How many more times am I gonna wake up with the only memory of the night before the club stamp on my hand? *Hmm*. I roll a joint. I figure I have to ask myself these questions but I'm in no rush to change my lifestyle.

I look in the mirror. I've got another split lip and a lump on my head. I don't remember getting into a fight and Bubba's was a friendly place. Musta been Mitchum again, the coward. Why can't he fight me in the daytime, or when I'm awake?

'I can't fight a shadow – I tried it: the competition's too tough.'
R M, *Holiday Affair*

I need a bus to Felton and onward to Jones Beach where Mitchum and his brother would hitch and spend the day fishing and catching crabs.

I don't know much about Delaware. I know it's the first state and that in its history it has been predominantly Dutch, Swedish, English and British. A cab could be a good thing if I can get a driver with local knowledge. The guy at City Cab promises he has just the man. He'll send Frank. Frank knows Felton and Felton knows Frank.

The cab arrives. I get in.

'How you doing Frank?'

'Well every day's a holiday.'

'That's a good attitude to have.'

'Well it may as well be. Wake up a little early, go to bed a little late. Apart from that, everything's the same.'

I ask Frank how far to Felton.

'About twenty miles.'

I explain what I need. He doesn't understand.

'*Why* do you wanna go to Felton?'

I give him the Mitchum spiel. In Bridgeport the boys had become increasingly uncontrollable so mother Mitchum decided to send them to join her family on their farm outside Felton.

'OK, well, where first?'

I tell him I want to visit the school. We pull away from the motel and head south.

The windows are open. The sun is warm but the wind is cold. It feels like winter.

'Round here used to be a nice quiet place. Only a few hundred thousand in the whole state. It was farmin' –

chickens. Gettin' far too populated. One of the most rapidly expanding states in the USA.'

Frank tells me people are moving here because there's no purchase tax, 'No seven percent or whatever it is.' This includes houses so to buy property here is substantially cheaper than in neighbouring states.

'But it's marshland, bein' mostly below sea level. An' we got a problem with termite infestations – bet the realtors don't tell purchasers *that*.'

Frank explains the money brought into the local economy through the presence of the USAF used to keep the place going. As for industry: 'Well Dover was home to Playtex girdles...'

I sing, 'You'll never get to heaven in a Playtex bra 'cos a Playtex bra won't stretch that far...'

Frank ignores me. 'And it was once known as the "Jello capital of the world..."'

How the mighty have fallen.

On the road to Felton we pass a sign for Barratt's Chapel. I gotta find where Mitchum got married. Some say it was in Dover. 'You know anything about that chapel, Frank?'

'That's one of the oldest – from 17-somethin'.'

I ask if there's a chapel in Rising Sun. He don't think so. He phones his wife. 'No, no chapel in Rising Sun.' She's certain.

Signs for Killens Pond, Frederica, Lloyd's Memorials. Frank points out where he used to live. 'I used to ride my skateboard six miles down to my grandfather's place to pick peppers. He'd plough the fields with a horse, and

327

barefoot, chewing snuff.'

'Pretty rural, huh?'

'It was rednecks and fast cars.'

We reach Felton. Just a smatter of buildings; a village on the side of the road. It's south of Dover and north of Murderkill River.

'Well, here we are,' Frank says, 'there's the school.'

Felton High School exists on the junction of 12 and 13, but no longer in name. Two schools, both small, combined so they could have a football team. This combined school is now called Lake Forest High and, even though it's been extended with architectural sympathy and has free-standing classrooms around it, at its heart is still the old red-brick, white-framed building and above its doors reads 'Felton High'. The name was a misnomer – kids of all ages attended.

'It used to be a pretty good basketball school...' says Frank. When Mitchum was here he was pretty useful at baseball but once he proved his worth he lost interest. I can't imagine he was much of a team-player.

'Now rather permanently domiciled on the Delaware farm, I continued to scribble essays, and while restricted by shyness and economy to the isolation of the farm, nursed my ego through participation in the literary and forensic projects of the school and church....'

R M, 1949 probation plea

Ah, school. Mitchum wasn't happy here. He was a troubled kid in an alien state, treated as an outsider. He walked

328

through those doors and regularly caused mischief but he was also commonly believed to be the most intelligent person there – of both pupils and staff. Often he would contradict his teachers and they could do little about it because he could argue his point and prove he was right. This was a boy who had been reading and writing since the age of three; who devoured books of his own free will; who gained a stepfather who told lurid tales of the wider world, sparking his imagination and desire to travel; who was already cynical enough to question what the world wanted him to believe. He became bored, dispirited, disaffected. He was a problem pupil. It was only a matter of time before he was expelled – and it happened more than once.

The Norwegian side of Mitchum's family, the Gundersons, had a history of producing performers – his grandfather's three sisters were all opera singers back home. Although his grandmother Petrine could only dream of appearing in the movies and his uncle Charles had any dreams of becoming a song-and-dance man beaten out of him at a young age, Mitchum and his siblings were fortunate their mother was a great advocate of artistic expression. All three children from the marriage of Ann and James went on to become professional performers and Robert's line of children and grandchildren produced several movie actors and performers who would achieve things in their own right. Sister Julie was first to hit the stage and became a successful dancer and cabaret performer from a young age, and both Robert and brother John became writers and Hollywood actors.

John became a well-respected character actor. He took

the professional name 'Mallory' to avoiding riding on his brother's rep, explaining later, 'It's definitely a problem being Robert Mitchum's brother. Psychologically, it's bad for me. Everyone expects me to look and act like him.' John reverted to his real name in the 1960s, once he established his own reputation. He appeared in over fifty movies – including several with his brother – and hundreds of TV shows including *Batman*, *Bewitched*, *Bonanza*, *Little House on the Prairie* and *The Waltons*.

According to Frank, Felton High – Lake Forest High – survived a tornado in the early sixties. 'We call things tornados but usually they're just small. This thing was big. It came 'cross the fields, hit the building opposite – sent it spinning to the other side of the highway. Demolished those buildings over there. Not *them*, but what *was* there.'

In school, Mitchum and his buddy Manuel Barque soon got reps as trouble-makers and young Bob found an enemy: the principal Mr Petrie. Bob wrote home to his mother in Connecticut that he was blamed for everything and anything that went on. 'Petrie is a coward... some day I am coming back and so help me I am going to ruin him as he ruined me....' Petrie might've been an ogre in Mitchum's eyes but rumour has it his wife was a dish.

The first time Mitchum was expelled it was for firing paperclips at a female teacher's nipples. With, according to his brother, 'unnerving accuracy'. The second time it was because someone left a fresh turd in a school-girl's swimming cap (or, depending which version you wish to believe, a teacher's hat). No one could say for certain who was responsible, but the accusatory finger pointed towards

Mitchum. He and his friends were taken to the principal's office for questioning. When the details of the 'crime' were outlined, Mitchum laughed – and wouldn't you? – but the others kept quiet. This was interpreted as a sign of guilt. He had nothing to lose – Petrie had already decided it was an act of Mitchum, so he may as well accept the blame. He was kicked out of school again.

But it didn't end there. On hearing of the events, Mitchum's uncle Willie stormed into the school. Brother John recalled the first he heard was his uncle's voice 'careening through the school like a tornado', insisting 'Bob didn't shit in no hat!' Willie had been a pro wrestler and was one tough cookie. He was out for blood. The football coach was called to throw him out of the building. Willie was looking forward to him trying. Wisely, they left before the police arrived. Mitchum would never return.

'I don't think I ever graduated. They gave me some sort of honorary graduation. I don't remember if it was from Haaren here in New York or from Felton High School down in Delaware... every other school claimed me, except the school I went to. Never heard of me. They erased me.'

R M

In 1976 the school invited Mitchum back to finally receive his diploma. He didn't return; didn't even reply. They sent him his diploma anyway. He probably stuffed it full of grass and smoked it.

We cruise past Lee's Market, its ice and cigarette machines, and across the rail tracks.

331

The line's at road level; easy to walk across or along. In this sense it's just another highway; a rare sidewalk. How much did this influence Mitchum? It ain't easy getting pulled out of your hometown to go live in some backwater shithole and he wanted out. Out *anywhere* – he didn't mind. Did he sit in school, looking out of the window, wishing he was on a train steaming by?

It was along this line Mitchum decided to escape the oppression and depression of rural Delaware. Dragging along brother John and Manuel Barque, he walked the line for twenty-five miles until their spirits broke. They called into a farmhouse. The sheriff was called. They were taken home. Their uncle cried, reiterating that he had promised on their father's grave the Mitchum boys 'Would not go hungry, never be without a roof over their heads, and would get an education,' exclaiming, 'and how do youse repay me? You run away!'

Their grandmother was left to carry out a superficial excuse for punishment, tentatively flicking a peach tree twig across their asses. John would recall, 'That "flogging" looms in our minds as the worst we've ever taken. "This hurts me more than it does you" was never more clearly defined than in our sainted grandmother's valiant attempt to "punish" us.'

'You're gonna try to fight a tornado with a peach-tree switch.'
Trevor Bardette in *Thunder Road*

The one-storey railway station still stands, vibrant red with yellow-painted wood; still holds the dynamic quality of a gateway to other worlds. These days it serves as something else. Frank thinks it might be a police station. I clamber out of the cab to take photographs.

We go down to the old sawmill. Frank used to play around here as a kid. It brings back memories.

'We used to have a street fair. We'd decorate our bikes with crêpe paper and baseball cards. Simple stuff. People want more these days.'

Flags are flying outside the town hall. It could pass for a house. Frank says it used to be a nursing home. Felton feels like the kind of town where you'd move to eke out your last days.

'Felton used to be the kinda place where everyone knew everyone else's affairs. Now it's being bought up by one family.'

The remains of a graveyard – only four stones remain, each with the name Simpson or Minner. No Mitchum, no Gunderson, no Tetrault, no Spence.

We drive back to the main street and the Methodist church. It's difficult to tell how old it is – it's been reclad. Two storeys, tall windows, wooden bell-tower, wooden cross above all except trees and the water tank on Walnut Street. The water tank and wooden cross – symbols at the heart of a rural American community.

Was it in this church Mitchum married his only wife? Possibly, but I'm not convinced; I still think they were wed four miles away in Rising Sun. So we head back north a little before turning east.

'What kind of place is Rising Sun?'

Frank pauses to think. 'A hole in the wall kinda place.'

We pass Canterbury Cemetery. Pointing west at a junction is a sign to Woodside.

Mitchum's grandfather Gustave bought Woodside Farm partly as investment and partly in hope it would provide his wife Petrine with so much to do she wouldn't have time to run away back to Norway. Gustave was a big man in shoulder and chest; a seaman who survived both shipwrecks and accusations of eating shipmates while lost at sea. Also living on the farm were Uncle Willie, his wife and kids.

Being sent away by his mother, to live in a different state with a more old-fashioned lifestyle and culture, must've been hard on young Bob. After all, under all the bad behaviour he was a sensitive kid. But being sent to the farm wasn't an act of maternal abandonment, although it's easy to imagine it appearing as such in the heart of a fatherless child. It was more about practicalities: this was the time of the Wall Street Crash and the beginnings of the great American Depression; to feed her family, his mother had to work and didn't have time to keep enough of an eye on two adventurous young boys in a dangerous, industrial city. If they moved to the farm they'd have fresh air, wholesome activities, less to lead them astray, she believed, and a tough uncle to bring them to heel. These 'wholesome' activities included getting expelled from school for the cack-in-a-hat incident, shooting a friend with a rifle and constantly having to prove themselves against the local boys who perceived Bob and John as 'city dudes'. They were outsiders and not allowed to forget it and soon tagged as 'them ornery Mitchum boys'.

The family were poor but being from Bridgeport the brothers were seen by their peers as city-slickers. John would write that Delaware taught them about 'bigotry and red-neck perverseness'.

'[We were] *always put in a position of proving ourselves. The trick was to push the challenger's nose to the back of his brain without giving him a cerebral hemorrhage.'*

R M

Uncle Willie was a tough disciplinarian towards his own children but because he had sworn never to harm Jimmy's kids resentment built within the home towards the Mitchum boys who continued to get away with everything.

The boys' behaviour didn't improve when their mother joined them at the farm. In 1927 she arrived in Delaware with the new man in her life and announced they were married.

The Major was a journalist on the *Bridgeport Post*. The boys had met him before – it was the Major who put Mitchum's poetry into print so he had already exerted a huge influence on young Bob's life. Mother Mitchum had kept the depth of their involvement secret. The boys immediately developed a sense of resentment towards this new family member; this newly imposed father figure.

Considering her disastrous relationship with Clancy, his mother might be expected to stay forever clear of journalists but the Major was different.

Hugh Cunningham Morris was from Land's End and was a man of great stories of land, sea and air. Stories which ranged from his time as 'St Elmo the Great' – circus bareback rider in Australia – to heroics in the army, navy, air force *and* as a spy.

According to his stories, he took part in both the Boer War and World War I, serving in Europe and Africa; was a qualified seaman with captain's papers; was chummy with Winston Churchill (and carried in his wallet an IOU he claimed was signed by Winny himself). He first served as a British spy in Belgium. Wounded by machine-gun fire he managed to make his way behind German lines. Once there he established himself as a shoe-shine and found himself cleaning the Red Baron's boots. Baron von Richtofen recognised Morris but, both being gentlemen, he refused to give him away. Morris then escaped back to Blighty hidden in a wicker basker on the back of a donkey. Thank god for the gentleman's code, eh?

Back home, he came up with the idea of using observation balloons to detect submarines before joining the Camel Corps in Africa, where his mount had its head blown off by a Bedouin gun. The Major watched the rest of the battle trapped beneath the headless corpse of a camel. Well, we've all been there. Then he joined the RAF but was shot down over North Africa, getting his stomach blown away in the process – a medic had to push his remaining intestines back in. After the war, Morris emigrated to Canada and then to the States, again serving as a spy for the British.

Hmm. Well if you're gonna bullshit, bullshit big. In today's climate of shallowness, cynicism and a high expectation of bullshit it's easy to sneer and dismiss these stories, and it's easy to see how Mitchum's taste for the tall tale could've developed early under the Major's influence, but there was evidence to support some of his claims – medals, photographs of him on a camel or climbing out of a biplane or on a boat off Australia... and the man was full of shrapnel – so to what extent the Major 'enhanced' these stories, as Mitchum would later do with his, is difficult to gauge.

Either way, there's enough evidence to prove the new stepfather was a 'man's man' in a way that seems to have completely vanished: charming, dapper, intelligent, entertaining, funny, non-threatening to others, yet with a war record to shame modern meat-headed marine or brutal bombadier.

Brother John described him as 'A totally fearless, indomitable man with a tremendous personality – and not a nerve in his entire body.' But for all the tales of derring-do the young Mitchum boys didn't want the man in their family – he was *not* their daddy. Not that they could recall much of their real father, even with Bob's photographic memory, and John wasn't even born when Jimmy died, but that didn't matter – they knew who *wasn't* their pappy.

'We kids didn't give this one much of a break for a long time. He had a box full of medals from World War I, photos of himself on camels in Egypt, climbing out of old biplanes in France, saluting the quarterdeck on wind-jammers in Australia. When we were very small we couldn't understand that he was full of shrapnel and couldn't work hard enough to keep us all together as a family unit. He was a very

interesting man, but I couldn't see it at first.'

R M

The Major was a resourceful man and figured out other ways to make ends meet.

'We were really hard up in the Depression. One day when we were living in Delaware he [the Major] *scrounged fifteen cents together and walked into Dover, and got into a poker game. He came home with forty dollars.'*

John Mitchum

On a fishing trip with some friends, Mitchum took the Major's gun and by shooting close to the fish so as to stun them, was having some success. Sat across from him, one of his friends was having less success with his own rifle so wanted to use Mitchum's. In one of those chance events which are always bound to happen, while passing the guns to each other Mitchum 'accidently' shot his buddy, the bullet going up his ass and out of his stomach. His buddy 'accidentally' ended up in hospital, on the critical list. And when he found out, Uncle Willie 'accidentally' came close to breaking his promise not to harm the boys.

I don't know: boys and their 'accidents'. I remember being 'accidentally' shot once. I remember being 'accidentally' stabbed too. And I remember both experiences 'accidentally' hurting like the devil was shafting me senseless.

According to John, this 'accident' ensured they would never shake off the 'ornery' tag they had acquired in

338

Delaware, and that the community's judgement that if the Mitchums were involved, it was certainly no accident, led to young Bob becoming even more introverted. Worse, they now believed them to be prejudiced because the boy who was shot was one of Delaware's rare Jews. In later years Robert would remain adamant it was an accident, 'It wasn't my fault... I was horrified, I thought if you were shot, you died.'

On another occasion Bob was trying to do the right thing. He had been sent to chop firewood so decided to chop down the biggest tree he could find but Uncle Willie had already sold it to the telegraph company as a future pole. He had to return the money to the telegraph company and once again bite his lip. Must've been pretty difficult for a violent man not to whop the living shit out of a continuously naughty kid.

We pass a combine trundling along. 'You see a lot of those in the summer,' says Frank, 'but the small farmer in the States is just about a thing of the past. It's all being eaten up by big business; it's all corporate now.' Which may explain why Frank, who lives in Woodside, has never heard of the possibly now-defunct Woodside Farm.

The road to Rising Sun is surrounded by flat green farmland but there's plenty of Christmas tree farms in the area and this is reflected in lane names like Douglas Fir Avenue. Frank points to a field: 'This is what Delaware *used* to be. It won't be long before it's all like *that*' – he points to a new housing development called Eagle's Nest.

We reach a crossroads. Frank says, 'Well, we're half way through town now – it's just an iddy-bitty place, there's not even a post office.' And he's right, it's even smaller than Felton. Dust flies in through the window and we're already heading back out of town.

It was while hanging out at Faulkner's Store that young brother John asked the men of Rising Sun just what, exactly, is 'poontang'? He received the reply, 'What's poontang? If the Lord made anything better'n poontang, he kept if for hisself.'

Another cemetery. Sure seems like a lot of dead people around here. Frank's wife was right: there is no church or chapel in Rising Sun, perhaps there never was. 'Are you sure it was in Rising Sun?' Frank asks.

'That's what the books say.'

'The history books may *say* he was married in Rising Sun but maybe it was here, in Camden.' And as soon as he finishes his sentence we're there. 'You see, these old towns were so close together they almost run into each other...'

'Much like the villages in the South Wales valleys...' I interrupt, 'the street starts in one village and ends in another'.

'Well, I can't comment on that.'

Jesus, an American who voices opinions on only subjects he knows about – I'm really getting to respect Frank, he's challenging my opinions of Americans which at times, to my shame, have been based on stereotypes and those who run away to New York to reinvent themselves.

It strikes me that the road we're travelling must be the one them 'ornery Mitchum boys' would rollerskate over, on their way to see Dorothy Spence.

Mitchum was already a drinker – since he was eight –

and Mary-Jane smoker; had already hobo'ed up and down the eastern seaboard; had already served time in jail. She was a good girl and younger. He was sixteen, she was fourteen – the age when, according to Mitchum, 'A girl falls for derelicts'. Because of her age, Mitchum would later claim, in jest, 'They busted me right out of the county'.

Dorothy would recall she didn't take to Robert at first; that he was a foul-mouthed smart-ass.

'He never thought of paying a compliment like the other boys. Instead, he teased. Yet every other boy I knew seemed dull by comparison.'

Dorothy Spence

'She was it, and that was that.'

R M

They married on 16 March 1940 and remained together until his death over fifty years later.

'Dorothy was everything to him when he was, gosh, fifteen or fourteen years; before he became anything and hopped trains to go out to California to make something of himself. He told her, "Stick with me and you'll be farting through silk," and they stayed together for over fifty years – and she was! So he kept his word, he was able to look in the mirror, he did what he said he was going to do.'

Bentley Mitchum

In 1973 daughter Trina told Rolling Stone magazine, 'My

mother's a great lady. Don't ask me how she puts up with Dad... she's stood by him through everything and I guess she's put up with a lot and suffered a lot, but she keeps on going. She's a beautiful lady, very stable, very steadfast... she's a Taurus, she just hangs in there.'

'Sure there were rough times. Sometimes the women would elbow me out of the way to get to Bob. But... whatever he does, he always comes back.'

Dorothy Mitchum

'Mitchum was born the kind of man that does not have to seek women because they come to him.'

Unknown newspaper columnist

'Were that true. They come to me with their troubles. I absorb some of them. Cheer 'em up a little.... My wife rather frowns on any dalliance with anyone else.'

R M

'It gave rise to a ceaseless suspicion in my poor wife. I live with it.'

R M

In the eighties Mitchum claimed, wryly, that their success as a couple was down to a 'lack of imagination' and on another occasion said, almost apologetically, 'I suppose with us it's a mutual forbearance... I think we have each continued to believe the other will do better tomorrow'.

Dick Cavett: *'What is the secret of a thirty-year marriage?'*
R M: *'Deviousness, I should think.'*

That Mitchum loved her deeply is unquestionable. But it didn't stop him putting it about. Mitchum liked women and women liked him; he never went short of 'poontang'. It couldn't have been easy for Dorothy but whomever he slept with, he was her man; she was his woman, and always would be.

'I knew Bob's faults. I don't care. When there is love, who needs perfection?'

Dorothy Mitchum

'That's a wife's profession: forgiving a husband.'

R M, *The Lusty Men*

> *With my shamed sad hope*
> *in my tell-tale eyes*
> *and the fleet fears trapped*
> *within my breast*
> *there is no last mercy*
> *there are no last lies*
> *for my sweet dumb dreaming*
> *is confessed.*

R M, untitled poem to Dorothy

'We've had our moments and she's come through a lot. But I guess after all the years we've been together she knows

what to expect and how to handle me. Not as though there
has been anyone else in my life except Dorothy. There's not
one of 'em – and I've met the best of 'em – worth lighting a
candle for, alongside her.'

R M

Aware of how he might seem to them, when Mitchum was first introduced to Dorothy's parents as a gangly youth with a troublesome reputation and a manky leg caused by the shackles he wore on the Georgia chain-gang, she lied about his injuries.

'[Bob] *wanted to make it sound classier than that for my mother, so I told her that he hurt his leg jumping off a freight train. That didn't go over too well, either.'*

Dorothy Mitchum

In some circles a hobo may have better standing than a felon but in theirs there was little difference. Her people still weren't keen on the match.

We pull up outside the old Methodist church, only now it's home to the Morning Star Institutional Church of God in Christ, Inc. Comes to something when a church is an 'Inc'. It was Methodist Episcopalian from 1856 until 1967. I can't help but agree with Frank; I reckon this is where they got married.

According to Mitchum (and he should know) they were married by 'Ignatius Cooper, Justice of the Peace at large, or something like that, Esquire. They have a square system. It said, "licenses – dogs, hunting, marriage: $2".

Solid. And that was it. We got married in the kitchen in the odor of burnt cabbage.'

We drive past Caesar Rodney High School where both Dorothy and John were pupils. 'I went there too,' says Frank.

Caesar Rodney is Delaware's great American hero. He was born (and died) in nearby Jones Neck. He was a farmer, lawyer, Sheriff of Kent County, militia major general, congressman, senator, President of Delaware during the revolution and signer of the Declaration of Independence. His father died when he was young.

In the eighteenth century the people of Delaware were split between those who wanted reconcilation with Britain and those who wanted independence. The latter – many of whom were originally from the British Celtic provinces – got their way, but the split created great animosity within the state.

Rodney had face cancer and asthma. He's famous for getting saddle-sore. Although warned by his doctor it might kill him, one night in 1776 he rode eighty miles through a thunderstorm to take part in a vote on whether Delaware should join the other states in favour of independence. He survived the ride and his vote was the decider. Independence won out.

'I think they made Delaware the First State jus' 'cos Rodney had cancer,' says Frank.

Ah, the sympathy vote. Rodney's condition was such he wore a scarf across his face to hide his cancerous disfigurement. He never married.

As President of Delaware, Rodney was responsible for

defending the state against the British military and keeping down local loyalist forces who would march on Dover. He would defeat the loyalists – many of whom were to leave the state rather than accept the outcome – and the Delaware Militia would go on to serve in the battles of Long Island; Monmouth; and Camden, South Carolina.

We head back up 13 to Dover.

'So where you headin' after here?'

'I ain't too sure. I got a woman in New York so I may go back there but I should really crack on and get down South. Exactly where South, I ain't decided yet.'

Frank warns me it'll soon be hurricane season in the South.

'If it comes, it comes,' I say.

'Well I'm jus' givin' you an early warnin'. If you're close to the coast: get away from it. The further inland the better. But you'll like it down there. It's the oldest part of the States, I reckon. And they're more laid back. They talk slow and they love to talk to you, but you better have all day to listen. I don't know what you like to eat but down there's good eatin'. Friendly people, very racial. They're good ole boys all right. Just stay away from the local authorities as best you can. When you get into the small towns: their brother is the sheriff, their uncle is the judge, their sister will be running your hotel. You think we got hick towns here, you just wait 'til you get down there.'

'You all kinda friendly, ain't you. A nice, tight, little corporation.'

R M, *Cape Fear*

'Like I said, when you get down South it's a whole different world but don't go letting your imagination run wild. They're good people, providing you don't go causing any trouble.'

'I've no intention of doing that, Frank.'

'No. Didn' think you would.'

We're interrupted by Frank's phone. It hasn't stopped ringing since we left the motel; it's red-hot with people wanting to know what he's doing driving some foreign guy around Felton and Rising Sun.

'We're lookin' for Robert Mitchum,' he tells them. From the following silence I guess they don't understand.

We stop at an ATM so I can pay the fare and give Frank a tip for sharing his knowledge. He drops me back at the Howard Johnson. We shake hands and I take his photo. 'See you again,' he says, 'good huntin'.'

I forgot to go to Jones Beach.

Around the bend
The quiet pool
Where waters gather
Deep and cool and gentle,
Marks
The melody
And echoes
Softly then
Its tune.
Mark then
How the stone
Is ever adding

Harmony –
Gentle –
Pleasant –
Mark it there
Forever.
Softened voice
To buff the swirls –

R M, extract from *To Jones*

The poem *To Jones* was not written for Dover but to mark the twenty-first birthday of his friend Elmer Ellsworth Jones. Jones was a drinking, fighting, womanising no-good hound. He fitted right in with the brothers Mitchum. Bob and Jones were great friends and referred to themselves as the 'Two Goniffs' (Yiddish for 'swindler' or 'scoundrel').

I can't help feel Mitchum, in need of imagery and metaphor, was referring back to the St Jones River here in Delaware. It can't be proved but it's not an unimaginable leap of logic: his friend is called Jones, the river is called Jones, the poem for his friend whirls around a watery image. The rest of the poem has a comical feel, as can be expected of a young man attempting to express emotions of comradeship towards a male friend, but this extract taken from the heart of the poem shows Mitchum had a fine understanding of tempo, mood and image, even as a teenager.

I call into Arby's for a fish sandwich. The server tells me there'll be a four minute wait so asks, 'Do you want to order something else?'

Again I'm thrown. I guess here fast-food means no

wait at all. I sit and read the ketchup sachet – 'Tomato Concentrate Made From Red Ripe Tomatoes'. I should hope so. Tomato ketchup once got Mitchum into a lot of trouble. *Confidential Magazine* even more so. In 1955, in an article titled 'Robert Mitchum, The Nude Who Came to Dinner', they reported that Mitchum showed up worse for wear at a party thrown by *Night of the Hunter* director Charles Laughton and producer Paul Gregory. The magazine claimed Mitchum stripped off, climbed on the dinner table, covered himself in ketchup and declared, 'This is a masquerade party, isn't it? Well, I'm a hamburger!' and then he and an unnamed female were promptly thrown out. Mitchum was furious; so furious he decided to make a stand and became the first Hollywood star to challenge the gossip magazines and make them defend what they had written. He took them to court, and won. It was a huge financial risk and cost him a lot of money but others followed his lead and *Confidential* was put out of business a few years later.

He explained his stance: 'I think it's a case of fighting for your own good name.... People are inclined to believe what they read in magazines. They say, "If it's printed it must be true. And if it's not true, how come they are able to get away with it?" And that's the whole point. they should not be able to get away with it.'

A more likely version of events was told by Mitchum himself. He was having dinner with Laughton and Gregory and they were both lusting after him. So, in true Mitchum style, he whipped out his old fella, layed it on a plate, covered it in ketchup and asked, 'Which of you guys wants to eat this first?' By the time *Confidential* got wind of it, the story had mutated and they were eager to print it.

I go outside, wait for a gap in the traffic and run for it across four lanes. The totems on the other side advertise the 'Family Restaurant / established 1945 / Fresh Sea Scallops $8.95', the 'Dover Inn / Rooms / God Bless America / Microwave / Fridg' [*sic*]. I reach the median then dash another four. Headlights flashin' and horns a-tootin'. There's a psychic – 'Walk-Ins Welcome' – and a DVD store.

I knock on the psychic's door. I don't want my palm read, I don't want my karma cleansed, but I do wanna find Mitchum. The neon says 'Open' but the door won't budge. I knock again. Still no answer. Seems these psychics just don't wanna talk.

I go next door. The guy behind the counter asks if I'm looking for anything in particular. He's big, bald and sporting a beard.

'Yeh. You got any Robert Mitchum films?'

'Rob-ert Mitch-um,' he muses. He pulls the name up on his computer and goes through the titles. It takes a little time. I ask if he knew Mitchum lived nearby. He didn't. I tell him about the cack in a hat and getting kicked out of Felton High. 'That's beautiful,' he chuckles, 'but I can honestly say I have no Robert Mitchum titles in the store.'

Too bad. I check out a cheerleader calendar while he lets a guy into the back room marked 'Over 18s only'. Maybe Mitchum's in there.

I leave and run back across the street intent on returning to my motel. I'm tempted to call into the Swedish massage parlour – research reasons, only – but it's only open weekends. Guess it ain't the weekend yet. Wish I could remember what day it is.

Back at my motel there's a black balloon. Stock-still. Just a normal kid's balloon but I don't recall seeing a black one before. I stop and watch, expect it to float away, let loose from some crying kid's grasp. But it just sits about twenty foot above the entrance. It's not tied to anything but still it don't move. Mitchum is that you, you bag of hot air? What you trying to tell me, *dad*? Screw this, I'm going for a beer.

But I don't. Not yet. I've never been to K-Mart before.

The big K. I take a cart from the corral and go pay my first visit. Pump-action shotguns sit alongside shoe laces and bubble gum. I check out the cheap DVDs. There's plenty of John Wayne, Dean Martin, Laurel and Hardy, but I don't expect to find a Mitchum. But I do, of sorts. A copy of *Minesweeper* – a patriotic B-movie set in 1941 – shoved to the back. I buy a cheap bag of chips and some soda, go back to my hotel room for a film and a joint.

I'm waiting for my cab and it's running late. I've phoned three times and they promise it's on its way. *Hmm*. I wouldn't mind but I ain't confident the Greyhound will wait until its stated departure time before leaving.

I consider my checklist for Delaware:

1. Felton – *yep*
2. Rising Sun – *yep*
3. Woodside Farm – *pah*
4. Barque, Gunderson, Petrie, Tetrault, Spence – *pah*
5. Murderkill River, Jones Beach – *pah*

351

6. Felton High School – *yep*
7. Methodist chapels – *kinda*
8. Local press – *no reply*
9. Cinemas – *pah*
10. Historical societies – *one day.*

Limited success. Ah well, at least I've been here and left word I'm on his trail.

Dorothy's family remained in Delaware so Mitchum's link would continue long after he left. He returned in 1948 with his wife and kids because Dorothy was fed up with him and Hollywood. Mitchum returned west, alone – his wife fed up of his behaviour. He went back to Hollywood and got himself busted.

My bus arrives forty-five minutes late. I've forgotten where's it going. Dover, for a little town, you sure gave me a lot to think about.

Take 22

We enter Maryland and the early evening sun; pass road signs for Cross Keys, Canton, Havre de Grace, Little Gunpowder Falls and Winters Run; head down Johns Hopkins highway towards Baltimore – a city named after curry greed, in my world at least.

'The people of Baltimore are extremely kind-hearted, and no man need starve if he has the courage to express his wants. The women seem to be as beautiful as they are good, for I have never seen finer women than those of Baltimore, and a man would not be making the worst of life if he idled all day in a principal street, reading the face of beauty, and studying the grace of forms that pass him by.'

W H Davies, *Autobiography of a Super-Tramp*

We stop at the station. There's the usual run of Best Western, McD's, Sbarro, KFC. I take the opportunity to stock up on water and nicotine and to empty my guts. Wonder if I'll find a Mitchum poem.

'You can find them in the men's rooms in filling stations all over the country.'

R M, on his poems

The walls of the cubicle are covered in graffiti. The usual 'I like suck cock' and phone numbers. There's also a wider and more opinionated range: 'NY bitch', 'Never lose faith in God – he cares for you', 'the white man the devil the truth', 'niggers lurkin'. Whether the latter is fact, threat or boast is open to interpretation. Personally, I can't see danger advertising itself. I add my own; ask if anyone's seen Mitchum lately.

In 1959 the Mitchums moved to a 300-acre farm here in Maryland. Dorothy was sick of Hollywood again and wanted to come back east. He began to breed horses and renamed his production company Talbot Productions after the county they lived in. Belmont Farm gave them privacy from callers but because Mitchum was frequently away filming it left her with too much work to do. While he was in Vietnam she sold up and moved back to California.

Also, Mitchum spent eight years in a Baltimore penitentiary. At least he did in *Cape Fear*. Gregory Peck withholds evidence which would've seen Mitchum clear. Instead, he's sent up and spends his time studying the law and plotting.

'I burned for eight years.'

R M, *Cape Fear*

When he's released, Mitchum heads down South to catch up with Peck and seek his revenge. And, boy, did he catch up with him.

Peck: *'What do you want?'*
R M: *'Didn' remember me right off, did ya? Well, I guess I changed a little. Where I been, uh, if you* don't *change they're real disappointed. You haven't changed a bit and you know something, that's just the way I wanted it.'*

Cape Fear

'Cape Fear *was one of those things where I told them I'd prefer it if they got someone else. Meanwhile, I demonstrated that I knew more about the behavior of the functional criminal than anyone they can get... no-mother-way would they try someone else. After I agreed, the story was drawn through a suck-hole, you know: given the Hollywood treatment. There had to be a heavy and a hero. So they made a hero of a crooked lawyer who had committed God knows how many trifling felonies.'*

R M

I too am heading down South from Baltimore, seeking my own revenge and something else; something intangible and emotional. Freedom, release. Understanding and a clean mental slate. An uncontaminated future. Stability. My feet.

I splash water over my face. Gotta get out of the

mindset. Walk outside, take one last smoke, board the bus, settle into my seat, try and find comfort.

We head south on 95, across railway lines. Next stop: Richmond, VA. The mother state.

So this is Virginia, huh? More museums than any other state and having problems overcoming its glorious past. I'm told they don't like change here.

Richmond is the birthplace of Shirley MacLaine. Like Dorothy Mitchum, MacLaine is a Taurean. She claimed her parents made her 'an investigator, a revolutionary' – not bad things to be. Not easy things, but not bad either.

MacLaine is a believer in astrology. Mitchum and his family had their own mystical leanings: Robert and his sister claimed there was a psychic link between them and when the family moved out of their Bridgeport home, they left behind a Ouija board.

In 1939, Mitchum toured the States as writer, barker and driver for celebrity astrologer Carroll Righter. Righter would give the performance and Mitchum would push the horoscopes. He was pretty good at it. While touring the eastern seaboard the car they were in ran off the road and into a bayou. They didn't see it coming. Mitchum got out before the car sank to the bottom but went back to rescue his employer who was trapped, the water rapidly rising around him. Righter would tell anyone who'd listen that Mitchum saved his life. Mitchum kept quiet; refused to discuss it.

'One day I asked the stargazer what the stars had in store

for me. He said, "Plenty. According to my calculations you're going to buy a hotel." I never did get that hotel.'

R M

Having saved $2,300 Mitchum left Righter's employ to return to Dorothy and ask her to be his wife. Righter compared their horoscopes and advised against it.

'Don't marry her. There will be great conflict. Your horoscopes are completely incompatible.'

Carroll Righter

Mitchum went ahead and did exactly what he wanted. Dorothy accepted. The lion and the bull joined forces.

Henry Hull: *'You know what you remind me of? No offence meant, of course. You remind me of a hungry lion I once seen pacing a cage.'*
R M: *'I'm hiding out.'*
Henry Hull: *'You? From what?'*
R M: *'Questions. That I can't answer.'*

Man with the Gun

I find a diner and walk in. It is dark and busy – in both custom and décor. My glasses steam up. I take a booth under a large poster of Marilyn Monroe. Wait for my server. She approaches, shy and clumsy. I order burger and fries and beer, settle in and watch her. She is attractive but doesn't realize. Something beautiful shines out of her but her status in the diner is apparent, in her attitude and that of her colleagues. They are disappointed in her and she knows it. I am pleasant to her, respectful – I know what it's like to be presumed less than I am. She returns with my order. I ask her name. Let's call her Ginny.

George Cooper: *'What did you say your name was?'*
Gloria Grahame: *'Ginny, 'cos I'm from Virginia.'*

Crossfire

I ask if she's local, whether there's anywhere else open.

'There's a club down the alley might be open, but that's it tonight.'

'Can you give me directions?'

'Sure.'

She explains how it ain't gonna be easy to find. I explain I'll give it my best shot.

Customers up and leave. My server continues to get bad-mouthed by her colleagues. They look at her with mock incredulity; enjoy their superiority. But what they do not see, or will not admit to seeing, is that they are diner staff and probably always will be whereas my server, from the look in her eyes, from the air about her, is due to become a lot more. She approaches to tell me it'll soon be last call. I order a final beer. State, 'You want more, don't you.'

She looks at me, recognizes I mean no disrespect, sighs, 'Yeh,' but tries not to weigh it with any tone that might reveal emotion.

She is Cinderella, the light under a bushel, a diamond in the raw. Who knows who or what she will become but the harsh treatment is getting to her, wearing her down, and she's in danger of believing its message for ever. I want to tell her how fantastic she is. How, even though I don't know her, it's plain to anyone who hasn't got shit in their eyes that's she is so much more than how people frame her.

When she returns with my beer I add, 'And you will – get more.'

She pauses for the merest fraction of time before turning to fetch a new order. I stub out my cigarette and down the beer. Best I'm soon gone – I'm interfering.

The blonde at the register is physically attractive but I have witnessed how she treats her colleague. She tries to be nice to me, charming. I ain't buying it. I tell her the service was excellent – it wasn't but no matter, there's an imbalance in these people's perception of Ginny which needs to be addressed.

Immediately, she smiles, 'Why, thank you!'

'Really. The food was OK but the service made up for it.'

She checks me ticket. 'You get served by Ginny?'

'Yep.'

'And it was good, huh?'

'No, not good; excellent. I've been through seven states to get here and the young woman who served me is as friendly and efficient as I've met.'

She rings my money through the register but doesn't believe me. 'Ginny, huh?'

'Yep.'

'So how much you giving your server?'

I give a good tip – not extravagant, but enough to send a message.

Like a dog perplexed by the tone of a human voice, she flips her head to one side. 'Ooooooooooo-Kay.'

You better believe, sister.

Mitchum was well known in the business for standing up for the crew and fellow cast members. If he, the star, got coffee and donuts on set, then everyone got coffee and donuts on set; if a dispute between him and the studio or director would result in the crew losing work, Mitchum swallowed his pride to protect their livelihoods; if a crew member was fired, Mitchum withdrew his labour; when crew members were injured during the filming of *Heaven Knows, Mr Allison*, Mitchum was the only cast member to visit them in hospital. For me, it is this which made Robert Charles Durman Mitchum a big man. Not the drinking, the womanizing, the fighting, the mouthing, the larger-than-life presence, but the willingness to sacrifice his own easy life and use his power to stand up for others against the powerful, the bullies, the egoists and money-men.

Out of respect and gratitude, the set builders and craftsmen at RKO built Mitchum a prototype mobile home on the back of a pick-up. The vehicle slept four and had all the available mod-cons. Mitchum was moved. The vehicle became his home on numerous hunting trips. He named it the 'Oochee-Papa-Poontang Wagon'.

'Bob wanted coffee on the set and they would bring coffee for him. And he says, "No, I want it for everybody." They said, "Well everybody's not going to have it..." Bob would get in his car and say, "I'm going to go for a cup of coffee..." two hours later he would come back. He didn't say, "I demand

*you have coffee on the set for everybody" but every morning
for three or four days he would do this. They finally got the
message and they had coffee on the set for everybody.'*

Anthony Caruso, co-star in *His Kind of Woman*

While filming *Macao*, the story goes that Mitchum took
director Joseph von Sternberg to one side and warned him,
'Don't make assholes out of the electricians and grips.'
Another time, director Henry Hathaway informed the
cast, 'I shout at actors, but it doesn't mean anything. The
next morning I've forgotten it.' Mitchum felt the need to
set boundaries on how they were to be treated. He replied,
'I punch people who shout at me, but it doesn't mean
anything. The next morning I've forgotten it.' Hathaway
took it on board.

As usual with tales of Mitchum, that's only one
version. Another, told by Mitchum himself, claims it was
Dale Robertson who put the director straight.

When filming *Angel Face* Mitchum had reason to stand
up for his co-star Jean Simmons.

*'In one scene Bob was supposed to smack Jean and she told
the really gentle Mitchum to really let go. Otto [Preminger]
insisted on take after take and poor Jean's cheek was getting
redder and redder. As Otto insisted on yet another take,
Mitchum turned to him and let him have one right across the
face. "Would you like another, Otto?" he said. Otto quickly
agreed to print the last take.'*

Stewart Grainger

While filming *One Minute to Zero* in 1951 Mitchum attempted to protect fellow actor Charlie McGraw from a pasting in the Red Fox bar, Colorado Springs. The aggressor was a drunken soldier called Bernie Reynolds. Reynolds was no ordinary soldier; he was a heavyweight prizefighter ranked in the world's top ten with nineteen KO's under his belt. Mitchum put him on his ass then cracked his head against a piano stool, giving the boxer concussion. Not only did Mitchum protect his colleague but he also stepped in to try, unsuccessfully, to protect Reynolds from army punishment.

'They were going to court-martial him and I really tried to help... the brig or the street were his only two options.'

R M

Mitchum didn't see his co-stars as threats to his status or importance; their success didn't undermine him. He appeared alongside some of the world's most talented and beautiful actresses. Often they were intimidated at first but grew to love him. Many never stopped claiming him as not only one of the best – and most supportive – actors they'd ever worked with, but one of the most sensitive and adorable men.

'This sort of macho thing about him being so tough – it's partly true, but underneath all that there's a gentleness you would never expect....'

Deborah Kerr

A Mitchum movie was usually followed by rumours of him sleeping with his co-star – the loudest regarding Ava Gardner, Shirley MacLaine and Sarah Miles. This was normal for Hollywood and encouraged by the studios.

'The public is secretly convinced that the leading man is always having an affair with his leading lady. And that's why they go to the theater – in the hope of catching them at it.'

Howard Hughes to R M

Mitchum starred opposite Oscar® winners and nominees Barbara Bel Geddes, Greer Garson, Gloria Grahame, Susan Heywood, Kim Hunter, Deborah Kerr, Janet Leigh, Myrna Loy, Shirley MacLaine, Jean Simmons, Shelley Winters, Teresa Wright and Loretta Young. Not to mention working with Sally Field, Olivia de Havilland, Katherine Hepburn, Anjelica Huston and Elizabeth Taylor; or appearing in the same films as Jessica Lange and Sharon Stone; or those beautiful, famous and/or talented actresses overlooked by the Academy: Lauren Bacall, Bo Derek, Angie Dickinson, Mia Farrow, Ava Gardner, Jane Greer, Rita Hayworth, Glynis Johns, Natassja Kinski, Julie London, Ali McGraw, Sarah Miles, Marilyn Monroe, Charlotte Rampling, Jane Russell, Theresa Russell, Jane Seymour and Victoria Tennant.

Quite how many of his co-stars Mitchum slept with is anyone's guess. With clinching and clutching a part of the job, and with these women as intimate colleagues, no wonder he kept going back to work.

Howard Hughes expected sex from the actresses he hired. Many gave him their bodies but never got to appear on screen. Hughes wanted Jean Simmons but she wasn't interested. What he lacked in morals he made up for in determination. He bought her contract from Rank and made it clear: no sex, no film roles. To get out of the situation she threatened legal action. A deal was struck: make three movies for RKO – within a specific time frame – and she could go. These included *She Couldn't Say No* and *Angel Face*, both opposite Mitchum.

Understandably Simmons felt resentful. Hughes was obsessed with her hair so, grasping what power was available to her, she cut most of it off. Hughes was furious and made her wear custom-made wigs.

Time was running out. Simmons would soon be free to leave RKO having made only two of the three movies. Hughes forged ahead and the film was made in eighteen days. After that, Simmons was free to go her own way. Meanwhile, Mitchum was cruising towards the end of his own contract.

In *Angel Face*, as in *Where Danger Lives*, Mitchum turns his back on a good girl to do the run-around with a conniving femme fatale. He plays an ex-racing driver turned ambulance driver – a 'dead-body jockey'; a working man who's tried doing the right things but still can't keep away from risk. That risk is a scheming, rich brunette played by Simmons; the spoiled daughter of a novelist, who hates her stepmother. After a foiled attempt to kill said stepmother, Simmons follows ambulance-driving Mitchum to a diner and talks him into taking her dancing. The next day she meets Mitchum's girl (Mona Freeman) with the sole intention of ensuring she knows he was with her the previous night, and not at home alone. Mitchum does himself no favours by continuing with the lie, telling good-girl Freeman, 'I would've been lousy company last night, honey. Ten minutes after I left Harry's I was in the sack.'

Freeman, having already met Simmons, replies, 'I can believe that.'

Simmons plots to kill her stepmother, succeeds, but accidentally also kills the father she adores. Mitchum gets implicated and railroaded into marriage. They both face the court but are found not guilty. Mitchum tries to escape his new wife but this gets him deeper involved in her scheming. Yes, Mitchum gets the woman. But he also gets all the trouble going. And then he ends up with nothing. Not even a pulse. Yet more cinematic evidence that, for the post-war male, the independent woman spelled G-R-I-E-F. The messages behind so many femme fatales was clear: good girls work, bad girls don't have to; the powerful, independent woman is bad and dangerous.

Angel Face received mixed reviews, some of which were scathing, but time has been kind to it. French director Jean Luke Goddard named it in his top ten greatest American talkies and these days it's seen as one of the greatest moments in film noir.

I follow the trail laid down by my server. Walk up and down streets, find an alley, go down it, my street-smarts on alert. I see no bar. I walk back around the block, try figure out if there's another alley. By the library there's some guy sat on a stoop with his dog.

''Scuse me, you know where the ODC is?'

'Sure, you a member?'

'No.'

'Best I walk you then.'

'Yeh?'

'Sure. My dog could do with a walk and you'll need me to get in. If it's open.'

That 'if' sounds too big to me.

We stroll around the block; past the big, period houses with their red brick and white wood, pillars and balustrades, and into a dingy parking lot.

'We have to go round the back,' he says and he leads me to a steel door. It's shut. He knocks but there's no answer. I look around. It's dark, cramped and there's a lot of crap piled in the corners. I'm aware I've just allowed a stranger to lead me down a blind alley; into a restricted space with only one route in or out; I'm aware of potential dangers but my instincts assure me all is well. No point presuming a person's a threat unless evidence pricks the senses, besides, he appears to love his dog so any tricky business and that'll be his Achilles' heel – I'll damage the dog and scarper.

'I thought it'd be closed. On the weekends it's lively – lots of women....' And as an afterthought adds, 'What day is it?'

I have no idea, but I know it's not a weekend.

Me, he and the dog walk back to where we met. He asks, 'So do you wanna drink?'

'Sure.'

'Well come up to my place. We can have a drink there.'
We go up to his place, pausing only while his dog relieves himself on the lobby carpet. He turns on the light to reveal a fair apartment. The stars and stripes is laid out across the back of the sofa and there's a baby's playpen for the dog. The dog is still a pup.

'What do you drink?'

'What you got?'

He pours two big glasses of Jim Beam and we settle down to smoke. We don't know each other's names but we talk freely.

'I been in the penitentiary,' he says, trying neither to impress, scare, nor apologise for it. I don't ask for what – I feel no danger and he's showing me hospitality. Besides, where else am I gonna get a drink and friendly conversation at three in a weekday Richmond morning?

He asks me what I'm doing here. I tell him about Mitchum.

'But why don't you just sit at home and write it?'

I have to think about that. I drink my Beam, light another cigarette. Exhale, slowly.

'Because... I need to see for myself.'

It hangs for a few moments.

'When you set off looking for someone else,' he says, 'you often get to find yourself. And their stories, well, you find they're very similar to your own. You better think about that and be careful what you look for.'

He doesn't have to tell me twice.

He refills my glass, tells me he's moved around a lot. I've done my fair share.

'How old are you?' he asks.

'Thirty-seven.'

'I'm fifty-four. I served in Vietnam. I've been stabbed, shot three times. I've killed people. I don't have tattoos or any of that shit but I don't get messed with. After Vietnam, what they gonna do to me?'

Mitchum went to Vietnam in 1966 and '67, going along on 150 missions. Approached by the US State Department, he volunteered to go as a morale booster and observer, spending time with the green berets and special forces. He'd arrive by chopper with bottles of brandy in each hand, troops asking, 'Why did you come here?'

'To get out of the house,' he replied. It was a standard, glib, Mitchum response which he usually pulled out when asked why he appeared in second-, third- or fourth-rate movies.

When he asked where the frontline was, they told him, 'You're standing on it'. They advised him to swap his red shirt for a green one.

Soon as Mitchum got back home, he'd be hot on the phone calling moms and wives, having promised to pass on messages of love and confirmation of continued existence. This is as close to the official, organised battle ground as Mitchum got. He had his own war to fight.

'Should we be in Vietnam? It's like cancer. Are we for it or against? We are in there, aren't we? It's a fact of our lives. So are unrest, disassociation from society, rebellion, propaganda on all sides.'

R M

We empty the bottle and fill up the ashtray.

'People say to me, "you walk your dog at two o'clock in the morning?" like I'm risking my life, but they don't scare me. Fear is all in the mind and it stops you from living. Fear will kill you. I've met some bad people, some BAD people, but they can't mess with me because I'm not scared of them; I'm not scared of dying.... I was robbed by three guys with knives. All I had was eleven dollars. I told them, "You can stab me if you want, you can kill me, but if you really need eleven dollars I would've given it to you." I asked if they needed eleven dollars – they said they did. So I gave them the money but I wasn't scared of them. A week later I run into one of the guys on his own. I said, "You owe me eleven dollars." He didn't understand. I reminded him, "You were with your buddies in the alley, you can give me back my eleven dollars or I can split your head right open." He said, "I think I might have eleven dollars" and pulled out a twenty. I took it and told him, "Next time you see me in the alley, I owe you change." Haven't seen him since.'

I chuckle and drink to his thinking.

He walks me back to my hotel. I don't need an escort but I welcome the company. We go past the library. I say, 'America seems to do libraries well.'

'Yep, libraries and churches.'

'Seems to be a lot of them.'

'A hell of a lot of churches.... It's good to talk to somebody normal.'

I know what he means. 'We're all fucking lunatics.'

'Amen to that.'

369

I thank him for his kindness and companionship.

He calls after me, 'Hey, you got a bar in that hotel?'

Sadly not, man, sadly not. I push open the door and he slopes back into the night. A decent man, walking the shadows.

'Came falling in at three o'clock in the morning, fell heavily on my bed of pain.'

R M

I wake. A miracle in itself. I can't say I've slept well but at least I slept.

Somebody recommended I go down to the James River but I don't have much time. I'm heading to Roanoke, up in the Blue Ridge Mountains and close to West Virginia. Ever since I was a kid I wanted to go see the mountains – because of the song I first heard performed by Laurel and Hardy. It had slipped onto my subconscious life-list and now I'm so close it seems dumb to not go see them for myself. Besides, Mitchum hobo'd through them on his way to somewhere, anywhere, everywhere and on.

Everybody:

'In... the... Blue Ridge Mountains of Virginia
On the Trail of the Lonesome Pine...'

Sitting in my cab, I consider the final conversation of the night. How, once you've seen how dark things can get, there's really nothing left to be afraid of.

We stop at lights. It's cold but the windows are open.

370

I can hear birdsong coming from Catherine Lane – joy to my ears, seems I haven't heard birdsong in a long, long time. There's a guy, about my age, hat and glasses, stood on the side of the road holding a sign saying, 'Stranded Please Help'. Man, I've been there. So has Mitchum. You'll get your ride – it may take a little time but don't worry about it.

We pass the Diamond – 'Home of the Richmond Braves' – and pull in to the depot. I tip the driver and drag out my case. On the floor of the ticket hall is a sizeable clump of brown hair from someone's weave – at least I hope it's a weave otherwise that's one painful grab. I trawl through the giftshop in an attempt to fill time. Consider buying my woman a 'Way-Cool' ring for 79c but fret in case the humour would be lost and she'd consider me a cheapskate. God-damit, she's met me – she knows I'm a cheapskate. I buy a postcard declaring, 'Virginia, Mother of Presidents' – the state having produced more US presidents than any other. Although, strictly speaking, Virginia is not a state but a commonwealth, along with Kentucky, Massachusetts and Pennsylvania.

The Carolina Trailways 12.05 arrives at door eighteen. I board it. Head away from False Cape and the Great Dismal Swamp in the east and towards Mount Hope in the west.

The route to Roanoke is a roundabout one. We pass through Goochland, Louisa, Fluvanna and Albemarle Counties; past settlements called Short Pump, Gum Spring and Shadwell, cross the Rivanna River and reach Charlottesville in under an hour.

371

All I see of towns like this are the bus stations; all I use is their air and the ashtrays.

The driver nudges past us as we smoke by the door, ''Scuse me fellas.' He starts her up. I guess he wants us back on board.

We climb up the land and to the south of Devil's Knob; head into Nelson County and get overtaken by a timber truck. It looks like rain and my cell-phone loses signal. I look out of the window: huddles of houses along a country road, front-yard dogs on chains; rusting tractors and pick-up trucks, disintegrating automobiles and farm machinery; the winding tracks up to isolated farms; the roll of the hills and the peaks of the mountains; trailer groupings between woods and forests; very few humans to be seen; the rain, the rain. Maybe the trees are a little taller, maybe it's not quite so green, maybe life is not so squeezed by the mountains... if it wasn't for Old Glory and Confederate flags flying from the eaves and the lack of sheep, I could be in Wales. The thought winds me. Virginia looks like my home country but the similarity seems not only visual – I feel something in the air. It is profoundly familiar. A resignation; an acceptance.

Here is Wales transposed. It makes me feel like I feel when I drive through the guts of my nation – both miserable and proud to my bones. Such a beautiful country but the weather affects the soul. The colours, the tones, the light and air, the living earth. My mood is mutated and controlled by surroundings. No longer am I a Welshman outside of Wales – so different to being a Welshman at home – but I have returned to my native mental state.

Although happy to be travelling; feeling neither isolated, alienated nor lonely, I feel a twinge of desire for my home, to be home now, just a second.

Lovingston.

Sweet Briar.

Monroe.

Vineyards; creeks and lakes and rivers; white, cream and green wood-slat houses; truckers riding Highway 210 and talking on their CB radios.

We pull into the cobbled station and the sun comes out at Lynchburg – 'City of the Seven Hills'. After the rural towns along the route it seems industrial here. It doesn't seem big enough but it has a university – Liberty – where they are 'Changing Things... One Life at a Time'. That's all we can do, one life at a time.

'We gotta go, man.'

The driver pulls me back down to land. I find no signs of Mitchum in town but I do catch up with the James River which has meandered along the same route as my thoughts.

I board the bus. It's 2.45pm. Lynchburg to Roanoke is about fifty miles. Out of the window I spot a diner called Mary-Jane's Café. Perhaps Mitchum is in there, smoking.

We shadow the rail-tracks. Black clouds return on the Salem road. The eagles and hawks swoop over Virginia as red kites do over Wales. Into the Blue Ridge and the outskirts of Roanoke. I meet my contact outside the bus depot on Campbell. Charlene is a woman of many depths and experiences, and is a frequent visitor to Wales. She offers me a tour of the town.

We pass the rail-lines, the farmers' market, the oldest

continuously used firehouse in the state, the local transvestite bar – all the big attractions. Charlene tells me I have to go see what the town's known for: 'When you come to Roanoke, you have to go see the star.'

In the 1930s the town felt it needed a tourist attraction so erected a big neon star overlooking the area. It declared itself 'The Star City of the South'. Still, today, it is the largest free-standing neon star in the world. I can't help but wonder how much competition there is.

We pass the old railway station, derelict and burned out. For a while, Roanoke was a rail town. It served as a major transportation hub, connecting routes and destinations and cultures since the railroad first arrived here in 1853. It's said the finest locomotives in the world were built here. The Norfolk & Western Line carried coal, lumber, tobacco, cotton; reefer wagons loaded with potatoes, apples, peaches, watermelons; passengers, who would alight and reside between trains within the mock-Tudor elegance of the Roanoke Hotel. The town bustled, it was an essential cog in the wheel; it was somewhere.

On coal and steel, industrial America was built. The discovery of the Pocahontas coal seam in 1881 created an urgent demand for railways to stretch into the mountains of south-west Virginia, West Virginia and Kentucky. In 1883 the first load of coal was transported by rail from Pocahontas Vein No.3. Another 100,000 tons would follow that same year. Within four years it would be nearer a million. By the 1940s it had reached over fifty-four million. Roanoke was necessary to the business of fuelling growth. Whether or not Mitchum stopped in Roanoke while hobo'ing is undocumented but it seems likely he would've found it a hot place to jump trains on his meandering trips south.

Although the railroad was a convenient, fast and wide-reaching method of travel, it wasn't without its dangers – for crew, passengers and hoboes.

'Train no.3 had left Roanoke en route for Huntington
These poor men did not know they were making their last run
Dad pulled his train, a smile on his face did beam
He didn't have to grumble, Frank sure kept him lots of steam
At eleven-fifty-two that day they'd just left Ingleside
An eastbound freight crushed them, they took their farewell
ride....'

Roy Harvey, from *The Wreck of the Virginian No.3*

'Often, when travelling through a hostile country, we rode
on the roof of a car so as not to give the brakesman an
opportunity of striking us off the bumpers.... It is nothing
unusual in some parts to find a man, always a stranger,
lying dead on the track, often cut in many pieces. At the
inquest they invariably bring in a verdict of accidental death,
but we know different.'

W H Davies, *Autobiography of a Super-Tramp*

These days Roanoke is no longer accessible via the line, the nearest station being almost forty miles away. Its rail heritage has been retired to the Virginia Museum of Transportation and the archives of the library on Jefferson. This here's a car town now, like just about all towns in the States.

'What's gonna happen to the station?' I ask.

'It'll get demolished. That whole site is gonna be a biomedical center.'

Of course it is. Roanoke's history is rail and manufacture, its present and future are health care.

'We've got the biggest gathering of hospitals and health facilities for two hundred miles, over three states.'

It makes no sense to me, but I guess it's a town likes to specialise.

We pass numerous examples of 1930s Sears and Roebuck pre-order houses and the 'Roanoke Box' – a perfectly square house containing three perfectly-square bedrooms. Women sit on their porches drinking red wine as the evening approaches. I ask if I can smoke in this state.

She laughs, 'This is where tobacco is grown! Getting asked not to smoke is, uh, very unlikely.'

In Mitchum's day, it wasn't only tobacco that grew through the South but marijuana, also.

'When I was a kid hoboing around America it grew on every countryside track and railway. All the bums I moved with rolled it – not much sense in picking up cigarette butts when this stuff grew free all over the South... it became the poor man's whiskey... then came the repeal of Prohibition. Marijuana became illegal in the 1930s. Naturally, the big boys moved in on it... and suddenly it became big business.'

R M

We cross the river which flows down to Roanoke Island in North Carolina; zigzag up the old switchback road to the star on Mill Mountain, so called because it was owned by Nathaniel Evans who established the town's first mill. Evans came here in 1715, from Wales. From what I've seen of the environment, I can understand why – the similarities have to be seen to be believed. It became a popular area for Welsh settlers and this is reflected in the county and town names that circle Roanoke – Craig, Pembroke, Newport, Montgomery, Cambria, Elliston, Floyd.

I mention how the area reminds me of Wales.

'No shit,' Charlene says. 'They're very friendly mountains, very old. They have nothing left to prove. The Snowdonia mountains in Wales are, well, they're the... the tip of the Blue Ridge Mountains – geologically speaking. We share the same range...'

So the belief that under the surface we're all the same refers also to mountains. Mountains, mountain men and men-mountains.

'Just as the coal in Virginia and Wales is similar – they come from the same seam.'

The same dirt, the same holes, the same raw material. The South is like Wales. Or Wales is like the South. The map lies about us both. We have been absorbed by the winning entity, our neighbour, and it doesn't seem likely either place will entirely cease its resentment. Part of a whole but a different place – mentally and physically – with an alternative sense of history, culture, strength. The North tells the world, 'This is America'; Englands tells the world, 'This is Britain'.

We pull up behind the star. It's just a big ole' neon light announcing the town but I greet it all friendly. I look down on the sprawl below.

Roanoke was a Native American hunting zone – the tribes had a peace treaty allowing all to hunt the plain free from attacks by their neighbours and the name 'Roanoke' meant 'trade goods' or 'barter'. No greenbacks for the natives. Then, when the settlers came down the Great Wagon Route, they called it Big Lick because the animals would come down from the Appalachian and Blue Ridge Mountains for a lick of salt.

We get back in and drive along the Blue Ridge Parkway, built during the Depression under orders of President Roosevelt to provide jobs.

We pull over to view Sharp Top – the M-shaped highest peak in the range. Mountains are often referred to as coloured. I've travelled from the Black Mountains of Wales to the Blue Mountains of New South Wales, Australia, but these... these Blue Ridge Mountains of Virginia, are truly deserving of their name – never have I seen such a spectrum of delicate blue and lilac shades. Pale yet vivid, bright, it's like they're plugged into the mains. Perhaps, at night when the light is down, the mountain blues power the star.

She asks if I've heard of the McCoy–Hatfield feud. I haven't.

'People think it was all over a pig,' she says, 'but it began earlier than that. Became one of the bloodiest feuds in American history.'

In 1863 the suspiciously named Devil Anse Hatfield formed a band of guerrillas which led raids on and thefts from the neighbouring McCoys, who did likewise in return.

In 1865, Asa Harmon McCoy was murdered. No one was prosecuted. Then, in 1878, Randolph McCoy accused Floyd Hatfield of stealing his pig. Hatfield won the court case thanks to testimony from Bill Staton. In 1880, Staton was murdered by Paris and Sam McCoy. Sam was tried and acquitted. Meanwhile Roseanna McCoy and Johnse Hatfield did the old Romeo and Juliet and broke family rules in their search for love. She left her family to go live with him. The following year, Roseanna returned home and Johnse was captured by the McCoys. Roseanna went to see Devil Anse and in doing so saved Johnse's life. In return, Johnse continued to work his way through the enemy clan by marrying Nancy McCoy. In 1882, Ellison Hatfield was killed by three of the McCoy boys who, in retribution, were ritually executed. Soon after, Jeff McCoy was also killed. Five years later, the Kentucky governor ordered the capture of the McCoys' murderers. On New Year's Day 1888 the McCoys were raided, two of their boys killed and their cabin burned to the ground. Roseanna died, without reaching thirty. 1889, the Hatfields were put on trial for the McCoy murders... and on it went. Jesus, I thought my family were bad. Memo to self: however tempting, don't steal Virginia ham.

'Family is what the South is about. When Southerners meet, we spend the first ten minutes working out how we're related.'

I know what she means but being part of a culture where you expect to be related to one another can lead to some very harsh judgements from outsiders. Knowing your cousins, kissing or otherwise, is oft viewed in a dim light in a cynical, self-conscious world.

On the other side of the Appalachian Mountains is West Virginia. This is where the 1955 release *Night of the Hunter* was set.

Based on a novel by West Virginian Davis Grubb, *Night of the Hunter* can be seen, in hindsight, as one of Mitchum's defining performances. He plays Preacher Powell – a murderous woman-hater hiding under the cloth of religion. These were still times when the hero-stars didn't dare tarnish their image by playing the immoral or evil enemy; didn't dare risk bringing their persona into question, but Mitchum's persona had already been questioned enough.

'You know what people say? "Where there's smoke, there's fire." Or, "He's got it in him, because he couldn't do that [otherwise]".'

R M

The image of Mitchum dressed in holy black, 'LOVE' and 'HATE' tattooed across his knuckles, a bible in one pocket and a switch-blade in the other, is iconic in American cinema.

Even though the children in the movie were scared of Mitchum's character, in reality they liked him, which is just as well as it was he who directed them.

'Charles was talking to the little boy and he says, "John, are you frightened of the preacher?" And the kid says, "No, not at all." And he says, "Well, I don't think you understand the character of the preacher in that case, and maybe not your

own character either." And the kid says, "Oh really, well maybe that's why I just won a couple of awards on Broadway!" And Laughton gets up and shouts, "Get that snot-nosed little brat out of here! I don't want to see him again!" So I ended up directing them.'

R M

Although the ending to *Night of the Hunter* is infuriatingly cloying, the film is a classic of American expressionist cinema. The softness of the final scenes was intended as an antidote to the evil of Mitchum's character, and to balance the black and white 'nightmarish Mother Goose tale'.

'After I was finished... Charles put in all those owls and pussycats, said he thought I was too horrific... so he reduced the effectiveness of the film, I think. It should've been right down the fucking line.'

R M, interviewed by Dick Lochte

There's good reason to agree with that.

As with so many classics, on its release *Night of the Hunter* was treated with indifference by both audience and critics. This disappointed Charles Laughton to such an extent that he would never direct another film. How ironic that if you mention Mitchum today, *Night of the Hunter* is often the first movie many film fans think of.

Take 23

At midnight Roanoke bus station is empty. Every town I stop at they ask how I'm travelling. When I tell them by Greyhound they warn me to be careful, watch my belongings and sleep with one eye open. I ain't worried.

Passengers gather. The bus arrives, our tickets are checked, we climb aboard. Cross the bridge just as a freight train passes beneath us, slow enough to jump. I'm travelling through the night on the first of four Greyhounds. The other passengers are just trying to get where they're going and a few hours shut-eye in the meantime. Watch my possessions? *P'shaw*, why? Where they gonna run to? They're sat on the same bus as me.

Roanoke, Salem, Elliston, Floyd.

The bus arrives at Wytheville at 1.45am – prompt to the minute. I alight and the driver hands me my case. He spots a colleague at the stop, 'Man, I ain't seen you in a hundred years!' They clap each other on the back and trade lines. There are no new passengers to board. The bus continues to Memphis.

The Greyhound office ain't no more than a shack, a hut at the side of a truck stop. McDonald's is closed, there's a gas station over the way but I can't be bothered to walk it. I know from my hitching days, gas stations never match the promise of their neon warmth. I ask if there's anywhere around here I can spend the next two hours before my bus arrives.

'Only here, sir.'

So here it is. The guy slinks behind his counter, gets absorbed in the internet. There's two vending machines, three benches, a door to a restroom. On one of the benches, a guy tries to sleep. He looks ragged, questionable. If you saw him walk towards you, you'd be cautious. That's the problem with carrying the air of a man trying to get somewhere, the travel film drawn across your face – you look a damn sight more shifty than you really are. He twists and turns, trying to find some comfort on a wobbly wooden bench. I sit. He gets up, goes to the restroom. Comes back, sits, shuffles, fidgets, gets back up and buys a drink from the machine. Goes outside for a cigarette, spits, flicks the butt, comes back in. Pulls things out and back into his case, looks around, clocks me, lies down, tries to get to sleep again, turns, sighs, sits up. He wants to sleep but his head won't let him. Nor will the bench, the brightness of the strip lights, the hum of the electrics.

A short woman in her fifties and a baggy grey leisure

suit enters the office. 'What time's the next bus?'

'To where, ma'am?'

'It doesn't matter!' she seems livid, 'what time's the next bus?'

The Greyhound guy is calm and polite, 'It's the 3.55 to South Carolina.'

'OK,' she snaps.

'You sure that's where you wanna go?'

I lean forward. That's my bus so I've got a vested interest in whether this bad-tempered hornet is heading my way.

'It doesn't matter where I wanna go – there's souls on that bus!'

Oh Christ, please don't try to convert us, save us, explain to us the error of our ways, how sin doesn't pay, or pray for our souls. Mine is split between a bar on the Upper West Side and a bed in Brooklyn. It's a little stained, soiled, singed around the edges but I'll do my best to survive myself without prayers or conversion. The door slams behind her. I'll give it a few minutes before I venture outside.

The frustrated snoozer speaks, 'God damn lunatic' and shakes his head.

'Yeh man,' I reply.

'You going to Charlotte?'

'Yes I am.'

'God damn, I've been waiting for that bus for nine hours.'

'Shit.'

'You got that. Man, I'm pissed. My boss dropped me

385

at the wrong bus station.'

'Where you heading?'

'Tampa, Florida. I rolled my truck down a cliff yesterday. Haven't had a vacation for two years. Told my boss I need a break. He offered to pay for my air ticket if I worked until Saturday. I said, "No man, I'm going TODAY." Wish I'd taken that fuckin' plane now. My leg's sore, my shoulder's all busted up, my head's cut open, I'm sore as all hell.'

'How did you roll your truck?'

'Well, I'm a logger. I was driving that truck down a grit track, hit some ice, swung the wheel so I would hit the bank. Thought I'd be OK. But the driver's wheel went over the edge. Thought that truck would never stop rolling. It went over and over. I ain't scared of dying but as that truck was tumbling I wasn't looking forward to getting hurt. Then when it stopped I was trapped under the steering wheel and all this stuff on top of me. And I could hear this trickling. Thought the gas tank was busted. Didn't realise I had landed in a creek. Managed to get out, after a while. Walked a mile and a half to get some help. They said, "Man, what's going on?" I said, "I just rolled the truck over a cliff." We went back down and they didn't believe I was in it. They said, "Man, you weren't in that truck." I said, "I was." They said, "If you'd been in that truck you'd be dead by now." I said, "No, if *your* pussy ass had been in it, *you'd* be dead." That's how they knew I was alright. So I told my boss, "I'm leaving today, I haven't had a vacation in two years." He said I can take as much time as I want but he wanted me to work 'til Saturday. He's a good boss but, hell, I know him. He wants me to work 'til Saturday 'cos he's hoping I'll forget or change my mind or something. Hell, I need a break. I ain't saying I got it harder than anyone else. Hell, a lot of people think everyone owes them something. Get off your ass and stop feeling sorry for yi'self.'

Nine hours alone with that tale to tell, I reckon I should just let him talk. Nothing harder than sitting on a tale to tell and no one to tell it to. I roll another cigarette and let him off-load. Shit, after nine hours sat in this hole I'd be talking to the cigarette butts.

'Going down to Tampa to see my family and my kids. That's if my ex will let me see 'em. But she's a bitch, so I ain't holding out on that one. And she went behind my back with a friend of mine then came crawling back, wanted to get back with me. Realised that green grass ain't so green after all. I said, "Fuck you, bitch." I guess that wasn't the reaction she was looking for. Stopped me seeing my kids. They got some fucked-up laws in Florida. I told her, "I ain't paying you nothing if I can't see my kids." She said, "I don't want ya fuckin' money!" I said, "Good! 'Cos you ain't gettin' it!" But I do miss ma kids. That's why I'm single. She's ruined me for every other woman. I ain't goin' back to that shit.'

He pauses to think. Spits accurately into the night.

'But I got two months vacation owing to me. My boss said I can take as long as I want. He asked me where I was going. I said, "Tampa; to see my kids." He knows how important they are to me. "And then maybe Vegas." He said, "Good! Go to Vegas! Gamble like shit." I said, "Why do you want me to do that?' he said, "'Cos then you'll be broke and you'll wanna come back to work." Like I say, he's a good boss but... shit....'

'You ever think about hitting New York?'

'Ah, I ain't too sure about New York...' he drifts through the city streets for a moment, 'besides, I'm tryna escape the cold, not go back to it. And I don't really enjoy those cities. I work in the forests and I like to be outside. If I'm not working, I go hunting. When you hunt you know what you eat. All that shit they put in store food – I reckon that's why people get so ill. All them chemicals to make the beast big. I don't have fear for anything but store food – living on that would scare me. Me, I like hunting but I don't think it's right to kill stuff if you ain't gonna eat it. But I would like to hunt some of them god damn tree-huggers, chaining themselves to my trees. You live in a house? Guess what it's made of. You read books? Guess what they're made of. You know, the forests are well organized – we log, we plant. It's under control.'

We stand and smoke, go back into the hut and talk, back outside to sit and smoke, watch the occasional passing traffic, the trucks lit up like rectangular Christmas trees.

Two buses show up at the same time. The first is heading north, to Boston; the second south, to Charlotte, Columbia, Jacksonville. The Greyhound guy emerges from his hut and busies himself getting cases off one and putting them on the other. The logger says, 'Shit, I just wanna get my case on the bus – I'm getting to know this place too well.' I'm with him on that. We board, knowing we'll have to wait again at Charlotte.

We arrive at 6am – a full half-hour ahead of schedule. Which ain't the good news it first appears to be – the bus don't continue on to Rock Hill until 7.30. So this is North Carolina. Wedged between Virginia and South Carolina it has been dubbed 'the valley of humility between two mountains of conceit', which says more about its neighbours than itself.

Mitchum once described himself and Ava Gardner as 'Native son and daughter of the Carolinas' – Gardner was from Brogden, North Carolina, while Mitchum had lived briefly in his father's home state of South Carolina. The two starred together in RKO's 1951 production *My Forbidden Past*, which was adapted from the best-selling novel *Carriage Entrance* by Polan Banks. It's set in turn-of-the-century N'Orleans. Gardner plays a Southern belle hiding a sordid family past, and Mitchum a Yankee doctor. Her family talks her out of marrying him, he leaves, returns with a wife, she is awarded an inheritance from a disgraced relative and wants him back. Ex-girlfriend and wife have a face-off. Her people want him to leave town. Ex-girlfriend gets cousin to seduce wife. Tragic accident. Yankee doctor dragged before the inquest. Ex-girlfriend reveals her secrets to all. Doctor's cleared of suspicion. Film ends suggesting they might, after all, share a future. Mitchum floats along through the middle of it not caring diddlysquat.

It wasn't long before the two stars began an affair. Knowing she was one of Hughes' regulars, Mitchum asked his boss whether he should sleep with her. Hughes replied, 'You might as well. Everyone'll think you're a fag if you don't.'

'You've been using your sex on me, I'd like to know why.'

R M to Ava Gardner, *My Forbidden Past*

Gardner's sexual appetite was legion and her pleasures came in many forms, not least water-sports. When it came to bedding Mitchum she wanted him all to herself, so telephoned his wife. According to legend Ava said to Dorothy, 'You've had him ten years, give someone else a chance.' What Dorothy said to Mitchum when he arrived home is anyone's guess.

I feel I should get something hot inside me, to wake me up. Maybe there's a woman here who feels the same way but I can't spot a single woman under sixty. And those over sixty all look done in, but then everyone does, me included. We've all been travelling and waiting all night. No one blows their nose – they snort the snot back up again.

The breakfast grill offers the expected burgers and pizza, as well as sausage, biscuits and gravy – a Southern staple of sausage meat and buttermilk bread. I choose not to eat.

I scan the street map on the wall: Lloyd Street, Flint Street, Johnson and Wales; Long Street, Shorter Avenue; Armour Drive, Atomic Place.

It was here that Mitchum filmed *Thunder Road* – in Asheville, north-west of Charlotte and within the Blue Ridge range.

Mitchum played a boot-legger, a transporter, a whiskey runner, one of those 'wild and reckless men' who drove moonshine through the backwoods of the South while the government revenue agents tried to catch up with them.

Not only did Mitchum play the lead but also it was the first movie from his newly formed production company DRM Productions; he wrote the story on which the screenplay was based; and he wrote the music for the song 'Whippoorwill' and the lyrics for the title song 'The Ballad of Thunder Road' – both of which are in the film (the latter reached number sixty-two in the American pop charts, and stayed in the top hundred for several months). 'Whippoorwill' had been with him for some time: Mitchum wrote it when he was only fourteen, for Dorothy, but it's based on an old Norwegian tune suggested by his mother.

Mitchum also gave his sixteen-year-old son Jim – the spit of a younger Bob – his movie debut as young brother Robin (Jim's real-life middle name).

'I remember when I was a little kid trailing my daddy... didn't have any noble notions then, of course – still don't... I don't remember anything dark and shameful... I was jus' a lil' ole boy following my daddy's footsteps up Sorrowful Mountain.'
R M in *Thunder Road*

Although he gave Jim his first break, Mitchum wasn't keen on any of his children following him into acting. Years later, when Jim had become an actor in his own right, Mitchum told the press, 'I wish I could tell you Jim is a famous surgeon or even a box-boy in a supermarket, but I can't.' Fathers: never satisfied.

Thunder Road set the pace for car-chase movies for years and is now seen by many as *the* boot-legger flick. It became hugely popular, especially in the South where it became a favourite at the drive-ins. What's weird is that it somehow appears older than it is – it would be easy to believe it was released in 1948, not 1958. Strictly speaking that's a criticism. But whereas the movie may've appeared out of date at the time the years have been kind to it and if you don't mind watching old-fashioned car chases where both car and driver are obviously sat in front of a studio backdrop rather than the screeching-the-streets norm of today's movies, then *Thunder Road* is a 'real stampeder'.

What's more important is the question of why it looked old in the first place. *Thunder Road* was Mitchum's pet project – never had he so much control over a movie, nor would he again. Perhaps it's the direction of old-hand Arthur Ripley. Perhaps the Mitchum of the late fifties was still caught, stylistically, behind the times. OK, so it was only three years since *Night of the Hunter*, six since *Angel Face*; but in the meantime he had made *Second Chance* in 3-D, *River of No Return* in CinemaScope and several 'modern' full-colour movies in unusual or exotic locations. And here he was churning out a noir-ish black and white, complete with cheapo driving scenes and inexperienced cast members, some of whom had never acted before.

Mitchum claimed *Thunder Road* only 'had a chance' of being a great movie and that was his own fault, admitting it could've been better.

'It wasn't great and I'm sorry about that. It was my design. My shots.'

R M

392

As producer, co-writer and lead actor he had to accept responsibility, but it's responsibility for a damn-fine film. For all its technical flaws, it works. Oh man, does it work. It's one of those great little movies which doesn't try to over-extend itself and does better because of it. It's a tale of the anti-hero doing his thing while looking out for his people, trying to keep those he cares for on the straight and narrow; the lone wolf taking it upon himself to stand up against authority; it's family and freedom versus 'the man'; bloody-mindedness versus control; intoxication versus sobriety; it's Mitchum to a T.

When it came to researching the subject, Mitchum worked hard to ensure the movie was steeped in authenticity. He already had some firsthand experience – as teenager hoboes, he and brother John got themselves hooked-up with moonshiners in the Alabama hills – and he gained access to real-life Revenue cases by fooling the Alcohol, Tobacco and Firearms Agency and the North Carolina Alcohol and Beverage Control Agency into believing he was going to play Revenue agent as hero, rather than moon-runner as hero. When they found out, they withdrew their co-operation.

The bus breaks down in Rock Hill, North Carolina. There's no point getting peeved by it – gotta roll with the drift. Besides, now I can drink. I've travelled from Massachusetts through Virginia to North Carolina; bus stop to bus stop to bus stop; Cape Cod to False Cape to Cape Fear. This here seems like a small town.

I got some time to kill; need to get me something to

eat. I walk into a diner. It's near empty. I take a table by the window. Out of the jukebox comes a personal favourite – 'The Most Beautiful Girl in the World'. It's one of those songs that serve as a time machine for me in just those few opening bars. But it's not the Charlie Rich version I grew up with, instead a twangy guitar has replaced the piano. I'm singing along to myself as I read through the menu. The waitress approaches. She's well into her sixties. Asks, 'You singing that for me, honey?'

'Sure am.'

'Well that's sweet of you. What can I get you – coffee?'

'Beer.'

'We got domestic.'

'Make it two.'

'You eatin'?'

'I'll have a steak, if I can.' I guess it's breakfast time for everyone else but after hours on a bus I got no sense of it.

'Sure you can. How do you like it?'

'Like my women: hot and blue, with a little sauce on the side. You got any sauce there, honey?'

She laughs and says, 'Honey, I got more sauce than you can handle.'

We share a smile and she returns to the kitchen. From the way her ass moves I'm tempted to believe her.

The guy on the next table eyes me as he shovels from plate to face. 'Where you from?'

I tell him.

'Huh. Long way from home.'

'Where the heart is.'

'You got that right.'

The waitress brings my steak. Blue is an understatement, this thing is still throbbing. Probably trying to crawl away from the grits. I scoop them away from the meat.

'That's grits,' the guy says between forkfuls of mush. 'Eat. They're good. You know what defines the South?'

'What?'

'The South is defined by the "grit line".'

'You got me. What's the grit line?'

'When you stop for breakfast, you get grits whether you ask for 'em or not – then you're in the South.'

Grits I've got a problem with. Even though the name has nothing to do with texture, referring to the fine grinding of corn, the sound of it and the sight of the substance, I'm yet to find appealing. Politely I say, 'I'm still learning to like grits.'

'Stone-ground are the best – they can cook for hours. Finely ground corn which, to a non-Southerner's taste, can seem bland and unsatisfying, like eating semolina. But if escargot are a vehicle for garlic and butter, then grits is a vehicle for butter and salt. It's cheap, filling food and there's always enough of it. Eat up.'

Grits is no longer just a food but has become a cultural and political statement. I watch him shovel it in. Eating can get messy when it's about more than texture and taste.

The South doesn't seem to be fixed but is referred to as that area beneath certain state lines – which particular state lines depends on your attitude and prejudice. In New York and New England it seems to be just about anywhere south of New Jersey and I have to admit, to my ignorant ears, Delaware sounded a damn sight more Southern than I expected. But then when I look at a map, Virginia doesn't strike me as a geographically southern state but it was Johnny Reb to the core. And Florida, way down at the bottom, well that's so southern it's got to be the South. I decide I need clarity so I ask the guy, 'So this is definitely the South, huh?'

'The South as an entity don' exist anymore,' he says, without looking up from his food. 'Virginia thinks it's the South but it ain't; it's southern but it ain't the South.'

He's not talking geographically, nor politically, but culturally. For many people who consider themselves to be of the old South, those territories are declining, shrinking. Change equates to dereliction; to betrayal and treason; to territory being taken away.

'And Florida, that's just a mix of New York and Cuba… see, today,' he points his fork at me, 'the South is the Carolinas and Georgia – but not Atlanta. Not even Mississippi and Alabama no more.'

I was under the impression I was in the South soon as I entered Virginia – that being where its loyalties lie and the state being so intrinsic to the Confederacy. And I can't help feel I've heard this all before. I guess, like in Wales, it depends who you ask.

So many Welsh people consider the major urban spread of Cardiff as not 'really' Welsh, nor the lowlands of Gwent, nor border towns like Chepstow and Monmouth, nor the north-east corner which comes under the influence of Merseyside. So what does this leave us with? Shrinkage. Geographically, culturally and emotionally. A different type of Wales – just as with a different type of the South – is viewed as a change too far. It's like saying, 'There is only one Wales, only one South – and you're not it, whatever you believe yourself to be.' And so we get smaller, and weaker. It reeks of the modern age being judged as robbing now-urban areas of their rightful heritage. Well, change happens – we either accept and develop or get very, very lonely in an ever-reducing club, sat all on our lonesome in our chilly *tai bach*. And that's where we'll stay for as long as the question remains: are you as Welsh, are you as Southern, as I am?

'I'm from Rock Hill. Ma family lived in this town since 1760, but ma children are the first generation to move away.'

Modern life eroding community and continuity? Fair point, but wasn't that the reason so many people moved to the States in the first place? To force change, to grasp the mettle, to grab adventure or to escape an inevitable and uncomfortable past, present or future? In so doing, weren't those early settlers escaping the old ways, eroding the old ways, and riding a wave of social evolution? He seems pretty staunch in his views and I'm finding it difficult to keep my mouth shut and listen. I guess to a hammer, everything looks like a nail.

I finish my steak. Tip the waitress and thank the guy for his conversation.

'Where you headin'?'

'Charleston. Then Savannah.'

'That's the South alright. You'll have no trouble there.'

So long as I keep my mouth shut.

397

A replacement bus shows up. I board it, find myself sandwiched between a big guy and the window. We're heading towards the state capital, Columbia. There's a spate of Confederate flags along the road. I ask the big guy, 'You local?'

'Fair Play, Anderson County.'

I presume that's local. 'The Confederate flag, is that still important?'

'To some people, I guess.'

'The Civil War, does that still play on people's minds?'

He guffaws. 'That "recent trouble"? We like to call it "The War of Northern Incursion". It's there, somewhere in the background. You here to study history?'

'Kinda.'

'This your first time in the States?'

'No, but it's my first time down South,'

'Up North, did they tell you it was about slavery?'

'Uh-huh.'

'Well, I thought as much. See, it wasn't about slavery – that's all a blind. It was about economics. The North was manufacture-based; the South, agriculture. That presented what you might call an economic dichotomy. Yu'see, the North wanted the South to sell its material to them so they could make the real money out of manufacture, but they also wanted the South to sell to them cheaply. But England and France were willing to offer the South more for our raw materials, so to stop them from dealing with the South, the North painted it as a moral war. They put England, France and the South over a barrel. We weren't too happy about that.'

This is all news to me. 'So do you think Lincoln's declaration was more an act of war, than humanity?'

'Damn right it was. Slavery... slavery was already being dismantled 'cos it was cheaper to employ than to house and feed. And Lincoln signed that thing under duress placed upon him by the Northern manufacturers and politicians – who were one and the same people, mind. You know, there were free black forces in the Confederate armies, as well as those of the North?'

I didn't know that. In fact, I know little of the subject except what popular, white-Western knowledge would have me believe. The one thing I do know is the common records of history are rarely to be trusted. And Frank was right: in the South, they do like to talk.

In Columbia there is much confusion alongside the bus. This bus is going to Orangeburg but so is another. The driver insists some passengers unload their luggage and change service. The porter asks for my ticket. I show it. He wants me to take the other bus. I ain' having it.

'Ma ticket says I stay on this service until I get to Orangeburg, so that's what I'm doin'.'

I'm pernickety like that. Don' wanna do what he says then find some jobsworth kicks me off, en route. He thrusts the ticket back at me and mumbles off to hassle somebody else. I get back on the bus, too tired to grumble.

We soon hit the road, the driver bitchin' about this an' that. Head down Gervais Street, past red or brown brick buildings; solid, low-level architecture; palm trees and wall murals. It's a beautiful looking city, but quiet. Can't help but wonder what it's like at night.

We cross the Congaree River on its way towards forming the Santee. Spanish conquistador Hernando DeSoto crossed this river in 1540, in search of the fabled Cofitachequi gold. When he landed in Florida in 1538, he was leading the largest European expedition North America had ever experienced. DeSoto brought with him hundreds of men and horses and left a trail of destruction throughout what would become known as the South. As he searched for gold, transportable valuables and land to colonise, DeSoto's behaviour towards the locals was ruthless, brutal, savage. Torture, rape, kidnapping, razed settlements, the desecration of sacred sites – on which he often erected Christian crosses in their stead – and looting, in fact the whole self-righteous, colonial shebang. Ah, praise the Lord, the civilised settler strikes again.

We travel alongside the Cherokee Path, which served as the main route from Charleston to Columbia until the demands of the combustion engine found it wanting. It began life as a series of animal tracks then became a major trading route for the native tribes and then, in the seventeenth century, for European fur traders. It found a new role as an important supply route during those 'recent troubles'. Routes and roads which travel through time don't appear out of nowhere. They each have their history, ghosts of those who travel to embrace the new or escape the old.

A call goes out from the back of the bus: 'Anyone know what time it is?'

'Eleven o'clock.'

'Damn! Appreciate that.'

'Four and a half more hours.'

Road-signs declare a 70mph limit and 'Life is short, eternity isn't – God.' Nobody likes a smart-ass.

Even more so than usual, time for me has melted into less than an abstract concept. We cross the bridge on Highway 26 and turn off for Orangeburg.

All I know is, the more I see and hear of the South, the more I like it. There ain't nothin' to be scared of.

Take 24

The bus pulls in to Orangeburg. The driver's in a rush to get those of us who are getting off, off, and those who want a cigarette back on. 'We thirty-five minutes late already.'

He ain't gonna hang around. My next bus don't get here for another three hours. It seems I've left my copy of Tully's *Beggars of Life* on the bus. On *a* bus. I guess I just gotta wait in the sun. Sit my ass down on the curb, kick stones and roll myself a smoke.

On one side of the station is the Piggly-Wiggly store – a poster advertises Maverick-brand cigarettes at $1.77 a pack. Well, Mitchum worked for less, once. On the other side there's a house selling items off the porch. Billy's Flea Market stocks baseball caps, T-shirts, leisure suits and puffa jackets all hanging from a tree. Sure looks like strange fruit to me.

A couple of pick-ups pull up and out get the bandana and goatie brigade. We watch a beautiful woman walk by. She's loping along, slapping her own ass with each step. OK, baby, you got our attention. We'd all like to lope along with you, slap your ass and see where you take us.

I could kill for a beer but sometimes you just gotta lay low and ride it out, which is just about what Mitchum told Marilyn Monroe when filming *River of No Return* – one of the first movies filmed in CinemaScope.

Mitchum plays a man with a violent past. His son finds out and shuns him as he grapples with the realisation that his father isn't the saint he thought he was.

'I thought he was the perfect guy to play the man in the River of No Return.... *a man's man and yet he had this enormous affection and yearning for the reunion with his son – even in the nature of his relationship and the way he treated his son, there was a poetic side to his character and therefore in Mitchum.'*

Stanley Rubin, producer, *River of No Return*

Mitchum took top billing from Marilyn even though she was already well into her fame. She was warned about working with Mitchum: 'Bob knows this business better than you do. He's all right if he likes you, but he's a scene-stealer if he doesn't.'

'Oh I'm not scared of Bob stealing scenes,' she replied, 'it's those darned hammy horses that worry me'.

The movie began as a nothing project but the studio decided to make it a big deal. They brought in Otto

Preminger to direct, with whom Mitchum had already developed an antagonistic relationship while filming *Angel Face*, but this previous trouble was put to one side to save *River* from Marilyn.

'[Marilyn] *rehearsed her lines with such grave ar-tic-yew-lay-shun that her violent lip movements made it impossible to photograph her... I pleaded with her to relax and speak naturally but she paid no attention... Mitchum saved the situation. During rehearsals, he ignored her studied affectation. Then, just as I was ready to shoot, he would slap her sharply on the bottom and snap, "Now stop that nonsense! Let's play it like human beings...."'*

Otto Preminger, Director, River of No Return

Although Marilyn's lip-quivering was an absurd affectation on which her speech coach, Natasha Lytess, insisted, it's worth remembering that the real Norma Jean spoke with a stammer, which might go some way to explaining why she would want to change how she spoke in the first place.

'*Natasha Lytess came into her life because...* [Marilyn] *felt she needed someone to support her, to tell her what she was doing right, when she did something right.*'

R M

While cast and crew were ready to perceive her non-appearance on set as awkwardness or prima donna behaviour, she was – according to Mitchum – doubled up with debilitating premenstrual cramps and 'falling deeper into the prison of agoraphobia.'

'She was a sweet, naïve girl with a wild sense of humour. She'd invite me to dinner sometimes. "What are we going to eat?" I'd say. "Who said anything about eating?" she'd say. I never went.'

R M

Rumours spread that the two stars were enjoying each other's company off, as well as on, set. Such was Mitchum's reputation that her then-boyfriend and future husband, Joe DiMaggio, unexpectedly joined them on location in Canada. But Mitchum didn't find her attractive. The nearest they got to having an affair was him educating her in the ways of anal sex.

'She was convinced that she was not terribly pretty or sexy, really, you know, and as a matter of fact she did not have an aura of sexiness about her.'

R M

'She was a funny girl... sort of asexual in terms of radiance, but then I'd known her since she was fifteen.'

R M

'She felt the whole lark of being a sex goddess or glamor queen was just that. She would play it, if that's what they wanted, and as a matter of fact she burlesqued it, really, because she felt the whole thing was very, very funny.... She really felt she didn't have the inner qualifications to fulfill the

image of the sex goddess. As a comedienne, I think she was very comfortable. But she thought that the whole thing was a lie because it was not her.'

R M

Between takes, Mitchum found Marilyn reading a dictionary of Freudian terms. He asked why she was reading it so she explained, 'I feel one should know how to discuss oneself.' He asks which chapter she was on. 'Anal Eroticism', she replied. 'Do you think that'll come up in conversation?' he asked, deadpan as ever. Marilyn pondered her answer then, a few minutes later, asked, 'What's "eroticism"?' Mitchum explained. Then she looked up at him again and asked, 'And what's "anal"?'

Marilyn was hurt while filming a raft scene and had her leg in plaster. Mitchum commented, 'Well, you can't say you haven't got a good supporting cast.'

He cared deeply for Marilyn and the stories suggest they went back a long way. Before fame had claimed either of them, Mitchum worked the graveyard shift at the Lockheed factory in Burbank, California. One of his colleagues was a guy called Jim Dougherty. While working at the plant, Jim married Norma Jean Baker.

Mitchum claimed the two workmates and their wives socialised and went together to hear big band concerts starring the likes of Sinatra, but after Mitchum had attained fame and failed to respond to Jim's attempts to re-establish contact with his old workmate, Jim would later deny they were that close.

One story loved by biographers is that such was

Mitchum's financial state at the time that Jim would share his sandwiches with him – sandwiches made by Norma Jean.

'Bob never did meet Norma Jean when I was married to her. The closest he came was to eat some of her sandwiches. He never had any lunch to bring to work and I'd give him one of Norma Jean's tuna salad or bologna and I'd tell her my buddy didn't have anything to eat and she started putting in an extra sandwich or two for Bob.'

Jim Dougherty

Mitchum's financial state was certainly ropey at the time but still better than his health. In 1941, insomnia was ruling his days as well as his nights, he was experiencing hallucinations and eventually went temporarily blind.

'Sometimes three days with only fifteen minutes sleep – couldn't make it.'

R M

In hospital a doctor told him there was nothing physically wrong with him but that his blindness was psychosomatic, brought on by exhaustion and the stress of the job. Mitchum had a family to support so didn't feel he could quit. The doctor told him, 'it's lose the job or lose your mind.'

'In April the Lockheed Aircraft Corp accepted me for employment... my mediocrity as a sheet-metal worker was early established and my utter inability to adjust myself

to the midnight-to-morning or "graveyard" shift resulted in an acute chronic insomnia... determined to re-establish my direction, I expended my sleepless hours in little-theater productions.... In April, 1942, the Lockheed medical supervisor advised my severance, in the interest of health, and in a memorable and profitable discussion prescribed that I recognize my impulse, and seek expression in the work I loved. To finance my speculation... I busied myself as a part-time shoe salesman.'

R M, 1948 probation plea

Mitchum left Lockheed. Dorothy got an office job and his mother suggested he try movie acting....

'I'd just quit Lockheed. Oh yeh, set out into the world to become a glamorous movie actress.'

R M

As for Marilyn, Mitchum felt she was 'too fragile for Hollywood', while she claimed, 'Mitch is one of the most interesting, fascinating men I have even known.'

Marilyn trusted Mitchum. Neither had known their fathers. He didn't want anything from her and felt protective towards her.

'She respected intellect... she was attracted [to] *maybe father figures but certainly older men who were very smart.'*

Shelley Winters

'At the time, I don't think she knew too many people who

were friendly to her. Growing up in an atmosphere of agents, directors and journalists, she seemed like a lost child. The whole thing to her, I mean her position in this atmosphere, was like Alice in Wonderland. The whole thing was through the looking glass and she could not believe that anybody was really very serious about her. She was a very special girl and she had an enormous feeling for, well, just for people.'

R M

The night before Marilyn sang at JFK's birthday party, she visited Mitchum at his New York hotel claiming she didn't want to go to the party. Mitchum convinced her to attend and that was the last he saw of her. She phoned him later, desperate to talk. Mitchum made himself unavailable. After her death he was told how important it had been to Marilyn that she speak to him. Mitchum wrote, 'I have never shed the guilt I felt at hearing that.'

'I find it difficult to accept the suicide ruling on Marilyn's death. She was a confused, troubled lady who, confronted with living the life of an artificial stranger, felt inadequate to the demands of deportment expected of her, but was never morose or despondent. I never saw her take a drink, and know nothing of any association with pills.'

R M

Clouds come over, the winds pick up. The bus is late. Mitchum, if you're driving this one I'm gonna kick your ass. I ask the guy on the counter if there's any news of the Charleston bus.

410

'It's thirty minutes late – that's all the man told me. But it's later than that now.'

Bells and horn sound – a freight train is coming. I feel the temptation to run for it, to feel that midair instant between foot leaving ground and hitting the iron steps of a Union Pacific, holding on, swinging one-handed, climbing onboard and accelerating out of here to anywhere fast, just to see where it takes me.

The restroom door says I need to request a token from the counter but the lock's long gone. I push open the door. Two urinals, a sit-down toilet, an eroding basin, a chipped mirror, an ancient, green, enamel condom dispenser advertising 'Skin Tights' and 'French Ticklers'. French Ticklers? Who knows how long they've been there. The graffiti reads 'Tell Rodney I need pussy and a good blow job from a bitch', 'Bishopville backstreet' and 'Baby Dee the baby-faced killer', but no poems from Mitchum. I look in the mirror and appear strangely healthy, but I'm pushing shandy-coloured piss. I swill my hands under the tap, wipe them on my trousers and go outside for a spliff. The sun comes back out, and out of it comes the bus.

A woman with whom I've shared every bus since Roanoke says her first words to me: 'This has been a *loooong* day, not just for us but for everyone.'

'Yeh, yeh.'

'Still, we back on our way now.'

We pull out of the station. Leave behind the line of barbers, beauty saloons and nail parlours on Magnolia and Russell – however small the town, there's always a nail parlour. Stop at the crossing where a Union Pacific claims

411

right of way – big, open-bed wagons offering lots of space to hoboes but little shelter. I count forty cars then my eyes and the train's accelerating movement mangle lines and definition. The barrier rises and we head east before turning south towards Charleston. Between Orangeburg to the south and Hopkins to the north, Eureka and Swansea to the west, Davis Station and Lane to the east, is the little town of Lone Star in Calhoun County.

In 1943 Mitchum appeared in *The Lone Star Trail*. The lone star to which the film refers is not this little town in South Carolina but Texas – the Lone Star State – and its flag, the colours of which represent those qualities most highly valued: blue for loyalty, red for bravery and white for strength.

The Lone Star Trail was the last of Johnny Mack Brown's cowboy movies for Universal and on its release was described by the press as 'a rip-snorting Western'. As Blaze Barker, Brown's sent down on trumped-up charges and, once freed, instead of falling into the trap of thinking, 'well, if I'm gonna be portrayed as bad I may as well be bad' he fights to clear his name.

'The West's Greatest Star Team... Roars Along a Lead-Swept Trail of Vengeance!'

Tag-line for *The Lone Star Trail*

Mitchum appeared alongside Brown and his usual team of Tex Ritter, Jennifer Holt, the Jimmy Wakely Trio and the wonderfully named Fuzzy Knight. It was Mitchum's thirteenth movie of the year and, although another Western following on his five previous appearances in Hoppy features, it was still a worthwhile supporting role for the emerging Bob Mitchum who was willing to try his hand at any role in any genre but still had to take whatever came along.

I could do with watching a good Mitchum movie now. Lay back and skin-up. Lose myself to the black and white. Until then: time, if not to sleep, then at least to drift.

Take 25

God knows how many hours since leaving Roanoke, I arrive in Charleston having zig-zagged through Virginia, North Carolina and South Carolina; through magnolias and angel oaks, tall trees and dense undergrowth sucking up swamp juice. Late, but here all the same. Man, someone should put this country on a hot wash – let it shrink a little. I forget: it's already underway; N'Orleans has come through a spin cycle and Malibu is slipping into the sea.

'How high's the river, mama? Five feet high and rising.'
Johnny Cash, *Five Feet High and Rising*

I feel like I should be catching yet another Greyhound but know I'm here to stay, temporarily at least.

A cab pulls up at the bus station. A woman piles her

kit in the trunk and slides into the back seat. I approach the driver, ask if he can call another cab. He asks where I'm going. He motions me into the front seat.

'You got a reservation?'

'Yep.'

'That's good. 'cos you won't find an empty room from here to hundred miles up. All the hotels and waffle houses are full. There's lots going on – the Flowertown Festival, the Bridge Run, the Air Expo, and auditions for some national TV talent show. It's pretty busy this weekend.'

'It's the weekend?'

'Not yet, it ain't.'

Dagnabit, I still don't know what day it is.

We drop off the lady at her sister's on Aberdeen. She's here for a funeral; feels torn between the pleasure of seeing her family for the first time in years and the sadness of the occasion. She wishes us good day and we continue on to my hotel.

For all its palm trees and pretensions, the hotel is just an airport motel, housing people waiting for a flight out of town. My room overlooks the parking lot. I don't care – it's got a lock on the door and a clean bed.

I take a snooze, shower, call a cab, head out to eat. The driver's wearing a straw cowboy hat. I ask if he can recommend somewhere to eat. He suggests an Italian off Rivers Avenue.

'I hear it's a good restaurant. I took my wife there once but my wife's a country girl, she don't like all that funny food.'

He drops me outside, tells me his name, gives me his

card. I agree to call him later.

I grab a table and begin rolling myself a cigarette.

'Hey, I'm Donna, I'll be serving you today...'

She watches my hands.

'What is that?! What you rolling in... in *that*?'

'It's just a cigarette.'

'Uh-huh, sure it is.'

She walks away and returns with a basket of bread. Pours olive oil onto a plate of herbs. 'You want me to put some herb in that "cigarette"?'

'Babe, if you got it, I wan' it.'

'I thought so – you look the type. Now what you wantin' to eat?'

I ask what's in the *pescatore*.

'Shrimp, scallops, mussels tossed in a spicy sauce.'

'Sounds good. I could do with having my muscle tossed.'

She laughs, despite herself. I figure she made the rules – if she can be cheeky, so can I. I watch her ass as she walks away. Boy, has she got it.

Charleston is a naval and air force town. I'm here to visit the naval yard; to find the truth of James Mitchum's death. The location, the culture, the detail. I haven't made any contacts, I have no one to meet. If I can get myself a little Southern belle action too, all the better.

Donna brings my food. It doesn't touch the sides. She comes back and says, 'You sure seemed to enjoy that.'

'I'm a man with an appetite.'

'Where you from?'

I tell her. She asks what I'm doing in Charleston.

417

'You remember Robert Mitchum?'

'Can't say I do. He live round here?'

'He was a famous movie actor. His father was from Lane.'

'Wait. This Robert Marshall...'

'Mitchum.'

'This Robert Mitchum was from Lane? Lane, South Carolina?'

'Uh-huh... no. His *father* was from Lane. Worked in the Naval Yard.'

'And he was an actor?'

'Uh-huh.'

'Well, I can't rightly remember him.'

'Your mama still alive?'

'Uh-huh.'

'Ask her. She'll remember him alright.'

'You sure?'

'Ask her, you'll soon find out. I tell you what: here's my card. Call me if she remembers Robert Mitchum from the movies.'

'What if she don't?'

'Call me anyway.'

It's amazing what a full stomach and beautiful server can do to a man's mood.

They're playing Sinatra over the speakers. 'I'll Take Romance'. I'll take it wherever I can find it.

I phone the cowboy cabbie for a ride back to my hotel. Go outside to wait.

'Thank you. You come back and see us, OK?'

'Donna, I will see you in my dreams if not before.'

The line embarrasses even me but as long as she keeps laughing, I'll keep at it.

After only a bottle of wine I'm still dry as a bone, so I hit the hotel bar. Order a cold one; ask the server if I can smoke.

'Sure.'

The woman sat next to me says, 'Huh! You're in a *bar*!' Like my two brain cells have died from friction. I explain I'm used to drinking up North.

'Well, I don't smoke,' she says, 'but I think if you need a drink, you should be able to smoke while you're doing it.'

'That's very civil and understanding of you, thank you.'

She introduces herself as Rebecca. And her husband as Ed. They're having a good ole time, downing liquor as soon as it arrives. She's a nurse and pissed with work. 'I've been instructed to stop calling patients "Sugar" and "Hun". It's disrespectful of the patient, they told me, but that's BS as far as I'm concerned.'

Ed's a photographer. I get talking about Mitchum. He says, hesitantly, that he might have some shots of Mitchum with Ronnie Reagan. I'm interested. Very interested.

Mitchum may've claimed to have been an anarchist but in the eighties he came out in support of Reagan. He didn't know what Reagan stood for but he had known him for forty-odd years. Whatever Mitchum may've said in interviews, he still didn't vote.

'I used to go to dinner on occasion with Ronnie when he was a great friend of Bob Taylor's, and it was always like we

were being monitored by an eagle scout. He didn't want to tell the bad joke. You always felt a little constricted with Dutch, at least I did.'

R M

I sure can't imagine those two out on the pop.

Ed says he'll go through his archives when he gets back home.

'That's very kind. Appreciate it.'

'If you need a hand, Southerners will give it.'

We carry on drinking until the bar kicks us out.

I wake in last night's clothes to the sound of trains troubling the rails. The hotel is situated between two main freight routes and their rumblings are comforting; remind me of home.

I breakfast on blueberries and water. Wait an hour in the sun for a cab, a cool breeze moving the warm air around me. I guess they do things a little slow around here.

'So where'd you wanna go?'

'You know the naval yard?'

'The naval yard? You mean the Denton ship yard?'

'I have no idea. It's the old naval yard, where they used to unload the trains.'

'Which gate?'

'Don't know. Just get me down there and we'll see where we go.'

He puts the cab into drive. 'What you doin' out here?'

'I'm investigating – researching – the death of a man here in 1919. Somebody's father.'

420

'I understand. I had to do something like that. Had to track down somebody's death certificate, be certain what he died of. My step-daddy died from asbestos and my sisters died from leukemia and cancer. I couldn't understand why I was still alive. Turns out I had a different daddy. Nobody told me that. Still, I'm alive. See, I look after *me*. I'm not putting a limit on how long I live and I ain't gonna let anyone put on a limit on it either. I reckon God put me on this Earth to live so that's what I'm gonna do, for as long as I can, 'cos I don't plan on dying. In *this* world, it's all about survival.'

We reach the yard; drive through McMillan Gate. Cruise slow over in-set rails, windows open so I can snap US Navy and Coastguard vessels at the dockside, just to see what happens. Nothing happens. Nobody takes a blind bit of notice.

We pull over to one side. So this is the North Charleston naval yard where James Mitchum died.

'It would've been real rough work down here in them days, yes sir.'

Jimmy had been in the army, posted in Connecticut where he met Mitchum's mother. After he was discharged he returned to his family home of Lane, in the South Carolina county of Williamsburg, with his young family. He needed to work and found a job working on the trains that loaded and unloaded in the North Charleston naval yard.

Baby Bob wasn't yet eighteen months old when his papa died. Who was at fault no longer matters. Either Jimmy gave the wrong signal or the driver misunderstood but instead of going forward, the train reversed and James

Thomas Mitchum was squashed between couplings, clinging onto life just long enough for the pregnant Ann to be brought to the naval yard so he could die in her arms.

'His father was coupled between two trains but was still alive. They went and gathered [Bob's] mother... and she went to say goodbye to him, and I believe he was there but he was only about two years old. She said goodbye to his father and then they uncoupled the trains, his guts spilled out and he died. I don't know if it scared him – I'm sure that if he actually saw those images they probably stuck with him. I do think it might've been a huge catalyst in him realizing that he is alone in this world and he's gotta be the man, and he can't show weakness. And I'm sure, psychologically, it's gotta define you in some way. Being robbed of a father at such an early age causes a lot of pain and confusion that might make you be the kind of person that he became... very strong and stoic. At that time he would stand up for himself and his brother a lot, maybe in honor of his father because his father wasn't around to protect the family. I don't know if he was ever scared – probably hurt and confused, which defined him, maybe.'

Bentley Mitchum

The tragedy had a huge effect on the family. Brother John was born two months premature; the Mitchums returned to Bridgeport so Ann could have the support of her family while trying to bring up three kids and scrape a living. Baby Bob screamed all the way north.

There's an irony in teen Robert turning to the trains.

He had step-daddies, he had uncles, but no father. The story goes that Mitchum's old man had died a brakeman, working on the trains. So Mitchum – as a young hobo, a student of the life – took on a role for whom the brakeman is the enemy, authority, the one who might catch you riding the tracks and, if you're lucky, hand you over to a rail bull. More likely, physically throw you from the train, at speed. The brakeman had the power of life or death over the hobo. If Mitchum had been caught, if Mitchum had been thrown, if Mitchum had died then as a fifteen-year-old boy, at what price to the brakeman's conscience to have killed the son of a dead colleague? Did Jimmy Mitchum ever throw a kid from a train?

Jimmy is described as half-Celtic, whatever that means. The American biographies tell it he was Irish-Scots, as if that narrows it down. And considering America's temperamental awareness of Wales and the reality of who or what constitutes the *United* Kingdom, there's nothing to say he ain't part-Welsh, or part-Cornish, or part-Manx. But Jimmy was definitely part-Blackfoot. The Blackfoot are mostly from Montana but somehow a group broke off and found themselves in the Carolinas.

'My Indian people came from South Carolina and I have seen it written that it's a great mystery about the presence of the Blackfoot Indians in South Carolina. First of all they were... not nomadic, but they were sort of the scout tribe... they knew what the weather conditions were and what grass conditions were all around the country. My father was Indian on both sides of his family. I had a great-grandmother or

grandmother named Alice Pat – that was it; flat out, that was her name…. "What's your grandmother's name?" Alice Pat. "What's her last name?" Tomahawk.'

R M

This big mouth who was often accused of being anti-Semitic, anti-Catholic; anti-this, anti-that – man, he wasn't anti-anyone in particular; he was disrespectful to everyone, even his own.

Would Mitchum have been better off had his father lived? Nobody can say. But if I'd had a choice between father or no father – I would've taken my chances without one. Fathers are strange creatures. I'm unsure I ever want to be one. To continue the mistakes, the bad advice, the damage? But life gets pretty shallow without taking on a role of such magnitude.

I find somewhere to grab a beer. Check my baggage at the train station, buy a ticket for later, stand on the side of Rivers Avenue awaiting a bus into town. This here was once all marsh, swampland, but now the creek runs through a tunnel just past Wendy's burger bar.

I've got eight hours left in town. The bus arrives. I board but I ain't got the dollar-twenty-five. I say to the driver, 'I guess I gotta put in a five?'

'No,' she says, 'don't do that, we'll get your fare.'

I thank her and walk to an empty seat. On it, someone has placed a dollar note. I pick it up. A guy leans forward and says, 'Hey.' He hands me a quarter. I pay the driver and everyone's happy without making a scene. Even if I'd paid with my own money, a dollar-twenty-five amounts to the cheapest ride I've had in a long time, but their generosity to a stranger resonates far more than a peach.

We travel down Rivers onto Meeting Street. Empty remnants of an industrial area surround Cool Blow Street. We pass Cooper River bridges to the left and hit downtown.

I take a glass of Palmetto Amber; a slice of banana and nut pound cake, wet and sticky and sexy in its own way. Unfold a street map. The directory lists dozens of churches but no library, even though I know there's one here. Good. Let the sheep take the pews, I'll find my truth in manuscript and microfiche.

I finish my beer and hit the bricks; follow my nose. I find my cathedral of print on Calhoun Street. Check out the archives for the Charleston *News and Courier* and *The Sunday News*, circa February 1919. First go through the front pages. Wade through a lot of stuff, a lot of dates. Then, on page two of the Friday morning edition, 21 February, towards the bottom of column one, I catch what I'm looking for.

'FATAL ACCIDENT AT YARD'

'Man Caught Between Box Cars and Dies of Injuries'

'James T. Mitchum was caught between two box cars at the Navy Yard yesterday afternoon and so crushed that he died about an hour later.

The accident occurred about 4.15 o'clock. The man was switching some cars about the yard when he fell between

425

them. The upper part of his body was horribly smashed. Coroner John O. Mansfield was notified and the inquest will be held later. The man was employed as a switchman at the yard. He died at the Navy Yard Dispensary.'

And that's it. An inch-or-so of newspaper type to record a man's horrific end. How much more coverage would it have got, had Jimmy Mitchum been a man of means, dead from obesity or the diseases of greed? I feel the need to raise a glass to him. The discovery saddens me.

I down my first beer, order a second and roll myself a cigarette. So Jimmy wasn't a brakeman. Bang goes the irony of Mitchum-as-hobo versus the authority-of-brakeman. Nor did Jimmy die on the steel. Order a third beer. A private thought escapes my mouth: Here's to Jimmy'.

'To Jimmy,' the guy next to me echoes and empties his glass.

Charleston sits between the Ashley and Cooper rivers, with the docks and old naval yard to the east and the more attractive Battery area at the end of the land and the city. It's surrounded by rivers, islands and marshes, referred to as 'the low country'. During the Civil War, these features provided the Confederacy port with a near-perfect defence system. Strongholds were built around the harbour – Castle Pinckney; Batteries Ripley, Gregg, Wagner and Beauregard; Forts Johnson, Moultrie and Sumter like the teeth of an open-mouthed 'gator waiting for ships on which to chomp.

I stroll past the Italianate and Georgia housing of the

Battery area and head back towards Marion Square. Traffic is steady. They like their cars down here. Between the obligatory pick-ups and SUVs there's plenty of Vipers, hotrods and customized motors. Even the police use Mustangs. The traffic stops to allow a funeral procession through. The shoppers and strollers and workers on a break stand respectfully then get on with their day.

I catch a bus from Mary Street. It's late but it's entitled to be at $1.25 a fare to anywhere en route. It fills up pretty fast. On board, everyone else is talking and heads are bobbing every time we drive past a pedestrian. It seems every block there's a railroad crossing. The guy in front turns to me; wants to examine my cell-phone. I let him.

'Is it contract?'

'Uh-huh. Only way I can afford it.'

'See, mine.' He explains the troubles he's having with his. The guy sat next to me wants to join in; wants to direct me to wherever I'm going. I ain't from around here and it obviously shows. And I guess I'm the only white guy on the bus. I'm grateful for the contact – gods know I'd be lost without others' local knowledge.

He gives me the nod when it's my stop.

'Appreciate it.'

I get off near the train station and, as the bus accelerates away, all heads turn to see where I'm going. I don't know where I'm going but spot a crab bar on the other side of the road. As long as they sell beer I don't care what I've gotta drink it out of.

I take a seat at the counter. The old guy behind it watches TV. The woman asks what I'd like to order.

'Can I just have a beer?'

'Have whatever you want.'

A freight train hoots, up the way. I roll myself a cigarette. Sip my Corona and crick my neck. Slip a tip in the bottle. Snap a couple of sly photographs with my cell-phone. A sign behind the bar reads, 'Beer – so much more than a breakfast drink'. Others list the price of the catch:

6/7 Crabs to a Bushel – $120 today

Crabs / Croakers / Red Snapper / Whole Flounder / Scallops / Shrimp / Florida Brim / Snow-Crab Clusters and Claws / Oysters – Singles, Buckets, Dozen, Bushel and Half-Bushel.

The staff are talking about a recently busted meth lab. A customer is hammering on crab claws. The door swings open.

'What's going on chief?'

'Hanging in there, man,' he says, between swings of the hammer.

'How you doing, young lady?' he says to the server, 'you going to that fish-fry tonight?'

She shrugs. I'm tempted to buy a baggie of crab seasoning and dollar-eighty-nine bottle of hot sauce but these days I rarely eat crab, having caught them three times in one unforgettable, teenage summer. Had to burn my bedding and underwear to get rid of the critters. Spread like wild-fire, you give 'em the chance.

I'm only on my third or fourth beer but suddenly the place

is full and there's a rush at the crab bar. Everybody's looking for take out. Crab, oysters, shrimp. The orders are wrapped in grease-proof paper then served up in brown paper bags, like a beer for the street. The server weighs up a pound of shrimp perfectly; not an ounce over or under.

'These stone-crab claws were swimming this mornin'.'

This town seems crazy for crab and within half hour the place is sold out – it's like a Cardiff chip shop at three in the morning except people here are queuing, respectful and sober.

And as soon as it's happening, it's over. I ask if it's always this busy.

'Yeh,' she says, 'we're always this busy on a Friday. All weekend, we got a lot of people in for their crabs.'

Ah. So it's a Friday.

'Oysters, too. When the weather's colder. We got three crabbers go out on the rivers – Stono and Cooper.'

The Stono River. The Stono Rebellion. In 1739 a group of eighty-or-so African-American people who were 'owned' as slaves marched in rebellion, killing over twenty white people along the way. They had been promised freedom by the Spanish if they could reach Florida. The motivation was not altruism but to stir up trouble in neighbouring colonies. What added fuel to the fire was the introduction of the Security Act, which in a climate of increasing fear of slave uprisings, required white men carry guns to church on a Sunday. Now *that* has a resonance.

After the alarm was raised, white settlers fought it out with the slaves, approximately half of whom were slaughtered. Those who escaped were caught and executed.

How easy it would be to reassure ourselves of this 'typical' Southern behaviour; how easily it fits with the stereotype. How easy to ignore the fact that most of the white people were first-generation British settlers. How easy it is for all of us, wherever we claim to be from, to dismiss bad actions as belonging only to others.

'You want another Corona, sir?'

'Please. I need it.'

A guy walks in and asks for four croakers.

'Six bucks.'

'OK, just give me two – I don't mind which.'

She wraps them up and he gives her his cash. She slips in some shrimp and says, 'A little snack for ya.' Nice touch. He's grateful and she knows, now that there's only me and a couple of boys supping on our cold ones, she can calm down after the rush; after good business and good acts.

She introduces herself as Christine, and me to Jimmy – the old guy in front of the TV. Christine tells me she was a semi-pro soccer player. Right-back and right-wing. She claims to be fifty, fifty-one soon, but she looks forty. I tell here so but I'm not tryna flatter. She looks good. And she's left handed, which is always attractive.

I talk about Mitchum. She's interested. Reaches for a worn paperback, turns the pages, reads out a biographical entry for Mitchum. I hand her a photocopy of the *News and Courier* article on the death of Jimmy Mitchum. She reads it out loud to Jimmy. Takes it and pins it to the wall. Two more people now feel linked to Mitchum. I drink my beer.

The door goes again. A blind guy walks in and orders

some shrimp. Asks Christine to describe them before she wraps.

'They're kinda brown-gray. Fresh, good size.'

'They sound good. I'll have some of them.'

And they do look fine eating.

She introduces me to Robert. 'Did you know Robert Mitchum's father was from Lane?'

'The actor?'

'Uh-huh.'

'Lane, South Carolina?'

'Uh-huh.'

'No I didn't.' He don't show much interest but then it's abstract information coming at him from outa the blue. Fair do's, he only walked in for a beer.

The crab trade is over for the night. I order one last beer before they close. Jimmy's complaining about the cop sat up a block, waiting for him to ride his bike with no lights.

'Shit, he gets me every night. I ain't buying lights – I only live round the corner. Why he keeps rassing me about it I'll never know. Every night we have the same conversation: "Jimmy, I've told you before...," "Yeh, and where were you when my bike got stolen?" Goddamn cops.'

He has my sympathy.

Christine gives me a card for a club in Savannah. Tells me to ask for her friend. 'Tell him Chris from Charleston sent you, he'll take good care of you.'

I say my goodnights and begin my stroll.

'Hey, where you going?'

I tell Christine I'm heading for my train.

'I'll take you to the station. At night, this ain't a good neighborhood and you being a writer, you're more important than the average Joe.'

I choke on my smoke. 'Lady, with that attitude I need to introduce you to everyone else in my life.'

She drives me to the station and I give her my thanks. People down here are sure real and friendly.

I thought I'd missed the 18.47 Atlantic Coast Service to Savannah but now it's gone 21.00 and it's still not arrived. This, and the fact the Amtrak station is eight miles from downtown Charleston, says a lot about the modern-day relevance of passenger trains in the States. The railroad, as Mitchum knew it, no longer exists.

The woman behind the glass has fantastic eyes – blue surrounded with a band of brown. I ask her if there's news of the Savannah train.

'Nine-fifteen.'

'Anything serious?'

'No, just freight traffic ahead of it.'

'Heading for the naval yard?'

'Naval yard? Boy, trains don' go there no more.'

I kick my heels. They still have the old-style phone booths with the hinged doors I'm so used to seeing in Mitchum films. I enter one and unfold the door behind me. Skin up. I feel I should be phoning Jane Greer.

I go sit outside and smoke. The crickets are at it tonight. It seems warmer than the daytime. A freight train rolls past. Most of the cars are marked up 'SSEX' like it wasn't on my mind enough. In amongst them and the tanker wagons there's an empty box car, doors slid back. It's travelling slowly enough to offer the temptation to jump, but fast enough to consider losing a limb. I watch sixty-plus cars roll past and cannot avoid the thrust of their rhythmic beating. What a jump it would be but it's heading in the wrong direction – it's Savannah I'm hitting.

Mitchum made nine trips across the USA as a hobo. No great plan at work, just existing. Just seeing. Just experiencing. He'd just grab a train heading in roughly the right direction, get off when he needed to – to eat, to escape the guards, to change lines.

'Moving around like I did... I could be just any place, not high maybe, but somehow alone and free.'

R M

Sometimes he'd ride the roofs, inside a car, on the girders. Wherever he could perch, unbothered, with his thoughts and his senses.

'I was sort of a traveling witness. I didn't have a trade and I didn't have a box of tricks. I had nothing to sell... I was principally concerned with keeping myself undetected and alive.'

R M

He was a young man not yet certain of what he wanted from life; what he needed from life; where he fitted in. So he did the sensible thing: go gathering. Fact-finding. I can

hear an echoed voice singing 'Bringing in the sheaves....'
He decided to see what was out there before signing
himself up to a role or a future or a set of values. He went
in search of the train with his name on it.

'I had no clear concept of myself. I didn't know if I had any
potential. All I wanted to do was eat enough to be strong
enough to survive. I had no particular notion. I was an
appreciator, largely. But not a very active participant.'

R M

In 1934, after Mitchum's adventures in Savannah, brother
John joined him on a trip from Delaware to California but
they were separated in Louisiana when a couple of rail
bulls held John at gunpoint. Brother Robert rode on into
the distance, leaving his brother behind. Desertion? Self
interest? Panic? A desire to rid himself of his companion
and the responsibility he brought? A desire for solitude?
Who knows what Bob's motivation was. He sent a postcard
from San Antonio, Texas, to his sister and her husband in
Long Beach.

'Dear Net 'n Ernie, So we're just lazin' along, takin' it easy.
Grabbed the wrong freight out of Birmingham and rode to
N. Orleans 'stead of Dallas, so I haven't been to Dallas for
my dough. P'raps Jack has, tho, he left me in Lake Chas. La.
Will grab a hot shot outa here tonite for El Paso. Write me in
El Paso. Love Bob'

Even in this easy prose scribbled on the back of a postcard,

434

there's a fantastically evocative poetic rhythm at play. And 'write me in El Paso' would be such a great end line to any cowboy flick.

Bob stopped off on his trips spending a little time here, a little time there. Earn a few bucks, try something out, little bit of this, little bit of that. When playing it straight he worked as a dish washer, ditch digger, truck driver, quarry man/coal miner, stevedore, bouncer, punch-press operator, driver, handyman, prize fighter, longshore-man and, eventually, freelance writer and movie extra.

'With what little money I had saved, I set out for California... where I began a series of odd jobs which included dish-washing, truck-loading, stevedoring and building maintenance and repair.'

R M, 1949 probation plea

When John eventually caught up with his big brother in California, Bob's response was, 'What kept you?'

Mitchum's wanderlust didn't fade just because be got a regular job, became famous or got married.

'Yeah I take off sometimes. I just float off like I used to when I was a kid. Dorothy? She understands. She'd better by now – she's had enough of it. I've been in a constant motion of escape my entire life. I've just never found the right corner to hide in. And now I've sold my anonymity to become a chromium-plated geek....'

R M

As for me, sat here waiting for the train with my name on it, I have seen the sun set over Charleston – a town I had always wanted to visit without knowing why. It's been an interesting addition to my life. Moving. Something unknown has been lifted from my shoulders.

Take 26

I get woken from my kip on the rails by a tune in my head – Duke Ellington's 'Happy-Go-Lucky Loco' – and the rolling rattle of empty beer bottles. It soon gets replaced by Johnny Cash's 'Orange Blossom Special'.

'I'll ride that Orange Blossom Special and lose these New York blues.'

At least on a train I can drink, unlike a Greyhound. Big seats to sleep in, lots of room, an open bar, somewhere to walk and the easiest, if not the most punctual, way for me to get to Georgia.

Savannah is an essential stop on the trail to Mitchum. It was there he was arrested as a teenager and sentenced to the chain-gang – an experience which profoundly affected

437

his attitudes towards authority, law and justice; and there they filmed one of the greatest ever Mitchum movies – *Cape Fear*.

I don't know what I will find when I get there. Whether it will be an old-fashioned surface civility; the class-led society I've been encouraged to believe still rules the roost in the South – and Savannah is most definitely the South; a culture of tassled loafers, linen worn only after the first day of spring, white shoes after Labor Day and women smoking only if sitting, in whose company I must wear clean clothes, avoid talking about religion or left-wing politics, not swear, and not get drunk. Which means if I stay true to form I'm gonna be right up the shitter. Or will it be the vibrant party city favoured by the younger generations of the Southern states?

Nancy Astor once described Savannah as a 'beautiful lady with a dirty face'.

'At one of the parties a real sassy magnolia belle tried to take a rise out of me because of the chain-gang episode and wanted me to know she knew all about it. "How'd you like it, back in Savannah?" she said. "Lady," I told her, "ah likes it anywhere I can get it...." They almost locked me away in the chain-gang again.'

R M

So my first port of call has to be the DeSoto Hilton where some of the *Cape Fear* interiors where shot and where the cast and crew stayed for the best part of a month. Although why it's named after a murderous Spanish conquistador is none of my business.

The train crew are preparing themselves. Looks like we're almost there. I bite into an apple to refresh my mouth. It's bad. The skin is fine but inside is dark and rotten. Looks can be deceiving. I hope it's not an omen.

We pull into the station. I alight, wait for my case to be unloaded. Grab it from the trolley and stroll over to wait for a cab. Roll myself a cigarette. The first words spoken to me in Savannah are heard.

'Is that a joint?'

Sat on the bench, looking at me, is a young woman, mid to late twenties, difficult to tell her figure sitting down, pretty face, smiling.

'No, just a cigarette.'

'I was gonna say, man, you got some balls. I was gonna ask if I could have some.'

Baby, you can have whatever I got.

She asks what I'm doing here. I explain I'm chasing a book.

'That's so cool!' she says, and gently squeezes my arm. She's heading into town for a wedding. We might catch up with each other later. A cab pulls in and she's on the back seat before it stops moving. She holds the door open. 'Come on, get in.'

I throw down my cigarette and climb in, trying not to catch the eye of those who waited longer.

I'm trying to talk to her but the driver insists on conversing. She's bubbly and excited and happy to talk to anyone. He wants to impart local knowledge. I want him to shut the fuck up so I can get her phone number.

'You go drinking: you don' wanna drive in Savannah. The cops are hot on drunken drivers.'

'Only place in the States if they are.'

'Oh they are. You don't wanna get caught behind the wheel in this town. You can get away with jus' about anythin' else, but don't get caught for that.'

'I'll bear it in mind.'

I have no intention of driving. I've come this far without getting behind the wheel and I don't intend to change now.

The driver pulls up outside the DeSoto Hilton. A rush of people near the door.

'Hey, that's my mom...'

We swap numbers just as she is pulled from the cab and into the throng of well-dressed family.

'That sure is a nice woman,' says the driver, 'but she'll cost you big money.'

'Yeh, you could be right.'

'Where you staying?'

'The Days Inn.'

He chuckles to himself and drives off.

'How long you staying?'

'As long as it takes.'

'Well, first thing you do, you phone that woman. Second thing you do, you give me a call.' He hands me his card. 'I'll drive you. Third thing you do, you go out with her and have a good time. Then call me again and tell me how it went.'

I guess Savannah doesn't keep secrets.

The town is long and skinny and I'm staying on

Southside. The Pipemaker Swamp through which Mitchum ran is over on the east. We arrive at the Days Inn. It's one of those cheap motels that always appears in movies – someone hiding out gets their door broken down by a renegade cop. Or the police arrive to find a corpse on the bed, on the floor, in the bath.

I drop my stuff. Change my clothes from Virginia mountain chill to Savannah evening warmth. Head back to the lobby. Stop a security guard in the parking lot and ask if there's a late-night bar close by. He directs me to Dacari Island. Says, 'But it might not be your kinda place.'

All the more reason to go there.

I stroll down Abercorn towards the bar. The sign outside the all-night diner declares, 'Welcome home troops – now hiring'. I slide between the loud cars and crowd outside the Dacari, past the doorman and up to the bar. Take a stool. Check out the cocktail dispensers – 'Georgia Peach', 'Hurricane', 'Thug Passion'. Order myself a beer and a plate of food.

The bar's full. Karaoke, food and pool. Now I see what the security guard meant: it's black to the button, except for the serving girls, but that's fine by me – I'm getting no stress; no one's staring, I get served – what more can I ask for.

People are sitting in booths and at the bar, eating fried food, drinking cocktails out of polystyrene cups; standing around tall tables; dancing in front of the stage in the corner. It's rap-karaoke night – you heard that right. The sexy woman singing has done well so far but she's made a bad decision in deciding to crucify Roberta Flack's 'Killing

Me Softly'. Unfortunately for her, and everyone else, the scales are dragging her through a minefield of bum notes.

'OK, let's give it up for our singer!' shouts the DJ. There's no response. Everyone's drinking and talking and watching the pool. A guy in shiny black shoes, pressed black pants and immaculate electric-blue blazer keeps pacing the floor, building the creative tension; working through his nervousness before his turn on stage. It's important to him. He appears to feel he's got something to lose. I hope he's good.

Some guy wears long bling and a shirt declaring 'Cash Rules Everything Around Me' like it's something to be proud of.

In walks a vision in pink and, man, she is see-through and knows it. The whole bar can see every crease of her pussy and how close she's shaved. Man, I don't know what kinda reaction she's after, but she's getting it. All the boys turn and comment.

'Man, she's finger-lickin' good!'

The comments from the women are not so positive.

But somebody else is the real belle of the bar. All in black, elegant in an informal venue but not overdressed. Gorgeous, bobbed. Not showing off. Not advertising. Not demanding attention. Just beautiful and peaceful and silent. And watching. Man, she may not be getting attention from anyone else, but I can't take my eyes off her. She is a stunner. Exudes beauty and a good soul. She's the only woman here without tattoos. Without visible tattoos. My concentration gets broken.

'You rollin' a cigarette?'

'What's that?'

'You rollin' a cigarette?'

'Yeh.'

'You ain't from Savannah, right?'

'Right.'

'Man, I knew you wasn' from Savannah – didn' I say? Didn' I say? I knew he wasn' from Savannah. My mama used to roll cigarettes when she first come from Germany. I knew you weren' from here.'

'Would you like one?'

'Hell no, I carry a baby.'

'That's right, man...' the big guy sat next to me at the bar puts his huge arms around her and continues, 'we want this baby to be healthy and I'm helpin' her.'

Congratulations. He's very proud and so he should be. There's a lot of love travelling between them.

'So, when you have the baby, when you become a daddy, d'you think you'll feel like a man?'

'Feel like a man? Hell, I don't know. I'll feel like *her* man, that's the truth.'

She giggles and they put their arms around each other, oblivious to anything outside themselves. I hope it works for them, I really do.

My food arrives. There seems to be layers of colour at play: the customers are black, the bar staff are white, the kitchen staff black. Intention or coincidence? I have no idea. All I know is, nobody's treating me like I don't belong here. I remember some advice I was given in Virginia: when you meet a Southerner for the first time, you'll never know what they really think of you unless you're from the South.

443

Well, I don't need my head kicked in and I don't rightly need any new best friends, so anything in between will suit me fine.

The guy stood between me and the pool table sports a football shirt named 'Williams'. Another, 'Jones'. The pregnant woman is touring the room, waves with one hand, carries a bottle of Hennessey with the other. The singer in the corner is in tune. I can smoke indoors. The world is good.

A uniformed gentleman from the Chatham Country Sheriff's Department walks behind the bar and helps himself to a drink. A soft drink, obviously. I finish off my plate of deep-fried oysters and order another beer.

Billy introduces himself between pool shots. We do the shake. Try to. God-damn handshakes change from town to town.

'I been tryna beat this motherfucker's ass, man. I'm gonna do him this time. Woop his ass.' His friends laugh. 'I am, I'm gonna woop his ass.'

'So who's the local champion?'

'There's a few of them. But I'm gonna be the one; I've gotta be the one.'

One of the servers pushes past the big guy alongside me: 'Move it, ton-o-fun.'

'You got one more fat joke, one more, just one more, then after that I'll beat your ass.'

A woman does a mean Prince impersonation to 'When Doves Cry'. She's enjoying herself and going for it. She reaches the end of the track and screams at the DJ, 'Next track, motherfucker – I wanna sing!' Next up, 'Purple Rain'.

Now she's loosening the wax from my ears. Give it a rest, baby, you shoulda quit while you were ahead.

Billy's ahead but his opponent fights back to pot three in a row, so it all comes down to the black. He misses. Billy lines it up, strikes the white and hits the black right down the hole. There's plenty of people to congratulate him and he's a happy man. I'll drink to his success until the server says no more.

The Savannah mid-morning sunlight is bright. I stroll through the parking lot towards Oglethorpe Mall. Next to my hotel is a putt-putt course full of fibreglass safari animals – an elephant, a giraffe; the usual suspects. Perhaps this is where they filmed the action for *White Witch Doctor*.

Mitchum was on loan from RKO. 20th Century-Fox had promised him a trip to Africa but only a film crew was sent, to capture location shots. The action was filmed on the studio back-lot and the result is as authentic-looking as if it'd been filmed here amongst the crazy golf. Mitchum knew he was in a dud.

'In the role of the hunter, Robert Mitchum is as dispassionate as a hippo.'

John McCarten, *The New Yorker*

I use the term 'action' loosely. Mitchum gets attacked by a gorilla or, rather, a man in a gorilla suit. You'd think they would've realised such things undermine a film's integrity, but in the 1978 release *Matilda*, Rank made the same mistake.

Matilda is the story of a boxing kangaroo brought to America to beat shit out of professional fighters. If that's not bad enough, instead of using a real kangaroo they employed actor Gary Morgan to wear a $30,000 kangaroo suit. And if that's still not bad enough, when the film was previewed the studio told the press it was a real kangaroo.

'When the press saw the picture it was like, "What, are you kidding?"... the reviews were like, "Fuck you!"'

Gary Morgan

Fortunately for Mitchum, top-billing went to Elliott Gould.

Matilda makes me laugh, though. In spite of myself. Perhaps because I can't help but watch Mitchum try and figure out if he's on set or in a stoned mirage. My advice is: if you're going to give an hour and a half to watching a glorified pillowcase bouncing around the screen, be in a stoned mirage.

I take a cab into town. The driver introduces himself as Philip. Drives slow. We get stopped every hundred yards.

'Oh Jesus, can't believe these lights.' He drawls his syllables without accelerating into second gear.

'So is Savannah still a seafood town?'

'Well, we got a lot of blue crab, king crab... but seafood not so good no more. Crabs ain't so big as they used to be. See, it's the pH. If it don' rain enough then the water's too salty and that ain't good for procreation – the sex act. And they don' reproduce so much and they don' grow so big. And it's been like that for about three, four, five years – it don' rain enough so the crabs don' grow. We used to sell blue crab for five dollar a dozen. Now it's forty-two dollar for two dozen. Forty-two dollar!'

He ain't happy about this particular effect of global warming.

We travel the hurricane evacuation route, in reverse; go over rail lines on Drayton and head for the historic quarter. He drops me at the DeSoto Hilton. I approach reception, ask them to call her room. There's no answer. Probably out with her mom. Just as well I'm here for research, not pleasure.

Situated on Bull and Harris Streets, the original, neo-romanesque DeSoto Hotel first opened on New Year's Eve 1890 and closed on New Year's Eve 1966, to be replaced by a modern building in which the interior design was modelled on its predecessor.

The hotel served as annual meeting place for the Savannah Hibernian Society. Now, Hibernian means Irish, right? So why does the framed menu from their 1928 dinner feature a drawing of a woman in traditional Welsh costume, complete with tall, black hat? Still further evidence of how America is confused about the homelands of its Celtic roots, perhaps.

Many powerful and famous guests have stayed at the DeSoto. Five US presidents – McKinley, Taft, Wilson, Hoover and Truman – as well as Henry Ford, Jack Dempsey, Margaret Mitchell, Sarah Bernhardt, Yehudi Menhuin and Katherine Hepburn. I wonder if anyone famous stayed at the Days Inn.

When *Cape Fear* came to town everyone stayed here:

447

the cast, including Mitchum, Gregory Peck, Martin Balsam and Telly Savalas; their entourages; the entire production crew, including wardrobe mistresses, nursemaids and school teachers.

According to the local press Mitchum spent most of the time in his room and the only incident occurred when Polly Bergen left her bath running, flooding the giftshop below. I find the idea of Mitchum keeping a low profile and out of trouble hard to believe but perhaps Mitchum's caution about returning to Savannah really affected him. What a contrast there must have been between the welcomes he received as a teenager in 1933 and a film star in 1962. No wonder the resentment still burned in him.

'Mitchum... felt a bitterness against the whole place; against the community. And he had a big chip on his shoulder so, again, he was explosive; always ready to explode, which was great for the picture. I mean, I didn't try to stop that.'

J Lee Thompson, director, *Cape Fear*

In 1933, Mitchum was heading for the Okefenokee Swamp. Hoboing on a train bound for Jacksonville he got off in Savannah, already wise to the dangers but in need of food.

'The family moved often and these moves I supplemented with occasional excursions of my own, one of which, in 1933, ended in the Chatham County Camp, in Savannah, GA. Riding freight trains in the company of a dozen other boys, I was arrested, convicted of what I recall as a technical charge

of vagrancy, and released approximately a week later. In fairness to the Georgia authorities, I must confesss that I falsified my age.'

R M, 1949 probation plea

Martin Balsam: *'What are you doing in our town?'*
R M: *'Well, they told me it was a pleasant climate; plenty of boating on the river; a lot of fine, stand-up citizens... I figured it'd be just the place for me.'*

Cape Fear

In the thirties the mere act of arriving as a hobo in a new town was just asking for trouble.

'I was charged with the common crime of poverty. I was a dangerous and suspicious character with no visible means of support – vagrancy; you know, begging. I probably asked a kind lady for a crust of bread or something.'

R M, *The David Frost Show*

'I was busted for mopery with intent to gawk.'

R M, *The Dick Cavett Show*

But Mitchum was no vagrant. He had thought ahead and had a plan. Before he was arrested he collected forty dollars forwarded by his mother. He had money for food and a bed for the night. When the police picked him up as a vagrant he produced the money as proof he had means of support. Having already decided his status, they arrested him anyway and he was kept in the cells for five days.

In *Cape Fear* Mitchum's character Max Cady goes through a similar experience. The police want him out of town so are willing to charge him with anything. He ain't broken no laws, ain't so far gone as to get thrown in the drunk tank, so they try and nail him for vagrancy. He's only got seven dollars in his wallet. The city limits are calling. He produces a bank-book which shows a balance of over five thousand dollars. The authorities can't touch him. Unlike in real life, Mitchum gets released. I bet he enjoyed filming that scene.

In reality there *was* a potency to Mitchum during filming. While Martin Balsam and Peck try and nail Mitchum, he stands in front of them as if wearing armour instead of only hat, boxer shorts and smoking a cigar. During the different takes, Mitchum realised Peck was avoiding eye contact. Mitchum asked him why. Peck replied, 'Because of the condition you were in. I was afraid you might try and fuck me.'

Back in 1933 Mitchum appeared before the Chatham County judge on a charge of robbery – how else could this vagrant have gotten the money?

'Suddenly I realize I'm listening to a burglary case. A couple of fuzz get up and describe the burglar that hit the shoe store, and it dawns on me that they're giving an exact description of me. Then in a daze I hear the fuzz that arrested me testify that forty dollars had been heisted from the shoe store and that when they took me in I still had thirty-eight on me.'

R M

The police had already proved to Mitchum their lack of interest in innocence and justice. He presumed he could rely on the judge and court. The judge was ready to sentence him to a lengthy spell, Mitchum explained he had the perfect alibi: he was in police custody at the time of the robbery. The courtroom filled with laughter. The judge was not impressed by the disruption or being made to look stupid by some skinny, Yankee upstart. According to Mitchum, the judge's response was, 'Well, I guess I can't hold you on that charge, but a nice little indeterminate sentence for vagrancy should straighten you out.'

How powerless he must have felt, having his status in society decided for him rather than being defined by his abilities, activities and merits. How righteous his anger, faced with such injustice. No wonder his beef with 'the man' played such a major factor on the path of his life.

'Robert sometimes has this little problem with authority.'
Dorothy Mitchum

Mitchum was carted off to Chatham County camp number one (or, according to other versions of the story, Brown County farm) to serve his time on the chain-gang. He lied about his age, claiming he was nineteen so he would be placed with the men rather than his peers. This was a curious decision considering it put him in the company of hardened criminals rather than naughty boys.

Who knows what Mitchum's motivation was but it strikes me as a very wise decision. Amongst his own age group he would no doubt get caught up in a battle for status as the boys sought to establish superiority and their position as king of the shit-heap. But amongst men he would pose no threat and maybe fare well out of their inherent need to act humanely. No man is entirely bad whatever crimes he's committed. A youth amongst men who have to live with their mistakes on a daily basis could be a very safe place to be. Provided his young ass didn't prove attractive.

'The fellows who were kind to me were the murderers, you know, the long-timers... they wouldn't let anyone take advantage of me.'

R M

The chain-gang were hired out as cheap labour; built roads, cleared swamps, rid gardens of snakes.... Local farmers and residents were not slow to exploit them. An inmate's perceived value was low – they weren't treated well.

'It wasn't much of a chain-gang. It's all we had, we called it home.'

R M

'They put you in chains and whacked you around for laughs.'

R M

On his first night Mitchum slept on the floor, next to a dying man.

'They kept him alive and turned him out on the road next day so he wouldn't die inside. They didn't want the fucking book-work and all that shit. They didn't want to dig him a hole.'

R M

If numbers were low, well, it was in Savannah's interests to round up some new faces.

'It cost them sixteen or thirty cents a day to feed you and they hired you out to the highway department for two dollars a day.'

R M

According to Mitchum the inmates were, 'Charmers all... victims of their own circumstances' kept under armed guard. Escape was not encouraged.

'My immediate detail captain – they called him Captain Friend.... He used to sit there all day long with an old broken Panama and a 30-30 across his knees. He said, "The reason y'all boys is here is 'cos y'all don't believe in God, y'all ain't got the holy spirit.... I got gonorrhea in my eyes and went blind. And I dropped down on my knees and I prayed to God for my sight. You think I can't see, take off across that field."'

R M, *The David Frost Show*

Quite how long Mitchum spent on the chain-gang is a moot point. Depending on which version you believe, he was sentenced to seven, thirty, ninety or one hundred and

453

eighty days. Equally vague is exactly how many he saw through before making his escape.

David Frost: *'How long were you actually on that chain-gang, Bob?'*
R M: *'No longer than it takes to tell. I wasn't there more than a week or two or three... it was a very short time. Maybe as much as thirty days. But at any rate, I got out of it.'*

How Mitchum escaped is hidden amongst many dramatic tellings of the story. Maybe he clobbered a guard with a shovel, maybe he waited until everyone was asleep. Maybe he escaped alone. Maybe he was with the tall Creole guy he was chained to. Maybe the bullets whistled past his head. Maybe nobody noticed. Whatever the truth, if you escape from a chain-gang I reckon you've earned the right to exploit it for the sake of a good tale.

Dick Cavett: *'How did you get out?'*
R M: *'That's a rather embarrassing question. They just forgot about me. I didn't turn up and they didn't miss me, I guess. Fired a few warning shots over my head....'*
Dick Cavett: *'Walked away?'*
R M: *'I ran; I didn't walk.'*
Dick Cavett: *'Did some lead follow you?'*
R M: *'I heard a lot of noise.'*
Dick Cavett: *'Do you owe them any time?'*
R M: *'No, no, they just applauded my nimbleness and my speed.'*

Did Mitchum owe them any time?

'When I went to work at Lockheed the FEI had to check me out and they said, "Look, there's a little item here about [the chain-gang]." Well, what do you suggest? That I go back? And they said, "No, they ain't gonna pay your fare back there," and I wasn't about to pay my own fare back there. They never did anything about it.'

R M

If he did, Savannah wasn't bothered enough to arrest a visiting movie star. He had caused them enough bad press already.

Mitchum didn't so much run as hobble. The shackles had rubbed away at his legs, or perhaps it was the ropes when they tied him up for a few days. The wounds became infected – some reports say gangrenous. Mitchum floundered through Pipemaker Swamp and across the border into South Carolina where he was befriended by two (or three) backwoods sisters who took care of him. Fed and washed, he made the slow trek north, hitching rides, sleeping in ditches, suffering from black tongue fever brought on by malnutrition, uncertain whether the Savannah authorities were still chasing him.

'I tried to tell myself I was really living, but on one or two nights I cried myself to sleep, wondering what my mother was thinking.'

R M

Eventually, he reached Washington DC in such a bad state

of health he had to ask a traffic cop for help. The irony wasn't lost on him.

'He took me to a hospital... they were talking about amputating... I quietly got up and put my clothes on and split that joint.'

R M

After escaping the hospital it took Mitchum weeks to get back to his family but when he arrived home in the fall, on the back of a truck, he received the love and care he'd been missing.

'I went back to Delaware and my mother boiled my foot – you know, made a little broth out of it.'

R M

'He looked terrible. He was white-faced and really in bad shape. His left leg had swelled up huge, as big around as a tree stump, where the shackle marks had let in dirt and poisoned it. Mother... went out and got herbs from the garden and made big hot poultices, put them round his leg and drew out literally quarts of pus. She bathed his leg and put these poultices on it day and night for a week and finally it drained completely and got better. He has the scars there even now.'

John Mitchum

And I bet those scars weren't just physical.

The maturity of the young man who had gone through

such experiences is evident in two statements. The first deserves a second reading – the poem he had previously sent home to his mother:

Trouble lies in sullen pools along the road I've taken
Sightless windows stare the empty street
No love beckons me save that which I've forsaken
The anguish of my solitude is sweet.

The second illustrates a wisdom only found through testing yourself and accepting responsibility:

'I became acquainted with death, with the knowledge that I too would die, very, very early. I had pellagra twice when I was wandering the face of this continent alone... but it was no one's fault but my own.'

R M

As much as Mitchum loved his solitude – even as an adult he would scoot off on his own to hide out in the hills somewhere – he never lost sight of the importance of family and the stability of a loving environment. Even the independent need a safe cave to hide in.

I leave the hotel and stroll across Liberty. In the heat I can't avoid adopting the Savannah swagger and stroll. A cool breeze steers me through a series of small park squares with their statues and monuments. General James Oglethorpe, who founded the colony of Georgia in 1733; George II proclaiming, 'Between the Savannah and the

Alatamaha and westward from the heads of the said rivers respectfully in direct lines to the south seas... we do by these presents make, erect and create one independent and separate province, by the name of Georgia.' The old king now stands surrounded by fallen leaves and covered in green silly-string. Georgia was a British penal colony, before some smart-ass thought of Australia.

Wright Square, Johnson Square. Tourist walking tours listening to their guides describe the statues, their relevance to the South, the wars, the English. Others go past in horse-drawn carriages. It's all so very civilised. A restaurant slogan catches my eye: 'Get some South in Your Mouth'. That's more like it. I must remember to try out that line tonight.

I take a seat in the sun, outside Jen's Bar and Grill. It's a little place in a street full of nothing, which suits me fine.

'You'll have to forgive me, I'm a little slow without my first drink.'

R M, *Cape Fear*

Cape Fear is a Hitchcock-style psychological thriller based on the novel *The Executioners* by John D MacDonald. You could say it's the best ever Hitchcock movie Hitchcock never made. You want proof? You got it. Of the *Cape Fear* crew the following all worked with Hitchcock: musical director, Bernard Hermann; editor, George Tamasini; art director, Robert Boyle; sound engineers, Corson Jowett and Waldon O Watson; set designer, Oliver Emert; hair stylist, Virginia Darcy; and stills photographer, Robert Willoughby.

458

Not just that, John D MacDonald wrote a short-story called 'The Morning After' which became an episode of *The Alfred Hitchcock Hour*, called 'Hangover'; and Martin Balsam played Detective Arbogist in *Psycho*. And Robert Mitchum was known to take a shower. Alfred must've felt he was being usurped.

If the choice of crew was one great decision, the choice of title was another. Working on the theory that geographical names were often successful, Gregory Peck – as co-producer – found the Cape Fear River in North Carolina. Although set there, location shooting took place here. 'Filmed in Beautiful Savannah' boasted the lights outside the local movie-house which hosted the movie's premiere. And beautiful it is. And beautiful is the perfect setting in which to portray a humanity so ugly, so vengeful, so bitter.

Yet another great decision was to film in black and white. It's the perfect medium for the script, direction and acting. Good, bad and the grey in between.

It's a film of two halves: the first, one of threat through dialogue; the second, one of action. In the opening shots, Mitchum strolls across a square and towards the court house, cigar in mouth, eyeing up the women as he goes. He wears a Panama hat, sports jacket, open-necked shirt, slacks, slip-on loafers. Everything about the man is laid-back yet forceful. He strolls but carries with him the weight of his mission. The smooth and unconcerned veneer covers a seething rape-fest of vengence.

On the stairs he knocks a book out of a woman's hand but doesn't break step. When he reaches the top he calls out

459

to a janitor. The first words he utters are, 'Hey, daddy...'.

In the court room Mitchum's face is like a clenched fist; his snidey, powerful sneer breaking through the rehearsed, superficial civility, establishing early the character of Max Cady as potent danger; reoccurring threat supreme. It's not long before we're left without doubt. When Mitchum looks into camera his stare and its meanings are unavoidable: Cady has a plan; Cady is determined; Cady is cunning, conniving and incendiary; Cady is intelligent and willing; Cady has burned and waited for an opportunity to go stirring and baiting; Cady knows how to unnerve; Cady knows how to tap an Achilles' heel; Cady intends to exact his revenge and nothing will stop him; Cady doesn't care who knows it.

Cady is a predator; a rapist, a psychological terrorist and, incidentally, a dog-poisoner. It is a role made for Mitchum. Not because of the 'no smoke without fire' theories about the real man but because he was just about the best in Hollywood at being human on screen, rather than acting. Cady needed to be a human to be that frightening. Mitchum took the role to heart.

'It was the first time I ever got to work with one of my heroes – Robert Mitchum – and I had the good fortune of having him in a great role. He did warn me right from the start, he said: "This part is a drunk, a rapist, a violent man, and I live my parts." Which was a warning we might have some stormy passages during the making of the film, and we did.'

J Lee Thompson

Daisy'. If it helps me sleep, it'll be worth it.

I talked with David about the state of the railways, the importance the railroad had to a port like Savannah, and Mitchum's arrest as a hobo. He packed the mug in a small cardboard box, and put it in a brown paper bag. I figure with its shape camouflaged it could, possibly, pass for a small explosive device. Or at least a suspicious package.

As I stroll around the riverfront I try leaving it places – stores, bars, ice cream parlours – to see whether it causes a reaction. It does, without fail. Every time I leave the premises, a member of staff runs after me, 'bomb' in hand, shouting, 'Sir, you forgot this.' A smile on their face, glad to be of service. I accept it with thanks, and try the next place. Maybe if I put a ticking clock in there.

I take it as a good sign. Here in Savannah normal Americans have not yet succumbed to instantly questioning innocent actions; whether or not a visitor's souvenir purchase is a suspect package. Instead, they rely on manners; they are pleasant, helpful, honest.

Right on cue, upriver comes a Saudi cargo ship, blowing its horn as brazen as they come. I wonder who and what it's bringing. Maybe I should be more concerned with what it will take away.

I stroll along the rail-track embedded in River Street. The cobbles once served as ballast on ships. The warehouses, once full of cotton. Both Savannah and the cotton trade depended upon those rails.

I call into Churchill's. It's a British bar. How I didn't see that coming I'll never know. They're showing highlights from the day's British football. This'll do for me. I take

The implication of Mitchum's statement is horrific but perhaps it was designed to unnerve. Just as, after filming *The Winds of War* in the early eighties, he told the press he was, 'Going down to Mexico for the raping season.'

I can't help but cringe at that one.

'[Mitchum] *really played the part... you know, he made people frightened... he was like a fireball, you felt any moment he would explode, an eruption.*'

J Lee Thompson

Cady attacks Barrie Chase and there's little doubt he rapes her. He also has plans for Bowden's (Peck's) wife (Polly Bergen) and daughter.

The censors had a field-day. They demanded all mentions of rape were cut, along with the rape scenes. The UK censors were even tougher. Marketing opportunities aside, perhaps this is one of the rare movies where the chance to see the director's cut would be of genuine interest.

In one scene Cady looks down on Bowden's daughter – played by fifteen-year-old Lori Martin – as she kneels on all fours, scrubbing the deck of the boat.

'*Say, she's getting to be...* [he sups from his beer can] *getting to be almost as juicy as ya wife, ain't she? He-he.*'
R M to Gregory Peck, *Cape Fear*

'*He looks at the girl – according to the censor – too lasciviously. Well, I thought it was just a very good Mitchum look... the censor saw there was some suggestion he was going to rape the girl. Well, of course. That really was the story.'*

J Lee Thompson

Thompson wanted Hayley Mills to play the daughter, having worked with her previously on *Tiger Bay* which was filmed in South Wales, but she was working on a Disney picture and unavailable.

When Mitchum gets around to attacking Polly Bergen (who would later star with him in *The Winds of War*), he throws her against a door, cutting open his hand in the process, and continuing with blood pouring from the wound well after Thompson had called 'cut'. She was scared; he knew what he could tap into. Afterwards he cradled her and apologised. He did what many actors won't or cannot do: convince us they are truly their character; reveal something of their animal self, which society would rather not witness and which many individuals refuse to admit exists.

Mitchum was convincing because the balance was right. He tried to portray a real man; a man we could believe exists and, so, a threat we could believe in – a bitter individual, a charmer with a vicious side, a fermenting brew of injustice and emotion.

But it wasn't just the attacks on women which were convincing. When filming the scene where Mitchum catches up with Peck and his family on the Cape Fear River, he didn't make it comfortable for his co-star. Peck didn't complain. It was him who wanted Mitchum in the film; who knew Mitch would be perfect as Cady; who knew

462

Mitch would steal the picture from under his nose.

'[Mitchum] really took it to the limit... it looked marvellous on film.'

Gregory Peck

'[There was] great teamwork between the two of them. Mitchum was playing it beautifully and Greg let him run with it. He never once came to me and suggested cutting any lines, in fact we added lines [to Mitchum's part].'

J Lee Thompson

'As the vengeful killer, Mitchum proves again that, given the opportunity, he can be a resourceful and expressive performer. His heavy-lidded eyes and petulant mouth here convey a depth of evil that is truly frightening.'

Arthur Knight, *Saturday Review*

I finish my beer. Stroll on down to the waterfront and River Street, reached via steep steps or cobbled ramp. With its mix of antiquity and lively bars, wrought iron street furniture and renovated warehouses, it reminds me of Plymouth's Barbican area. Only bigger. And warmer. River Street follows the banks of the Savannah, upon which sit paddle steamers and, upriver, the docks.

Earlier I bought myself a souvenir mug from a store called Bull Street Station. It's run by a guy called David Meredith who specialises in selling railway memorabilia. The mug bore the advertising slogan of the Chesapeake and Ohio Lines – 'Sleep like a Kitten and arrive Fresh as a

463

a stool at the bar, order myself a beer, settle in for the duration.

There's a blonde woman sat on my right who talks like a Southern Paris Hilton and dresses about the same. As pleasant as she is to look at, the thought of having a conversation with her fills me with... nothing. She faces away from me, turning occasionally – first to check who's sat behind her, then to make sure I'm aware of her. She's used to the attention. Each swivel on her stool gives me a view of her legs way up to a short skirt, and gives her an opportunity to emphasise motion. But she appears to be with the guy on her right. They talk, laugh, drink. Suddenly go at it full-tilt. Two bodies becoming one, as much as is legal. I'm trying to watch the football and leave them to it but the lengths to which they go demand attention. I look around the bar – everybody's watching, commenting, gossiping. I turn to the barman. He raises his eyes to the ceiling. I order another beer and watch the game.

Try to watch the game. As the guy leans further into her, she leans further back. Her hair is almost in my beer. She's wearing so much hairspray I put my cigarette in the ashtray to save her going up in flames. Her hand is on my knee. I presume she's in danger of falling off her stool. But no. It does not have the force behind it of someone trying to remain upright. It slides up my thigh. Back down to my knee. Up my thigh, down to my knee. Up my thigh, up and in and a gentle squeeze. I'm amused, bemused and titillated. It's nothing to do with me, she just wants the attention; needs the attention – of men.

I turn to the girls stood behind me and grin. They

don't know what to make of it. Nor do I, but my cock doesn't complain. All I know is, if her boyfriend realises what his woman's up to behind her own back, I may get a kicking.

They disengage and drink. Her beau orders another round then heads to the bathroom. She turns to me. I say, 'Hi'. She gives me her best smile. This one's trouble, alright. I reckon she'd consider me and her beau fighting over her to be a successful night.

Albert Dekker: '*Stay out of trouble.*'
R M: '*What kind of trouble?*'
Albert Dekker: '*Oh, well, there are all kinds of trouble. You know one kind – you've been living in it all your life. Then there's another kind of trouble doesn't look like trouble at all. Sometimes it looks as pretty as a picture.*'

The Wonderful Country

'You look as pretty as a picture,' I tell her.

She gives me the mock-coy look; lowers her eyes. Raises them again without raising her head. 'Why thank you.'

Her beau returns so she turns back to him. Takes a sip of her drink. Starts talking before he can say anything.

In *Cape Fear* Mitchum sits at the bar of a jazz joint called the Boar's Head, bottle of Bud in hand, eyeing up women. He establishes lingering eye contact with a bobbed brunette played by Barrie Chase in her first movie role. She's sat with another man but thinks Mitchum looks exciting. He thinks she looks like his next victim.

466

The police enter and shake him down. A uniformed cop pulls out a billy club. Mitchum gets to his feet and says, 'You start reaching for those, you better call for the riot squad, man. I don't mind a little talk, I just don't like being pawed, ya know?' That wasn't just Cady talking; it was also Mitchum.

As they escort him off the premises he says to Chase, 'I'll give you one hour to lose your friend.'

'Are you trying to pick me up?' she asks.

'Yes.'

She's so enamoured, you know the sight of Mitchum being led away by the police won't put her off one bit. She's looking to slum it; for a bit of rough.

Mitchum lowers his hat over his eyes and allows the police to stroll beside him as he leaves.

'You're rock bottom. I wouldn't expect you to understand this, but it's a great comfort for a girl to know that she couldn't possibly sink any lower.'

Barrie Chase to R M, *Cape Fear*

I order another Sweet Water pale ale. The randy couple beside me whisper. They decide to leave. Stand and sweep past me, the skin of her arm brushing mine. The barman wishes them a good night, clears away their glasses, wipes down the bar. Holds out a wet cloth and says to me in his Irish-English, 'Would you do me a favour and wipe down those seats – I don't want the next people sat there complaining.'

'It's pretty certain he'll have a good night.'

467

'Thank God they've gone. It's like, get a room, man! Still...' he looks at his credit card slip, 'he tipped well so what the hell. But she was a stripper, don't you think?'

No wonder she's used to getting the whole room's attention.

The football's over. I need somewhere else to direct my attention. The woman sat to my left is a beauty but there's a wedding band on her finger and I've promised myself I won't get involved with the married no more. Is it a moral decision? Perhaps. Maybe I just want a simpler life; maybe the hassle ain't worth the effort.

R M: *'That ring mean anything?'*
Joan Staley: *'It means plenty.'*

Cape Fear

She orders a cocktail. Takes a big sip then asks for a fresh glass. 'This one has a chip in it.' A tiny, intsy-bitsy chip in it. Lady, I'd drink it out of your sweaty shoe. In fact, you pour it into your mouth, slosh it around and spit it into mine – that'd be fine by me.

A guy arrives and kisses her. Her husband, maybe. He sees me checking her out. 'Hey, how you doing?'

'I'm doing just fine, thanks.' (Just getting an eyeful of your woman.)

He doesn't seem phased or offended. Maybe he considers it a compliment. Maybe he's trying to avoid conflict or defuse a situation; prevent something before it happens. Maybe he's so confident in their relationship that nothing I can do will disturb him. Maybe his Southern

The implication of Mitchum's statement is horrific but perhaps it was designed to unnerve. Just as, after filming *The Winds of War* in the early eighties, he told the press he was, 'Going down to Mexico for the raping season.'

I can't help but cringe at that one.

'[Mitchum] *really played the part... you know, he made people frightened... he was like a fireball, you felt any moment he would explode, an eruption.*'

J Lee Thompson

Cady attacks Barrie Chase and there's little doubt he rapes her. He also has plans for Bowden's (Peck's) wife (Polly Bergen) and daughter.

The censors had a field-day. They demanded all mentions of rape were cut, along with the rape scenes. The UK censors were even tougher. Marketing opportunities aside, perhaps this is one of the rare movies where the chance to see the director's cut would be of genuine interest.

In one scene Cady looks down on Bowden's daughter – played by fifteen-year-old Lori Martin – as she kneels on all fours, scrubbing the deck of the boat.

'*Say, she's getting to be...* [he sups from his beer can] *getting to be almost as juicy as ya wife, ain't she? He-he.*'

R M to Gregory Peck, *Cape Fear*

'*He looks at the girl – according to the censor – too lasciviously. Well, I thought it was just a very good Mitchum look... the*' *censor saw there was some suggestion he was going to rape the girl. Well, of course. That really was the story.'*

J Lee Thompson

Thompson wanted Hayley Mills to play the daughter, having worked with her previously on *Tiger Bay* which was filmed in South Wales, but she was working on a Disney picture and unavailable.

When Mitchum gets around to attacking Polly Bergen (who would later star with him in *The Winds of War*), he throws her against a door, cutting open his hand in the process, and continuing with blood pouring from the wound well after Thompson had called 'cut'. She was scared; he knew what he could tap into. Afterwards he cradled her and apologised. He did what many actors won't or cannot do: convince us they are truly their character; reveal something of their animal self, which society would rather not witness and which many individuals refuse to admit exists.

Mitchum was convincing because the balance was right. He tried to portray a real man; a man we could believe exists and, so, a threat we could believe in – a bitter individual, a charmer with a vicious side, a fermenting brew of injustice and emotion.

But it wasn't just the attacks on women which were convincing. When filming the scene where Mitchum catches up with Peck and his family on the Cape Fear River, he didn't make it comfortable for his co-star. Peck didn't complain. It was him who wanted Mitchum in the film; who knew Mitch would be perfect as Cady; who knew

Mitch would steal the picture from under his nose.

'[Mitchum] *really took it to the limit... it looked marvellous on film.*'

Gregory Peck

'[There was] *great teamwork between the two of them. Mitchum was playing it beautifully and Greg let him run with it. He never once came to me and suggested cutting any lines, in fact we added lines* [to Mitchum's part].'

J Lee Thompson

'*As the vengeful killer, Mitchum proves again that, given the opportunity, he can be a resourceful and expressive performer. His heavy-lidded eyes and petulant mouth here convey a depth of evil that is truly frightening.*'

Arthur Knight, *Saturday Review*

I finish my beer. Stroll on down to the waterfront and River Street, reached via steep steps or cobbled ramp. With its mix of antiquity and lively bars, wrought iron street furniture and renovated warehouses, it reminds me of Plymouth's Barbican area. Only bigger. And warmer. River Street follows the banks of the Savannah, upon which sit paddle steamers and, upriver, the docks.

Earlier I bought myself a souvenir mug from a store called Bull Street Station. It's run by a guy called David Meredith who specialises in selling railway memorabilia. The mug bore the advertising slogan of the Chesapeake and Ohio Lines – 'Sleep like a Kitten and arrive Fresh as a

Daisy'. If it helps me sleep, it'll be worth it.

I talked with David about the state of the railways, the importance the railroad had to a port like Savannah, and Mitchum's arrest as a hobo. He packed the mug in a small cardboard box, and put it in a brown paper bag. I figure with its shape camouflaged it could, possibly, pass for a small explosive device. Or at least a suspicious package.

As I stroll around the riverfront I try leaving it places – stores, bars, ice cream parlours – to see whether it causes a reaction. It does, without fail. Every time I leave the premises, a member of staff runs after me, 'bomb' in hand, shouting, 'Sir, you forgot this.' A smile on their face, glad to be of service. I accept it with thanks, and try the next place. Maybe if I put a ticking clock in there.

I take it as a good sign. Here in Savannah normal Americans have not yet succumbed to instantly questioning innocent actions; whether or not a visitor's souvenir purchase is a suspect package. Instead, they rely on manners; they are pleasant, helpful, honest.

Right on cue, upriver comes a Saudi cargo ship, blowing its horn as brazen as they come. I wonder who and what it's bringing. Maybe I should be more concerned with what it will take away.

I stroll along the rail-track embedded in River Street. The cobbles once served as ballast on ships. The warehouses, once full of cotton. Both Savannah and the cotton trade depended upon those rails.

I call into Churchill's. It's a British bar. How I didn't see that coming I'll never know. They're showing highlights from the day's British football. This'll do for me. I take

a stool at the bar, order myself a beer, settle in for the duration.

There's a blonde woman sat on my right who talks like a Southern Paris Hilton and dresses about the same. As pleasant as she is to look at, the thought of having a conversation with her fills me with... nothing. She faces away from me, turning occasionally – first to check who's sat behind her, then to make sure I'm aware of her. She's used to the attention. Each swivel on her stool gives me a view of her legs way up to a short skirt, and gives her an opportunity to emphasise motion. But she appears to be with the guy on her right. They talk, laugh, drink. Suddenly go at it full-tilt. Two bodies becoming one, as much as is legal. I'm trying to watch the football and leave them to it but the lengths to which they go demand attention. I look around the bar – everybody's watching, commenting, gossiping. I turn to the barman. He raises his eyes to the ceiling. I order another beer and watch the game.

Try to watch the game. As the guy leans further into her, she leans further back. Her hair is almost in my beer. She's wearing so much hairspray I put my cigarette in the ashtray to save her going up in flames. Her hand is on my knee. I presume she's in danger of falling off her stool. But no. It does not have the force behind it of someone trying to remain upright. It slides up my thigh. Back down to my knee. Up my thigh, down to my knee. Up my thigh, up and in and a gentle squeeze. I'm amused, bemused and titillated. It's nothing to do with me, she just wants the attention; needs the attention – of men.

I turn to the girls stood behind me and grin. They

don't know what to make of it. Nor do I, but my cock doesn't complain. All I know is, if her boyfriend realises what his woman's up to behind her own back, I may get a kicking.

They disengage and drink. Her beau orders another round then heads to the bathroom. She turns to me. I say, 'Hi'. She gives me her best smile. This one's trouble, alright. I reckon she'd consider me and her beau fighting over her to be a successful night.

Albert Dekker: '*Stay out of trouble.*'
R M: '*What kind of trouble?*'
Albert Dekker: '*Oh, well, there are all kinds of trouble. You know one kind – you've been living in it all your life. Then there's another kind of trouble doesn't look like trouble at all. Sometimes it looks as pretty as a picture.*'

The Wonderful Country

'You look as pretty as a picture,' I tell her.

She gives me the mock-coy look; lowers her eyes. Raises them again without raising her head. 'Why thank you.'

Her beau returns so she turns back to him. Takes a sip of her drink. Starts talking before he can say anything.

In *Cape Fear* Mitchum sits at the bar of a jazz joint called the Boar's Head, bottle of Bud in hand, eyeing up women. He establishes lingering eye contact with a bobbed brunette played by Barrie Chase in her first movie role. She's sat with another man but thinks Mitchum looks exciting. He thinks she looks like his next victim.

466

The police enter and shake him down. A uniformed cop pulls out a billy club. Mitchum gets to his feet and says, 'You start reaching for those, you better call for the riot squad, man. I don't mind a little talk, I just don't like being pawed, ya know?' That wasn't just Cady talking; it was also Mitchum.

As they escort him off the premises he says to Chase, 'I'll give you one hour to lose your friend.'

'Are you trying to pick me up?' she asks.

'Yes.'

She's so enamoured, you know the sight of Mitchum being led away by the police won't put her off one bit. She's looking to slum it; for a bit of rough.

Mitchum lowers his hat over his eyes and allows the police to stroll beside him as he leaves.

'You're rock bottom. I wouldn't expect you to understand this, but it's a great comfort for a girl to know that she couldn't possibly sink any lower.'

Barrie Chase to R M, *Cape Fear*

I order another Sweet Water pale ale. The randy couple beside me whisper. They decide to leave. Stand and sweep past me, the skin of her arm brushing mine. The barman wishes them a good night, clears away their glasses, wipes down the bar. Holds out a wet cloth and says to me in his Irish-English, 'Would you do me a favour and wipe down those seats – I don't want the next people sat there complaining.'

'It's pretty certain he'll have a good night.'

467

'Thank God they've gone. It's like, get a room, man! Still...' he looks at his credit card slip, 'he tipped well so what the hell. But she was a stripper, don't you think?'

No wonder she's used to getting the whole room's attention.

The football's over. I need somewhere else to direct my attention. The woman sat to my left is a beauty but there's a wedding band on her finger and I've promised myself I won't get involved with the married no more. Is it a moral decision? Perhaps. Maybe I just want a simpler life; maybe the hassle ain't worth the effort.

R M: *'That ring mean anything?'*
Joan Staley: *'It means plenty.'*

Cape Fear

She orders a cocktail. Takes a big sip then asks for a fresh glass. 'This one has a chip in it.' A tiny, intsy-bitsy chip in it. Lady, I'd drink it out of your sweaty shoe. In fact, you pour it into your mouth, slosh it around and spit it into mine – that'd be fine by me.

A guy arrives and kisses her. Her husband, maybe. He sees me checking her out. 'Hey, how you doing?'

'I'm doing just fine, thanks.' (Just getting an eyeful of your woman.)

He doesn't seem phased or offended. Maybe he considers it a compliment. Maybe he's trying to avoid conflict or defuse a situation; prevent something before it happens. Maybe he's so confident in their relationship that nothing I can do will disturb him. Maybe his Southern

response is too subtle, compared to the sledgehammer British response I am used to: 'Wada fuck you lookin' at?'

The fact is, I'm hot for a woman. Please tell me Southern belle is on the menu, tonight.

'You ought to be kept in a cage.'

R M, *Crossfire*

Says you.

I pay up, leave, hit the Moon River Brewery and take a stool at the bar. Order me a draft of Swamp Fox. The woman sat next to me is stroking the stem of her glass. She knows I'm watching. I ask if she wants a refill.

'Where you from?'

I tell her. And ask where she's from.

'You know, you shouldn't ask where I'm from. Down here we say, "In Charleston they ask, who are your people? In Atlanta, who is your firm? And in Savannah, what do you drink?"'

'And what's the right answer?'

'Buy me that drink and I'll tell you.'

I order two drinks.

'That's kind of you, appreciate it.'

'You know, in the North they say, "In Boston they ask, what do you know? In Philadelphia, who do you know? In New York, how much do you earn?"'

'Then I'm happy to be from Savannah.'

She introduces herself as Faith.

'So what's a Savannah drink?'

'I guess a mint julip, or a bourbon would do.'

Ah, the mint julip – drink of the Southern gentry.

'You're wearing the suit for it.'

It's true, I'm the only linen suit on show in Savannah – I guess it's not yet spring.

'But I ain't got the shotgun on my knee.'

'Don't worry about that, you get a Southern girl pregnant and her daddy will supply all the firepower needed.'

'I guess, down here, safe sex consists of being able to run fast.'

'Can't do you no harm. Is it any different where you come from?'

'I reckon it's the same the world over.'

'I know that's the truth. All men run away when things get tough.'

'Some of us run towards it.' I order more drinks. 'So, your daddy got a shotgun?'

She laughs, stands, and as she walks to the restroom turns and says, 'Every girl's daddy got a shotgun – this is Georgia.'

Well, I guess I'm running already, so what harm if I gotta run faster?

A guy leans over, says, 'That's some beautiful woman.'

'Yes she is.'

'But don' matter how beautiful, she still gonna fuck you up.'

'Reckon?'

'They always do. I wouldn't take a million for my wife, but I wouldn't give you a nickel for another just like her.'

'I guess I'm just a blind optimist.'

'You don't know truth from lies, you're just a love-sick crank.'

R M, *The Locket*

'Ain't you realized yet, they're all the same?'

'I guess I need more evidence.'

'You're fooling yourself, you know that. The problem with women is: one is too many, but a million ain't enough.'

If that's true, then I reckon it's probably more a problem with men. But there's still value to what he says. 'Yeh, you might have something there. I just can't stop trying for more.'

'More what?'

'I ain't sure. Experience I guess. My own experience. I love women. I love lust. I love falling in love. And that ain't as healthy as it might sound.'

'You see,' he points to Faith returning from the rest-room, 'she's fuckin' you up, already.'

Faith comes back and asks if I wanna eat. There's only one answer to that. As we leave, the guy at the bar tips his hat.

'For a bright fella, you sure are slow getting the picture sometimes.'

R M, *Cape Fear*

She takes me to a restaurant a few doors down. We order conch in a key lime sauce and get talking. She hesitantly and vaguely tells me she works for the government. I'm

471

intrigued but choose not to waltz into that particular mine-field. I ask her what she wants in a man. It seems safer.

'Money.'

'Ain' it surprising about how romantic women can get about money?'

R M, The Lusty Men

'He don' have to be rich but I'm done with men who drink my grocery money. And I'm done with men who expect me to help them but don't help me back. They expect me to listen to their shit but do they listen to mine? Uh-uh. I'm always gonna be there to help 'cos that's what I do, right? But when I need help, all of a sudden they deaf and stone gone.'

'Do you need a protector?'

'Need? Hell, no.'

'Do you *want* a protector?'

'Sure I wan' a protector. Don' all women?'

R M: *'You wanna be safe?'*
Linda Darnell: *'Who doesn't?'*

Second Chance

'If I'm in danger, he's gotta step up to the plate. But I don't want no thug, no damage man.'

'Does he have to be sensitive, compassionate, empathic?'

'Sure would help. But not all the time – he's still gotta be a man, yu'know?

'How so?'

472

'Well, I don' want no mama's boy. Yeh, he's gotta have feelings and show he's a human being, but I don't wanna be no man's mama. He's gotta be strong. Sure, he can lean once in a while, but thass all. I'm gonna need to lean on him sometimes, too, but if he's already leaning on me, we gonna fall over.'

The conch is chewy like calamari, only less sweet. Lucky for me, Faith adds the flavour. She's got spirit, humour and a damn fine figure. She shines into the night.

'How about sex?'

'If he the right man, sex'll take care of itself.'

'No, I mean how about sex, right now?'

She gives me a look, 'I hope you don' mean in the restaurant?'

'Well, not unless you really want to. I was thinking more along the lines of my hotel room.'

'Well, OK, if you think you can handle a Southern woman. But on one condition.'

'What's that?'

'Remember my daddy's got a gun.'

The Hibernian Society

Take 27

I get woken by the sun bursting through the drapes and the Asian cleaner bursting through my door. He looks concerned for my health.

Faith has gone. There's a note on the bedside table. I have no idea what time it is but the sun has been up for some hours. Seems a woman in my bed is only way I get some sleep these days.

I contemplate getting up but feel as useless, as pointless, as the sharks' teeth washed up on the banks of the Savannah. I am slobbed-out and sweaty, feel like I've woken to find a paddle-steamer passing overhead, thwacking me with each turn of the wheel; locked in that moment immediately following a clip round the ear from my old man. I pull my imaginary skipper's cap down over my eyes. I am a captain without industry; a captain of *un*industry;   *in*industry;   *dustry*.   Unindustriousness. Industriousnessless.   Unindustrialisationalitinouslessness. I'm still learning to speak American.

It was a good night. Good drink, good town, good sex. But the hangover is brutal. It doesn't matter how sweet the shovel, you're still being hit over the head with a shovel. Wakey-wakey, Welshman. It's time to suffer; to pay the cost.

'Hubba-hubba, chop-chop.'

R M, *One Minute to Zero*

The worst thing about hotel rooms – pricey or cheap – is the stickiness of the carpets. Nothing worse than climbing out of bed and having to peel your soles from the floor. It makes me wanna go straight back to bed. But the clock says it's three, or perhaps it's four, or two. The clocks changed last night but I don't know which way. I need to find my glasses.

I breakfast on a number one combo from Hardees. Pocket the free pencil. Thank gods I'm a writer – there's no other trade I can think of for which so many places wanna give you a free tool. And today, in the Savannah spring Sunday sun, strolling around with little to do except write and recover from last night's drinking, I feel like a free tool.

The stretch of Mall Boulevard between my motel and Water Street consists of drive-thro banks and fast-food restaurants – at least a dozen of each; graphics studios, insurance offices, a roller-skating park, a gun shop. A fairly representative collection of American businesses. I arrive at the Lan Sharks Gaming Center and ask for web access.

The guy behind the counter looks me up and down, asks, 'You have a good night?'

'When you wake deep in the afternoon, still drunk, you know it's time to change your lifestyle.'

'Nah, there's no need to do that.'

A voice emerges from behind a computer, 'Spoken like a true Baptist. Good man.'

Seems I'm amongst friends.

I settle into my seat and sign in. Fanny around the internet for a couple of hours, searching for details of Brown Farm, prison records and warrants, movie locations, mediums and séances. I had toyed with the idea of trying to raise Mitchum's ghost and trap him in Savannah.

'There's no way to trap a ghost.'

R M, *White Witch Doctor*

But it was a moment of bitter haste. I couldn't do that to him – he served his time and deserves his freedom and I don't feel the resentment I had for him in my youth.

I could search police and county records for the facts of his arrest and incarceration but time is short and I don't reckon on finding Mitchum in a filing cabinet, real or hyper.

An email awaits me, from Bridgeport library. There's a photo attached. It shows the class of 1931, McKinley Elementary School. Third row down, second from the end, there's a boy looks suspiciously like Mitchum. This is all I need.

McKinley School, Bridgeport, Class of 1931...

and, lurking near the end of the
row, a young Bob Mitchum?

In 1931-32, Mitchum would've been fourteen going on fifteen. According to the records and biographies, Mitchum would've been living in Manhattan, or Delaware, or Fall River, but certainly not Bridgeport. Perhaps it's not Mitchum, but the hair, the face shape, those eyes suggest otherwise.

I want to ignore it; pretend it doesn't exist. It seems however much I investigate, however certain I am of the truth of Mitchum, there's always an extra layer waiting to be uncovered. Well, I'm running out of time. Mitchum, you ain't ever gonna let me find the truth in your details, your travels and overlapping existences, but you haven't won yet. I've tried the professional way – libraries and press archives, research and contacts; I've investigated location, life-style, love. I've drank and robbed and fucked. There's only one more place I'm gonna find answers. I need to get down to the swamp.

'When the dogs start running he'll head for the thicket. He'll likely run downhill, instead of up. He'll try to get into the swamp.... You'll just have to follow along the best you can.'
R M, *Home from the Hill*

I ask the guy behind the desk how I can get to Okefenokee.
'Why would you want to go to the swamp?'

'I don't know why. It's just that I gotta go where I've not been and where I can say, "This far I've come, I can't go no farther." You understand that?'
Richard Widmark, *The Way West*

479

He pulls up a map and prints it. Even though it's in Georgia the easiest way on public transport appears to be via Florida, so Florida it must be. The thirteenth state I'll visit on this trip. Down into the land of Fargo and the Suwannee.

I have twenty-one bucks in my pocket. That's all I've got. My traveller's cheques are spent, my cards maxed out, I know if I get home there'll just be a whack of bills blocking the door. I email my publisher to wire me some funds. If they want me back, they gotta pay the ransom. I know he'll just ask what happened to the advance.

'I didn't throw it away – it just sort of floated.'

R M, *The Lusty Men*

I leave Lan Sharks and light a smoke. It's cooler tonight, down to seventy-five degrees. My knee's playing up. Sharp pains shooting through the cap tell me there's gonna be a downpour soon.

As I walk past the soft Spanish moss coating Shadows of Plantation Oaks, its ghostly shapes hanging down, the crickets stop and there is silence. Complete and utter silence. I look up at the moon. Its crescent vivid in a deep blue evening sky. I'm suddenly conscious of how much I've dreamed of this – this quiet moment in the South; the collective effect of oaks and moss and moon, crickets and an open sky. How it must have felt to the teenage Mitchum, escaping Georgia; escaping capture and danger and predators under a canopy of wonder.

The crickets crank up. I look around the sky. Clouds

gather to the south.

'Everything's quiet. Too quiet, I can hear the crickets.'
R M, Where Danger Lives

I get back to the motel. Splash my face and phone a cab. He's just around the corner but he's already got passengers.

'How many of you?'

'Just me.'

I run around to the street and get in the front seat. The driver chows down on some gum; wears a straw hat and wife-beater vest. There's a woman and man in the back. I tell them I appreciate it.

All the way downtown the woman's asking questions of the driver but doesn't wait for him to answer before changing the subject. You want people to take you seriously and respond positively: be choosy about what falls out of your cakehole. Some people like to dominate conversation; some like to make the most noise. Me, I'm a big mouth on my day but generally happy to be shouted down or told to shut up when I deserve it; sit back and listen to others hang themselves. Depending on the mood I'm in. Right now I feel like quiet. And reckon having your say may be a right but being listened to is a privilege people take for granted.

I get dropped at the Six Pence pub. There's a Welsh flag hanging outside. I take a stool at the bar and order a beer. Watch the TV news. President Bush has landed in Bridgeport to talk about Connecticut's health plan crisis which, it's claimed, is in 'dire straits'. Comes to something when the richest country in the world can't look after the health of its own. Not *can't*; won't. Just ask N'Orleans.

I ask the server if she knows somewhere good to eat seafood. She recommends the Shrimp Factory.

'The Shrimp Factory, huh? What about with the Octopus Depot?'

'Savannah doesn't have an Octopus Depot.'

Figured not. 'No good asking about the Calimari Call Center, then?'

She doesn't find me funny. I find this reassuring. Nor do I.

After a few beers the rain still hasn't come and I feel the need for air. I pay my tab and stroll the streets: Montgomery, Jefferson, Price; Jones, Harris, Perry. I try and relive the night with Faith but something's bugging my brain; fermenting. It ain't the hangover or the travel fatigue. I just gotta leave it alone until it's ready to tell me what's going on. I was advised, when I got down South, to be quiet and listen. Well, I done that. I followed the local saying: 'It is better to be silent and thought an idiot, than to open your mouth and remove all doubt.'

The South prides itself on friendliness, just as Wales likes to milk the idea of 'a welcome in the hillsides'. But it's a hard one to judge. For instance, for superficial camaraderie, nowhere matches Manhattan. In Boston, it didn't seem friendly but nor did it feel hostile. Perhaps, there, friendships are slower coming and deeper reaching. In the South, from my short stay here, I'd say the friendliness is present, somewhere. Not as overt as Manhattan, and it feels as if I'm being checked out underneath the smile, but there's something present. A little slowness is reassuring – these days I ain't sure I'd trust a friendship made in an instant.

But where do I feel most at home? Virginia is the most like Wales but that doesn't mean it feels most like my home. As an urban boy I feel most comfortable in New York, no question. But in terms of social politics, my first thoughts are that I'm more akin to the South than the North. I'm just not sure which South. The people here seem unimpressed with pretension but I bet if I got me an invite to the old, civilised class I'd drown in it there. And, instinctively, I feel I'm being misjudged down here and that hits me like a shovel across the head. Or maybe I'm just carrying some of Mitchum's resentment?

But the question remains: is the South so friendly? I'm still not certain. Everyone says, 'Hi', 'How you doing?' 'How are you today?' 'Thank you', 'Appreciate it', but that advice keeps coming back to me: 'you don't really known what a Southerner thinks of you unless you're from the South.'

All I have to go on is my own personal experience. I've seen no street fights; encountered reticence but not attitude. No racism either. From what I've seen of the South, if 'racial' means 'racist' then I ain't seen it. Everybody's been civil to one another, whether black or white. I wonder how the Asian cleaning staff get treated.

It's possible the North finds it convenient to place America's racism firmly and solely on the shoulders of the South. OK, so prejudice is often inherent rather than obvious but I see more overt racism in New York City than in Georgia or the Carolinas. I suspect the issues of race and class are confused. People need someone to look down on – I'm as guilty as the next. But I look down on those who think aspiration equates to promotion in the social order. Sure, improve yourself and the quality of your life, but don't think that makes you better or more worthy than you were, or anyone else is. We're all animals making the best of it and everbody's shit stinks. Doesn't mean you have to rub others' noses in it, but the fact remains.

Mitchum believed in this. He was often more at home with the hobo, the survivor, the working-class. Although he was wise enough to drop his prejudices as he aged and got to understand that even in a world as shallow as Hollywood there were still quality and sincerity to be found in individuals.

He claimed he didn't mix with actors, which is not entirely accurate. What is true is he would often prefer to keep company with the film crew rather than the egos in front of camera. But his ability to mix with all, to camouflage himself to suit the surroundings, I find admirable. It is the times when he lost touch with that, when he acted like a drunken, borish bastard, that people often recollect. But for a working-class kid to find himself mixing with the self-proclaimed elite of society, well, you can't expect him not to react at times; for his surroundings to conflict with his upbringing and values. For those factors to emerge through anti-social practise. Discomfort with one's self or one's surroundings.

R M: '*Why don't you take that chip off your shoulder?*'

Jane Russell: '*Everytime I do somebody hits me over the head with it.*'

Macao

I get frustrated with the fester and churn. Call into a bar on Bay. I'm just ordering my first beer when somebody speaks to me – a couple sat next to me, enjoying themselves. I haven't eyed her up so I can presume the contact's friendly.

'What's that?'

'I said are you local?'

'No, just passing through.'

'We're from Michigan.'

'From Mitchum?'

'Michigan. I don't know where Mitchum is.'

Tell me about it. 'So what you two doing down here?'

'We're looking to move. Michigan's cold. Too much snow. Here it's warm and there's a slower way of life.'

'That appeal to ya, huh?'

'Hell, yes. All our friends think we're mad, but winter in Michigan is suicide-central. We wanna come down here and ride our bikes.'

'Freedom, huh? There's a lot of people looking for that.'

They're heading to an Irish bar to listen to some music. Invite me to join them. Hell, I ain't got nothing but solitude to lose.

She's late teens, he's early twenties. They've been together five years. Lucky to find each other so young. Or maybe not. Someday they may want to experience more of the world and have to decide whether to sacrifice what they have and go for it, or not. A heart-breaking choice. I hope they never have to go through it. Maybe they'll get to see and do it all, together. He's served some time and is looking for a fresh start. She wants to follow.

We reach the bar on Congress. The menu chalked behind the bar offers a drink called an 'Irish Car Bomb'. God-damn America, I thought *I* had bad taste.

The band are country and pretty good. Between songs I catch slivers of conversation between drinkers.

'I ain't droppin' my gun. That's Georgia, baby.'

'He was goddamn sit-down ignorant.'

'I know that's the truth.'

'You can kiss my rebel red, white and blue ass.'

'Hundred'n'forty for a pool cue? What's it made out of, diamond? It won't break when I hit it over someone's head, but will it do my dishes?'

I'm getting drunk for the sake of it and it ain't satisfying. The thought of those Irish Car Bombs has blown away my pleasure. Besides, if I wanna get to the swamp I got an early bus to catch tomorrow. Tonight. In a few hours. I drink up and make my goodbyes. I hate to leave a bar in a mood but I need some time to myself. Myself and Mitchum.

It's difficult to fathom the depth of Mitchum's sociability. After the drugs bust in '49 he decided to distance himself from some of his less socially acceptable compadres, choosing instead to hang out at private parties given by his wife or their neighbours.

'Do I miss the Hollywood life? What Hollywood life? I never

traveled with the mob. I've been to only one movie star's
home – Kirk Douglas's – and that was for all of ten minutes.'

R M

Mitchum said that two years after he and Douglas appeared in *Out of the Past*. Mitchum had been enthusiastic about working with the promising young actor, but when it came to filming, Douglas decided to take on Mitchum at his own game and underplay in front of camera. Mitchum wasn't having it and under-underplayed. Eventually director Jacques Tourneur had to step in and tell them to focus on the scene, not the competition. So Douglas tried other tricks to try and steal the scene, like flipping a coin. Mitchum remained one step ahead of him. Tourneur stood by Mitchum.

By 1967, when they had to work closely in *The Way West*, it was pretty clear they didn't see eye to eye and that Mitchum felt he had the upper hand over Douglas. Also in the cast was brother John, playing one of the shotgun-carrying Henry brothers. His opinion was that it was 'Only [Bob and Kirk's] professionalism kept them from open warfare.'

It was not only Mitchum that Douglas antagonised. During rehearsals he tried to direct Richard Widmark, moving him around and showing him where to stand. Widmark responded aggressively. Widmark, an introverted ex-middleweight, got in Douglas's face and whispered, 'Don't direct *me*, Kirk' and, pointing to the director Andrew V McLaglen, added, 'There's our director. If he wants to tell me something, I'm prepared to listen, but you-don't-direct-me.'

Not knowing how to react to the uncomfortable and destablising situation, some of the young actors laughed. Douglas turned on them like a little man trying to save face. The whole crew turned against Douglas. John rushed to his brother's trailer and suggested he was the one to do something about it. Bob said he'd take care of things – tomorrow.

On set the next day, instead of taking Douglas to task, Mitchum told to no one in particular the story of a young actor who asked how he could become a director. Mitchum explained it was simple. 'Just put on your wardrobe and appear on the set. It seems that qualifies anyone for the job.' The point was taken. Douglas fumed and, later, kept the movie out of his memoirs.

Later in life, when asked how he got along with Douglas, Mitchum told another story of how, in 1987 while filming *Queenie*, Douglas complained to the movie's producer that another actor on set was taller than him, adding, 'No one is taller than I am!' Ditches were dug so Douglas would appear taller. Although satisfied that he was now the tallest on screen, Douglas again approached the producer, declaring, 'The man has a cleft chin – I have the cleft chin!'

'How can you compete with that kind of ego?' asked Mitchum. 'We get along perfunctorily. I say "hello" and the emperor acknowledges my greeting.'

Mitchum was never one to tolerate egos. Perhaps the last word on this should be given to to the script of *The Way West*:

Kirk Douglas: *'Sir, you're a liar.'*
R M: *'I believe you're beginning to get a bit personal.'*
Kirk Douglas: *'No, sir, because the best man bar none is you.'*

I hope saying that rankled.

It could be argued that only one actor ever managed to up-stage Mitchum, and that was in death. Mitchum died on 1 July 1997 – less than a month short of his eightieth birthday. He had lung cancer and emphysema as a result of a lifetime of tobacco, marijuana and alcohol use.

'That's one cashed-in dog.'

Florenz Ames, *Man with the Gun*

His passing filled the papers but within twenty-four hours the fall guy had been replaced by the little man: the reports and obits for Mitchum had been quickly replaced by those covering the death of Jimmy Stewart – the stammering friend of invisible rabbits; the all-round good guy (and also a poet) who died soon after Mitchum. It was as if the on-screen personifications of the polarised extremes of humanity couldn't exist without the other.

'Stewart was the heart and Mitchum was the soul.'

Roger Egbert, *Awake in the Dark*

Two great actors, two secret poets, two great examples to men. Two cashed-in dogs, both chasing a bone to the grave.

Take 28

'Tonight's a long time ago.'

Gloria Grahame, Crossfire

The alarms go off at four. I drag myself out of my pit at four-thirty. Swill my face, throw my kit in my bag, light a smoke and phone a cab.

I take a last look around my hotel room; the last roof over my head. I drag my case out to the curb, lift it into the trunk of the cab.

'You good to go?'

'As good as I can be. Bus station. Quick, please.'

'It's gonna be one hell of a long day for me.'

R M, Home from the Hill

I approach the window and buy a ticket. Confirm departure time and bus bay. There's four of us waiting for the Greyhound to Jacksonville. Greyhounds arrive, fill up, depart. No bus parks in our bay. The time comes and goes. We look at each other, hoping to find confidence to continue the wait. We smoke, throw down our butt ends, huff and sigh. One by one the others head for the window. A crowd gathers. I join them. Wait my turn. Ask about the bus to Jackonsville.

'That bus has gone.'

'But I been waiting by the bay, I ain't seen no bus.'

'It went from bay five.'

'You told me bay eight.'

'It went from bay five.'

'*Dog-gone, I'm always missing something.*'

Richard Quine, *We've Never Been Licked*

'So you gonna accept any responsibility for that?'

'Uh-uh.'

She ain't gonna apologise for nothin'. Goddamn Savannah fucked with Mitchum, tried to keep him here, and now it's doing it to me. Admittedly, not catching a bus ain't the same as getting sent down to the farm but it still means we're both kept from reaching the Okefenokee.

'What time's the next service?'

'Few hours.'

'Well, what are we supposed to do 'til then?'

She gives me a look.

'Baby, I don't care.'

R M, *Out of the Past*

'Well you have a good day, too. Knowing you've fucked four people before breakfast.'

She ignores me. Dagnabit. We're hovering around the window having been truly done over by the bitch on the other side. I'm over-riding my anger. I got bigger fish to fry. I go outside for a cigarette.

Well, now I'm here for a while I may as well settle in. I take a seat. The guy sat opposite me has a fish-shaped Stars and Stripes on his T-shirt, underneath it the words 'Trout Fishing'. *Hmm*. Didn't someone write a book about that, *Trout Fishing in America*? Damn fine read if I remember. I drag out a health bar from my bag; a 'Bible Bar' – 'Contains the seven foods of Deuteronomy'. The bits get stuck in my teeth.

The big-mouth NY-Latino sat next to me is bitching about the state of the station and the quality of service.

'They got a real attitude,' she says of the Greyhound staff. I have to agree with her. It's the cheapest form of long-distance transport so we, the passengers, get treated like we're cheap. 'I nearly missed my bus here because they give me the wrong gate number.'

I tell her the same happened to me.

'An' they don' apologise. And look at the filth. They don't clean the buses, either. You look at the windows and there's bacteria all along the edges, and we breathing it. They don' look after their passengers like they do on the planes. I was gonna fly but I was late gettin' my ticket and

493

I gotta get there tomorrow for my mother's birthday. Twenty-six hours. Twenty-six hours on a stinkin' bus to New York City. It's filthy and they don' let you off.'

She has a point, but bacteria? That's New Yorkers for you: human existence is just an excuse to moan. For a city which serves as home to so much creativity and invention it doesn't half have a negative attitude. I can't think of one New York friend who really, *really* enjoys living in the city but there's no way you'll ever convince them to live anywhere else.

Her bus arrives. I offer to help her with her bag. She declines, keeps it tight to her chest.

'Than' k'you, no. I got my medication in here. I gotta keep hold of it all times.'

The bus pulls in. I can't resist singing my own words to Johnny Cash's 'Jackson': 'I'm gonna Jackson(ville), Ok-e fen-o-kee, too. I'm gonna Jackson(ville), I'm gonna get there too....' Now where in the hell did I last hear that tune?

I take a seat and get joined by a pregnant woman. I slide over to the window. She squeezes her bag between her legs which presses her thigh against mine. The bus gets going. We head down the Okefenoke Parkway. Roadsigns advertise 'Cheap Cigarettes', 'UV's Welcome', '10ft Shark!', '17ft Gator!' – the usual things. Over the Big Satilla River. The woman next to me falls asleep. Her head on my shoulder, her thigh against mine. The warmth of her flesh is appealing. As is the gentleness of her sleeping breath. I join her in sleep. It is what it is; nothing more. The intimacy of the Greyhound. You either accept it or have an uncomfortable trip.

We pull into Jacksonville. I wake bathed in the citric sweat of Florida and the imagined strains of Johnny Allen's 'The Promised Land'. The woman next to me is complaining to nobody about the heat. She stands to let me off the bus. Speaks to the driver and asks, politely, that when they leave he turn up the a/c.

'I'll call you an ambulance,' he says.

He ain't listening. She explains again: 'I don' need no amb'lence, I jus' wan' you to turn the air up.'

'Lady, if you're unfit to travel, get off the bus.'

And that's that. She's a pregnant woman for chrissake. I wanna support her case but I know if I join in I'm just gonna fuel the fire; he's gonna feel out-numbered, ganged-up against, and he's gonna over-react and then I'll over-react and break his fucking face or get arrested in the process. She'll get kicked off the bus, I'll get kicked out of the country.

'I got told two things yesterday. One of them was to keep my big nose out of other people's business. That's pretty good advice all round.'

R M, *The Lusty Men*

I'm learning to think things through. The real-life Mitchum would've pinned him to a wall by now and got his point across. At least if she deals with it alone the driver will get chance to feel superior and powerful and this is the only way she'll get what she needs. I tell her to make sure he looks after her.

She says, 'Oh yeh, I will.' And lights up a cigarette.

I board the bus to Lake City. We head sixty miles west, on 90. Through the Osceola National Forest, past the Olustee battlefield. Mitchum may've lived in Florida for a while, when his father was still alive. The details are sketchy. Even Mitchum was uncertain.

My knees are killing me – weeks spent on the Greyhound. I feel drawn, unwell. All this travel, this unsettled lifestyle, this lack of sleep, this searching, all this thinking.

'You're sick in body, because you can't face the sickness of your soul…. Meet this inner conflict, understand it and then set it right.'

Cecil Humphreys, *Desire Me*

The guy next to me is taking up the leg space and the guy opposite has his legs in the aisle. They both snore. I stretch the best I can. The scabs on my toes have stuck to my shoes. They rip away from my flesh as I stretch. My legs need to escape to an open space, to run and climb and dive and tense.

Roy Roberts: *'Alright, whadda ya wanna do, spend the rest of your life remembering Jackson? If that's it then let's hang up the gloves, let's get through with it. Stop kidding ourselves about ever going back to the garden.'*
R M: *'We'll be back there soon enough.'*
Roy Roberts: *'You've been promising me that ever since we left New York. When is soon? When the peanut money runs out, or when your legs won't carry you the distance?'*

Second Chance

Add a 'ville' to that Jackson and I'm there.

The bus pulls into Lake City – 'Gateway to Florida'. It sure don' look like no city, don' feel like no city. Lake City? Fake City. Slat houses along a semi-rural road, the bleakness of the Greyhound station is fast becoming too familiar – another run-down, country stop. The toilets don't work and the vending machines are sold out. The walls are covered with photographs of bus drivers alongside their mounts. Travellers between rides wait for a way out of town and sit under the canopy smoking cigarettes. They cough, they toss their butts on the floor, they don't say too much. The next bus to Jacksonville don't leave for another five hours. Plenty of time for me to get to the swamp. Who knows, I may even come back.

My cell-phone is dead. I pull out a quarter and reach for the payphone. I dial a number taped to the window. The local cab company has only one driver and, according to the woman on the other end of the line, he refuses to take me to the swamp.

'Why not?'

'There ain't no other driver to cover for him while he's outa town.'

'But he'll be on a solid meter; he'll make more money driving me for a couple of hours than short trips around town. Explain that, will you? Ask him what it'll take; what it'll cost.'

She puts me on hold, comes back: 'I'm sorry sir, he still says no.'

Bizarre, but there's no point me arguing – regular custom, I guess. I phone a cab from Live Oak – thirty miles away – but they refuse to come this far out. I figure I'll phone the wildlife center to see if they can give me some advice on how to reach those moist roots. I ask the guy behind the counter to break a dollar into quarters. He refuses me too.

'Hell, I only got six left.'

So I got no transport, no coin for the phone. I always thought this search would end in tragedy, instead it looks like it's ending in farce. I accept it; am fatalistic, I may be this close but until I'm there I may as well be on the other side of the ocean. I don't know what my next move is. I do have tobacco. I roll and light in the sun. A gust tries to blow out my light but I inhale and encourage the flame. Mitchum tried to get to the swamp and got arrested for his trouble. OK, so I ain't getting sent down to the farm but I am stranded in a one-horse town with no way of getting to the swamp; I am – literally – up the Suwannee.

The tin drum used as a communal ashtray is at odds with the surroundings. Its chocolate-box art shows an American farmhouse, barn, wooden fence – all covered in snow. Something to dream of, in the sun. Does it snow here? Does snow ever settle on the swamp?

We sit and kick up dirt; listen to the de-dum, de-dum of occasional traffic pummelling the concrete road. To the side of the station, a couple of rusting wheelchairs. Above, a tattered Stars and Stripes – the first single flag I've seen for a while, all others down here were twinned with one depicting the Southern states.

Opposite me sits a bald guy in his fifties; grey suit, open-necked shirt, polished tasseled loafers, no socks on his feet. His trousers too short for his legs. A big, battered, leather-bound King James Bible in his hands. His head is bowed. I ain't sure if he's prayin' or sleepin' but every so often he raises his head to stare into me. I nod, say, 'How ya doin'?' but he lowers his head without speaking. We all got our burdens and I don't wanna interrupt his but, man, every time I look up his eyes are burrowing into me. There's no hate there, no disdain, no racial judgements, no questioning. It's as if he understands something and wants me to know it. As if he can see into me; as if he can see my swamp and knows there's no way out of it. That travelling to see it doesn't fool anyone – I live in it every day, and it in me. That I can't just board a bus and go visit or leave it behind.

An SUV pulls into a bus space. The Bible man looks up, opens his mouth for the first time and says, 'Him parked there? He a bad man.' A harsh judgement, it rings like a warning. I don't think he's talking about the choice of parking space. I cannot see the driver sat behind his tinted screens. The bible man goes back to prayer-sleep.

Around us patient passengers shuffle positions. A Grateful Dead-head in straw cowboy hat; a woman with braids; a boy with a rat's tail down the back of his neck; various men in baseball caps, doo-rags, bandanas; a little old lady in a string of pearls; a teenage couple running away to get married – 'we're going to get married,' they say to anyone who'll listen, hugging each other and sharing their cigarette.

A tattoo'd guy cracks his knuckles. I crick my neck. The subtle communications of masculinity take the place of camaraderie or friendship.

What to do. What to do. I'm not fretting, ain't concerned, certainly not worried, but I'm disappointed at having to think again. My brain doesn't want to take the lead; would rather follow snap decisions made by instinct, emotion and Mitchum's trail.

I could hitch. Hitching to a city is one thing but hitching to isolated regions is another. The dangers change. Whatever, as long as I get to the swamp. I gotta go see that swamp, for Mitchum. Or to get one over on Mitchum. I can't be sure of my motivation.

I hear a train's airhorn. Decide to follow its reverberation in search of a solution. Reach downtown. On the corner of the sunny thoroughfare there's a diner claiming they're 'Serving you & the Kingdom of God.' That's gotta be one long queue. I wonder what they serve in there? Wine and wafer? Fish and chips wrapped in newspaper? Biscuit and gravy wrapped in *The Watchtower*? A messy meal if ever there was.

I walk the town. It doesn't take long. The Bible bookstore has closed down – seems this town ain't open to good news. Bric-a-brac shops for nosing around out of the rain, if it was raining; coffee shops and diners to chat in; a parking lot; Lake DeSoto not two minutes walk to sit by and eat lunch. The fountain gushing, birds singing and shitting over the memorial to local police officers who gave their lives. Nice to have a lake; every city should have a lake. But I maintain, Lake City ain't no 'city', however many lakes they got. I'd be offended at the con if I could be bothered; if I wasn' too busy with my own concerns. Too small, too quiet. Not much to offer the pedestrian traveller but seems like a pleasant stop if I wasn't on a mission to somewheres else.

What to do. I have nothing to say. Nothing to think. All urgency gone. No plan, no idea if I'm pissed off or resigned or just waiting for things to fall into place. Maybe it's walkin' in the good heat and Southern sun – unusual for the season, I'm told. If only I could get that train whistle out of my head – it's like Mitchum's watching me the whole way, seeing what nonsense I get up to, what mistakes I make, thinking about how he would do it and do it right, having a chuckle at my expense.

Douglas V Fowley: *'So what no-good you been up to?'*
R M: *'Oh, the usual.'*

The Good Guys and the Bad Guys

It's like that airhorn, that train whistle, is my Preacher Powell, singing in the distance.

'Bringing in the sheaves, bringing in the sheaves,
We shall come rejoicing, bringing in the sheaves...'

R M, *Night of the Hunter*

It serves as reminder of his presence; his oppressive threat, the long cast of his shadow – the stronger example of my gender, the competition he presents, the model he set and his growing proximity, his success. Where now then, Mitch, you old drunken bastard? Follow the road or follow the rail? Give me a sign, *daddio*, you brought me here, this is your trail; lead and I'll follow. Tell me where.

I stop for homemade lemonade. I'm not hungry but I haven't eaten today and if I'm gonna stomp off into the swamp I better get something decent inside me. What did Frank tell me? 'When you're down South just shut up and eat. They'll do the talkin' for ya, while you get good eatin'.' Yeh, well maybe I should do just that.

I find a café at the back of a hippy store – crystals, therapy books, things which may or may not help people to help themselves. Goddamn pseudo-spirituality. Mitchum's mother and sister were in some cult – maybe that's unfair, an 'alternative belief system'. They would tap up Mitchum's mom, Mitchum's mom would tap up her son, they'd all get to go on some 'retreat' somewhere. Happy days.

Whatever. I'm past throwing stones at all that. Each to their own, I reckon. I mean, look at me: I'm running up and down the States looking in the bottom of a bottle for the dregs of a dead man as if he's gonna give me answers and tell me how to be a man, the real deal, the *dad*, or at least how to stop asking the question. Well how the hell is that any different to burning incense and surrounding yourself with a mishmash of bric-a-brac from various religions in the hope they will cleanse your aura? Jesus, glass houses – I gotta be careful.

At least it ain't traditional religion. I was brought up in that and it did me no good at all. From a young age I was surrounded by the self-righteous, the pompous, the hypocritical; the guilty, the camouflaged, the perverts in cassocks, those who are disgusted with themselves and humanity; a belief system which told me I was bad before I'd even had the chance to prove it. As a kid Mitch was often blamed for anything bad that happened so he figured, 'Well if I'm gonna get blamed for it, I may as well do it.' It granted him freedom but it also gave him a chip on his shoulder he would never get rid of.

Western religions – belief systems which told the bad they were bad already, so as long as they apologise they may as well get on with it. Free rein for the evil. A corrupter of the normal. Guilty conscience for those who don't deserve it and free rein for those who do. How the hell is that a healthy environment in which to bring up a kid? How is that a healthy environment in which to live?

Mitchum registered himself as a druid – an ancient, Welsh, stone-worshipping, mountainside religious man.

Yeh, I hate religion. But as a kid I hated Mitchum too. He represented the whole male thing that I, as a quiet loner of a bike-riding, poem-writing kid could not stand up to. It was too big, like Mitchum was too big when his frame entered a scene. The sound of him singing 'Bringing in the sheaves...' too threatening; the knowing look in his eyes too condescending – you don't know me, Mitchum, so wipe off that grin. OK, now you know me too well so buy me a beer. He was the epitome of all I couldn't be. He was someone I could hate, admiringly. Now Jimmy Stewart was harmless; usually stood up for the little guy; all us people with invisible friends, the stammerers like myself. Stewart I could tolerate, as long as he didn't get too sickly sweet. But Mitchum, hell, I wanted to punch his lights out every time he came on TV. At least I was a child when I felt this

– a lot of men in pubs and bars wanted to do the same; test their strength against him, in front of their girls, as if he were a circus sideshow bell to ring, and they were old enough to know better. Mitch would often resist; give them the first hit for free then warn them to sit down and get on with their night, but they'd persist and Mitch would put them down. The next day the papers would carry headlines like 'Mitchum in Bar Brawl', 'Mitchum Floors Drinkers', 'Mitchum Throws Marine out of Window'.

Masculinity. What we teach kids; what we show kids, or allow them to fuck up with guidance. A whole range of expectations placed upon me simply because I was male? Leave me alone, I was just tryna ride my bike, play football, write a poem, invent my own language, exist in my imagination or just clear my brain. Achieve emptiness. Calm. So when the penny drops, if it ever would, it might just get heard. No, I gotta be a man, I was told. So I tried. I got into fights but it took me well into my adulthood before I could hate anyone else enough to want to make them bleed.

Maleness, the search for manliness, seems to be something handed down with urgency from father to son, as if to say, 'Here, I'm sick of this, it's your responsibility now. Me? I have a son and that makes me a man – I no longer have to ask the question, that's your problem now.' Fathers can't get rid of it fast enough. Cowards, every one of them. After mine split town, I was left the 'man' of the house, even before my balls had dropped. I brought in the coal, took care of the chickens, I was surrounded by women.

Perhaps therein lies the answer to maleness: the

contrast to, and the treatment of, women. But a man cannot rely only on women to define him, he must also learn how to exist within a male world and define himself. Mitchum achieved this. He managed to get men to believe he was one of them, and women to believe he wasn't. He was a man's man; a lady's man. A man in everyone's eyes, but maybe not his own – not man enough to get away with writing poetry. Well Mitchum, you shoulda been a poet first and a man second. You succumbed, Mitch, you hid yourself and played up to the big icon. *The Big Sleep*, *The Big Steal*, the big con. Yeh, you were a real man, a real man too scared of something as basic and essential as poetry. Man, if you had opened your wise-ass mouth and admitted your sensitivity, think what a hero you would've been. A real man – no one could argue that – who admitted to the range of existence and created artistic, honest expression out of it, if only for his own ends and means. Man, you don't get much closer to a real man than a poet – fucked up as we may be. One who admits to existing. And for all your fighting, your womanising, your drinking, your drugging; perhaps only in loving your woman, in having children, were you ever as close to achieving your manhood as when writing a poem: as when revealing yourself to yourself, in the artistic. Art is not a process of intelligence; it is a spiritual, emotional ceremony of self and existence. It is looking yourself in the eye. Being brave enough to be honest, to admit what you are and what you aren't. It is knowing and not wanting to end it. It is feeling. And men continue to rob themselves of this; rob themselves of the opportunity to use creativity as a tool to assist us in understanding our own existence and reason. Without this outlet there can only be lunacy.

I roll a cigarette and drink my tea. The woman dusting crumbs from my table recommends the bell peppers and rice. So I take the peppers, the rice, the green leaf salad, the sunflower seeds, the garlic, the olive oil, the finely chopped tomato flesh, the spinach leaves – mustn't forget the spinach leaves, they do their job magnificently – the half-grapes and strawberry. Yeh, Frank was right, down South is good eatin'.

She asks me if I like it. I like it a lot. Her name is Tammy. She is smiling and has beautiful, glittering blue eyes. She tells me she loves my accent. I tell her I love her food.

'I invented the salad only this morning. Y'u know, I jus' couldn't face making another soup an' it's spring outside so I thought I'd make this. If everyone likes it I guess I'll keep it on the list.'

'Do you have a recipe?'

'Naw, I don't follow recipes; just put in things I like.'

I explain I'm trying to get to the Okefenokee Swamp. She's never heard of it. A guy enters through the side door, a woman follows. Tammy turns and calls him over, 'Hey Charlie, this guy needs to get to the Oak-ee-se-bo-kee Swamp?'

'Hey, that's way down south...'

Having been told Florida ain't really the South I don't know if he means geographically or culturally. So I ask, 'You mean further, in Florida?'

'Yep.'

'Nah man, you must be thinking of someplace else. I'm looking for the Okefenokee, it's in Georgia.'

'Oh, yeh, the Okefenokee. Hell, that's in Georgia. You need to go to Georgia.'

I can't fault his logic but add, 'Well according to this map,' I show him my map, 'it also comes over the state line into Florida, not too far north of here....' I leave it hanging.

'Hm.' He's thinking. He turns to speak to his girlfriend who's sat at the bar, 'You thinkin' what I'm thinkin'?'

'Yep.'

'If you've got a map I can drive you up to Fargo, the swamp should be somewhere round there, if *you* pay the gas....'

Easy deal.

'Man, I'll pay for the gas, the soda, the cigarettes, I'll put your kids through college – if you can get me to that swamp.'

'OK, let's do it.'

So we do it. Charlie seems more excited about this unexpected adventure than I am. Although it ain't no adventure for him – he lives just off highway 441, along which we bomb towards Fargo. He wants to talk, to laugh. He's good company, has spent some time in Britain, drops in British slang at every opportunity, as he remembers words not used in ages. It's good to hear him use them; good to hear old friends; entertaining to hear words like 'bonkers' again. How long has it been, bonkers, since we last met? Many moons, although your presence is still felt. I check to make sure I'm not thinking out loud but if I am he hasn't noticed. He's telling me about some of

507

the scrapes he's had. I don't wanna think about scrapes – enough of those of my own. I wanna think about the swamp. Where is it? What does it look like? Will I recognise it when I see it? Will it recognise me? Will it try to drag me back; try and force me into returning so I can continue evolution from where it left off – man still needs some work done. Will it smell? A swamp's gotta smell, surely. Whatever. I reckon a swamp's as good a place as any to try to get answers.

If I'm here for answers it means I can no longer avoid the question: what have I learned? Knowing me, nothing. But perhaps, perhaps by following Mitchum's trail, by uncovering his past and his formative years, I've gained some handle on my own history and upbringing. And future. Perhaps, perhaps I need to bury the past out there in the swamp. Perhaps, perhaps I need to leave something of myself; something old, cantankerous, cankerous, cancerous and debilitating; an out-of-date burden; a previous self. Perhaps I need to dig me that shallow grave after all.

Charlie reckons they're all rednecks around here. He can say that 'cos he's local. 'I'm tellin' you, they're all rednecks round here. You gotta watch yourself, bein' an outsider.'

There are no longer any dangers for me to face.

We drive through the Osceola National Forest; pass lanes named Iron Horse, Frogs Garden, Desperado and Deadend; pass routes to Big Gum Swamp and Pinhook. Continue on the 441 towards Fargo and Colon.

'Is that the same Fargo where a Japanese tourist went

missing a few years ago?' I ask. 'Did they ever solve that case?'

'Nah, I think that's another Fargo. You never know, though, strange things happen round here, too.'

I think about it. Nah, it was to do with the film, her being in Fargo. And the film took place in the snow.

In truth, it was North Dakota. In 2001, a twenty-eight year old Japanese dreamer, thinker and feeler named Konishi Takako took a bus to Bismarck. A local man, thinking she was lost, took her to the police. She showed them a treasure map with the detail of a tree next to a highway. She was heading to Fargo. She had seen the movie – the Coen brothers' *Fargo* – which they claimed was based on a true story. They weren't trying to fool anyone, just trying to add to its depth. In the movie, Steve Buscemi buries his treasure – a whack of cash – in the snow. Konishi wanted to find it. The police tried to explain it was only a movie; that the Steve Buscemi character wasn't real and therefore nor was his treasure. They could not detain her – she had a visa – so they took her back to the station. She boarded the bus to Fargo. Within days, her body had been found by a hunter in a grove of trees. There was no specific cause of death ascertained so she was ruled a suicide. At least she was Japanese. In Japan, suicide ain't no crime against the gods; no immoral act; to the greater society, just a nuisance which delays the trains. There's that whistle again.

We pull off the highway and down a dirt track, follow a sign to Deep Creek. There ain't nothing here but a church and a cemetery but according to my map Deep Creek is in the Okefenokee Swamp area. I don't see no swamp and I can't see anyone burying their loved ones in a swamp either, not if they want the bodies found again.

We get back on the highway and travel north, turn off at Fargo onto the 177 spur. Pass Edith; Strange Island and Sweetwater Roads.

'You wanna go to the official entrance?'

'No. Stop before.'

We turn up a sand road between trees and swamp. One side has been logged. The memory of a forest still fresh in the piles of branches and the thick rug of twigs and leaves and... the emptiness left is ghostly. The contrast between the stark and the swamp is vast and dramatic.

Charlie starts talking about the movie *Deliverance*. 'Hell, people round here are like in *Deliverance* – you ever see that movie? Man, that scared the shit outa me. I was like, "Mama, what you showing me this fo'?"'

He's referring to the male rape scene, the 'squeal like a piggy', but he ain't trying to put the shits up me – he don't see himself as a local or a redneck, he just wants to share a laugh at the environment and its people. But I'm not sure I'd wanna be out here on my own, at night, running through the swamp, escaping the authorities, unsure of those individuals you come across and whether they intend to aid, hinder or obliterate your ass.

'A man checks into this world where and when his time comes. I reckon he checks out the same way. That can happen most any time in this neck of the woods.'

R M, *West of the Pecos*

Mitchum was resourceful and determined; fell on his feet like the cat he was. Escaping the prison farm, the chain gang, the swamp, but that was the Pipemaker. This one, the Okefenokee, this was the lure; what drew him to the South in the first place and into trouble, and this one, this Okefenokee, he never got to see. Well, *I'm* almost there, Mitchum, now let's hear you bringing in those sheaves.

The jeep slides on the sand but its wide tyres keep us from going into either of the deep gullies trammelling the track. There's a house out here, in the middle of nowhere. No signs of life. But swamp. There *is* swamp. The edge of it. An edge which has receded over years.

'It ain't as wet as it used to be,' says Charlie. 'The water basin, or somethin'.'

The edge is all I need.

'Oh the sun never shines in Walker's Woods
I doubt that it want to come in even if it could
The gators and the cottonmouths, the sand that pulls you down
Makes Walker's Woods a haven for the damned.'
R M, Walker's Woods

We pull over. Charlie stops the engine and begins singing. I climb out and shut the door behind me. Light a cigarette. Look the swamp right in the eye; am face to face with everything. All senses numb. Okey-dokey, Okefenokee, you have my full attention. Tell me what I need to know.

There is no flash of light, no dramatic moment of clarity, no deliverance. Detail is fogged and a murmuring thought slowly reaching focus: now that I'm here I can't remember why it was so important. I don't know what to do with myself. I am looking but not seeing. I am not gathering information or judging the experience through my physical senses. There is a direct link between the swamp and something internal and the experience is bypassing my brain. I am at the swamp but feel I have always been. Being here proves nothing. There are no secrets to be told, no answers to behold. There is little to gather that I haven't gathered already. It is still, calm except for the occasional inexplicable movement, currents, small bubbling. Understated. Its potential threatening. All that dynamic activity under the surface, the subtlety of existence under one ominous fug. The deep air. The beauty in the dowdy tones of primordial mud; the reliance on water, plant, earth. Resilient roots and juice. The lull. The false sense of security. The attraction of complexity. The kind of place which comes alive at night: movements in the dark; eyes watching; the camouflage of lurking; the warmth of a predator; the danger of getting sucked in. There are no answers here, only confirmation of detail, the interlinking ingredients, the questions. The questions. I hope I can leave mine here.

My senses strain. The swamp does not smell like I expected. The insects are quiet. The water makes an effort but has nothing to prove.

'You wanna ride back to Lake City?'

'No. Just leave me here.'

'Leave you here? How you gonna get back?'

'Back where?'

'Lake City.'

'There ain't no going back to Lake City.'

'Now remember, he's gonna be in thick cover. You're not gonna be able to see him until you get really close to him. That is, until he gets close to you. The minute he sees you, he's gonna charge you.... By the look of him and the size of him, you'd think he's bound to be slow. Don't you believe it. He's one of the fastest things that moves.... Make that first shot count. Because that's the last one you're likely to get.'

'Man, you're sure lookin' to make it hard on yourself.'
    I turn to face him. 'No. Now it gets easy.'

'Son, his daddy told him, make this run your last
your tank is filled with hundred proof
you're all tuned up and gassed
now don't take any chances
if you can't get through
I'd rather have you home again
Than all that mountain dew.'

I pay him for the gas and reassure him I'll be OK. He's not keen to leave; curious as to what I'm up to. I stand with my back to the swamp, as if guarding it; preventing him from perceiving my intentions or route. He reverses the jeep, accelerates and leaves dust in the air. I wait for it to settle. I am alone, for now. I step towards the thriving suckatash of life lapping and bubbling and calling.

'You walk in there, you'll never walk out.'

'Sure you don't wanna go back?'
 'Made it this far, dad.'

So here I am, at the ragged edge of the planet. The place is
bursting and bustling with life. I'm in danger of going from
one extreme to another. From comatose to too much alive.
Every cell bursting. Not just energy but a desire to merge.
But first I've got Mitchum to visit, or deliver.

I find a spot to sit down. Roll a joint. Inhale deeply.
Hold long.

'Well, I'm here, Mitch, I'm here.'

There are prints in the mud. Something is moving. I
hear rustling. A tail twitching. What to do? Play possum or
chase? Possum I ain't.

'Is that you, Mitchum?'

His voice buzzes me like spring insects across the
water.

'Did you wanna talk to me about something?'

'Where you been hiding?'
 'Where nobody found me.'
 'Those are the best places.'

*'If you think my inviting myself here was an imposition,
you're right, it was.'*

'On the level, Jim, what are you doing here?'
 'Running out.'
 'Any reason?'

I don't know what to say. Too many reasons, and not enough.

'*Say something, gringo.*'
    '*What can I say?*'
    '*Whatever is in your heart.*'

'I'm looking for answers.'

'*I haven't found an answer. But when I do, I promise you'll be the first to know.*'

'Not good enough, Mitchum.'

'*Still paying me back?*'
    '*For what, for something you couldn't help? ... I'm not paying you back, I'm punishing myself.*'

'*Time to quit this business. There's gotta be an easier way to make a living.*'

'This isn't business; this is life.'

'*This time I'm staying until you tell me everything I wanna know.*'

'*There's no use trying to explain anything to you like an adult human being so let's just forget it; let's forget ever seeing each other again; let's say goodbye now and leave it alone.*'

'No dice, *dad*. You don't get to shake me so easy until I get answers.'

'What would you care for?'
    'An explanation.'

'You a fighter?'
    'I'm a poet.'
    'That ain't answering my question.'
    'If you wanna get physical I'm sure you could snap me in two. But each time you put me down, I'm just gonna get straight back up again. Someone like you, well, you might call me a worm – you can keep cutting me in half but I'll keep surviving. You'll never get rid of the likes of me, you'll just get tired of punching. Eventually, I'm gonna break your hand. Then who you gonna hit?'

He looks me in the eye. I look right back. He's only got two ways to go. He makes the smart choice. Starts laughing.

'You know, you haven't turned out half bad. You know how to stand on your own two feet. You get along in the world. I'll tell you something: you got my respect for that.'

I need more than respect, I need answers.

'Son, when you get a little older you'll realize there's certain things that's best left alone and by and by they jus' take care of themselves.'

'I'm almost forty. We've gone past that.'

'Well if you haven't got it yet, you never will.'

'I refuse to accept that dismissal.'

'Do you know what makes life hard? The fact that it always forces us into making a choice and if we do not make a choice it is always made for us.'

'Yeh, well I'm sick of living the results of choices taken away from me. I'm sick of living a reaction.'

'The only cure for this sickness lies within you... you can either learn and grow from what has happened to you or you can be destroyed. The choice is yours.'

'I ain't used to freedom.'

'When you're dead, you're dead, buddy. That's all there is to it. Now, you keep that in your head. It might help keep you careful.'

'You think I'm afraid of death?'

'Your mouth dry? Tastes kinda like brass, doesn't it.'
 'How did you know that?
 'Well, I guess every man's tasted it at one time or another. That's fear.'

517

'Or maybe it's just this Yankee grass I'm smoking.'

'A man's life is his own truth – I guess we both knew it would end up like this some day.'

'I expected that of you: typically cryptic. You ever had a fear, Mitch?'

    'I was just as scared as the next man.'

    'You?'

'Yeh, I'm really a three-year-old girl. I weep all the time.'

'Still hiding under that humour, huh?'

'I've got the same attitude I had when I started. I haven't changed anything but my underwear.'

'Well you should have. You should've revealed yourself. Shown those meat-heads you were an artistic man; a poet; a deep and sensitive being as well as all the other things you were. You ever think you might be letting people down?'

    'I promised nothing. I guess I delivered.'

    'Things could change.'

'It's too late now.'

    'Well, you gotta start sometime.'

'You do it for me. You're still alive.'

    'Listen, *dad*. You've been riding my ass since I was a

518

kid. Now I'm getting rid of you so the least you can do is give me some nugget of wisdom to send me on my way.'

'Hell, how can I call to mind just one of a million things I've learned? How many schisms are there, or philosophies, that express just one thing? It's too much... the only thing I've really learned is that easy does it.'

'You're chickening out, Mitch. Commit yourself.'

'Would you like me to tell you the story of right hand, left hand? The story of good and evil? H – A – T – E, it was with this left hand that old brother Cain struck the blow that laid his brother low. L – O – V – E, you see these fingers, dear-hearts, these fingers has veins which run straight to the soul of man. The right hand, friends, the hand of Love. Now watch and I'll show you the story of life. These fingers, dear-hearts, is always a-warring and a-tugging, one against t'other. Now watch 'em. Old brother left hand, left hand Hate's a-fighting and it looks like Love's a goner but wait a minute, waaaaait a minute, hot dog, Love's doing it, yesiree, it's Love that won and old left hand Hate is down for the count.'

'Heard it all before, *dad*. Tell me something that'll make all this worthwhile; that'll make returning worth it.'

'Don't be a sucker. What's more important than staying alive?

'Swimming in choppy waters.'

'All anybody wants is for you to live in the present, not be afraid of the future. Yunno, maybe it can happen again if you quit pretending that something that's dead is still alive.'

'Yeh, well you might have something there, I'll give you that.'

I light another joint and absorb what he's saying. Look around at the foliage, the light through the branches and reflected in water.

'You didn't know where you were going or if everybody else was going to the same place or what difference it would make. Well now we're... rugged individuals with nobody to tell us what to do or when to do it. We're on our own.... Well, we been yapping for it, now we got it.'

'I guess you're right, this is decision time, huh? Just one last question: don't you confuse yourself?'

'Oh, no. I have the key.'

'I did ask him at one time what the key was, and he thought for a second and said, "Life is a playground – that's the key."'

Bentley Mitchum

I need to disappear; replace the fog of existence with swamp gas; act Japanese soldier who don't realise the war is over, Crusoe, cave dweller, escapist, hermit, coward.

What's to stop me rotting and fermenting here? Seems the perfect place. No black panthers to chase. No 'phantom of failure'. For this moment I have nothing more to think about. Is this peace? Tranquillity? Serenity? Contentment? The safety and reassurance of mental silence? Is this what it feels like?

'Mitch, I've learned a lot from you, I just don't know what it is.'

'Sounds like a line.'

'One of yours?'

'Perhaps.'

'I delivered it better.'

'Yeh. Yeh, you did, kid. What of it?'

'You got me there, Mitch, you got me. You know, I came here to free you as much as myself. You're free to go now whenever you like.'

'Go where?'

'That's for you to decide. Any reason to hang around?'

'I just wanna see one guy in this world get what he wants.'

'Yeh, well I've spent so many years thinking about what I don't want that I ain't too sure of what I do want.'

'I escaped my swamp a long time ago, now it's your turn.'

'Well, OK. Thanks for the ride, Mitchum. Now *vamos* will ya. Go on. Go taunt the alligators or something.'

'I'd like to finish this my own way.'

I toss my butt in a pool and set a trail for myself. Get down to the water. Kneel. Sink my head into the dark brown juice. Pull up and shake it from my head. Look. Focus. Watch the reaction to my intrusion settle; the waters calm. Delve without touching. What is there? What is there? All I see is mirror; my face in the ripples. Look through the eyes for substance. See nothing, and all. So there you are, you bastard. I've been looking for you.

'That man right there looks rejected, looks dejected, looks downright neglected... like a boozer, like a blueser, like a long-gone loser that man right there, he looks a lot like me.'

The reflection offers a moment of clarity in a swamp-fug of thought and feeling. All I see is a man looking back at me. A man alone. No father, no Mitchum. Just, just a man surrounded by swamp but no thickets. I don't recognise him. 'Hey, what's your story?'

I stand up. Throw my cell-phone away. Strip and stretch out my arms, crick my neck. It's good to be naked in the swamp.

'Smell that air – did you ever breathe anything like it?'
    'Sounds like a man going home.'

Take a deep breath. A man could suffocate under all the layers he builds up over the years. I put one foot in front of the other and keep going, enter the wet. *How high's the water, mama?* Not high enough. If I can swim the swamp and survive I'll have my answer. If I'm 'gator food? What the hell. If I'm bitten by a cottonmouth? It'll slither off and die.

'People are always telling me, "Watch it boy, play it safe. Be careful." But that chokes me off. What for? Being careful's not living – that's for the cemetery.'

I dive under. Stay there until my lungs feel they'll burst. Explode back to the surface. Sing as I pull strokes.

*'Leaning, leaning, safe and secure from all alarms
Leaning, leaning, leaning on the everlasting arms...'*

'I know you're still there, Mitch,' I shout. 'Any last words of wisdom? Wanna take this final opportunity of a captive audience?'

'You gave it your best shot, chief.'

'Thanks, Mitch. Thanks. That means a lot to me. I guess I'll see you on the other side.'

I lower my head under water, one last time. And laugh.

Forest clearance

The road to the swamp

Acknowledgements

Huge thanks are due to many people who provided support, understanding and assistance during the writing of this book. Most notably, Richard Davies at Parthian, Catherine Fletcher, Sally Ogut and my family. I couldn't have done it without you.

Also, to the Welsh Assembly Government and the Welsh Books Council for the commission; the John Masefield Trust and the Society of Authors for helping to pull me out of a hole; Jon Gower at Boomerang for being such a fab and enthusiastic producer on *Oh Dad! A Search for Robert Mitchum* (BBC Radio 4); and my editors.

Thanks are also due to Richard Gwyn, who was intrinsic to me beginning this book – although I doubt the result is what he had in mind; everyone with whom I shared a drink and a conversation about Mitchum – gods know there were lots of you; all the wonderful people who appear in this book – yes folks, they're real, mostly (although some names have been changed); everyone who proffered their own personal tales of Mitchum; and all the beautiful, enriching women who helped save my life for another day.

And to everyone at Parthian; Catrin Brace, Janine Murphy and everyone at Wales Trade International, NYC; Chris Torrance; Elizabeth, Mary, Roseanne and the staff in the Historical Collections dept of Bridgeport Public Library, and all the other libraries I pestered; Joe Meyers at the *Connecticut Post* who proved such an enthusiastic and supportive contact; Alan Neigher; John and the others at Books, Fall River; Frank the great cab driver in Dover; Bob Siler; Michael Howard, Delmar; Charlene and Bob Hutchinson, Roanoke; the gents at the Lan Sharks Gaming Center, Savannah; Michelangelo Verso and Michelangelo Verso Jnr; Danny and Lucy Kilbride for the info; David Bagwell for being such a good teacher and introducing me to *Autobiography of a Super-Tramp* at such a young age; me uncle Geoff for his thoughts on Mitchum; Bella Kemble; and all the eBayers who helped me find – and occasionally donated – rare movies and memorabilia.

The McKinley Elementary School class of 1931 photo was provided by Stewart Farber and is owned by the estate of Ann Levinsky Farber.

Extracts from this work – or a previous version of it – have appeared in *FCUK* and *Poetry Wales* magazines.

Sources
&
Recommended Reading,
Watching, Listening

An Open Book, John Huston
Anatomy of the Movies, ed. David Pirie
Awake in the Dark, Roger Egbert
Baby I Don't Care, Lee Server
Beggars of Life, Jim Tully
Behaving Badly, Cliff Goodwin
Bridgeport (Images of America series)
Civil War Handbook, William H Price
Close-Ups, ed. Danny Peary
Faithfull, Marianne Faithfull
Film Noir, Paul Duncan
Hollywood Anecdotes, Paul F Boller Jnr and Ronald L Davis
Jane Russell, My Autobiography, Jane Russell
Kiss Kiss Bang Bang, Pauline Kael
Mitchum in His Own Words, ed. Jerry Roberts

My Lucky Stars, Shirley MacLaine
Oh Dad! A Search for Robert Mitchum (Lloyd Robson/
                              Boomerang for BBC Radio 4)
OK You Mugs, ed. Luc Sante and Melissa Holbrook Pierson
Rebel, Donald Spoto
Richard Burton, John Cottrell and Fergus Cashin
Robert Bolt, Scenes from Two Lives, Adrian Turner
Robert Mitchum, David Downing
Robert Mitchum, Derek Malcolm
Robert Mitchum, A Biography, George Eels
Robert Mitchum on the Screen, Alvin H Marill
Robert Mitchum, Poet with an Ax, 20th Century-Fox
Solid, Dad, Crazy, Damien Love
That Man Robert Mitchum... Sings, Robert Mitchum
The Autobiography of a Super-Tramp, W H Davies
The Cinema of Otto Preminger, Gerald Pratley
The Dick Cavett Show: Hollywood Greats
The Film Career of Robert Mitchum, Bruce Crowther
The Little Black & White Book of Film Noir, Peg Thompson
                              and Saeko Usukawa
The Men who Murdered Marilyn, Matthew Smith
The MGM Story, John Douglas Eames
The New York Public Library, Ingrid Steffensen
The Oscars, John Atkinson
The RKO Story, Richard B Jewell and Vernon Harbin
The Robert Mitchum Story, Mike Tomkies

Quotes from Mitchum movies and DVDs originally released by American-International, A-pix, Avco-Embassy, Candice Productions, Cannon, Capstone, Columbia Pictures, Golden Harvest, Samuel Goldwyn, Jensen Farley, Hollywood (Disney), Maverick, MGM, Miramax, Monogram, Nu Image, Paramount, Republic, RKO, 20th Century-Fox, Universal, United Artists, Warner Bros, Yellow Cottage/Norsk Film.

The BBC radio and TV archive.

Innumerable websites, notably mitchumgirl3, who were most helpful.

Many quotes are from old newspaper and magazine cuttings. Details of the original authors and publications have proved difficult to pin down. To any journalist or author whose works I have unwittingly omitted from this list of sources I apologise profusely but, Jesus, I'm surrounded by photocopies, print-outs, archive material and scribbled scraps of paper here. No disrespect intended.